WITHDRAWN

Tarrying with the Negative

Post-Contemporary Interventions

Series Editors:

Stanley Fish and Fredric Jameson

TARRYING *with the* NEGATIVE

Kant, Hegel, and the Critique of Ideology

Slavoj Žižek

Duke University Press   *Durham 1993*

Fourth printing, 1998

© 1993 Duke University Press   All rights reserved

Printed in the United States of America on acid-free paper ∞

Typeset in Dante by Keystone Typesetting, Inc.

Library of Congress Cataloging-in-Publication Data

appear on the last printed page of this book.

Contents

Lacking strength, Beauty hates the Understanding for asking of her what it cannot do. But the life of Spirit is not the life that shrinks from death and keeps itself untouched by devastation, but rather the life that endures it and maintains itself in it. It wins its truth only when, in utter dismemberment, it finds itself. This tarrying with the negative *is the magical power that converts it into being.*—G. W. F. Hegel, *"Preface"* to Phenomenology of Spirit

Tarrying with the Negative

Introduction

The most sublime image that emerged in the political upheavals of the last years—and the term "sublime" is to be conceived here in the strictest Kantian sense—was undoubtedly the unique picture from the time of the violent overthrow of Ceauşescu in Romania: the rebels waving the national flag with the red star, the Communist symbol, cut out, so that instead of the symbol standing for the organizing principle of the national life, there was nothing but a hole in its center. It is difficult to imagine a more salient index of the "open" character of a historical situation "in its becoming," as Kierkegaard would have put it, of that intermediate phase when the former Master-Signifier, although it has already lost the hegemonical power, has not yet been replaced by the new one. The sublime enthusiasm this picture bears witness to is in no way affected by the fact that we now know how the events were actually manipulated (ultimately it had to do with a coup of Securitate, the Communist secret police, against itself, against its own signifier; that is, the old apparatus survived by casting off its symbolic clothing): for us as well as for most of the participants themselves, all this became visible in retrospect, and what really matters is that the masses who poured into the streets of Bucharest "experienced" the situation as "open," that they participated in the unique intermediate state of passage from one discourse (social link) to another, when, for a brief, passing moment, the hole in the big Other, the symbolic order, became visible. The enthusiasm which carried them was literally the enthusiasm over this hole, not yet hegemonized by any positive ideological project; all ideological appropriations (from the nationalistic to the liberal-democratic) entered the stage afterwards and endeavored to "kidnap" the process which originally was not their own. At this point, perhaps, the enthusiasm of the masses and the attitude of a critical intellectual overlap for a brief moment. And the duty of the critical intellectual—if, in today's "postmodern" universe, this syntagm has any meaning left—is precisely *to occupy all the time,* even when the new order (the "new harmony") stabilizes itself and again renders invisible the hole as such, *the place of this hole,* i.e., to maintain a distance toward every reigning Master-Signifier. In this precise sense, Lacan points out that, in the passage from one discourse (social link) to another, the "discourse of the analyst" always emerges for a brief moment: the aim of this discourse is precisely to "produce" the Master-Signifier, that is to say, to render visible its "produced," artificial, contingent character.[1]

This maintaining of a distance with regard to the Master-Signifier characterizes the basic attitude of philosophy. It is no accident that Lacan, in his Seminar on Transference, refers to Socrates, "the first philosopher," as the paradigm of the analyst: in Plato's *Symposium,* Socrates refuses to be identified with *agalma,* the hidden treasure in himself, with the unknown ingredient responsible for the Master's charisma, and persists in the void filled out by *agalma.*[2] It is against this background that we have to locate the "amazement" that marks the origins of philosophy: philosophy begins the moment we do not simply accept what exists as given ("It's like that!", "Law is law!", etc.), but raise the question of how is what we encounter as actual also possible. What characterizes philosophy is this "step back" from actuality into possibility—the attitude best rendered by Adorno's and Horkheimer's motto quoted by Fredric Jameson: "Not Italy itself is given here, but the proof that it exists."[3] Nothing is more antiphilosophical than the well-known anecdote about Diogenes the cynic who, when confronted with the Eleatic proofs of the nonexistence and inherent impossibility of movement, answered by simply standing up and taking a walk. (As Hegel points out, the standard version of this anecdote passes over in silence its denouement: Diogenes soundly thrashed his pupil who applauded the Master's gesture, punishing him for accepting the reference to a pretheoretical *factum brutum* as a proof.) Theory involves the power to abstract from our starting point in order to reconstruct it subsequently on the basis of its presuppositions, its transcendental "conditions of possibility"—theory as such, by definition, requires the suspension of the Master-Signifier.

In this precise sense, Rodolphe Gasché is fully justified in claiming that

Derrida remains thoroughly a "transcendental" philosopher: notions like *différance*, supplement, etc., endeavor to provide an answer to the question of the "conditions of possibility" of the philosophical discourse.[4] That is to say, the strategy of the Derridean "deconstruction" is not to dilute philosophical stringency in the unrestrained playfulness of "writing," but to undermine the philosophical procedure by means of its most rigorous self-application: its aim is to demonstrate that the "condition of impossibility" of a philosophical system (i.e., what, within the horizon of this system, appears as the hindrance to be surmounted, the secondary moment to be subdued) actually functions as its inherent condition of possibility (there is no pure *logos* without writing, no origin without its supplement, etc.). And why should we not also claim for Lacan the title of "transcendental philosopher"? Is not his entire work an endeavor to answer the question of how *desire* is possible? Does he not offer a kind of "critique of pure desire," of the pure faculty of desiring?[5] Are not all his fundamental concepts so many keys to the enigma of desire? Desire is constituted by "symbolic castration," the original loss of the *Thing;* the void of this loss is filled out by *objet petit a,* the fantasy-object; this loss occurs on account of our being "embedded" in the symbolic universe which derails the "natural" circuit of our needs; etc., etc.

This thesis that Lacan is essentially a philosopher seems nonetheless all too hazardous, since it blatantly contradicts Lacan's repeated statements which explicitly dismiss philosophy as a version of the "discourse of the Master."[6] Did Lacan not emphasize again and again the radically antiphilosophical character of his teaching, up to the pathetic "Je m'insurge contre la philosophie" from the last years of his life? However, things get complicated the moment we recall that it is already the post-Hegelian philosophy itself which, in its three main branches (analytical philosophy, phenomenology, Marxism), conceives of itself as "antiphilosophy," "not-anymore-philosophy." In his *German Ideology,* Marx mockingly observes that philosophy relates to "actual life" as masturbation to sexual act; the positivist tradition claims to replace philosophy (metaphysics) with the scientific analysis of concepts; the Heideggerian phenomenologists endeavor to "pass through philosophy" toward the post-philosophical "thought." In short, what is today practiced as "philosophy" are precisely different attempts to "deconstruct" something referred to as the classical philosophical corpus ("metaphysics," "logocentrism," etc.). One is therefore tempted to risk the hypothesis that what Lacan's "antiphilosophy" opposes is this very philosophy qua antiphilosophy: what if Lacan's own theoretical *practice* involves a kind of *return to philosophy?*

According to Alain Badiou, we live today in the age of the "new sophists."[7] The two crucial breaks in the history of philosophy, Plato's and Kant's, occurred as a reaction to new relativistic attitudes which threatened to demolish the traditional corpus of knowledge: in Plato's case, the logical argumentation of the sophists undermined the mythical foundations of the traditional mores; in Kant's case, empiricists (such as Hume) undermined the foundations of the Leibnizean-Wolfian rationalist metaphysics. In both cases, the solution offered is not a return to the traditional attitude but a new founding gesture which "beats the sophists at their own game," i.e., which surmounts the relativism of the sophists by way of its own radicalization (Plato *accepts* the argumentative procedure of the sophists; Kant *accepts* Hume's burial of the traditional metaphysics). And it is our hypothesis that Lacan opens up the possibility of another repetition of the same gesture. That is to say, the "postmodern theory" which predominates today is a mixture of neopragmatism and deconstruction best epitomized by names such as Rorty or Lyotard; their works emphasize the "anti-essentialist" refusal of universal Foundation, the dissolving of "truth" into an effect of plural language-games, the relativization of its scope to historically specified intersubjective community, etc., etc. Isolated desperate endeavors of a "postmodern" return to the Sacred are quickly reduced to just another language game, to another way we "tell stories about ourselves." Lacan, however, is not part of this "postmodern theory": in this respect, his position is homologous to that of Plato or Kant. The perception of Lacan as an "anti-essentialist" or "deconstructionist" falls prey to the same illusion as that of perceiving Plato as just one among the sophists. Plato accepts from the sophists their logic of discursive argumentation, but uses it to affirm his commitment to Truth; Kant accepts the breakdown of the traditional metaphysics, but uses it to perform his transcendental turn; along the same lines, Lacan accepts the "deconstructionist" motif of radical contingency, but turns this motif against itself, using it to assert his commitment to Truth *as contingent*. For that very reason, deconstructionists and neopragmatists, in dealing with Lacan, are always bothered by what they perceive as some remainder of "essentialism" (in the guise of "phallogocentrism," etc.)—as if Lacan were uncannily close to them, but somehow not "one of them."

To ask "Is Lacan one among the postmodern new sophists?" is to pose a question far beyond the tedium of a specialized academic discussion. One is tempted to risk a hyperbole and to affirm that, in a sense, *everything*, from the fate of so-called "Western civilization" up to the survival of humanity in the ecological crisis, hangs on the answer to this related question: is it possible today, apropos of the postmodern age of new sophists, to repeat mutatis mutandis the Kantian gesture?

PART I

COGITO *The Void Called Subject*

1 "I or He or It (the Thing) Which Thinks"

The Noir *Subject . . .*

One way to take note of the historical gap separating the 1980s from the 1950s is to compare the classic *film noir* to the new wave of *noir* in the eighties. What I have in mind here are not primarily direct or indirect remakes (the two *DOA*'s; *Against All Odds* as a remake of *Out of the Past*; *Body Heat* as a remake of *Double Indemnity*; *No Way Out* as a remake of *The Big Clock*, etc., up to *Basic Instinct* as a distant remake of *Vertigo*)[1] but rather those films which endeavor to resuscitate the *noir* universe by way of combining it with another genre, as if *noir* today is a vampirelike entity which, in order to survive, needs an influx of fresh blood from other sources. Two cases are exemplary here: Alan Parker's *Angel Heart*, which combines *noir* with the occult-supernatural, and Ridley Scott's *Blade Runner*, which combines *noir* with science fiction.

Cinema theory has for a long time been haunted by the question: is *noir* a genre of its own or a kind of anamorphic distortion affecting different genres? From the very beginning, *noir* was not limited to hard-boiled detective stories: reverberations of *noir* motifs are easily discernible in comedies (*Arsenic and Old Lace*), in westerns (*Pursued*), in political and social dramas (*All the King's Men, The Lost Weekend*), etc. Do we have here a secondary impact of something that originally constitutes a genre of its own (the *noir* crime universe), or is the crime film only one of the possible fields of application of the *noir* logic? That is, is *noir* a predicate that entertains toward the crime universe the same relationship as toward comedy or western, a kind of logical operator introducing the same anamorphic distortion in every genre to which it is applied, so that finding its strongest application in the crime film turns on nothing but historical contingency? To raise these questions in no way means indulging in hairsplitting sophistry: our thesis is that the "proper," detective *noir* as it were *arrives at its truth*—in Hegelese: realizes its notion—only by way of its fusion with another genre, specifically science fiction or the occult.

What, then, do *Blade Runner* and *Angel Heart* have in common? Both films deal with memory and subverted personal identity: the hero, the hard-boiled investigator, is sent on a quest whose final outcome involves discovering that he himself was from the very beginning implicated in the object of his quest. In *Angel Heart,* he ascertains that the dead singer he was looking for is none other than himself (in an occult ritual performed long ago, he exchanged hearts and souls with an ex-soldier, who he now thinks he is). In *Blade Runner,* he is after a group of replicants at large in L.A. of 2012; upon accomplishing his mission, he is told that he is himself a replicant. The outcome of the quest is therefore in both cases the radical undermining of self-identity masterminded by a mysterious, all-powerful agency, in the first case the Devil himself ("Louis Cipher"), in the second case the Tyrell corporation, which succeeded in fabricating replicants unaware of their replicant status, i.e., replicants misperceiving themselves as humans.[2] The world depicted in both films is the world in which the corporate Capital succeeded in penetrating and dominating the very fantasy-kernel of our being: none of our features is really "ours"; even our memories and fantasies are artificially planted. It is as if Fredric Jameson's thesis on postmodernism as the epoch in which Capital colonizes the last resorts hitherto excluded from its circuit is here brought to its hyperbolic conclusion: the fusion of Capital and Knowledge brings about a new type of proletarian, as it were the absolute proletarian bereft of the last pockets of private resistance; everything, up to the most intimate memories, is planted, so that what remains is now literally the void of pure substanceless subjectivity (*substanzlose Subjektivitaet*—Marx's definition of the proletarian). Ironically, one might say that *Blade Runner* is a film about the emergence of class consciousness.

This truth is concealed, in one film metaphorically, in the other metonymically: in *Angel Heart,* corporate Capital is substituted by the metaphorical figure of the Devil, whereas in *Blade Runner,* a metonymical impediment prevents the film from carrying out its inherent logic. That is to say, the director's cut of *Blade Runner* differs in two crucial features from the version released in 1982: there is no voiceover, and at the end, Deckard (Harrison Ford) discovers that he also is a replicant.[3] But even in the two released versions, especially in the version released in 1992, a whole series of features points toward Deckard's true status: strong accent falls on the visual parallelism between Deckard and Leon Kowalski, a replicant questioned in the Tyrell building at the beginning of the film; after Deckard proves to Rachael (Sean Young) that she is a replicant by quoting her most intimate child-recollections she did not share with anyone, the camera provides a brief survey of *his* personal mythologies (old childhood pictures on the piano, his dream-recollection of a unicorn), with a clear implication that they also are fabricated, not "true" memories or dreams, so that when Rachael mockingly asks him if he also underwent the replicant test, the question resounds with ominous undertones; the patronizing-cynical attitude of the policeman who serves as Deckard's contact to the police chief, as well as the fact that he makes small paper models of unicorns, clearly indicates his awareness that Deckard is a replicant (and we can safely surmise that in the true director's cut he viciously informs Deckard of this fact). The paradox here is that the subversive effect (the blurring of the line of distinction between humans and androids) hinges on the narrative closure, on the loop by means of which the beginning metaphorically augurs the end (when, at the beginning of the film, Deckard replays the tape of Kowalski's interrogation, he is yet unaware that at the end he will himself occupy Kowalski's place), whereas the evasion of the narrative closure (in the 1982 version, the hints of Deckard's replicant status are barely perceptible) functions as a conformist compromise which cuts off the subversive edge.

How, then, are we to diagnose the position of the hero at the end of his quest, after the recovery of memory deprives him of his very self-identity? It is here that the gap separating the classical *noir* from the *noir* of the eighties emerges in its purest form. Today, even the mass media is aware of the extent to which our perception of reality, including the reality of our innermost self-experience, depends upon symbolic fictions. Suffice it to quote from a recent issue of *Time* magazine: "Stories are precious, indispensable. Everyone must have his history, her narrative. You do not know who you are until you possess the imaginative version of yourself. You almost do not exist without it." Classical *noirs* remain within these confines: they abound with cases of amnesia in which the hero does not know who he is or what he did during his blackout. Yet amnesia is here a deficiency measured by the standard of integration into the field of intersubjectivity, of symbolic community: a successful recollection means that, by way of organizing his life-experience into a consistent narrative, the hero exorcizes the dark demons of the past. But in the universe of *Blade Runner* or *Angel Heart*, recollection designates something incomparably more radical: the total loss of the hero's symbolic identity. He is forced to assume that he is not what he thought himself to be, but somebody-something else. For that reason, the "director's cut" of *Blade Runner* is fully justified in dispensing with the voice-off of Deckard (homophonous with Descartes!): in the *noir* universe, the voice-off narrative realizes the integration of the subject's experience into the big Other, the field of intersubjective symbolic tradition.

One of the commonplaces about the classic *noir* sets its philosophical background in French existentialism; however, in order to grasp the implications of the radical shift at work in the *noir* of the eighties, one has to reach back farther, to the Cartesian-Kantian problematic of the subject qua pure, substanceless "I think."

. . . Out of Joint

Descartes was the first to introduce a crack in the ontologically consistent universe: contracting absolute certainty to the punctum of "I think" opens up, for a brief moment, the hypothesis of Evil Genius (*le malin génie*) who, behind my back, dominates me and pulls the strings of what I experience as "reality"—the prototype of the Scientist-Maker who creates an artificial man, from Dr. Frankenstein to Tyrell in *Blade Runner*. However, by reducing his *cogito* to *res cogitans*, Descartes, as it were, patches up the wound he cut into the texture of reality. Only Kant fully articulates the inherent paradoxes of self-consciousness. What Kant's "transcendental turn" renders manifest is the impossibility of locating the subject in the "great chain of being," into the Whole of the universe—all those notions of the universe as a harmonious Whole in which every element has its own place (today, they abound in ecological ideology). In contrast to it, subject is in the most radical sense "out of joint"; it constitutively lacks its own place, which is why Lacan designates it by the mathem $, the "barred" *S*.

In Descartes, this "out of joint" state is still concealed. The Cartesian universe stays within the confines of what Foucault, in his *The Order of Things*, called "classical episteme," that epistemological field regulated by the problematic of representations—their causal enchainment, their clarity and evidence, the connection between representation and represented content, etc.[4] Upon reaching the point of absolute certainty in *cogito ergo sum,* Descartes does not yet conceive of the *cogito* as correlative to the whole of reality, i.e., as the point external to reality, exempted from it, which delineates reality's horizon (in the sense of Wittgenstein's well-known *Tractatus* metaphor on the eye that can never be part of the seen reality). Rather than the autonomous agent which "spontaneously" constitutes the objective world opposed to itself, the Cartesian *cogito* is a representation which, by following the inherent notional enchainment, leads us to other, superior representations. The subject first ascertains that *cogito* is a representation which belongs to an inherently deficient being (doubt is a sign of imperfection); as such, it entails the representation of a perfect being free of incertitude. Since it is obvious that a deficient, inferior entity or representation cannot be the cause of a superior entity or representation, the perfect being (God) had to exist. The veracious nature of God furthermore assures the reliability of our representations of external reality, and so forth. In Descartes' final vision of the universe, *cogito* is therefore just one among many representations in an intricate totality, *part* of reality and not yet (or, in Hegelese, only "in itself") correlative to the whole of reality.

What, then, marks the break between Descartes' *cogito* and Kant's "I" of transcendental apperception? The key to it is offered by Kant's Wittgensteinian remark, aimed at Descartes, that it is not legitimate to use "I think" as a complete phrase, since it calls for a continuation—"I think that . . . (it will rain, you are right, we shall win . . .)." According to Kant, Descartes falls prey to the "subreption of the hypostasized consciousness": he wrongly concludes that, in the empty "I think" which accompanies every representation of an object, we get hold of a positive phenomenal entity, *res cogitans* (a "small piece of the world," as Husserl put it), which thinks and is transparent to itself in its capacity to think. In other words, self-consciousness renders self-present and self-transparent the "thing" in me which thinks. What is lost thereby is the topological discord between the form "I think" and the substance which thinks, i.e., the distinction between the analytical proposition on the identity of the logical subject of thought, contained in "I think," and the synthetical proposition on the identity of a *person* qua thinking thing-substance. By articulating this distinction, Kant logically *precedes* Descartes: he brings to light a kind of "vanishing mediator," a moment which has to disappear if the Cartesian *res cogitans* is to emerge (*CPR*, A 354–56).[5] This Kantian distinction is revived by Lacan in the guise of the distinction between the subject of the enunciation (*sujet de l'énonciation*) and the subject of the enunciated (*sujet de l'énoncé*): the Lacanian subject of the enunciation (*$) is also an empty, nonsubstantial logical variable (not function), whereas the subject of the enunciated (the "person") consists of the fantasmatic "stuff" which fills out the void of $.

This gap which separates the empirical I's self-experience from the I of transcendental apperception coincides with the distinction between existence qua experiential reality and existence qua logical construction, i.e., existence in the mathematical sense ("there exists an X which . . ."). The status of Kant's I of transcendental apperception is that of a *necessary* and simultaneously *impossible* logical construction ("impossible" in the precise sense that its notion can never be filled out with intuited experiential reality), in short: of the Lacanian *real*. Descartes' error was precisely to confuse experiential reality with logical construction qua the real-impossible.[6]

Kant's reasoning is here far more refined than it may appear. In order to appreciate fully its finesse, one has to make use of Lacan's formula of fantasy ($ ◊ a): "I think" only insofar as I am inaccessible to myself qua noumenal Thing which thinks. The Thing is originally lost and the fantasy-object (*a*) fills out its void (in this precise Kantian sense Lacan remarks that *a* is "the stuff of the I").[7] The act of "I think" is trans-phenomenal, it is not an object of inner experience or intuition; yet for all that, it is not a noumenal Thing, but rather the void of its lack: it is not sufficient to say about the I of pure apperception that "of it, apart from them [the thoughts which are its predicates], we cannot have any concept whatsoever" (*CPR*, A 346). One has to add that *this lack of intuited content is constitutive of the I; the inaccessibility to the I of its own "kernel of being" makes it an I.*[8] This is what Kant is not quite clear about, which is why he again and again yields to the temptation of conceiving of the relationship between the I of pure apperception and the I of self-experience as the relationship between a Thing-in-itself and an experiential phenomenon.[9]

When, consequently, Kant remarks that, "in the synthetic original unity of apperception, I am conscious of myself, not as I appear to myself, nor as I am in myself, but only that I am" (*CPR*, B 157), the first thing one has to notice here is the fundamental paradox of this formulation: I encounter *being* devoid of all determinations-of-thought at the very moment when, by way of the utmost abstraction, I confine myself to the empty form of *thought* which accompanies every representation of mine. Thus, the empty form of thought coincides with being, which lacks any formal determination-of-thought. Here, however, where Kant seems at his closest to Descartes, the distance that separates them is infinite: in Kant, this coincidence of thought and being in the act of self-consciousness in no way implies access to myself qua thinking substance: "Through this I or he or it (the thing) which thinks, nothing further is represented than a transcendental subject of the thoughts = X. It is known only through the thoughts which are its predicates, and of it, apart from them, we cannot have any concept whatsoever" (*CPR*, A 346). In short: we can provide no possible answer to the question "How is the Thing which thinks structured?" The paradox of self-consciousness is that *it is possible only against the background of its own impossibility:* I am conscious of myself only insofar as I am out of reach to myself qua the real kernel of my being ("I or he or it (the thing) which thinks"). I cannot acquire consciousness of myself in my capacity of the "Thing which thinks."[10] In *Blade Runner*, Deckard, after learning that Rachael is a replicant who (mis)perceives herself as human, asks in astonishment: "How can it not know what it is?" We can see, now, how, more than two hundred years ago, Kant's philosophy outlined an answer to this enigma: the very notion of self-consciousness implies the subject's self-decenterment, which is far more radical than the opposition between subject and object. This is what Kant's theory of metaphysics ultimately is about: metaphysics endeavors to heal the wound of the "primordial repression" (the inaccessibility of the "Thing which thinks") by allocating to the subject a place in the "great chain of being." What metaphysics fails to notice is the price to be paid for this allocation: the loss of the very capacity it wanted to account for, i.e., human freedom. Kant himself commits an error when, in his *Critique of Practical Reason*, he conceives of freedom (the postulate of practical reason) as a noumenal Thing; what gets obfuscated thereby is his fundamental insight according to which I retain my capacity of a spontaneous-autonomous agent precisely and only insofar as I am not accessible to myself as a Thing.

On closer examination, what makes up the inconsistencies which emerge when the I of pure apperception is identified with the noumenal Self (the "Thing which thinks")? As Henry Allison puts it in his perspicuous summary of Strawson's critique of Kant,[11] in the case of this identification, the phenomenal I (the empirical subject) has to be conceived of simultaneously as something which (in the guise of an object of experience) appears *to* the noumenal subject and as the appearance *of* the noumenal subject. That is to say, everything that appears as part of the constituted reality appears to the transcendental subject (which is here conceived as identical with the noumenal subject); on the other hand, the empirical subject is, as is the case with every intuited reality, a phenomenal appearance of some noumenal entity, in this case, of the noumenal subject. This doubling, however, is a nonsensical, self-canceling short-circuit: if the noumenal subject appears *to itself,* the distance that separates appearance from noumena falls away. The agency which perceives something as an appearance cannot itself be an appearance. In such a case, we find ourselves in the nonsensical vicious circle described by Alphonse Allais, where two appearances mutually recognize themselves as appearances (Raoul and Marguerite make an appointment at a masked ball; in a secret corner, they both take off their masks and utter a cry of surprise—Raoul, since his partner is not Marguerite, and Marguerite, since her partner is not Raoul). Thus, the only way out of this impasse is to distinguish between the I of pure apperception and the Thing-which-thinks: what I experience, what is given to me phenomenally in my intuition, the content of my person (the object of empirical psychology), is, of course, as with every phenomenon, the appearing of a Thing (in this case of the Thing-which-thinks), *but this Thing cannot be the I of pure apperception, the transcendental subject to whom the "Thing which thinks" appears as the empirical I.*

With this crucial point in mind, we can give a precise account of the difference between the inaccessibility of the noumenal Self and of any object of perception. When Kant says that the transcendental subject "is known only through the thoughts which are its predicates, and of it, apart from them, we cannot have any concept whatsoever" (*CPR*, A 346), does not the same also hold true for the table in front of me, for example? The table is also known only through the thoughts which are its predicates, and of it, apart from them, we cannot have any concept whatsoever. However, due to the above-described self-referential doubling of the appearing in the case of the I, *"I think" must also remain empty on the phenomenal level.* The I's apperception is by definition devoid of any intuitional content; it is an empty representation which carves a hole into the field of representations. To put it concisely: Kant is compelled to define the I of transcendental apperception as neither phenomenal nor noumenal because of the paradox of *auto-affection; if I were given to myself phenomenally, as an object of experience, I would simultaneously have to be given to myself noumenally.*

Another way to arrive at the same result is via the duality of discursive and intuitive intellect: on account of his finitude, the subject disposes only of discursive intellect. He is affected by things-in-themselves, and he makes use of the discursive intellect (the network of formal transcendental categories) to structure the multitude of formless affects into objective reality: this structuring is his own "spontaneous," autonomous act. If the subject were to possess intuitive intellect, it would fill out the abyss which separates intellect from intuition and would thus gain access to things as they are in themselves. However, "while I can coherently, if vacuously, claim that if I had an intuitive instead of a discursive intellect, I could know *other* things (objects) as they are in themselves, I cannot similarly claim that I could know myself as object in my capacity as a spontaneous, thinking subject."[12] Why not? If I were to possess an intuition of myself qua "Thing which thinks," i.e., if I were to have an access to my noumenal Self, *I would thereby lose the very feature which makes me an I of pure apperception;* I would cease to be the spontaneous transcendental agent that constitutes reality.[13]

The same paradox repeats itself apropos of the transcendental object qua correlate to the I of pure apperception. That is to say, how does Kant arrive at the notion of transcendental object? Why can't he get by with transcendental categories on the one hand and the affects which bear witness to our being acted upon by Things-in-themselves on the other hand? The "transcendental object, that is, the completely indeterminate thought of *something* in general," has the function of conferring "upon all our empirical concepts in general relation to an object, that is, objective validity" (*CPR,* A 109). In other words, without this paradoxical object which "can be thought only as something in general = X" (*CPR,* A 109), the difference between formal and transcendental logic would fall off, that is, the table of a priori categories would remain a mere formal-logical network, bereft of the transcendental power to constitute "objective reality." Transcendental object is the form of the object in general by means of a reference to which a priori categories synthesize the multitude of sensible intuitions into the representation of a unified object: it marks the point at which the general form of every possible object reverts to the empty representation of the "object in general." For that reason, the notion of the transcendental object undermines the standard Kantian distinction between the formless stuff which descends from the transcendent Thing (sensible affects which bear witness to how the subject is passively affected by some noumenal entities), and the transcendental form by means of which the subject molds this intuited stuff into "reality": it is an object entirely "created" by the subject, the "unity which thought projects in front of itself as the shadow of an object,"[14] an intelligible form which is its own stuff. As such, it is the semblance of an object, i.e., *stricto sensu* a metonymical object: the space for it is opened up by the simultaneous (actual) finitude and (potential) infinitude of our experience. The transcendental object gives a body to the gap which forever separates the universal formal-transcendental frame of "empty" categories from the finite scope of our actual experience, of the affects that provide our intuition with positive content. Its function is thus eminently anti-Humean, anti-skeptical: it guarantees that transcendental categories will refer to all possible future objects of experience. This distinction between *Ding-an-sich* and the transcendental object corresponds perfectly to the Lacanian distinction between the Real qua *Ding* and *objet petit a:* the latter is precisely such a metonymical object which gives a body to the lack of positive objects.[15]

Apropos of "the transcendental object, that is, the completely indeterminate thought of *something* in general," Kant says: "This cannot be entitled the *noumenon;* for I know nothing of what it is in itself, and have no concept of it save as merely the object of a sensible intuition in general" (*CPR,* A 253). In a first approach, Kant seems to contradict his own basic premise, citing as proof of the non-noumenal status of the transcendental object the fact that we know nothing of what it is in itself: isn't this unknowableness the very definition of the noumenal object? However, this apparent inconsistency is easily dispelled by taking into account the precise nature of the transcendental object:[16] insofar as it gives body to the object in general, i.e., insofar as it functions as a metonymical place-holder of the objectivity *in whole,* it is *an object which, if given to me in intuition, would simultaneously have to be given to me as it is in itself.* (We may recall that herein also lies the fundamental feature of the I of pure apperception: its representation is empty since, were it to be given phenomenally, it would also be given noumenally.)[17]

From Kant to Hegel

This ambiguity of Kant's concerning the transcendental object (Kant oscillates between conceiving of it as a Thing and as something which is neither phenomenal nor noumenal) is the reverse of the ambiguity concerning the transcendental subject; and, furthermore, it is not a simple default whose correction would enable us to formulate the "proper" Kantian theory, but a *necessary* equivocality whose roots became visible only with hindsight, from a Hegelian perspective: if we choose any of the two poles of the alternative, Kant's system in its entirety disintegrates. That is to say, if, on the one hand, we stick to the identification of the transcendental I with the noumenal Thing-Self, *the noumenal Self phenomenally appears to itself,* which means that the difference between phenomena and noumena dissolves— "I" becomes the singular subject-object given to itself in the "intellectual intuition," the "eye which sees itself" (the step accomplished by Fichte and Schelling, but unconditionally prohibited by Kant: *intelektuelle Anschauung* as the "absolute starting-point" of philosophizing). If, on the other hand, the I of apperception—this autonomous agent of the constitution of reality—is *not* a noumenal Thing, then the difference between phenomena and noumena again dissolves, yet in a wholly different way: in Hegel's way. What we have to bear in mind here is that Hegel rejects the very notion of "intellectual intuition" as an inadequate, "immediate" synthesis, i.e., that he remains thoroughly Kantian in his insistence on the irreducible gap that separates discursive intellect (the level of the Notion) from intuition. Far from simply healing the Kantian split, Hegel even radicalizes it—how?

At this point, it is advisable to forget the standard textbook phrases on Hegel's "absolute idealism" in which—or so the story goes—the Notion's self-movement overcomes formalism by generating the entire content out of itself and thus becoming able to dispense with the external instigation of the Thing-in-itself. Instead of directly plunging into such "fundamental Hegelian propositions," let us rather return to the Kantian duality of the transcendental network of categories and of Things-in-themselves: transcendental categories mold the affects which originate in noumenal things into "objective reality." However, as we have already seen, the problem lies in the radical finitude of the affects: they are never "all," since the totality of affects is never given to us; if this totality were to be given, we would have access to Things-in-themselves. At this precise point, Hegel's critique of Kantian "formalism" intervenes: he identifies as the site of insufficiency not the finite nature of affects, but the abstract character of thought itself. The very need for affects (i.e., for a heterogeneous material to provide content to our intellect) bears witness to the fact that our thought is abstract-formal, that it has not yet achieved the level of what Hegel calls "absolute form."

This way, the transcendental object radically changes its function: from the index of a deficiency on the side of intuition—i.e., of the fact that our representations are forever branded by our finitude, that the world of intuited objects is never given in its totality—it shifts into the index of the deficiency of the very *discursive form*. In this precise sense Hegel's "absolute idealism" is nothing but the Kantian "criticism" brought to its utmost consequences: "there is no metalanguage"; it is never possible for us to occupy the neutral place from which we could measure the distance that separates our semblance of knowledge from the In-itself of Truth. In short, Hegel carries to its extreme Kant's criticism at the very point where he seems to regress into absolute "panlogicism": by way of affirming that *every tension between Notion and reality, every relationship of the Notion to what appears as its irreducible Other encountered in the sensible, extra-notional experience, already is an intra-notional tension, i.e., already implies a minimal notional determination of this "otherness."*[18] The most obvious example of this notional determination, of course, is the empiricist counterposition of primary (shape) and secondary (color, taste) qualities of the perceived object: the subject has in itself the measure which allows him to distinguish between what are merely its "subjective impressions" and what "objectively exists." Yet the same goes for the Kantian Thing-in-itself: how does the subject arrive at it? In abstracting from every sensible determination that pertains to the objects of experience, what remains is the object of pure abstraction, the pure "thing-of-thought" (*Gedankending*). In short, our search for a pure presupposition, unaffected by the subject's spontaneous activity, produces an entity which is pure positedness.

Therein consists Hegel's "idealist" wager: what appears in and to our experience as the extra-notional surplus, as the "otherness" of the object irreducible to the subject's notional framework, impenetrable to it, is always-already the fetishistic, "reified" (mis)perception of an inconsistency of the notion to itself. In this sense, Hegel points out, in his Introduction to *Phenomenology of Spirit*, how the very measure we use to test the truth of our knowledge-claims is always caught in the process of testing: if our knowledge is proved inadequate, if it does not fit our measure of what counts as True, then we must not only exchange our knowledge for its more adequate form, but we must simultaneously replace the very measuring-rod of Truth, the In-itself which our knowledge failed to attain.[19] Hegel's point is not a delirious solipsism, but rather a simple insight into how we—finite, historical subjects—forever lack any measuring-rod which would guarantee our contact with the Thing itself. The dogmatic-rationalist intuition of eternal Truths, the empiricist sensible perceptions, the a priori categorial framework of the transcendental reflection, or—two examples whose value is not purely historical, since they indicate positions still claimed by contemporary philosophy—the phenomenological notion of *Lebenswelt* (life-world) as the always-already presupposed foundation of our reasoning, and the intersubjective speech-community, all are false attempts to break the vicious circle of what Hegel called "experience."[20]

In a first approach, what Hegel accomplishes here may strike us as a simple reversal of Kant: instead of the gap separating forever the subject from the substantial Thing, we get their identity (the Absolute qua substance = subject). Hegel is nonetheless the most consequential of Kantians: the Hegelian subject—i.e., what Hegel designates as absolute, self-relating negativity—is nothing but the very gap which separates phenomena from the Thing, the abyss beyond phenomena conceived in its negative mode, i.e., the purely negative gesture of limiting phenomena without providing any positive content which would fill out the space beyond the limit. For that reason, we must be very attentive if we are not to miss what Hegel has in mind when he insists that the Absolute has to be conceived also as subject, not only as substance: the standard notion of the gradual becoming-subject of the substance (of the "active" subject leaving its "imprint" on the substance, molding it, mediating it, expressing in it his subjective content) is here doubly misleading. First, we must bear in mind that with Hegel this subjectivization of the object never "turns out": there is always a remainder of the substance which eludes the grasp of "subjective mediation"; and far from being a simple impediment preventing the subject's full actualization, this remainder is *stricto sensu* correlative to the very being of the subject. We reach thereby one of the possible definitions of *objet a:* that surplus of the Substance, that "bone," which *resists subjectivization; objet a* is correlative to the subject in its very radical incommensurability with it. Secondly, we have the opposite notion according to which the subject is that very "nothing," the purely formal void which is left over after the substantial content has wholly "passed over" into its predicates-determinations: in the "subjectivization" of Substance, its compact In-itself is dissolved into the multitude of its particular predicates-determinations, of its "beings-for-other," and "subject" is that very X, the empty form of a "container," which remains after all its content was "subjectivized." These two conceptions are strictly correlative, i.e., "subject" and "object" are the two left-overs of this same process, or, rather, the two sides of the same left-over conceived either in the modality of form (subject) or in the modality of content, of "stuff" (object): *a* is the "stuff" of the subject qua empty form.

The Nonequivalent Exchange

The same paradox pertains to the Hegelian notion of infinite judgment in its opposition to negative judgment.[21] With reference to the infamous thesis on "determinate negation," one would expect negative judgment to *succeed* infinite judgment as a "higher," more concrete form of dialectical unity-within-difference: by affirming a non-predicate, the infinite judgment merely posits an abstract, wholly indeterminate, empty Beyond, whereas negative judgment negates positive judgment in a determinate way (i.e., by saying that a thing is an object of nonsensible intuition, we not only abstractly negate one of its predicates, we also invert abstract negation into positive determination: we delineate the field of "nonsensible intuition" as that to which the thing in question belongs). For Hegel, however, it is infinite judgment with its abstract, indeterminate negation which brings forth the "truth" of negative judgment—why? Perhaps what offers a key to this enigma is the logic of *exchange* at work here: negative judgment remains within the confines of an "equivalent exchange"; implicitly at least, we get something in exchange for what we renounce (by saying that a thing is "an object of nonsensible intuition," we obtain in exchange for the loss of the domain of sensible intuition another positively determined domain, that of nonsensible intuition), whereas in the case of infinite judgment the loss is pure; we get nothing in exchange.

Let us examine more closely the paradigmatic case of this logic of exchange, the dialectic of *Bildung* (culture-education) in the chapter on Spirit from the *Phenomenology of Spirit*.[22] The starting point of this dialectic is the state of extreme alienation, of the splitting between subject and substance, which are here opposed under the guises of "noble consciousness" and the State. As a matter of fact, this very opposition already results from an implicit act of exchange: in exchange for his utter alienation (for his yielding all substantial content to the Other, to the State), the subject—self-consciousness—receives honor (the honor of serving the common Good embodied in the State). Between these two extremes a process of exchange / mediation takes place: the "noble consciousness" alienates its pure For-itself (its silent honorable serving of the State) in language qua medium of the universality of thought (flattery to the Monarch, the head of the State); in exchange for this alienation, substance itself accomplishes a first step toward its "subjectivization," i.e., it changes from the unattainable State, abstractly opposed to us, into wealth qua substantial content which already is at our disposal (money we get for flattering the Monarch). On the other hand, Substance itself (the State) is not only subordinated to the subjectivity of self-consciousness via its transformation into wealth: in exchange for this subordination, it acquires itself the form of subjectivity— the impersonal State is replaced by the absolute Monarchy; it becomes identified with the person of the Monarch (*"L'Etat, c'est moi."*). Throughout the entire dialectic of *Bildung,* the appearance of an equivalent exchange between subject (self-consciousness) and substance is thus maintained: in exchange for his increasing alienation, for sacrificing a further substantial part of himself, the subject receives honor, wealth, the language of Spirit and insight, the heaven of Faith, the Utility of the Enlightenment. However, when we reach the apogee of this dialectic, "absolute freedom," the exchange between the particular and the universal Will, the subject "gets nothing in exchange for everything." He "passes into an empty nothing"; his alienation becomes an abstract negation which offers no positive, determinate content in exchange. (The historical epoch which stands for this moment of "absolute freedom" is, of course, the Jacobinical Reign of Terror, in which, for no apparent reason, I could be proclaimed traitor and have my head cut off at any moment: the chapter on Spirit encompasses the entire spiritual development of Europe from the medieval feudal state to the French Revolution.) Yet it is precisely this falling apart of the appearance of a symmetrical, balanced exchange that makes possible the speculative-dialectical reversal: self-consciousness has only to become aware of how this Nothingness which appears to a particular Will as an abstract, opposed, external threat coincides with its own force of negativity; it has to internalize this force of negativity and recognize in it its own essence, the very kernel of its own being. "Subject" emerges at this very point of utterly meaningless voidance brought about by a negativity which explodes the frame of balanced exchange. That is to say, what is "subject" if not the infinite power of absolute negativity / mediation: in contrast to a mere biological life, self-consciousness contains in itself its own negation, it maintains itself by way of negative self-relating. This way, we pass from absolute freedom (of the revolutionary *citoyen*) into "the Spirit certain of itself" epitomized by the Kantian moral subject: the external negativity of the revolutionary Terror is internalized into the power of moral Law, into the pure Knowledge and Will qua Universality, which is not something externally opposed to the subject but something which constitutes the very axis of his self-certainty; "Free Will" is a Will that acts in accordance with the universal moral Law, not in accordance with particular ("pathological") motivations which enslave it to the world of objects. Here is the passage from *Phenomenology* which recapitulates this movement:

> In the world of culture (*Bildung*) itself, it [self-consciousness] does not get as far as to behold its negation or alienation in this form of pure abstraction; on the contrary, its negation is filled with a content, either honour or wealth, which it gains in place of the self that it has alienated from itself; or the language of Spirit and insight which the disrupted consciousness acquires; or it is the heaven of faith, or the Utility of the Enlightenment. All these determinations have vanished in the loss suffered by the self in absolute freedom; its negation is the death that is without meaning, the sheer terror of the negative that contains nothing positive, nothing that fills it with a content. At the same time, however, this negation in its real existence is not something alien; it is neither the universal inaccessible *necessity* in which the ethical world perishes, nor the particular accident of private possession, nor the whim of the owner on which the disrupted consciousness sees itself dependent; on the contrary, it is the *universal will* which in this its ultimate abstraction has nothing positive and therefore can give nothing in return for the sacrifice. But for that very reason it is immediately one with self-consciousness, or it is the pure positive, because it is the pure negative; and the meaningless death, the unfilled negativity of the self, changes round in its inner Notion into absolute positivity.[23]

The logic of this internalization of negativity usually undergoes two types of criticism. The standard Marxist approach cites it as the supreme proof of Hegel's "hidden positivism," of his "acceptance of the existing order [*das Bestehende*]": it sees in it the repetition of the Protestant gesture of dislocating actual social freedom into "inner" moral freedom, which leaves untouched all the distortions of actual social life. According to this approach, the Hegelian "reconciliation" qua internalization of negativity bears witness to an indelible mark of renunciation, of a resigned acceptance of "irrational," perverted social conditions: by way of this internalization of the French social revolution into the German philosophical revolution, Reason is compelled to recognize itself in the un-Reason of the world. In a different vein, the deconstructionist reading insists on how this passage, from external revolutionary Terror into the pressure of moral conscience which terrorizes us from within, hinges on a "closed economy" which enables us to internalize-domesticate the radical Externality of the Terror, to transform it into a subordinated moment of our self-relating.

This second reading fails to appreciate the extent to which the "internalization" of the Terror into the moral Law, far from "gentrifying" its traumatic impact, gives rise to a kind of parasitical, malign foreign body in the very kernel of the subject's being. Hegel's implicit lesson here is that the "external" revolutionary Terror would not be able to hold the subject in check were he not already terrorized "from within," by the inexorable superego-agency whose demands can never be met since, in its eyes, our very existence is branded by guilt. The result of this "internalization" is the Kantian subject: the subject condemned to an eternal split, i.e., forever doomed to contend with "pathological" impulses. The pressure exerted on the subject, which first seemed to come from the outside, is now experienced as something which defines—or, rather, subverts—the very kernel of his self-identity. The subject who, in the Jacobinical Terror, had to accept his worthlessness in the eyes of the State, must now, in his capacity as moral subject, sacrifice what he most cherishes to a Demon within. Therein consists the Hegelian "negation of negation": what first appears as an external obstacle reveals itself to be an inherent hindrance, i.e., an outside force turns into an inner compulsion.[24]

The reproach, according to which the Hegelian dialectical process implies a "closed economy" where every loss is in advance recompensed, "sublated" into a moment of self-mediation, thus results from a misreading. Paradoxically, the one to whom such a "closed economy" can legitimately be attributed is Marx himself. What I have in mind here, of course, is the unique moment when Marx is at his most Hegelian: his formulation of the proletarian as "substanceless subjectivity" in the famous manuscript-fragment on "Precapitalist epochs" from *Grundrisse*.[25] After deploying his grandiose conception of the proletariat as the apogee of the historical process of "alienation," of the gradual disengaging of the labor force from the domination of the "organic," substantial conditions of the process of production (the double freedom of the proletarian: he stands for the abstract subjectivity freed from all substantial-organic ties, yet at the same time he is dispossessed and thus obliged to sell on the market his own labor force in order to survive), Marx conceives of the proletarian revolution as a "materialist" version of the Hegelian reconciliation of subject and substance: it reestablishes the unity of the subject (labor force) with the objective conditions of the process of production, yet not under the hegemony of these objective conditions (where individuals figure as mere subordinated moments of their social totality), but with collective subjectivity as the mediating force of this unity. In socialism, the collective subject is bound to render transparent and control the process of production and social reproduction in its entirety.

From this Marxian perspective, of course, the Hegelian "reconciliation" emerges as a mere "reconciliation in the medium of thought" that leaves social reality undisturbed. Perhaps, however, after more than a century of polemics on the Marxist "materialist reversal of Hegel," the time has come to raise the inverse possibility of a Hegelian critique of Marx. Does not Hegel enable us to discern, in the very foundation of the Marxian notion of the proletarian revolution, a kind of perspective-illusion which hinges precisely on the "closed economy" of the dialectical reversal? It was possible for Marx to imagine "dis-alienation" as the reversal by means of which the subject reappropriates the entire substantial content. However, such a reversal is precisely what Hegel precludes: in Hegel's philosophy, "reconciliation" does not designate the moment when "substance becomes subject," when absolute subjectivity is elevated into the productive ground of all entities, but rather the acknowledgment that the dimension of subjectivity is inscribed into the very core of Substance in the guise of an irreducible lack which forever prevents it from achieving full self-identity. "Substance as subject" ultimately means that a kind of ontological "crack" forever denounces as a semblance every "world-view," every notion of the universe qua totality of the "great chain of being." One must therefore draw the conclusion that Marx himself, under the guise of combating Hegel, retroactively constructs the figure of Hegel qua the philosopher who elevates self-mediating Notion into the Ground and Substance of the universe: what Marx boxes with is ultimately the idealistic shadow of his own ontological premises. In short, "Hegel as absolute idealist" is a *displacement* of Marx's own disavowed ontology. Is not the symptom of this displacement, and thereby of the inherent impossibility of the Marxian project, the radically ambiguous character of Marx's reference to Hegel? That is to say, in his endeavor to delineate the Capital-universe by means of the categories of Hegel's logic, Marx continually and systematically oscillates between two possibilities:

–The qualification of Capital as the alienated Substance of the historical process which reigns over the atomized subjects (see the famous formulae from *Grundrisse* on the proletariat qua "substanceless subjectivity" which posits Capital as its own nonbeing); within this perspective, Revolution necessarily appears as an act by means of which the historical Subject appropriates to himself his alienated substantial content, i.e., recognizes in it his own product. This motif achieved its ultimate expression in Georg Lukács' *History and Class Consciousness.*[26]

–The opposite qualification of Capital as Substance which is already in itself Subject, i.e., which is not anymore an empty-abstract universality but an universality reproducing itself through the circular process of its self-mediation and self-positing (see the definition of Capital as "money which begets more money": Money-Commodity-Money)—in short, Capital is Money-which-became-Subject. This theme of "Hegel's logic as the notional structure of the movement of Capital" assumes its ultimate expression in the Hegelian reading of the "critique of political economy," which flourished in West Germany in the early seventies.[27]

Money and Subjectivity

Let us then return to Hegel: revolutionary Terror designates the turning point at which the appearance of an equivalent exchange collapses, the point at which the subject gets nothing in exchange for its sacrifice. Here, however, at this very point at which negation ceases to be "determinate" and becomes "absolute," the subject *encounters itself,* since the subject qua *cogito* is this very negativity prior to every act of exchange. The crucial move from revolutionary Terror to the Kantian subject is thus simply the move from S to $: at the level of Terror, the subject is not yet barred but remains a full, substantial entity, identical to a particular content which is threatened by the external pressure of the Terror's abstract and arbitrary negativity. The Kantian subject, on the contrary, is this very abyss, this void of absolute negativity to whom every "pathological," particular positive content appears as "posited," as something externally assumed and thus ultimately contingent. Consequently, the move from S to $ entails a radical shift in the very notion of the subject's self-identity: in it, I identify myself to that very void which a moment ago threatened to swallow the most

precious particular kernel of my being. This is how the subject qua $
emerges from the structure of exchange: it emerges when "something is
exchanged for nothing," that is to say, it is the very "nothing" I get from the
symbolic structure, from the Other, in exchange for sacrificing my "pathological" particularity, the kernel of my being. When I get nothing in return,
I get myself qua $, qua the empty point of self-relating.[28]

   It would be of great theoretical interest to establish the conceptual link
between this genesis of self-consciousness and the modern notion of paper
money. In the Middle Ages, money was a commodity which so to speak
guaranteed its own value: a gold coin—like any other commodity—was
simply worth its "actual" value. How did we get from that value to today's
paper money, which is intrinsically worthless, yet universally used to pur-
chase commodities? Brian Rotman[29] demonstrated the necessity of an
intermediate term, the so-called "imaginary money." The problem with
the gold money was that of physical debasement: a gap necessarily arose
between "good" money (the pure unsullied issue of the state) and "bad"
money (the worn and diminished coins in circulation); this gap between
the good standard money and the worn currency was known as *agio*. On
the basis of this difference between "good" and "bad" money, a new form
of money emerged in mercantile states, a so-called "bank-money": it represented money exactly according to the standard of mint, i.e., money insofar
as it has not yet been devalued by use; however, for this very reason, it was
not embodied but existed only as an imaginary point of reference. More
precisely, it existed as a convention between a bank and an individual: as a
paper by means of which a bank promised to pay a particular merchant a
certain amount upon his presenting this paper. This way, the merchant was
guaranteed that the money he gave to the bank would keep its "real" value.

   There are two crucial points to be noted here. The first is that, by way of
this operation, "money entered into a relation with itself and became a
commodity":[30] the duplication into "good," but only imaginary, money
and "bad," empirically existing gold money, subjected to wear and tear,
made it possible to measure the "price of money itself." It was possible to
say that this gold coin that I hold in my hand, due to its wear and tear, is
worth only so much, only a percentage of "good" money, of its own "true"
value. The second point is that this imaginary money was "deictically
rooted in the signature of a particular named payee":[31] the paper issued by
the bank was a monetary promise made by it to a named, individual
merchant. In order to arrive at paper money as we know it today, this

deictic promise with concrete dates and names has to be depersonalized into a promise made to the anonymous "bearer" to pay the gold-equivalent of the sum written on paper money—thus, the anchoring, the link to a concrete individual was cut loose. And the subject who came to recognize itself as this anonymous "bearer" is the very subject of self-consciousness— why? What is at stake here is not simply that this "bearer" designates a neutral universal function which can be filled in by any individual; if we are to attain self-consciousness, the empty universality of the "bearer" has to assume actual existence, it has to be posited as such, i.e., *the subject has to relate to itself, to conceive of itself, as (to) an empty "bearer," and to perceive his empirical features which constitute the positive content of his particular "person" as a contingent variable.* This shift is again the very shift from S to $, from the fullness of the "pathological" subject to *cogito* qua empty self-relating which experiences its own positive, empirical content as something "posited," i.e., contingent and ultimately indifferent.[32]

From Subject to Substance . . . and Back

The gap that separates Marx from Hegel, i.e., the crucial dimension of what Hegel calls "subject" (as opposed to empirical individuals), becomes visible the moment one traverses the path "from substance to subject" in the opposite direction. What we have in mind here is the reproach usually addressed to Hegel by his nominalist adversaries, from Feuerbach and young Marx onwards, whose basic premise is that "actually existing individuals" realize their potentials in the social network of their mutual relationships ("the essence of man is the totality of his social relationships," as Marx put it). According to this reproach, Hegel's "idealist mystification" proceeds in two steps. First, Hegel transposes-translates this multitude of relations between subjects qua concrete individuals into the relationship of the subject-individual to the Substance: social relationships *between* individuals undergo a sudden transsubstantiation and change into the relationship of *the* individual to *the* Society qua substance. Thereupon, in a second move, Hegel transposes this relationship of the individual-subject to the Substance into the relationship of the Substance *to itself.* The paradigmatic case of this "unmasking of the idealist mystification" is provided by the critique of religious consciousness elaborated by Feuerbach and young Marx, which conceives of God as the alienated, inverted, "substantialized" expression of the basic structure of social relations between actual and active individuals. According to this critique, the first step of the religious mystification is to "ground" the individual's relations to his social environs, to other individuals, in his relationship to God: when I relate to God, I relate in an inverted-alienated form to my own social essence, i.e., what I (mis)perceive as "God" is nothing but a "reified," externalized expression of the fundamental way I am related to my fellow creatures. Once this step is accomplished, the next step that follows automatically is that I, a concrete individual, identify my relating to God with God's self-relating. Suffice it to recall mystical formulas on how the eye through which I see God is the very eye through which God is looking at Himself.

From the proper Hegelian perspective, however, we are here at the very opposite point of losing the specific dimension of subjectivity, i.e., of reducing the subject to a subordinated moment of the Substance's self-relating. It is precisely and only here that we encounter *subject* as distinct from the "individual": the Hegelian "subject" is ultimately nothing but a name for the externality of the Substance to itself, for the "crack" by way of which the Substance becomes "alien" to itself, (mis)perceiving itself through human eyes as the inaccessible-reified Otherness. That is to say, insofar as the relationship of the subject to the Substance overlaps with the Substance's self-relating, the fact that Substance appears to subject as an alien-external-inaccessible entity bears witness to a self-splitting of the Substance itself.[33] In his *Ecrits*, Lacan resolves the worn-out problem of the relationship between the individual and society via an elegant reference to precisely this moment of Hegel's philosophy: psychoanalytical theory enables us to recognize their "reconciliation"—the "mediation" of the Individual and the Universal—in the very splitting that runs through both of them.[34] In other words, the problem remains unsolvable as long as we insist upon either the individual or Society as an organic, self-enclosed Whole: the first step toward the solution is to relate the splitting which traverses the social Substance ("social antagonism") to the splitting which is constitutive of the subject (in the Lacanian theory, the subject is precisely *not* "in-dividual," an indivisible One, but constitutively divided, $). This reading of Hegel which locates the "reconciliation" of the Universal and the Particular into the very splitting which cuts through them and thus unites them, also provides an answer to the eternal problem of solipsism and the possibility of communication (between different subjects or, at a more general level, between different cultures): what begs the question in the solipsist hypothesis is the presupposed self-enclosure of the individual or society. In other words, communication is rendered possible by the very feature which may seem to undermine most radically its possibility: I can communicate with the Other, I am "open" to him (or it), precisely and only insofar as I am already in myself split, branded by "repression," i.e., insofar as (to put it in a somewhat naive-pathetic way) *I cannot ever truly communicate with myself;* the Other is originally the decentered Other Place of my own splitting. In classical Freudian terms: "others" are here only because and insofar as I am not simply identical to myself but have an unconscious, insofar as I am prevented from having direct access to the truth of my own being. It is this truth that I am looking for in others: what propels me to "communicate" with them is the hope that I will receive from them the truth about myself, about my own desire. And the same goes for the no less worn-out problem of "communication between different cultures." The common ground that allows cultures to talk to each other, to exchange messages, is not some presupposed shared set of universal values, etc., but rather its opposite, some shared *deadlock;* cultures "communicate" insofar as they can recognize in each other a different answer to the same fundamental "antagonism," deadlock, point of failure.[35]

What is therefore crucial for Hegel's notion of *act* is that an act always, by definition, involves a moment of externalization, self-objectivization, of the jump into the unknown. To "pass to the act" means to assume the risk that what I am about to do will be inscribed into a framework whose contours elude my grasp, that it may set in motion an unforeseeable train of events, that it will acquire a meaning different from or even totally opposed to what I intended to accomplish—in short, it means to assume one's role in the game of the "cunning of reason." (And what is at stake in *la passe,* the concluding moment of the psychoanalytical process, is precisely the analysand's readiness to fully assume this radical self-externalization, i.e., "subjective destitution": I am only what I am for the others, which is why I have to renounce the fantasy-support of my being, my clinging to "my own private Idaho," to some hidden treasure in me, inaccessible to others.)[36] The basic problem with the act in Hegel is therefore not its necessary ultimate failure (due to the interference of the Other subverting every intended meaning, one can never adequately externalize, transpose into the mode of intersubjective actuality, our internal project), but rather its exact opposite: *a wholly successful act (an act "corresponding to its notion") would bring about catastrophe,* i.e., either a suicide (the accomplished self-objectivization, the transformation of the subject into a thing) or a lapse into madness (the "short-circuit," the immediate sign of equality, between Inside and Outside, i.e., the (mis)perception of the Law of my Heart as the Law of the World). In other words, if the subject is to survive his act, he is compelled to organize its ultimate failure, to accomplish it "with fingers crossed," to avoid totally identifying with it, to inscribe it into an overall economy which subverts its proclaimed goal, so that what appears as a failure is actually its true aim.

The common notion of the "cunning of reason" reduces it to a relation-ship of technological manipulation: instead of acting directly upon the object, we interpose between ourselves and the object another object and let them interact freely; the frictional wear and tear of objects realizes our aim, while we maintain a safe distance, keeping ourselves out of the melee. One has only to recall Adam Smith's "invisible hand of the market": every individual pursues his or her egotistical interests, but their interaction realizes the Common Good of increasing the nation's welfare. The idea is that the Hegelian Absolute entertains the same relationship toward con-crete individuals engaging in historical struggles:

> It is not the general idea that is implicated in opposition and combat, and that is exposed to danger. It remains in the background, un-touched and uninjured. This may be called the *cunning of reason*—that it sets the passions to work for itself, while that which develops its exis-tence through such impulsion pays the penalty, and suffers loss. . . . The particular is for the most part of too trifling value as compared with the general: individuals are sacrificed and abandoned. The Idea pays the penalty of determinate existence and corruptibility, not from itself, but from the passions of individuals.[37]

This quotation from Hegel's *The Philosophy of History* fits perfectly the common notion of the "cunning of reason": individuals who follow their particular aims are unknowingly instruments of the realization of the Divine plan. But certain elements disturb this seemingly clear picture. Usually passed over in silence is the very main point of Hegel's argumenta-tion apropos of the "cunning of reason": the ultimate *impossibility* of it. It is impossible for any determinate subject to occupy the place of the "cunning of reason" and to exploit another's passions without getting involved in their labor, i.e., without paying in flesh the price for his exploitation. In this precise sense, the "cunning of reason" is always redoubled: an artisan, for example, makes use of the forces of nature (water, steam . . .) and lets them interact for ends external to them, to mold the raw material into a form appropriate for human consumption; for him, the aim of the process of production is the satisfaction of human needs. It is here, however, that he is as it were the victim of his own ruse: the true aim of the process of social production is not the satisfaction of individual needs but the very development of productive forces, what Hegel refers to as the "objectivization of the Spirit." Hegel's thesis is therefore that *the manipulator himself is always-already manipulated:* the artisan who exploits nature by way of the "cunning of reason" is in turn exploited by the "objective spirit." And, according to Hegel, the supreme proof of this impossibility of occupying the position of the "cunning of reason" is provided by God himself: Christ's suffering on the cross explodes the logic of Divinity who keeps itself in the background and pulls the strings of the theater of History from a safe distance. Crucifixion designates the point at which it is no longer possible for the divine Idea to "remain in the background, untouched and uninjured": it is God himself who, by way of "becoming man" and dying on the cross, "pays the penalty."

The Subject as "Vanishing Mediator"

This paradoxical relationship of subject and substance, where the subject emerges as the crack in the universal Substance, hinges on the notion of the subject as the "vanishing mediator" in the precise sense of the Freudian-Lacanian Real, i.e., the structure of an element which, although nowhere actually present and as such inaccessible to our experience, nonetheless has to be retroactively constructed, presupposed, if all other elements are to retain their consistency. In Hegel's *Phenomenology of Spirit,* we encounter more than once this structure of the "vanishing mediator." Suffice it to mention two such loci: the passage of the dialectic of Lord and Bondsman into stoicism; the passage of "phrenology," the last form of the "observing Reason," into "active Reason":

—In the dialectic of Lord (Master) and Bondsman, Knowledge first belongs to the Bondsman in the guise of his "savoir-faire" (know-how), of his practical skills about handling things in order to provide satisfaction for the Lord-Master. It may seem that the passage from this technical "know-how" to Thought (and thereby to stoicism as the position of the thinking Bondsman-Slave: it is clear from Hegel's presentation that it is the Slave, not the Master, who arrives at the "labor of the Notion" by means of the "notion of labor") is direct and unambiguous: we attain the universality of Thought qua form of actuality by way of the typically Hegelian reversal of external finality into self-finality, i.e., of external form into absolute form. Through his effort to mold, to form, external objects so that they fit the end of satisfying the Master's needs, the Slave becomes aware of how Thought as such is already the form of every possible objectivity. What is missing from this account, however, is the very moment exposed, isolated by Lacan as the inaugural moment of philosophy: the "appropriation of Knowledge by the Master." According to Lacan, philosophy emerges when the Master appropriates to himself the Slave's "know-how" and transforms it into a universal *episteme* disengaged from utilitarian interests, i.e., into philosophical ontology.[38] In the history of philosophy, this moment roughly corresponds to Plato and Aristotle, whereas stoicism, which follows them, stands for an attempt of the Slave to participate in the Master's disinterested Knowledge (stoicism is the philosophy of the Slave who posits his "inner freedom" as the only level at which he is equal to the Master). Why then is this intermediate term, this inaugural gesture of philosophical discourse, missing from Hegel's account? Perhaps the reason can be sought in the fact that the position of Philosopher qua "Master who thinks (who possesses knowledge)" is inherently impossible *and as such is a mere fantasy of philosophy* which can never be realized? Was it not already Plato who, clinging to his dream of a knowing Master (the "Philosopher-King"), was bound to new and newer disappointments, finding himself again and again reduced to the role of a court jester, whispering advice in the ignorant Master's ear?[39]

—Phrenology ends with the infinite judgment "Spirit is a bone,"[40] whose speculative content is the identity of the subject and object, i.e., the power of the Spirit to "become" an inert thing, to "mediate" it; what then follows is the passage into active Reason which endeavors to consummate, to implement, to "realize," this truth of the observing Reason, i.e., to transpose it from its In-itself into its For-itself: by means of his activity of molding objects, the subject actualizes himself, "changes into an object"; he acquires an existence independent of his subjective Inwardness in the guise of the human shape of the objects around him. There is again, however, a certain bump which belies the smooth run of this passage and introduces a note of compulsive neurosis into the dialectical process, which otherwise follows the matrix of hystericization: the subject escapes into activity, he transposes what he already possessed into an infinite task to be gradually realized through his continuous effort. In other words, we encounter here a case of what psychoanalytic theory calls *acting out*. By way of shifting from phrenology into "active Reason," the subject effectively puts off the uneasy encounter with what is already here, with the Real: he transposes his identity with the dead, inert object (which, at the end of the phrenological experience, is already realized) into the goal of his infinite activity—the same as in courtly love where the knight again and again assumes new tasks in order to adjourn the final moment of the sexual encounter with the lady. In both cases, the aim of flight is the same: to avoid confronting an unbearable trauma, in the first case the uncanny abyss of the subject *qua* $, the void of absolute self-contradiction, in the second case the traumatic fact that "there is no sexual relationship." If, however, this is how things stand, then between the immediate naiveté of the phrenological attitude (which "truly believes" that the key to the secrets of the Spirit is contained in the skull's convexities and is thus unaware of the speculative content of the equation "Spirit is a bone") and the attitude of "active Reason" (which endeavors to realize this speculative content by way of bestowing on the objects the form which suits spiritual ends) we must interpose a brief, evanescent, yet for structural reasons necessary moment at which consciousness has a foreboding of the speculative truth of phrenology, but *is unable to endure it and therefore runs away from it into activity.*[41]

Limitation Precedes Transcendence

Against the background of this shift from Kant's subject qua the I of pure apperception to Hegel's subject qua the crack in the universal Substance, it is possible to delineate the exact nature of the relationship between the Real and the object small *a* (*objet petit a*). The obvious solution, of course, is to conceive of the Real as the substance of *jouissance* radically external to the symbolic order, and of the status of *objet a* as that of a semblance: the semblance of being. The translation into Kantian terms seems no less obvious: the Real is the *Ding-an-sich*, the inaccessible substance, and *a* the transcendental object. This translation seems imposed by the way Kant differentiates between the transcendental object and the *Ding-an-sich*: they are of the same nature, yet in the case of the Thing the accent is on its independence from the subject's perception, from the subject's being affected by it (the Thing is what it is "in itself," irrespective of us); whereas in the case of transcendental object, the accent shifts imperceptibly, but crucially: the transcendental object is the underlying, unknown ground of appearance, i.e., of what we perceive as an object of experience. However, it is this ground conceived of in the mode of our thinking; that is, it is the unknown X that has to be thought of as an X (a sensuously unfulfilled conception) if our experience is to retain its consistency. The point is, precisely, that *it has to be thought*. In other words, the transcendental object is a *Gedankending:* it is as it were the "In-itself insofar as it is for us, for the consciousness," i.e., it designates the way the In-itself is present in thought.[42]

The problem with this seemingly obvious solution is that it leads to the "substantialization" of the Thing: it compels us to conceive the Thing as the fullness of the In-itself and the transcendental object as the way this fullness is present in our experience—in the guise of its opposite, of an empty thought devoid of any intuitive content. In this perspective, the status of the transcendental object is strictly secondary; it designates the negative way the Thing is present in the field of our experience: as the empty thought of an underlying, inaccessible X. And are things not homologous in the relationship between the Lacanian Thing qua substance of *jouissance* and *objet petit a*, the surplus-enjoyment? Is not the Real Thing a kind of preexisting substance "cultivated," "gentrified" by the Symbolic, and is not *a* the semblance of the lost *jouissance*, i.e., what remains in the Symbolic of the lost Real? It is here that the fate of our comprehension of Lacan and Kant is decided. That is to say, a certain fundamental ambiguity pertains to the notion of the Real in Lacan: the Real designates a substantial hard kernel that precedes and resists symbolization and, simultaneously, it designates the left-over, which is posited or "produced" by symbolization itself.[43] However, what we must avoid at any price is conceiving of this left-over as simply secondary, as if we have *first* the substantial fullness of the Real and *then* the process of symbolization which "evacuates" *jouissance*, yet not entirely, leaving behind isolated remainders, islands of enjoyment, *objets petit a*. If we succumb to this notion, we lose the paradox of the Lacanian Real: there is no substance of enjoyment without, prior to, the surplus of enjoyment. *The substance is a mirage retroactively invoked by the surplus.* The illusion that pertains to *a* qua surplus-enjoyment is therefore the very illusion that, behind it, there is the lost substance of *jouissance*. In other words, *a* qua semblance deceives in a Lacanian way: not because it is a deceitful substitute of the Real, but precisely because it invokes the impression of some substantial Real behind it; it deceives by posing as a shadow of the underlying Real.[44] And the same goes for Kant: what Kant fails to notice is that *das Ding* is a mirage invoked by the transcendental object. *Limitation precedes transcendence:* all that "actually exists" is the field of phenomena and its limitation, whereas *das Ding* is nothing but a phantasm which, subsequently, fills out the void of the transcendental object.

Lacan's ultimate point in his reading of Kant is that *the distinction between phenomena and the Thing can be sustained only within the space of desire as structured by the intervention of the signifier:* it is this intervention that brings about the split separating the accessible, symbolically structured, reality from the void of the Real, the index of the lost Thing. What we experience as "reality" discloses itself against the background of the lack, of the absence of it, of the Thing, of the mythical object whose encounter would bring about the full satisfaction of the drive. This lack of the Thing constitutive of "reality" is therefore, in its fundamental dimension, not epistemological, but rather pertains to the paradoxical logic of desire—the paradox being that this Thing is retroactively produced by the very process of symbolization, i.e., that it emerges in the very gesture of its loss. In other (Hegel's) words, there is nothing—no positive substantial entity—behind the phenomenal curtain, only the gaze whose phantasmagorias assume the different shapes of the Thing. Lacan is for that reason far from falling prey to a theoretically illegitimate short-circuit between the psychoanalytical problematic of the unattainable lost object of desire and the epistemological problematic of the object of knowledge, of its unknowable character.[45] Quite to the contrary, what he aims to do is to demonstrate precisely how this short-circuit results from a kind of perspective illusion which generates an illegitimate (although structurally necessary) "substantivization" of the Thing. The status of the Thing-*jouissance* becomes epistemological; its unattainable character is perceived as unknowableness the moment we "substantivize" it and assume that it ontologically precedes its loss, i.e., that there is something to see "behind the curtain" (of the phenomena).

This priority of limitation over transcendence also sheds a new (Hegelian) light on the Kantian sublime: what we experience as the positive sublime content (the moral law in ourselves, the dignity of the free will) is of a strictly secondary nature; it is something which merely fills out the original void opened up by the breakdown of the field of representations. In other words, the Sublime does *not* involve the breakdown of the field of phenomena, i.e., the experience of how no phenomenon, even the mightiest one, can appropriately express the suprasensible Idea. This notion—

that, in the experience of the Sublime, phenomena prove unfit to render the Idea—results from a kind of perspective-illusion. What actually breaks down in the experience of the Sublime is the very notion that, behind the field of phenomena, lies some inaccessible positive, substantial Thing. In other words, this experience demonstrates that phenomena and noumena are not to be conceived as two positive domains separated by a frontier: the field of phenomena as such is limited, yet this limitation is its inherent determination, so that there is nothing "beyond" this limit. The limit ontologically *precedes* its Beyond: the object which we experience as "sublime," its elevated glitter, *Schein*, is a mere secondary positivization of the "nothing," the void, beyond the limit. And—as demonstrated by Lacan in his Seminar on the Ethic of Psychoanalysis—this Kantian notion of the Sublime is wholly compatible with the Freudian notion of sublimation: in the Freudian theory, the "sublime" designates an empirical object that occupies, fills in, the void, the empty place, of the "primordially repressed" Thing, becoming "elevated to the dignity of the Thing." In this precise sense, the sublime object is simultaneously the surface *Schein* or "grimace," a pure semblance devoid of any substantial support, *and* something "more real than reality itself": in its very capacity of a pure semblance, it "gives body" to a boundary which fixes the limits of (what we experience as) reality, i.e., it holds the place of, stands in for, what has to be excluded, foreclosed, if "reality" is to retain its consistency.[46]

As regards Hegel's critique of Kant, the crucial thing is to avoid the seemingly obvious conclusion that Hegel "delivers," makes a foray into, what Kant shirks from and designates as inaccessible. That is to say, according to Kant, we, finite beings, are condemned to the gap that separates intuition from concept; it is this very gap which defines our finitude. Kant's point is that transcendental constitution (i.e., the subject's "spontaneity") can occur only within this horizon of finitude: in an infinite being (God), intuition and intellect would coincide, which is why such a being would overcome the opposition of theoretical and practical reason (and, consequently, the need for their mediation in the "capacity of judging"). Such a being would be capable of "intellectual intuition" or, to put it in another way, of productive perception: the very act of perception would create (not merely "constitute" in the transcendental sense) the perceived objects. How does Hegel respond to this splitting? He in no way asserts that this intellectual intuition, the unity of concept and intuition, posited by Kant in the inaccessible divine Beyond, is already actual, present, in the I of pure self-consciousness; if this were the case, we would have to do with a senseless solipsistic creationism, with the notion of an I directly creating objects. Hegel's point here is far more refined: according to him, the very notion of "intellectual intuition" belongs to the level of abstract Understanding (as opposed to dialectical Reason), i.e., it presents the synthesis of the Sensible and the Intellectual as something that takes place in a separate domain beyond their splitting. The actual synthesis of the Sensible and of the Intellectual is already effectuated in what was for Kant their splitting, since the suprasensible Idea is *nothing but* the inherent limitation of the intuited phenomena. Hegel thus can be said to reaffirm the Kantian gap that forever separates intuition and intellect: for an "object" to emerge in the field of what we experience as reality, the multitude of sensible intuitions which provide its content must be supplemented by the "sensuously unfulfilled conception" of an X qua *Gedankending*, i.e., the void which no empirical, positive feature can fill out, since it is a correlative, a "reified" effect, of the *subject's* synthetic act of apperception.[47]

The very tetrad of Kant-Fichte-Schelling-Hegel appears thus in a new light. When Kant formulated the problematic of transcendental constitution, of the I qua pure apperception, he opened up a new domain, yet he advanced only half-way into it and thus got stuck in inconsistencies; both Fichte and Schelling endeavored to overcome these Kantian inconsistencies by conceiving of the Kantian split between intellect and (sensible) intuition as the lapse from some original unity, the true starting point of philosophy, which, of course, is none other than intellectual intuition (*intelektuelle Anschauung*), the unity of intuition and intellect, of object and subject, of theory and praxis, etc. Hegel, however, paradoxically *returns to Kant*, i.e., he *rejects* these post-Kantian attempts of a beforehand, precipitate, "immediate" synthesis and proposes to overcome Kant's inconsistencies in a different, "Hegelian" way: by demonstrating how synthesis already is actualized where Kant saw only the splitting, so that there is no need to postulate a separate, additional act of synthesis in the "intellectual intuition." We do not pass from Kant to Hegel by *filling out* the empty place of the Thing, i.e., the black void perceptible in the crack of the half-opened window in Magritte's *Lunette d'approche*,[48] but *by affirming this void as such, in its priority to any positive entity that strives to fill it out*.

"Total Recall": Knowledge in the Real

And—to return to *noir*—it is this void, standing for the irreducible gap between the I of apperception and the noumenal "Thing which thinks," which opens up the possibility of a "paranoiac" attitude according to which noumenally—qua "Thing which thinks"—I am an artifact, a plaything in the hands of an unknown Maker. The last impersonation of this figure occurs in the *noir*-renewal of the eighties, in the guise of the new type of father which characterizes "postindustrial," corporate late capitalism, a father epitomized by Tyrell in *Blade Runner,* a lone figure of uncanny, ethereal, frail materiality, devoid of a sexual partner. This father clearly materializes the Cartesian Evil Genius: a father who exerts domination over me not at the level of my symbolic identity, but at the level of what I am qua "Thing which thinks."[49] In others words, a father who is not anymore S_1, Master-Signifier whose Name guarantees my symbolic identity, my place in the texture of symbolic tradition, but S_2, Knowledge which created me as its artifact. The moment father changes his status from S_1 to S_2, from empty Master-Signifier to Knowledge, I, the son, become a monster.[50] Herefrom the hystericization of the monster-son: the questions monsters address to their Maker, from Dr. Frankenstein's creature to the Rutger Hauer character in *Blade Runner,* ultimately vary one and the same motif: "Why did you screw me up? Why did you create me the way you did, incomplete, crippled?" Or, to quote the lines from Milton's *Paradise Lost* which served as the motto to the first edition of *Frankenstein:* "Did I request thee, Maker, from my clay / To mould me man? Did I solicit thee / From darkness to promote me?"[51]

This paradox of the "subject who knows he is a replicant" renders clear what the "nonsubstantial status of the subject" amounts to: with regard to every substantial, positive content of my being, I "am" nothing but a replicant, i.e., the difference which makes me "human" and not a replicant is to be discerned nowhere in "reality." Therein consists the implicit philosophical lesson of *Blade Runner* attested to by numerous allusions to the Cartesian *cogito* (like when the replicant-character played by Darryl Hannah ironically points out "I think, therefore I am"): where is the *cogito,* the place of my self-consciousness, when everything that I actually am is an artifact—not only my body, my eyes, but even my most intimate memories and fantasies? It is here that we again encounter the Lacanian distinction between the subject of enunciation and the subject of enunciated: everything that I positively am, every enunciated content I can point at and say "that's *me,*" is not "I"; I am only the void that remains, the empty distance toward every content.

Blade Runner thus gives a double twist to the commonsense distinction between human and android. Man is a replicant who does not know it; yet if this were all, the film would involve a simplistic reductionist notion that our self-experience qua free "human" agents is an illusion founded upon our ignorance of the causal nexus which regulates our lives. For that reason, we should supplement the former statement: it is only when, at the level of the enunciated content, I assume my replicant-status, that, at the level of enunciation, I become a truly human subject. "I am a replicant" is the statement of the subject in its purest—the same as in Althusser's theory of ideology where the statement "I am in ideology" is the only way for me to truly avoid the vicious circle of ideology (or the Spinozean version of it: the awareness that nothing can ever escape the grasp of necessity is the only way for us to be truly free).[52] In short, the implicit thesis of *Blade Runner* is that replicants are pure subjects precisely insofar as they testify that every positive, substantial content, inclusive of the most intimate fantasies, is not "their own" but already implanted. In this precise sense, subject is by definition nostalgic, a subject of loss. Let us recall how, in *Blade Runner,* Rachael silently starts to cry when Deckard proves to her that she is a replicant. The silent grief over the loss of her "humanity," the infinite longing to be or to become human again, although she knows this will never happen; or, conversely, the eternal gnawing doubt over whether I am truly human or just an android—it is these very undecided, intermediate states which make me human.[53]

What is of crucial importance here is that we do not confuse this radical "decenteredness" characterizing the replicants with the decenteredness characterizing the subject of the signifier with regard to the big Other, to the symbolic order. We can, of course, read *Blade Runner* as a film about the process of subjectivization of the replicants: despite the fact that their most intimate memories are not "true" but only implanted, replicants subjectivize themselves by way of combining these memories into an individual myth, a narrative which allows them to construct their place in the symbolic universe. Furthermore, are not our "human" memories also "implanted" in the sense that we all borrow the elements of our individual myths from the treasury of the big Other? Are we not, prior to our speaking, *spoken* by the discourse of the Other? As to the truth of our memories, does not, according to Lacan, truth have the structure of a fiction? Even if its ingredients are invented or implanted, not "really ours," what remains "ours" is the unique way we subjectivize them, we integrate them into our symbolic universe. From this perspective, the lesson of *Blade*

Runner is that manipulation is ultimately doomed to fail: even if Tyrell artificially implanted every element of our memory, what he was not able to foresee is the way replicants will organize these elements into a mythical narrative which will then give rise to the hysterical question.[54] What Lacan has in mind with *cogito*, however, is *the exact opposite of this gesture of subjectivization:* the "subject" qua $ emerges not via subjectivization-narrativization, i.e., via the "individual myth" constructed from the decentered pieces of tradition; instead, the subject emerges *at the very moment when the individual loses its support in the network of tradition;* it coincides with the void that remains after the framework of symbolic memory is suspended. The emergence of *cogito* thus undermines the subject's inveterateness in the symbolic tradition by way of opening up an irreducible gap between the horizon of meaning, of narrative tradition, and an impossible knowledge whose possession would enable me to gain access to the Thing I am in the Real, beyond all narrativization, all symbolization or historicization. A full recollection ("total recall") would therefore amount to filling out the void which constitutes me qua $, subject of self-consciousness, i.e., to identifying-recognizing myself as "he or it, the Thing which thinks." In Lacanian terms, "total recall" would amount to the "knowledge in the Real."[55]

Replicants know their life span is limited to four years. This certainty saps the openness of their "being-towards-death"; it bears witness to their arrival at the impossible point of knowing how they are structured qua "thing-machine which thinks." For that reason, replicants are ultimately the impossible fantasy-formation of us human mortals: the fantasy of a being conscious of itself qua Thing, of a being which does not have to pay for access to self-consciousness with $, with the loss of its substantial support. A crack in this fantasy therefore enables us to broach the question of "artificial intelligence": do computers think?

What is crucial to the debates on artificial intelligence is that an inversion has taken place, which is the fate of every successful metaphor: one first tries to simulate human thought with the computer, bringing the model as close as possible to the human "original," until at a certain point matters reverse and the question emerges: *what if this "model" is already a model of the "original" itself,* what if human intelligence itself operates like a computer, is "programmed," etc.? (Therein consists also the intriguing implication of the computer-generated "virtual reality": what if our "true" reality itself has to be virtualized, conceived as an artifact?) The computer raises in pure form the question of semblance, of a discourse which would not be that of a semblance: it is clear that the computer in some sense only "simulates" thought; yet *how does the total simulation of thought differ from "real" thought?* No wonder, then, that the specter of "artificial intelligence" appears as an entity which is simultaneously *prohibited* and considered *impossible*: we assert that it is not possible for a machine to think; at the same time, we try to prohibit research in these directions, on the grounds that it is dangerous, ethically dubious, etc.

Do then "computers think" or not? The answer hinges precisely on this logic of the reversed metaphor where, instead of conceiving of the computer as the model for the human brain, we conceive of the brain itself as a "computer made of flesh and blood," where, instead of defining the robot as the artificial man, we define man himself as a "natural robot," etc. This reversal could be further exemplified by resorting to the domain of sexuality. We usually consider masturbation as an "imaginary sexual act," i.e., an act where the bodily contact with a partner is only imagined; is it not possible to reverse the terms and to conceive the "proper" sexual act, the act with an "actual" partner, as a kind of "masturbation with a real (instead of only imagined) partner"? The whole point of Lacan's insistence on the "impossibility of sexual relationship" is that this, precisely, is what the "actual" sexual act is; man's partner is never a woman in the real kernel of her being, but woman qua *a*, reduced to the fantasy-object (let us just recall Lacan's definition of the phallic enjoyment as essentially masturbatory)!

It is against this background that we can provide one of the possible definitions of the Lacanian Real: the Real designates the very remainder which resists this reversal (of computer qua model of human brains into brains themselves qua blood-and-flesh computer; of masturbation qua imaginary sexual act into the actual sexual act qua masturbation with a real partner). The Real is that X on whose account this "squaring of the circle" ultimately is doomed to fail. This reversal relies on a kind of realization of the metaphor: what at first appears as a mere metaphorical simulation, a pale imitation, of the true reality (computer as a metaphor of the true brains, etc.) becomes the original paradigm imitated by blood-and-flesh reality (brains follow in an always imperfect way the functioning of the computer, etc.). What we experience as "reality" is constituted by such a reversal: as Lacan puts it, "reality" is always framed by a fantasy, i.e., for something real to be experienced as part of "reality," it must fit the preordained coordinates of our fantasy-space (a sexual act must fit the coordinates of our imagined fantasy-scripts, a brain must fit the functioning of a computer, etc.). This way, we can propose a second definition of the Real: a surplus, a hard kernel, which resists any process of modeling, simulation, or metaphoricization.

Let us recall how, apropos of *Alien³*, some reviewers quoted a series of features (the action takes place in a closed male community where even Ripley has to shave her head in order to become part of it; humans are utterly defenseless against the threat of the "alien," etc.) as an argument for conceiving the "alien" as a metaphor of AIDS. What one has to add, from the Lacanian perspective, is that all the talk about "alien," the monster, as a metaphor of AIDS falls short of the crucial fact that AIDS itself owes its tremendous impact not to its raw reality of an illness, to its immediate physical impact, however horrifying it may be, but to the extraordinary libidinal energy invested in it (AIDS is perceived as irresistible, it strikes suddenly, as if from nowhere, it seems to function perfectly as God's punishment for our promiscuous way of life . . .). In short, AIDS occupies a certain preordained place in our ideological fantasy-space, and the monstrous "alien" ultimately just materializes, gives body to, this fantasy-dimension which from the very beginning was at work in the AIDS-phenomenon.

Our point is thus a very elementary one: true, the computer-generated "virtual reality" is a semblance, it does foreclose the Real; but what we experience as the "true, hard, external reality" is based upon exactly the same exclusion. The ultimate lesson of "virtual reality" is the virtualization of the very "true" reality: by the mirage of "virtual reality," the "true" reality itself is posited as a semblance of itself, as a pure symbolic edifice. The fact that "a computer doesn't think" means that the price for our access to "reality" is that *something must remain unthought.*

2 *Cogito* and the Sexual Difference

■

The Kantian Crack in the Universal

It may seem paradoxical to evoke a "crack in the universal" apropos of Kant: was Kant not obsessed by the Universal, was not his fundamental aim to establish the universal form (constitutive) of knowledge, does his ethics not propose the universal form of the rule which regulates our activity as the sole criterion of morality, etc.? Yet as soon as the Thing-in-itself is posited as unattainable, *every universal is potentially suspended.* Every universal implies a point of exception at which its validity, its hold, is canceled; or, to put it in the language of contemporary physics, it implies a point of singularity. This "singularity" is ultimately *the Kantian subject himself,* namely the empty subject of the transcendental apperception. On account of this singularity, each of Kant's three critiques "stumbles" against universalization. In "pure reason," antinomies emerge when, in the use of categories, we reach beyond our finite experience and endeavor to apply them to the *totality* of the universe: if we endeavor to conceive the universe as a *Whole,* it appears simultaneously as finite and infinite, as an all-embracing causal nexus and containing free beings. In "practical reason," the "crack" is introduced by the possibility of "radical Evil," of an Evil which, as to its form, *coincides with the Good* (the free will qua will which follows universal self-posited rules can choose to be "evil" out of principle, not on account of "pathological," empirical impulses). In the "capacity of judging" qua "synthesis" of pure and practical reason, the split occurs twice. First, we have the opposition of aesthetics and teleology, the two poles which, together, do *not* form a harmonious Whole. Beauty is "purposefulness without purpose": a product of man's conscious activity, it bears the mark of purposefulness, yet an object appears as "beautiful" only insofar as it is experienced as something which serves no definite purpose, which is here without reason or end. In other words, Beauty designates the paradoxical point at which human activity (which is otherwise instrumental, directed at realizing conscious aims) starts to function as a spontaneous natural force: a true work of art never proceeds from a conscious plan, it must "grow out spontaneously." Teleology, on the other hand, deals with discerning hidden purposes at work in a nature submitted to blind mechanical laws, i.e., ontologically constituted as "objective reality" by means of transcendental categories among which there is no place for purposefulness.[1]

The Sublime is to be conceived precisely as the index of the failed "synthesis" of Beauty and Purpose—or, to use elementary mathematical language, as the intersection of the two sets, the set of what is "beautiful" and the set of what is "purposeful"—a negative intersection, to be sure, i.e., an intersection containing elements which are neither beautiful nor purposeful. Sublime phenomena (more precisely, phenomena which arouse in the subject the sentiment of the Sublime) are in no way beautiful; they are chaotic, formless, the very opposite of a harmonious form, and they also serve no purpose, i.e., they are the very opposite of those features that bear witness to a hidden purposefulness in nature (they are monstrous in the sense of the inexpediently excessive, overblown character of an organ or an object). As such, the Sublime is the site of the inscription of pure subjectivity whose abyss both Beauty and Teleology endeavor to conceal by way of the appearance of Harmony.

How then, on a closer look, is the Sublime related to the two sets of Beauty and Teleology whose intersection it is? As to the relationship between the Beautiful and the Sublime, Kant, as is well known, conceives of beauty as the symbol of the Good; at the same time, he points out that what is truly sublime is not the object which arouses the feeling of sublimity but the moral Law in us, our suprasensible nature. Are then beauty and sublimity simply to be conceived as two different symbols of the Good? Or is it not, on the contrary, that this duality points toward a certain chasm which must pertain to the moral Law itself? Lacan draws a line of demarcation between the two facets of law: on the one hand, law qua symbolic Ego-Ideal—i.e., law in its pacifying function, law qua guarantee of the social pact, qua the intermediating Third which dissolves the impasse of imaginary aggressivity; on the other hand, law in its superego dimension—i.e., law qua "irrational" pressure, the force of culpabilitization totally incommensurable with our actual responsibility, the agency in whose eyes we are a priori guilty and which gives body to the impossible imperative of enjoyment. It is this distinction between Ego-Ideal and superego which enables us to specify how Beauty and Sublimity are differently related to the domain of ethics. Beauty is the symbol of the Good, i.e., of the moral Law as the pacifying agency which reins in our egotism and renders possible harmonious social coexistence. In contrast, the dynamical sublime—volcanic eruptions, stormy seas, mountain precipices, etc.—by its very failure to symbolize (to represent symbolically) the suprasensible moral Law evokes its superego dimension. The logic at work in the experience of the dynamical sublime is therefore: true, I may be a tiny particle of dust thrown around by wind and sea, powerless in face of the raging forces of nature, *yet all this fury of nature pales in comparison with the absolute pressure exerted on me by the superego, which humiliates me and compels me to act against my fundamental interests!* (What we encounter here is the basic paradox of the Kantian autonomy: I am a free and autonomous subject, delivered from the constraints of my pathological nature, precisely and only insofar as my feeling of self-esteem is crushed down by the humiliating pressure of the moral Law.) Therein consists also the superego dimension of the Jewish God evoked by the high priest Abner in Racine's *Athaliah:* "Je crains Dieu et n'ai point d'autre crainte . . ."—the fear of raging nature and of the pain other men can inflict on me converts into sublime peace not simply by my becoming aware of the suprasensible nature in me beyond the reach of the forces of nature but by my realizing how the pressure of the moral Law is stronger than even the mightiest of natural forces.

The unavoidable conclusion to be drawn from all this is: if Beauty is the symbol of the Good, the Sublime is the symbol of . . . Here, already, the homology gets stuck. The problem with the sublime object (more precisely: with the object which arouses in us the feeling of the Sublime) is that it *fails* as a symbol; it evokes its Beyond by the very failure of its symbolic representation. So, if Beauty is the symbol of the Good, the Sublime evokes—what? There is only one answer possible: the nonpathological, ethical, suprasensible dimension, for sure, but *the suprasensible, the ethical stance, insofar as it eludes the domain of the Good*—in short: radical Evil, Evil as an ethical attitude.[2]

In today's popular ideology, this paradox of the Kantian Sublime is what perhaps enables us to detect the roots of the public fascination with figures like Hannibal Lecter, the cannibal serial killer from Thomas Harris's novels: what this fascination ultimately bears witness to is a deep longing for a Lacanian psychoanalyst. That is to say, Hannibal Lecter is a sublime figure in the strict Kantian sense: a desperate, ultimately failed attempt of the popular imagination to represent to itself the idea of a Lacanian analyst. The correlation between Lecter and the Lacanian analyst corresponds perfectly to the relation which, according to Kant, defines the experience of the "dynamic sublime": the relation between wild, chaotic, untamed, raging nature and the suprasensible Idea of Reason beyond any natural constraints. True, Lecter's evil—he not only kills his victims, but then goes on to eat parts of their entrails—strains to its limits our capacity to imagine the horrors we can inflict on our fellow creatures; yet even the utmost effort to represent to ourselves Lecter's cruelty fails to capture the true dimension of the act of the analyst: by bringing about *la traversée du fantasme* (the crossing of our fundamental fantasy), he literally "steals the kernel of our being," the *object small a,* the secret treasure, *agalma,* what we consider most precious in ourselves, denouncing it as a mere semblance. Lacan defines the *object small a* as the fantasmatic "stuff of the I," as that which confers on the $, on the fissure in the symbolic order, on the ontological void that we call "subject," the ontological consistency of a "person," the semblance of a fullness of being—and it is precisely this "stuff" that the analyst pulverizes, "swallows." This is the reason for the unexpected "eucharistic" element at work in Lacan's definition of the analyst, namely his repeated ironic allusion to Heidegger: "Mange ton *Dasein!*"—"Eat your being-there!" Therein resides the power of fascination that pertains to the figure of Hannibal Lecter: by its very failure to attain the absolute limit of what Lacan calls "subjective destitution," this figure enables us to get a presentiment of the Idea of the analyst. So, in *The Silence of the Lambs,* Lecter is truly cannibalistic not in relation to his victims but in relation to Clarice Sterling: their relationship is a mocking imitation of the analytic situation, since in exchange for his helping her to capture "Buffalo Bill," he wants her to confide in him—what? Precisely what the analysand confides to the analyst, the kernel of her being, her fundamental fantasy (the crying of the lambs). The quid pro quo proposed by Lecter to Clarice is therefore: "I'll help you if you let me eat your *Dasein!*" The inversion of the proper analytic relation turns on the fact that Lecter compensates Clarice by helping her track down "Buffalo Bill." Thus, he is not cruel enough to be a Lacanian analyst, since in psychoanalysis, we must pay the analyst so that he allows us to offer him our *Dasein* on a plate.

If, consequently, the Sublime is opposed to the Beautiful with regard to the two sides of the moral Law (the pacifying Ego-Ideal versus the ferocious superego), how are we to distinguish it from its counterpole in the *Critique of Judgement,* from teleology in nature? The Sublime designates nature in its purposeless raging, in the expenditure of its forces which *does not serve anything* (Lacan's definition of enjoyment from the first pages of *Encore*), whereas the teleological observation discovers in nature a presupposed (merely reflexive, not constitutive) *knowledge,* i.e., the regulative hypothesis of teleology is that "nature knows" (the flow of events does not follow "blind" mechanic causality; it is guided by some conscious purposefulness).[3] In the Sublime, nature does not know—and where "it doesn't know," *it enjoys* (we are thereby again at the superego qua law which *enjoys,* qua the agency of law permeated with obscene enjoyment). The secret connection between such an outburst of the "enjoyment of nature" and the superego is the key to John Ford's *The Hurricane* (1937), the story of a sandbar, once an island paradise run by the French governor De Laage (Raymond Massey)[4] who denies mercy to Terangi, an aborigine condemned for hitting back at a Frenchman. When Terangi escapes from the prison to rejoin his wife, De Laage pursues him mercilessly until a hurricane destroys everything. De Laage, of course, is an irrational law-and-order extremist, infested with myopic arrogance—in short, a superego figure if there ever was one. From this perspective, the function of the hurricane should be to teach De Laage that there are things more important than the penal code: when De Laage is confronted by the ruination caused by the hurricane, he humbly grants Terangi his freedom. Yet the paradox is that the hurricane destroys the native dwellings and their island paradise, while De Laage is spared; so the hurricane must rather be conceived as a manifestation of *De Laage's* patriarchal-superego wrath! In other words, what sobers De Laage is his confrontation with the destructive nature of the fury which dwells in him; the hurricane makes him aware of the wild, untamed *enjoyment* that pertains to his fanatical devotion to the law. He is able to grant amnesty to Terangi not because he gained an insight into the nullity of human laws in comparison with the immensity of the forces of nature as they manifest themselves in the hurricane, but because he realized that the hidden reverse of what he perceived as his moral rectitude is radical Evil whose destructive power overshadows even the ferocity of the hurricane.

The Christian Sublime, or, the "Downward-Synthesis"

Although Christianity remains within the confines of the Sublime, it brings about the sublime effect in a way exactly opposite to that of Kant: not through the extreme exertions of our capacity to represent (which nonetheless fails to render the suprasensible Idea and thus paradoxically succeeds in delineating its space), but as it were *a contrario*, through the reduction of the representative content to the lowest imaginable level: at the level of representation, Christ was the "son of a man," a ragged, miserable creature crucified between two common brigands; and it is against the background of this utterly wretched character of his earthly appearance that his divine essence shines through all the more powerfully. In the late Victorian age, the same mechanism was responsible for the ideological impact of the tragic figure of the "elephant-man," as the subtitle of one of the books about him suggests (*A Study in Human Dignity*): it was the very monstrous and nauseating distortion of his body which rendered visible the simple dignity of his inner spiritual life. And is not the same logic the essential ingredient of the tremendous success of Stephen Hawking's *A Brief History of Time?* Would his ruminations about the fate of the universe remain so attractive to the public if it were not for the fact that they belong to a crippled, paralyzed body communicating with the world only through the feeble movement of one finger and speaking with a machine-generated impersonal voice? Therein consists the "Christian Sublime": in this wretched "little piece of the real" lies the necessary counterpart (form of appearance) of pure spirituality. That is to say, we must be very careful here not to miss Hegel's point: what Hegel aims at is not the simple fact that, since the Suprasensible is indifferent to the domain of sensible representations, it can appear even in the guise of the lowest representation. Hegel insists again and again that there is no special "suprasensible realm" beyond or apart from our universe of sensible experience; the reduction to the nauseating "little piece of the real" is thus *stricto sensu* performative, productive of the spiritual dimension; the spiritual "depth" is *generated* by the monstrous distortion of the surface. In other words, the point is not only that God's embodiment in a ragged creature renders visible to us, human mortals, His true nature by way of the contrast, of the ridiculous, extreme discord, between Him and the lowest form of human existence; the point is rather that this extreme discord, this absolute gap, *is* the divine power of "absolute negativity." Both Jewish and

Christian religions insist on the absolute discord between God (Spirit) and the domain of (sensible) representations; their difference is of a purely formal nature: in Jewish religion God dwells in a Beyond unattainable through representations, separated from us by an unbridgeable gap, whereas the Christian God *is this gap itself.* It is this shift that causes the change in the logic of the Sublime, from the prohibition of representation to the acceptance of the most null representation.[5]

This "Christian Sublime" involves a specific mode of the dialectical movement which might be called the "downward-synthesis": the concluding moment is here not a triumphant "synthesis," but the lowest point at which the very common ground of position and negation is worn away. What we get stuck with is a remainder which falls out from the symbolic order: the order of universal symbolic mediation as it were collapses into an inert left-over. Apart from the Christian Sublime, the further examples of it are the triad of positive-negative-infinite judgment, the dialectic of phrenology ("Spirit is a bone"), and, of course, the triad of Law which concludes the chapter on Reason and sets the passage into Spirit, into History, in Hegel's *Phenomenology of Spirit:* reason as lawgiver; reason as testing laws; the acceptance of law for the simple fact that it is law. Reason first directly *posits* laws qua universal ethical precepts ("Everyone ought to speak the truth," etc.); once it gains an insight into the contingent content and the possible conflictual nature of these laws (different ethical norms may impose on us mutually exclusive forms of behavior), it assumes a kind of *reflective* distance and limits itself to their testing, to assessing how they fit formal standards of universality and consistency; finally, Reason becomes aware of the empty, purely formal character of this procedure, of its incapacity to procure actual spiritual substance filled out with concrete, positive content. Reason is thus compelled to reconcile itself to the fact that it can neither posit nor reflect upon laws without presupposing our inveteratedness in some concrete, *determinate* ethical substance, in a law which is in force simply *because it is law,* i.e., because it is accepted as a constitutive part of our community's historical tradition. We pass to history *stricto sensu,* to the succession of actual historical figures of Spirit, only on the basis of our accepting that we are embedded in some historically specified "spiritual substance."[6] The logic of these three stages follows the triad of positing, external and determinate reflection, and, what may surprise somebody not versed in Hegel, the third, concluding moment that consists of an immediate acceptance of the given ethical substance; one would rather expect it to constitute the "lowest" moment, the immediate starting point from which we then "progress" by way of reflective mediation. The triad of Law in its entirety thus exemplifies the breakdown of reflection: it ends with the reflecting subject getting accustomed to the ethical substance qua universal, presupposed medium which mediates his very attempts at reflective mediation. This resigned acceptance of the immediate character of the very totality-of-mediation is what Hegel has in mind with "determinate reflection": reflective totality is "held together" by a contingent, nonreflected remainder which is "simply there."[7]

As to its formal structure, this effect of the Christian Sublime hinges on a certain temporal inversion: a material which, presented in "normal" linear succession, in no way affects our sensitivity to the Sublime nonetheless acquires the aura of the "Sublime" the moment it undergoes a purely temporal manipulation. An exemplary case is Paul Newman's melodrama *The Effect of Gamma-rays on Man-in-the-Moon Marigolds,* the story of Mathilda, a girl in her early teens who lives in a poor family with her older sister, the victim of epileptic attacks by means of which she acts out her frustrations, and her mother, a resigned, cynical eccentric who "hates the world"; she escapes domestic misery by investing her energy in biological experiments with seeds exposed to radioactive rays. Mathilda presents the results of her experiments at a school competition and, unexpectedly, wins. Upon returning home, she finds her pet rabbit, given to her by the biology teacher, dead on her bed: her mother has killed it in revenge for the daughter's public success. Mathilda puts the rabbit on a pillow and brings it down the stairs to the garden to be buried, while her mother continues her cynical wise-cracking. A standard pedagogical melodrama of the daughter's moral victory over her resigned mother who failed in her attempt to contaminate the daughter with her hatred: the daughter transcends her degraded home atmosphere by way of biological experiments which made her aware of the mysteries of the universe. What distinguishes this film is a simple temporal manipulation in its last half hour: the scene of the school competition is interrupted at the most tense moment, with Mathilda stumbling in her speech; we pass immediately to the aftermath, when her drunken mother enters the hall and asks a passer-by who won. We hear the missing part of Mathilda's speech, expressing her belief in the mysterious charm of the universe, at the very end of the film: it accompanies the painful events we see on the screen (Mathilda carrying the dead rabbit past the drunk mother). And it is this simple confrontation, this contrast between the visual level (the humiliated child carrying the dead animal) and the soundtrack (a truly Kantian triumphant speech on the mysteries of the "starry sky above us"), which brings about the sublime effect.

Philip Kaufman's *The Unbearable Lightness of Being* resorts to a similar temporal displacement which successfully condenses the ending of Kundera's novel. Late at night, the hero, a dissident doctor exiled to the Czech countryside, returns home with his wife from a dance in a nearby small town; the last sight of them is the point-of-view shot of the dark macadam road illuminated by the lights of their truck. Then, a sudden cut to California a couple of weeks later: their friend Sabina, who lives there as a sculptor, receives a letter informing her of their death in a traffic accident when returning home from a dance, and comments that they must have been happy at the time of their death. What then follows is a cut which transposes us back to the previous scene: a simple continuation of the point-of-view shot, from the driver's seat, of the road into which our gaze penetrates. Here, as well as in *Gamma-rays,* the sublime effect of this last shot which ends the film results from a temporal displacement: it hinges on the coexistence of our, the spectator's, knowledge that the hero and his wife are already dead, with their forward-moving gaze on a strangely illuminated road. The point is not only that the allure of this strange illumination acquires the meaning of death, but rather that this last point-of-view shot belongs to somebody who is still alive although we know that he is already dead: after the flash-forward to California informing us of their death, the hero and his wife dwell in the domain "between the two deaths," i.e., the same shot which was, prior to the flash-forward, a simple point-of-view shot of a living subject renders now the gaze of the "living dead."

The "Formulae of Sexuation"

The problem with this account, however, is that it privileges one mode of the Sublime (the "dynamical" superego-Sublime manifested in raging nature, in the display of intense, concentrated Force which threatens to overwhelm us) to the detriment of its second mode, the "mathematical" Sublime (the dizziness that seizes us when we are confronted with an infinite series whose totality lies beyond our grasp). This split of the Sublime itself, of the intersection of Beauty and Teleology, into "mathematical" and "dynamical" Sublime, is far from negligible since it directly concerns sexual difference. The "official" theory of the Sublime sustained not only by Kant but already by Burke, his forerunner and source, links the opposition masculine / feminine to the opposition Sublime / Beautiful;[8] in contrast, our aim is to demonstrate that, *prior to the opposition Sublime / Beautiful, sexual difference is inscribed in the inherent split of the Sublime into mathematical and dynamical.*

As is well known, the conceptual matrix that underlies the opposition of the two modes of the Sublime is set up already in the *Critique of Pure Reason,* in the guise of the difference between the two types of antinomies of pure reason (*CPR,* B 454–88). When, in its use of transcendental categories, Reason goes beyond the field of possible experience by way of applying the categories to entities which cannot ever become objects of possible experience (the universe as a Whole, God, soul), it gets entangled in antinomies, i.e., it necessarily arrives at two contradictory conclusions: the universe is finite and infinite; God exists and does not exist. Kant arranges these antinomies into two groups: mathematical antinomies arise when categories are applied to the universe as a Whole (the totality of phenomena which is never given to our finite intuition), whereas dynamical antinomies emerge when we apply categories to objects which do not belong to the phenomenal order at all (God, soul). What is of crucial importance here is the different logic of the two types of antinomies. This difference concerns first of all the modality of the link between the elements of the series whose synthesis brings about the antinomy: in the case of mathematical antinomies, we are dealing with a multitude (*das Mannigfaltige*) accessible to sensible intuition, i.e., with a simple *coexistence* of the elements given in the intuition (what is at stake here is their divisibility and their infinitude); in the case of dynamical antinomies, we are dealing with intellect, a synthetic power which reaches beyond a mere sensible intuition, that is to say, with the necessary logical *interconnection* (*Verknuepfung*) of the elements (notions of cause and effect).

This difference of the two types of antinomies can be further specified with reference to the opposition homogeneity / heterogeneity: in the mathematical antinomy, all elements belong to the same spatiotemporal series; in the dynamical antinomy, on the contrary, we progress from effect to cause or ground which (in principle, at least) can belong to a different (nonsensible, intelligible) ontological order. The fact that a cause may (also) not be a cause within the series allows for the possibility that both poles of the antinomy are true: conceived phenomenally, the event X—say, my giving a hand to a drowning person—is determined by the universal causal nexus (as a material event, it is submitted to physical causality); conceived noumenally, this same event is brought about by a heterogeneous, intelligible cause (as an ethical act, it depends on the free will of the autonomous subject). Another aspect of the same opposition is that mathematical antinomies concern the *real existence* of their object (the universe as a Whole), i.e., they extend the scope of reality beyond the limits of possible experience, whereas dynamical antinomies concern an object which does not belong to "reality" conceived of as the field of possible experience (God, the soul furnished with free will . . .).

This difference in the structure of mathematical and dynamical antinomies hinges on the double negation which defines the status of phenomena: noumenon is a non-phenomenon, a limitation of phenomena, and, furthermore, the field of phenomena itself is never complete or whole. Mathematical antinomies are antinomies of the "non-all" of the phenomenal field: they result from the paradox that, although there is no object given to us in intuition which does not belong to the phenomenal field, this field is never "all," never complete. Dynamical antinomies, on the contrary, are antinomies of universality: logical connection of the phenomena in the universal causal nexus necessarily involves an exception, the noumenal act of freedom which "sticks out," suspending the causal nexus and starting a new causal series "spontaneously," out of itself. The status of the disputed object therefore differs radically: the "universe as a Whole" is the *totality of phenomena*, whereas "God" or "soul" are noumenal entities *beyond phenomena*. Consequently, the solution of the antinomies is also different in each of the two cases. In the first case, both the thesis and the antithesis are false, since the very object to which the thesis attributes finitude and the antithesis infinitude does not exist (the universe as the Whole of phenomenal reality is a self-contradictory entity: it speaks of "reality," i.e., it uses transcendental categories constitutive for the field of possible experience, yet simultaneously it reaches beyond possible experience, since the universe in its entirety can never be the object of our finite experience). In the second case, where the disputed object (soul, God) is not conceived as an object of possible experience, i.e., as a part of reality, it is possible for both the thesis and the antithesis to be true. This duality of mathematical and dynamical reproduces the duality of object and subject, of theoretical and practical reason: theoretical reason aims at *completing* the causal chain, i.e., at rendering the entire causal nexus which led to the event to be explained (the regulative Ideal of pure reason), whereas practical reason aims at *suspending* the causal nexus by way of a free act which begins "out of itself" and therefore cannot be explained by the preceding causal chain.

What has all this to do with sexual difference?[9] Lacan endeavored to formalize sexual difference qua discursive fact by means of his "formulae of sexuation," in which on the "masculine" side the universal function (Vx.Fx: all x are submitted to the function F) implies the existence of an exception (Ex.notFx: there is at least one x which is exempted from the function F), whereas on the feminine side a particular negation (notVx.Fx: not-all x are submitted to the function F) implies that there is no exception (notEx.notFx: there is no x which could be exempted from the function F):

$$\exists x.\ \overline{\Phi x} \qquad \overline{\exists x.\ \Phi x}$$
$$\forall x.\ \Phi x \qquad \overline{\forall x.\ \Phi x}$$

What we have to be attentive to apropos of these formulae of sexuation is that they are structured like antinomies in the Kantian sense, not like contrary poles: the relationship of contrariety is excluded here. (In the case of the "masculine" antinomy, for example, the contrary to "all x are submitted to the function F" is not "there is at least one x which is exempted from the function F," but "no x is submitted to the function F.") Common sense would therefore suggest that the formulae are, if linked in two diagonal pairs, equivalent: is not "all x are submitted to the function F" strictly equivalent to "there is no x which could be exempted from the function F"? And, on the other hand, is not "not-all x are submitted to the function F" strictly equivalent to "there is (at least) one x which is exempted from the function F"?[10] Lacan's aim, on the contrary, is to call into question these two signs of equation: the universal function *implies* a constitutive exception; the lack of exception to the function F *prevents* its universal span.[11]

What precise notion of sexuality underlies these "formulae of sexuation"? Lacan's answer is: sexuality is the effect on the living being of the impasses which emerge when it gets entangled in the symbolic order, i.e., the effect on the living body of the deadlock or inconsistency that pertains to the symbolic order qua order of universality. Kant was the first philosopher to formulate the "crack in the universal," which is why his antinomies of pure reason—antinomies, precisely, of universalization—directly herald Lacan's formulae of sexuation. Paradoxical as it may sound, *the Kantian antinomies designate the moment at which sexual difference is for the first time inscribed in the philosophical discourse,* not in the guise of the opposition between the two contradictory poles of every antinomy (the universe is finite / the universe is infinite, etc.), but in the guise of the difference in the two types of antinomies.[12] The first two ("mathematical") antinomies are "feminine" and reproduce the paradoxes of the Lacanian logic of "not-all"; whereas the last two ("dynamical") antinomies are "masculine" and reproduce the paradoxes of universality constituted through exception. That is to say, a Lacanian translation of the mathematical antinomies yields the two formulae of the "feminine" side of sexuation. The thesis on the infinity of the universe has to be read as a double negation, not as a universal affirmation: (insofar as we read the function F as "to be preceded by another phenomenon in time") *"there is no* phenomenon *which is not* preceded by another phenomenon" (there is no x exempted from the function F), not *"all x are* submitted to the function F." The thesis on the finitude of the universe has to be read as *"not-all x are* submitted to the function F" (i.e., all phenomena are not infinitely divisible and / or preceded by other phenomena), not as *"there is one x which is* exempted from the function F." Dynamical antinomies, on the contrary, display the structure of the "masculine" paradoxes of sexuation: *"all x are* submitted to the function F" (everything in the universe is caught in the universal network of causes and effects) on condition that *there is one x which is exempted* from this function (i.e., freedom is possible; there is an element which escapes the universal chain of causes and is capable of starting autonomously, out of itself, a new causal chain).[13]

Feminists are usually repulsed by Lacan's insistence on the feminine "not-all." Does it not imply that women are somehow excluded from fully participating in the Symbolic order, unable to wholly integrate themselves into it, condemned to leading a parasitical existence? And, truly, do not these propositions belong to the best vein of patriarchal ideology, do they not bear witness to a hidden normativity to the detriment of woman? Man is able to find his identity in the Symbolic, to assume fully his symbolic mandate, whereas woman is condemned to hysterical splitting, to wearing masks, to not wanting what she pretends to want. How are we to conceive of this feminine resistance to symbolic identification? We would commit a fatal mistake if we were to read such resistance as the effect of a preexistent feminine substance opposing symbolization, as if woman is split between her true Nature and the imposed symbolic mask. A cursory glance at Lacan's "formulae of sexuation" tells us that woman's exclusion does not mean that some positive entity is prevented from being integrated into the symbolic order: it would be wrong to conclude, from "not-all woman is submitted to the phallic signifier," that there is something in her which is not submitted to it; there is no exception, and "woman" is this very nonexistent "nothing" which nonetheless makes the existing elements "not-all."[14] And the subject qua $, qua pure "I think" of substanceless self-relating, is precisely such a "nothingness" without any positive ontological consistency of its own, yet nonetheless introducing a gap into the fullness of being.

We are thereby at the paradoxical dialectic of the Limit and its Beyond.[15] Lacan's point is the logical priority of the not-all to the All, of the Limit to what lies Beyond: it is only afterwards, in a second time, that the void opened up by the Limit is filled out by a positive Beyond. Therein consists the anti-Cartesian sting of the Lacanian logic of "not-all" (as opposed to Descartes' premise that the less perfect cannot act as the cause of what is more perfect, the premise which serves as the foundation for his proof of God's existence): the incomplete "causes" the complete, the Imperfect opens up the place subsequently filled out by the mirage of the Perfect. From this perspective, the seemingly misogynist definition of woman as truncated man actually asserts her ontological priority: her "place" is that of a gap, of an abyss rendered invisible the moment "man" fills it out. Man is defined by the dynamic antinomy: beyond his phenomenal, bodily existence, he possesses a noumenal soul. If, in opposition to it, "woman has no soul," this in no way entails that she is simply an object devoid of soul. The point is rather that this negativity, this lack as such, defines her: she is the Limit, the abyss, retroactively filled out by the mirage of soul.

"I Am Not Where I Think"

Both "feminine" and "masculine" positions are therefore defined by a fundamental antinomy: the "masculine" universe involves the universal network of causes and effects founded in an exception (the "free" subject which theoretically grasps its object, the causal universe of the Newtonian physics); the "feminine" universe is the universe of boundless dispersion and divisibility which, for that very reason, can never be rounded off into a universal Whole. In Kant, mathematical antinomy finds its solution in the nonexistence of its very object (universe qua totality of the objects of possible experience); no wonder, then, that in Lacan also "la Femme n'existe pas." How does this notion of sexual difference affect the Cartesian *cogito* and Kant's criticism of it? A commonplace of deconstructionist feminism is that the neutrality of the Cartesian *cogito* is false and conceals male primacy (on account of its abstract-universal character, etc.). What this critique fails to take into account is the moment of the "vanishing mediator," the void of the pure "I think" which logically precedes the Cartesian *res cogitans:* the Cartesian *cogito* is "masculine" not because of its abstract-universal character, but because it is not "abstract" enough. In *res cogitans*, the nonsubstantial void of "I think" is already obfuscated, surreptitiously transformed into a "thinking substance" — and, to put it succinctly, sexual difference is equivalent to the difference between the Cartesian *res cogitans* and the Kantian pure form of "I think."

In the span of three years, Lacan elaborated two opposed readings of the *cogito*. In both cases, he broke up the unity of *cogito ergo sum: cogito* is conceived of as the result of the forced choice between thought and being, i.e., "I am not where I think." However, in the Seminar on the four fundamental concepts (1964–65), the choice is that of thought; the access to thought ("I think") is paid for by the loss of being.[16] Whereas in the unpublished Seminar on the logic of fantasy (1966–67), the choice is that of being; the access to being ("I am") is paid for by the relegation of thought to the Unconscious. "I am not where I think" can thus be read in two ways: either as the Kantian "I think" qua pure form of apperception founded on the inaccessibility of the I's being, of the "Thing which thinks," or as the Cartesian affirmation of the subject's being founded on the exclusion of thought. Our idea is to read these two versions of "I am not where I think" *synchronously*, as the duality which registers sexual difference: the "masculine" *cogito* results from the "subreption of the hypostasized consciousness"; it chooses being and thus relegates thought to the Unconscious ("I am, therefore it thinks"), whereas "la femme n'existe pas" involves a *cogito* which chooses thought and is thus reduced to the empty point of apperception prior to its "substantialization" in a *res cogitans* ("I think, therefore it ex-sists").

This duality in the Lacanian thematization of *cogito* is the effect of a radical shift in his teaching which can be located in a very precise way: it occurs somewhere between the Seminar on the ethics of psychoanalysis[17] and the *écrit* "Kant avec Sade," written two years later as the résumé of some ideas first proposed in the Seminar.[18] The effects of this shift can be discerned at a multitude of levels. Let us begin with the motif of the sublime body dwelling in the uncanny space "between the two deaths." This body is first identified as that of the sadist's victim — the body of the

innocent young woman who magically retains her beauty while under-
going endless unspeakable sufferings. In "Kant avec Sade," however, suddenly the sadist executioner himself is conceived of as an object-instrument
(of the Other's *jouissance*): he acquires this status of *objet a* by way of
transposing his subjective splitting onto his victim, $. Closely connected
with this change in the motif of the sublime body is the ambiguous status of
Antigone: on the one hand, she epitomizes desire qua desire of the Other
(the desire with regard to which she does not yield is the desire of the big
Other, of mores, which demands that the (brother's) body be integrated
into the symbolic tradition by way of the appropriate funeral rite); on the
other hand, her suicidal act involves a willing self-exclusion from the big
Other, a suspension of the Other's existence. On a more general level, this
shift generates a fundamental tension in Lacan's approach to ethics. On the
one hand, we have an ethics of desire, of "not giving way as to one's desire"
(*ne pas céder sur son désir*)—to put it briefly, yielding to enjoyment (*jouissance*) means compromising our desire, so the authentic ethical attitude
involves sacrificing enjoyment for the sake of the purity of our desire.[19] On
the other hand, desire itself is conceived of as a defense against enjoyment,
i.e., as a mode of compromise (we take flight into the endless symbolic
metonymy of desire in order to avoid the real of *jouissance*), so that the only
true ethics is that of *drive,* of our commitment to the *sinthome*[20] which
defines the contours of our relation to enjoyment. This tension between an
ethics of desire and an ethics of drive further determines Lacan's shift from
distancing to identification. That is to say, up to the last stage of his
teaching, the predominant ethical attitude of Lacanian psychoanalysis involved a kind of Brechtian gesture of distancing: first the distancing from
imaginary fascination through the work of symbolic "mediation"; then the
assumption of symbolic castration, of the lack constitutive of desire; then
the "going through the fantasy": the assumption of the inconsistency of the
Other concealed by the fantasy-scenario. What all these definitions have in
common is that they conceive of the concluding moment of the psychoanalytic cure as a kind of "exit": as a move *out,* out from imaginary captivation,
out from the Other. In his very last phase, however, Lacan outlines a
reversal of perspective, unheard of as to its radicality: the concluding moment of the psychoanalytic cure is attained when the subject fully assumes
his or her identification with the sinthome, when he or she unreservedly
"yields" to it, rejoins the place where "it was," giving up the false distance
which defines our everyday life.

For that reason, we should avoid the trap of interpreting the second version of the *cogito* choice as Lacan's "last word" in this matter, devalorizing the first version, or vice versa; instead, we should maintain their irreducible antagonism—again—as an index of the inscription of the sexual difference.

But isn't such a link between *cogito* and sexual difference all too abstract, all too nonhistorical? We can answer this reproach by referring to Marx, who in the Introduction to *Grundrisse,* demonstrated how an abstract category, which on account of its abstract-universal character is valid for all epochs, acquires social actuality only at a precisely determined historical moment. What Marx had in mind was the abstract notion of work, of using one's working force, irrespective of its particular qualitative determination: this notion realizes itself, "becomes actual," only in capitalism, where the working force is offered on the market as a commodity, exchangeable for money and as such indifferent to its particular determinations.[21] What we encounter here is the logic of *in itself / for itself* in which a thing *becomes* what it *always-already was:* in capitalism, "work" becomes what it always-already was. And the same holds for the logic of sexual difference: it is only in Kant—i.e., at the moment when the subject is for the first time explicitly conceived of as nonsubstance, not as "part of the world"—that sexual difference becomes what it always-already was, not a difference of two substantial, positive entities, but the "ontological scandal" of the two types of antinomies and thereby the difference of the two modalities of *cogito.*

Cogito *as the Fantasy-Gaze*

In his critique of Foucault's reading of Descartes, Derrida conceives *cogito* as a hyperbolic, excessive moment of madness, the vortex of pure "I think . . ." in its absolute seclusion which is not yet the inwardness, the self-presence, of a thinking substance.[22] This *cogito,* prior to *res cogitans,* is the "feminine" *cogito.* The choice between feminine and masculine *cogito* is therefore more intricate than it may seem; it eludes the clear-cut alternative of "thought or being":

—The "masculine" *cogito* chooses being, the "I am," yet what it gets is being which is merely thought, not real being (*cogito "ergo sum,"* I think "therefore I am," as Lacan writes it), i.e., it gets the fantasy-being, the being of a "person," the being in "reality" whose frame is structured by fantasy.

—The "feminine" *cogito* chooses thought, the pure "I think," yet what it gets is thought bereft of any further predicates, thought which coincides with pure being, or, more precisely, the hyperbolic point which is neither thought nor being. When, consequently, in his Seminar *Encore*, Lacan speaks of *jouissance feminine*, of woman enjoying it without knowing it, this in no way entails her access to some ineffable fullness of being: as he explicitly points out, *jouissance feminine* is nonexistent.

The publicity poster for *Alien³* (on the left side the head of the ET-monster, the slimy metal skull, fixing its gaze on Sigourney Weaver; on the right the terrified face of Sigourney Weaver with her eyes lowered, diverting her gaze from the monster, yet her whole attention fixed on it) could be titled "death and the maiden": here we encounter *cogito* at its purest when (what will become) the subject constitutes itself by rejecting the slimy substance of *jouissance*.²³ It is therefore not sufficient to say that It (the alien Thing) is a "projection of our own repressed": the I itself constitutes itself by way of rejection of the Thing, by way of assuming a distance toward the substance of enjoyment. In this punctuality of pure horror she *thinks;* she is reduced to pure thought: the moment we abstain from the confrontation with the "alien," the moment we recoil from this stain of horror and retreat to the haven of our "being," at some decentered place "it" begins to think. This, then, is Lacan's version of "the spirit is a bone": the pure "I think" takes place only when the subject endures the confrontation with the senseless stain of *jouissance*. And do we not encounter another version of it in E. A. Poe's "The Facts in the Case of M. Valdemar," one of the recurrent references of Lacan? When Valdemar, for a brief moment awakened from the sleep of death, utters the "impossible" statement "I am dead!", his body, which hitherto retained the frozen, stiff beauty of a Dorian Gray, all of a sudden changes into "a nearly liquid mass of loathsome—of detestable putrescence," in short, into a pure, formless, slimy substance of enjoyment. The necessary correlate of this slimy substance which exists in its fullness of being is the position of enunciation from which Valdemar pronounces his "I am dead!", the pure-impossible thought, *cogito* qua the point of thought bereft of being, qua nonexistent-impossible fantasy-gaze by way of which I observe my own nonbeing. At the very moment of my reduction to a pure *cogito* qua impossible gaze, a formless slime of the substance of *jouissance* had to emerge somewhere else. This is what Lacan aims at with his formula $ \$ \Diamond a $.

Eventually, everything that has hitherto been said is condensed in Frank Capra's *It's a Wonderful Life*, a film whose unmistakable *noir* undertones belie the common reduction of Capra's universe to a New Deal populist humanism. When, out of utter despair, the hero (James Stewart) is on the brink of committing suicide, the angel Clarence stops him and submits him to a Kripkean mental experiment with possible universes: he sends him back to his small Massachusetts town, but renders him unrecognizable and devoid of his identity, including his past history, so that he can witness how things might have turned out in the case of his nonexistence. This way, the hero regains his optimism, since the catastrophic consequences of his absence are made manifest: his brother is dead, having drowned long ago (the hero was not there to save him), the old good-hearted pharmacist is rotting in jail (the hero was not there to warn him of inadvertently putting in poison when mixing a medicine), his wife is a despairing old maid, and, above all, his father's small loan society, providing credits to working-class families and thus serving as the last shield of the popular community against the ruthless local capitalist who wants to control the entire town, goes bankrupt (the hero was not there to take his father's business over). So, instead of a community where solidarity prevails and every poor family has a modest home of its own, the hero finds himself in a bursting, violent American small town, full of rude drunkards and noisy night clubs, totally controlled by the local magnate. What immediately strikes the eye here is that the America encountered by the hero when he witnesses the way things would turn out in his absence is the actual America, i.e., its features are taken from grim social reality (the dissolution of communal solidarity, the boastful vulgarity of the nightlife, etc.). The relationship of dream and reality is thus reversed: in the mental experiment that the hero is subjected to, what he experiences as a nightmarish dream is the actual life. We see him encounter the real in the filmic dream, and it is precisely in order to escape this traumatic real that the hero takes refuge within the (diegetic) "reality," i.e., the ideological fantasy of an idyllic town community still able to resist the ruthless pressure of big Capital. This is what Lacan means when he says that the traumatic Real is encountered in dreams; this is the way ideology structures our experience of reality.

However, of primary interest here is the Cartesian dimension of this mental experiment. That is to say, when Stewart is sent back to his town as a stranger, he is bereft of his entire symbolic identity, reduced to a pure *cogito*: as the angel Clarence points out, he has no family, no personal history; even the small wound on his lips has disappeared. The only remaining kernel of certainty, the kernel of the Real which remains "the same" in the two different symbolic universes, is his *cogito*, the pure form of self-consciousness devoid of any content. *Cogito* designates this very point at which the "I" loses its support in the symbolic network of tradition and thus, in a sense which is far from metaphorical, ceases to exist. And the crucial point is that this pure *cogito* corresponds perfectly to the fantasy-gaze: in it, I found myself reduced to a nonexistent gaze, i.e., after losing all my effective predicates, I am nothing but a gaze paradoxically entitled to observe the world in which I do not exist (like, say, the fantasy of parental coitus where I am reduced to a gaze which observes my own conception, prior to my actual existence, or the fantasy of witnessing my own funeral). In this precise sense one can say that *fantasy,* in its most basic dimension, implies *the choice of thought at the expense of being:* in fantasy, I find myself reduced to the evanescent point of a thought contemplating the course of events during my absence, my nonbeing—in contrast to *symptom,* which implies *the choice of being,* since (as we shall see apropos of Freud's case of the wife who cuts her left ring-finger) what emerges in a symptom is precisely the thought which was lost, "repressed," when we chose being.

There is a further feature which confirms this fantasy-status of the Cartesian *cogito.* The fundamental structure of the fantasy-gaze involves a kind of self-duplication of the gaze: it is as if we are observing the "primordial scene" from behind our own eyes, as if we are not immediately identified with our look but stand somewhere "behind" it. Which is why, in Hitchcock's *Rear Window,* the window itself clearly acts as a gigantic eye (the curtain raising during the credits stands for opening the eyelids upon our awakening, etc.): Jefferies (James Stewart) is immobilized precisely insofar as he is reduced to the object-gaze behind his own gigantic eye, i.e., insofar as he occupies this space outside reality seen by the eye. What is crucial, however, is that Descartes, in his optical writings, outlined the same fantasy: that of a man interposing between himself and reality a dead animal's eye and, instead of directly observing reality, observing pictures that emerge in the back of the animal eye.[24] Is not the same *dispositif* at work in a series of gothic or costume films: there is a gigantic eye up on the wall, usually a relief sculpture, and all of a sudden, we become aware that there actually is somebody hidden behind the eye and observing what is going on? The paradox here is that *the gaze is concealed by an eye,* i.e., *by its very organ.* And is not the same economy at work in the (deservedly) most famous scene of David Lynch's *Blue Velvet,* with Kyle MacLachlan observing the sadomasochistic erotic game of Isabella Rossellini and Dennis

Hopper through the crack in the wardrobe, the crack which clearly functions as a half-opened eye and thus posits the viewer behind his own eye? Our point here is the ultimate coincidence between this fantasy-gaze which immobilizes the subject, deprives him of his existence in reality, and reduces him to an object-gaze observing reality from which he is missing, and the Cartesian *cogito* which, at the height of its radical doubt, is also reduced to a nonexisting gaze acquiring distance from its own bodily presence, i.e., observing reality from "behind its own retina."

"Self-consciousness Is an Object"

This, then, is the first of Lacan's two versions of *cogito:* "I think, therefore it is." How are we to conceive of the other version, "I am, therefore it thinks"? Let us recall a small symptomatic act described in Freud's *Psychopathology of Everyday Life:*

During a session a young married woman mentioned by way of association that she had been cutting her nails the day before and "had cut into the flesh while she was trying to remove the soft cuticle at the bottom of the nail". This is of so little interest that we ask ourselves in surprise why it was recalled and mentioned at all, and we begin to suspect that what we are dealing with is a symptomatic act. And in fact it turned out that the finger which was the victim of her small act of clumsiness was the ring-finger, the one on which a wedding ring is worn. What is more, it was her wedding anniversary; and in the light of this the injury to the soft cuticle takes on a very definite meaning, which can easily be guessed. At the same time, too, she related a dream which alluded to her husband's clumsiness and her anesthesia as a wife. But why was it the ring-finger on her *left* hand which she injured, whereas a wedding ring is worn [in her country] on the *right* hand? Her husband is a lawyer, a "doctor of law" ["*Doktor der Rechte,*" literally "doctor of right(s)"], and as a girl her affections belonged in secret to a physician (jokingly called *"Doktor der Linke"* ["doctor of the left"]). A "left-handed marriage", too, has a definite meaning.[25]

A trifling slip, a tiny cut on the ring finger, can well condense an entire chain of articulated *reasoning* about the subject's most intimate fate: it bears witness to the knowledge that her marriage is a failure, to the regret for not choosing the true love, the "doctor of the left." This tiny blood stain marks the place where her unconscious thought dwells, and what she is unable to do is to recognize herself in it, to say "I am there," where this thought is articulated. Instead, the stain has to remain a blot which means nothing to her, if she is to retain the consistency of her self-identity. Or, as Lacan would put it, there is no I without the stain: "I am" only insofar as I am not where I think, that is to say, only insofar as the picture I am looking at contains a stain which condenses the decentered thought—only insofar as this stain remains a stain, i.e., insofar as I do not recognize myself in it, insofar as I am not there, in it. For this reason, Lacan returns again and again to the notion of anamorphosis: I perceive "normal" reality only insofar as the point at which the "it thinks" remains a formless stain.[26]

The theoretical temptation to avoid here, of course, is that of identifying this stain too hastily with *objet petit a: a* is not the stain itself but rather the gaze in the precise sense of the point of view from which the stain can be perceived in its "true meaning," the point from which, instead of the anamorphic distortion, it would be possible to discern the true contours of what the subject perceives as a formless stain. For that reason, the analyst occupies the place of *objet a:* he is supposed to know—to know what? The true meaning of the stain, precisely. Consequently, Lacan is quite justified in claiming that in paranoia *objet a* "becomes visible": in the person of the persecutor, the object qua gaze assumes the palpable, empirical existence of an agency which "sees into me," is able to read my thoughts.

In this sense, *objet petit a* stands for the point of self-consciousness: if I were able to occupy this point, it would be possible for me to abolish the stain, to say that "I am where I think." It is here that the subversive potential of the Lacanian critique of self-consciousness qua self-transparency becomes visible: *self-consciousness as such is literally decentered;* the slip—the stain—bears witness to the ex-sistence of a certain decentered, external place where I *do* arrive at self-consciousness (Freud's patient articulates the truth of herself, of her failed marriage, at a place that remains external to her sense of self-identity). Herein lies the scandal of psychoanalysis, unbearable for philosophy: what is at stake in the Lacanian critique of self-consciousness is not the commonplace according to which the subject is never fully transparent to itself, or can never arrive at full awareness of what is going on in its psyche; Lacan's point is not that full self-consciousness is impossible since something always eludes the grasp of my conscious ego. Instead, it is the far more paradoxical thesis that *this decentered hard kernel which eludes my grasp is ultimately self-consciousness itself;* as to its status, self-consciousness is an external object out of my reach.[27] More precisely, self-consciousness is the object qua *objet petit a,* qua the gaze able to perceive the true meaning of the stain which gives body to the unbearable truth about myself.[28]

We can now see why self-consciousness is the very opposite of self-transparency: I am aware of myself only insofar as outside of me a place exists where the truth about me is articulated. What is not possible is for these two places (mine and the stain's) to coincide: the stain is not an unreflected remainder, something one could abolish via self-reflection, via a deeper insight into one's psychic life, since it is the very product of my self-awareness, its objective correlative. This is what Lacan has in mind when he writes "symptom" as "sinthome": the symptom qua ciphered message waits to be dissolved by way of its interpretation, whereas the "sinthome" is a stain correlative to the very (non)being of the subject.

In order to exemplify this distinction, let us recall the two versions of *Cape Fear,* J. Lee Thompson's original from the early sixties and Martin Scorcese's remake from 1991. Although repelled by Scorcese's patronizing self-conscious attitude toward the original film, reviewers nonetheless approvingly noted how Scorcese accomplished a crucial shift. In the original version, the ex-convict (Robert Mitchum) is a figure of Evil who simply invades from outside the idyllic all-American family and derails its daily routine; whereas in Scorcese's remake, the ex-convict (Robert de Niro) materializes, gives body, to traumas and antagonistic tensions that already glow in the very heart of the family: the wife's sexual dissatisfaction, the daughter's awakened femininity and sense of independence. In short, Scorcese's version incorporates an interpretation homologous to the reading of Hitchcock's *Birds* that conceives of the ferocious birds' attacks as the materialization of the maternal superego, of the disturbance that already dwells in family life. Although such a reading may appear "deeper" than the allegedly "superficial" reduction of the force of Evil to an external threat, what gets lost with such a reading is precisely the remainder of an Outside that cannot be reduced to a secondary effect of inherent intersubjective tensions, since its exclusion is constitutive of the subject: such a remainder or object always adds itself to the intersubjective network, as a kind of "fellow traveler" of every intersubjective community. Consider the birds in Hitchcock's *The Birds.* Are they not, notwithstanding their intersubjective status, at their most radical such an overblown stain on a finger? When, upon crossing the bay for the first time, Melanie (Tippi Hedren) is attacked by a gull which strikes her head, she feels her head with a gloved hand and perceives on the tip of her forefinger a small red blood-stain; all the birds who later attack the town could be said to arise out of this tiny stain, the same as in *North-by-Northwest,* where the plane attacking Cary Grant on the empty cornfield is first perceived as a tiny, barely visible spot on the horizon.

This original doubling of self-consciousness provides the foundation of "intersubjectivity": if, as the Hegelian commonplace goes, self-consciousness is self-consciousness only through the mediation of another self-consciousness, then my self-awareness—precisely insofar as this self-awareness is not the same as self-transparency—causes the emergence of a decentered "it thinks." When the split between "I am" and "it thinks" is translated into the standard motif of intersubjectivity, what gets lost is the radical *asymmetry* of the two terms. The "other" is originally an *object,* an opaque stain which hinders my self-transparency by giving a body to what has to be excluded if I am to emerge. In other words, the ultimate paradox of the dialectics of self-consciousness is that it inverts the standard doxa according to which "consciousness" relates to a heterogeneous, external object, while "self-consciousness" abolishes this decenteredness: instead, *the object is* stricto sensu *the correlate of self-consciousness.* No object exists prior to self-consciousness, since *the object originally emerges as that opaque kernel which has to be excluded if I am to gain awareness of myself.* Or, to put it in Lacanian terms, the original intersubjective correlate of the subject—of the barred $\$$—is not another $\$$, but S, the opaque, full Other possessing what the subject constitutively lacks (being, knowledge). In this precise sense the Other—the other human being—is originally the impenetrable, substantial Thing.

A radical conclusion thus can be drawn: the reproach according to which the Cartesian-Kantian *cogito* is "monological" and as such "represses" an original intersubjectivity totally misses the point. It is the exact opposite which is true: the pre-Cartesian individual immediately, inherently belongs to a community, but intersubjectivity and (belonging to a) community are to be strictly opposed, i.e., *intersubjectivity* senso strictu *becomes possible, thinkable, only with Kant, with the notion of subject qua $\$$, the empty form of apperception which needs S as correlative to its nonbeing.* In other words, intersubjectivity *stricto sensu* involves the subject's radical decenteredness: only when my self-consciousness is externalized in an object do I begin to look for it in another subject. What we have prior to the Kantian subject is not the intersubjectivity proper but a community of individuals who share a common universal-substantial ground and participate in it. It is only with Kant, with his notion of the subject as $, as the empty form of self-apperception, as an entity which constitutively "does not know what it is," that the Other Subject is needed in order for me to define my own identity: what the Other thinks I am is inscribed into the very heart of my own most intimate self-identity. The ambiguity that sticks to the Lacanian notion of the big Other—another subject in its impenetrable opacity, yet at the same time the very symbolic structure, the neutral field in which I encounter other subjects—is therefore far from being the result of a simple confusion: it gives expression to a deep structural necessity. Precisely insofar as I am $, I cannot conceive of myself as participating at some common substance, i.e., this substance necessarily opposes itself to me in the guise of the Other Subject.

"I Doubt, Therefore I Am"

Lacan's achievement with regard to *cogito* and doubt could be summed up in the elementary, but nonetheless far-reaching operation of perceiving (and then drawing theoretical consequences from) the affinity between the Cartesian doubt and the doubt that dwells at the very heart of compulsive (obsessive) neurosis. This step in no way amounts to a "psychiatrization of philosophy"—the reduction of philosophical attitudes to an expression of pathological states of mind—but rather to its exact contrary, the "philosophization" of clinical categories: with Lacan, compulsive neurosis, perversion, hysteria, etc., cease to function as simple clinical designations and become names for existential-ontological positions, for what Hegel, in the Introduction to his *Encyclopaedia of Philosophical Sciences,* called *Stellungen des Gedankens zur Objektivitaet,* "attitudes of thought toward objectivity." In short, Lacan as it were supplements Descartes' *I doubt, therefore I am*—the absolute certainty provided by the fact that my most radical doubt implies my existence qua thinking subject—with another turn of the screw, reversing its logic: *I am only insofar as I doubt.* This way, we obtain the elementary formula of the compulsive neurotic's attitude: the neurotic clings to his doubt, to his indeterminate status, as the only firm support of his being, and is extremely apprehensive of the prospect of being compelled to make a decision which would cut short his oscillation, his neither-nor status. Far from undermining the subject's composure or even threatening to disintegrate his self-identity, this uncertainty provides his minimal ontological consistency. Suffice it to recall Lina, the heroine of Hitchcock's *Suspicion*. Tormented by suspicions that her husband is about to kill her, she persists in her indecision, putting off indefinitely the act which would instantly enable her to dissolve the unbearable tension. In the famous final scene, her gaze becomes transfixed upon the white glass of milk containing the answer to the doubts and suspicions that are tormenting her, yet she is totally immobilized, unable to act—why? Because by finding an answer to her suspicions she would thereby lose her status as a subject.[29] It is this inherent dialectical inversion that characterizes the subject of doubt and suspicion: "officially," he strives desperately for certainty, for an unambiguous answer that would provide the remedy against the worm of doubt that is consuming him; actually, the true catastrophe he is trying to evade at any price is this very solution, the emergence of a final, unambiguous answer, which is why he endlessly sticks to his uncertain, indeterminate, oscillating status. There is a kind of reflective reversal at work here: the subject persists in his indecision and puts off the choice not because he is afraid that, by choosing one pole of the alternative, he would lose the other pole (that, in the case of Lina, by opting for innocence, she would have to accept the fact that her husband is a mere small-time crook, devoid of any inner strength, even in the direction of Evil). What he truly fears to lose is doubt as such, the uncertainty, the open state where everything is still possible, where none of the options are precluded. It is for that reason that Lacan confers on the act the status of *object:* far from designating the very dimension of subjectivity ("subjects act, objects are acted upon"), the act cuts short the indeterminacy which provides the distance that separates the subject from the world of objects.

These considerations enable us to approach from a new perspective the motif of "Kant avec Sade." Today, it is a commonplace to qualify Kant as a compulsive neurotic: the uncertain status of the subject is inscribed into the very heart of the Kantian ethics, i.e., the Kantian subject is by definition never "at the height of his task"; he is forever tortured by the possibility that his ethical act, although *in accordance with* duty, was not accomplished *for the sake of* duty itself, but was motivated by some hidden "pathological" considerations (that, by accomplishing my duty, I will arouse respect and veneration in others, for example). What remains hidden to Kant, what he renders invisible by way of his logic of the Ought (*Sollen*), i.e., of the infinite, asymptotic process of realizing the moral Ideal, is that it is this very stain of uncertainty which sustains the dimension of ethical universality: the Kantian subject desperately clings to his doubt, to his uncertainty, in order to retain his ethical status. What we have in mind here is not the commonplace according to which, once the Ideal is realized, all life-tension is lost and there is nothing but lethargic boredom in store for us. Something far more precise is at stake: *once the "pathological" stain is missing, the universal collapses into the particular.* This, precisely, is what occurs in Sadeian perversion, which, for that very reason, reverses the Kantian compulsive uncertainty into absolute certainty: a pervert knows perfectly what he is doing, what the Other wants from him, since he conceives of himself as an instrument-object of the Other's Will-to-Enjoy. In this precise sense Sade stages the truth of Kant: you want an ethical act free of any compulsive doubt? Here you have the Sadeian perversion![30]

Of what, more exactly, does this ontological uncertainty of the subject consist? The key to it is provided by the link between anxiety and the desire of the Other: anxiety is aroused by the desire of the Other in the sense that "I do not know what *object a* I am for the desire of the Other." What does the Other want from me, what is there "in me more than myself" on account of which I am an object of the Other's desire—or, in philosophical terms, which is my place in the substance, in the "great chain of being"? The core of anxiety is this absolute uncertainty as to what I am: "I do not know what I am (for the Other, since I am what I am only for the Other)." This uncertainty *defines* the subject: the subject "is" only as a "crack in the substance," only insofar as his status in the Other oscillates. And the position of the masochist pervert is ultimately an attempt to elude this uncertainty, which is why it involves the loss of the status of the subject, i.e., a radical self-objectivization: the pervert *knows what he is for the Other,* since he posits himself as the object-instrument of the Other's *jouissance.*[31]

In this regard, the position of the pervert is uncannily close to that of the analyst: they are separated only by a thin, almost invisible line. It is by no accident that the upper level of Lacan's mathem of the discourse of the analyst reproduces the formula of perversion ($a \lozenge \$$). On account of his or her passivity, the analyst functions as *objet a* for the analysand, as the latter's fantasy-frame, as a kind of blank screen onto which the analysand projects his or her fantasies. This is also why the formula of perversion inverts that of the fantasy ($\$ \lozenge a$): the pervert's ultimate fantasy is to be a perfect servant of his other's (partner's) fantasies, to offer himself as an instrument of the *other's* Will-to-Enjoy (like Don Giovanni, for example, who seduces women by enacting one by one the specific fantasy of each of them: Lacan was quite right in pointing out that Don Giovanni is a feminine myth). The entire difference between the pervert and the analyst hinges on a certain invisible limit, on a certain "nothing" that separates them: the pervert confirms the subject's fantasy, whereas the analyst induces him or her to "traverse" it, to gain a minimal distance toward it, by way of rendering visible the void (the lack in the Other) covered up by the fantasy-scenario.

For that reason, it is quite legitimate to associate perversion, in its fundamental dimension, with the "masochism" of the anal phase. In his Seminar on transference,[32] Lacan made it clear how the passage from the oral into the anal phase has nothing whatsoever to do with the process of biological maturation, but is entirely founded in a certain dialectical shift in the intersubjective symbolic economy. The anal phase is defined by the adaptation of the subject's desire to the demand of the Other, i.e., the object-cause of the subject's desire (a) coincides with the Other's demand, which is why Lacan's mathem for the "anal" compulsive neurosis is that of drive, $\mathcal{S} \Diamond D$. True, the oral phase does imply an attitude of wanting to "devour it all" and thereby satisfy all needs; however, due to the child's dependency, caused by the premature birth of the human animal, satisfying its needs, from the very beginning, is "mediated" by, hinges upon, the *demand addressed to the Other* (primarily mother) to provide the objects which meet the child's needs. What then occurs in the anal phase is a dialectical reversal in this relationship between need and demand: *the satisfaction of a need is subordinated to the demand of the Other,* i.e., the subject (child) can only satisfy his need on condition that he thereby complies with the Other's demand. Let us recall the notorious case of defecation: the child enters the "anal phase" when he strives to satisfy his need to defecate in a way that complies with the mother's demand to do it regularly, into the chamber-pot and not into his pants, etc. The same holds for food: the child eats in order to demonstrate how well-behaved he is, ready to fulfill his mother's demand to finish the plate and to do it properly, without dirtying his hands and the table. In short, we satisfy our needs in order to earn our place in the social order. Therein lies the fundamental impediment of the anal phase: pleasure is "barred," prohibited, in its immediacy, i.e., insofar as it involves taking a direct satisfaction in the object; pleasure is permitted only in the function of complying with the Other's demand. In this precise sense, the anal phase provides the basic matrix for the obsessional, compulsive attitude. It would be easy to quote here further examples from adult life; suffice it to recall what is perhaps its clearest case in "postmodern" theory, namely the obsession with Hitchcock, the endless flow of books and conferences which endeavor to discern theoretical finesses even in his minor films (the "save-the-failures" movement). Can't we account, at least partially, for this obsession by way of a compulsive "bad conscience" on the part of intellectuals who, prevented from simply yielding to the pleasures of Hitchcock's films, feel obliged to prove that they actually watch Hitchcock in order to demonstrate some theoretical point (the mechanism of the spectator's identification, the vicissitudes of male voyeurism, etc.)? I am allowed to enjoy something only insofar as it serves Theory qua my big Other.[33] The Hegelian character of this reversal of oral into anal economy cannot but strike the eye: the satisfaction of our need by means of the Other who answers our demand "attains its truth" when complying with the Other's demand is directly posited as the sine qua non, the "transcendental frame," the condition of possibility, of satisfying our needs. And the function of the third, "phallic," phase, of course, is precisely to disengage the subject from this enslavement to the demand of the Other.

The Precipitous Identification

The Althusserian "ideological interpellation"[34] designates the retroactive illusion of "always-already": the reverse of the ideological recognition is the misrecognition of the performative dimension. That is to say, when the subject recognizes himself in an ideological call, he automatically overlooks the fact that this very formal act of recognition creates the content one recognizes oneself in. (Suffice it to evoke the classical case of the Stalinist Communist: when he recognizes himself as the instrument of the "objective necessity of the historical progress toward communism," he misrecognizes the fact that this "objective necessity" exists only insofar as it is created by the Communist discourse, only insofar as Communists invoke it as the legitimization of their activity.) What is missing from the Althusserian account of this gesture of symbolic identification, of recognizing oneself in a symbolic mandate, is that it is a move aimed at resolving the deadlock of the subject's radical uncertainty as to its status (what am I qua object for the Other?). The first thing to do apropos of interpellation in a Lacanian approach is therefore to reverse Althusser's formula of ideology which "interpellates individuals into subjects": it is never the individual which is interpellated as subject, *into* subject; it is on the contrary the subject itself who is interpellated as x (some specific subject-position, symbolic identity or mandate), thereby eluding the abyss of $. In classical liberal ideology, the subject is interpellated precisely as "individual." The often quoted Marx-brothers joke on Ravelli ("You look like Ravelli.—But I am Ravelli!—No wonder, then, that you look like him!") ends with Ravelli jubilantly concluding "So I do look alike!" This joyful assumption of a mandate, this triumphant ascertaining that I am like my own symbolic figure, gives expression to the relief that I succeeded in avoiding the uncertainty of "Che vuoi?".[35]

For that reason, the subject's symbolic identification always has an *anticipatory*, hastening character (similar to, yet not to be confused with, the anticipatory recognition of "myself" in the mirror image). As pointed out by Lacan already in the forties, in his famous paper on logical time,[36] the fundamental form of symbolic identification, i.e., of assuming a symbolic mandate, is for me to "recognize myself as X," to proclaim, to promulgate myself as X, in order to overtake others who might expel me from the community of those who "belong to X." Here is the somewhat simplified and abbreviated version of the logical puzzle of three prisoners apropos of which Lacan develops the three modalities of the logical time: The head of a prison can, on the basis of amnesty, release one of the three prisoners. In order to decide which one, he makes them pass a logical test. The prisoners know that there are five hats, three of them white and two black. Three of these hats are distributed to the prisoners who then sit down in a triangle, so that each of them can see the color of the hats of the two others, but not the color of the hat on his own head. The winner is the one who first guesses the color of his own hat, which he signifies by standing up and leaving the room. We have three possible situations:

–If one prisoner has a white hat and the other two black hats, the one with the white hat can immediately "see" that his is white by way of a simple reasoning: "There are only two black hats; I see them on the others' heads, so mine is white." So there is no time involved here, only an "instant of the gaze."

–The second possibility is that there are two white and one black hat. If mine is white, I will reason this way: "I see one black and one white hat, so mine is either white or black. However, if mine is black, then the prisoner with the white hat would see two black hats and immediately conclude that his is white; since he does not do it, mine is also white." Here, some time had to elapse, i.e., we already need a certain "time for understanding":

I as it were "transpose" myself into the reasoning of the other; I arrive at my conclusion on the basis of the fact that the other does not act.

—The third possibility—three white hats—is the most complex. The reasoning goes here like this: "I see two white hats, so mine is either white or black. If mine is black, then any of the two remaining prisoners would reason the following way: 'I see a black and a white hat. So if mine is black, the prisoner with the white hat would see two black hats and would stand up and leave immediately. However, he does not do it. So mine is white. I shall stand up and leave.' But since none of the other two prisoners stands up, mine is also white."

Here, however, Lacan points out how this solution requires a double delay and a hindered, interrupted gesture. That is to say, if all three prisoners are of equal intelligence, then, after the first delay, i.e., upon noticing that none of the others is making any move, they will all rise at the same moment—and then stiffen, exchanging perplexed glances: the problem is that they will not know the meaning of the other's gesture (each of them will ask himself: "Did the others rise for the same reason as me, or did they do it because they saw on my head a *black* hat?"). Only now, upon noticing that they all share the same hesitation, they will be able to jump to the final conclusion: the very fact of the shared hesitation is a proof that they are all in the same situation, i.e., that they all have white hats on their heads. At this precise moment, delay shifts into haste, with each of the prisoners saying to himself "Let me rush to the door before the others overtake me!"[37]

It is easy to recognize how a specific mode of subjectivity corresponds to each of the three moments of the logical time: the "instant of gaze" implies the impersonal "one" ("one sees"), the neutral subject of logical reasoning without any intersubjective dialectic; the "time for understanding" already involves intersubjectivity, i.e., in order for me to arrive at the conclusion that my hat is white, I have to "transpose" myself into the other's reasoning (if the other with the white hat were to see on my head a black hat, he would immediately know that his must be black and stand up; since he does not do it, mine is also white). However, this intersubjectivity remains that of the "indefinite reciprocal subject," as Lacan puts it: a simple reciprocal capability of taking into account the other's reasoning. It is only the third moment, the "moment of conclusion," which provides the true "genesis of the I": what takes place in it is the shift from $\$$ to S_1, from the void of the subject epitomized by the radical uncertainty as to what I am, i.e., by the utter undecidability of my status, to the conclusion that I am white, to the assumption of the symbolic identity—"That's me!"

We must bear in mind here the anti-Lévi-Straussian thrust of these Lacan's ruminations. Claude Lévi-Strauss conceived the symbolic order as an asubjective structure, an objective field in which every individual occupies, fills in, his or her preordained place; what Lacan invokes is the "genesis" of this objective socio-symbolic identity: if we simply wait for a symbolic place to be allotted to us, we will never live to see it. That is, in the case of a symbolic mandate, we never simply ascertain what we are; we "become what we are" by means of a precipitous subjective gesture. This precipitous identification involves the shift from object to signifier: the (white or black) hat is the object I am, and its invisibility to me renders the fact that I can never get an insight into "what I am as an object" (i.e., $ and a are topologically incompatible). When I say "I am white," I assume a symbolic identity which fills out the void of the uncertainty as to my being. What accounts for this anticipatory overtaking is the *inconclusive* character of the causal chain: the symbolic order is ruled by the "principle of insufficient reason": within the space of symbolic intersubjectivity, I can never simply ascertain what I am, which is why my "objective" social identity is established by means of "subjective" anticipation. The significant detail usually passed over in silence is that Lacan, in his text on logical time, quotes as the exemplary political case of such collective identification the Stalinist Communist's affirmation of orthodoxy: I hasten to promulgate my true Communist credentials out of fear that others will expel me as a revisionist traitor.[38]

Therein resides the ambiguous link between the Symbolic and death: by assuming a symbolic identity, i.e., by identifying myself with a symbol which is potentially my epitaph, I as it were "outpass myself into death." However, this precipitation toward death at the same time functions as its opposite; it is designed to forestall death, to assure my posthumous life in the symbolic tradition which will outlive my death—an obsessive strategy, if there ever was one: in an act of precipitous identification *I hasten to assume death in order to avoid it.*

Anticipatory identification is therefore a kind of preemptive strike, an attempt to provide in advance an answer to "what I am for the Other" and thus to assuage the anxiety that pertains to the desire of the Other: the *signifier* which represents me in the Other resolves the impasse of *what object I am for the Other.* What I actually overtake by way of symbolic identification is therefore *objet a* in myself; as to its formal structure, symbolic identification is always a "flight forward" from the object that I am. By way of saying "You are my wife," for example, I elude and obliterate my radical uncertainty as to what you are in the very kernel of your being, qua Thing.[39] This is what is missing from Althusser's account of interpellation: it does justice to the moment of retroactivity, to the illusion of the "always-already," yet it leaves out of consideration the anticipatory overtaking qua inherent reverse of this retroactivity.

One of the ways to make this crucial point clear is via a detour, a foray into one of the finest achievements of analytical philosophy, Grice's elaboration of the structure of (intentional) meaning.[40] According to Grice, when we mean to say something in the full sense of the term, this involves an intricate four-level structure: (1) we say X; (2) the addressee must perceive that we intentionally said X, i.e., that the enunciation of X was an intentional act on our part; (3) we must intend that the addressee must perceive not only our saying X, but that we want him to perceive that we intentionally wanted to say X; (4) the addressee must perceive (must be aware of) (3), i.e., our intention that we want him to perceive our saying X, as an intentional act. In short, our saying "This room is bright" is a case of successful communication only if the addressee is aware that, by saying "This room is bright," we not only wanted to say that the room is bright, but also wanted him to be aware that we wanted him to perceive our saying "This room is bright" as an intentional act. If this seems a hair-splitting, contrived, useless analysis, suffice it to recall a situation when, lost in a foreign city, we listen to one of its inhabitants desperately trying to make us understand something in his native language: what we encounter here is level 4 in its pure, as it were distilled form. That is to say, although we do not know what, precisely, the inhabitant wants to tell us, we are well aware not only of the fact that he wants to tell us *something,* but also of the fact that *he wants us to notice his very endeavor to tell us something.* Our point is that the structure of a hysterical symptom is exactly homologous to Grice's level 4: what is at stake in a symptom is not only the hysteric's attempt to deliver a message (the meaning of the symptom that waits to be deciphered), but, at a more fundamental level, his desperate endeavor to affirm himself, to be accepted as a partner in communication. What he ultimately wants to tell us is that his symptom is not a meaningless physiological disturbance, i.e., that we have to lend him an ear since he has something to tell us. In short, the ultimate meaning of the symptom is that the Other should take notice of the fact that it has a meaning.

Perhaps it is with regard to this feature that a computer message differs from human intersubjectivity: what the computer lacks is precisely this self-referentiality (in Hegelese: reflectivity) of meaning. And, again, it is not difficult to discern in this self-referentiality the contours of a logical tem-porality: by means of the signifier of this reflective meaning, i.e., of the signifier which "means" only the presence of meaning, we are able as it were to "overtake" ourselves and, in an anticipatory move, establish our identity not in some positive content but in a pure self-referential signifying form alluding to a meaning-to-come.[41] Such is, in the last resort, the logic of every ideological Master-Signifier in the name of which we fight our battles: fatherland, America, socialism, etc.—do they not all designate an identification not with a clearly defined positive content but with the very gesture of identification? When we say "I believe in x (America, social-ism . . .)," the ultimate meaning of it is pure intersubjectivity: it means that I believe that I am not alone, that I believe that there are also others who believe in x. The ideological Cause is *stricto sensu* an effect of the belief poured into it from the side of its subjects.[42]

This paradox of the "precipitated" identification with the unknown is what Lacan has in mind when he determines the phallic (paternal) signifier as the signifier of the lack of the signifier. If this reflective reversal of the lack of the signifier into the signifier of the lack seems contrived, suffice it to recall the story of Malcolm X, the legendary African-American leader. Here are some excerpts from a *New York Times* article apropos of Spike Lee's film *Malcolm X*—and the *New York Times* for sure cannot be accused of a Laca-nian bias:

> X stands for the unknown. The unknown language, religion, ances-tors and cultures of the African American. X is a replacement for the last name given to the slaves by the slave master. . . . "X" can denote experimentation, danger, poison, obscenity and the drug ecstasy. It is also the signature of a person who cannot write his or her name. . . . The irony is that Malcolm X, like many of the Nation of Islam and other blacks in the 60's, assumed the letter—now held to represent his identity—as an expression of a lack of identity.[43]

The gesture of Malcolm X, his act of replacing the imposed family name, the Name-of-the-Father, with the symbol of the unknown, is far more complex than it may seem. What we must avoid is getting lured into the "search for the lost origins": we totally miss the point if we reduce the gesture of Malcolm X to a simple case of longing for the lost Origins (for the "true" African ethnic identity, lost when blacks were torn out of their original environs by slave traders). The point is rather that this reference to the lost Origins enables the subject to elude the grasp of the imposed symbolic identity and to "choose freedom," the lack of fixed identity. X qua void exceeds every positive symbolic identity: the moment its gap emerges, we find ourselves in the fantasy domain of "experimentation, danger, poison, obscenity and the drug ecstasy" that no new symbolic identity can fill out.

The further point to be made, however, is that this identification with the unknown, far from being an exception, *brings to light the feature constitutive of symbolic identification as such:* every symbolic identification is ultimately identification with an X, with an "empty" signifier which stands for the unknown content, i.e., it makes us identify with the very symbol of a lack of identity. The Name-of-the-Father, the signifier of symbolic identity par excellence, is, as Lacan emphasizes again and again, the "signifier without a signified." What this means with regard to Malcolm X is that although X is meant to stand for the lost African Origins, at the same time it stands for their irrevocable *loss:* by way of identifying ourselves with X, we "consummate" the loss of Origins. The irony therefore is that in the very act of returning to "maternal" Origins, of marking our commitment to them, we irrevocably renounce them. Or, to put it in Lacanian terms, Malcolm X's gesture is the Oedipal gesture at its purest: the gesture of substituting Name-of-the-Father for the desire of the mother:[44]

$$\frac{\text{Name-of-the-Father}}{\text{the desire of the mother}}$$

What is crucial here is the virtual character of the Name-of-the-Father: the paternal metaphor is an "X" in the sense that it opens up the space of virtual meaning; it stands for all possible future meanings. As to this virtual character that pertains to the symbolic order, the parallel to the capitalist financial system is most instructive. As we know from Keynes onwards, the capitalist economy is "virtual" in a very precise sense: Keynes's favorite maxim was that in the long term we are all dead; the paradox of the capitalist economics is that our borrowing from the (virtual) future, i.e., our printing of money "uncovered" in "real" values, can bring about real effects (growth). Herein lies the crucial difference between Keynes and economic "fundamentalists" who favor the actual "settling of accounts" (reimbursing the credits, abolishing the "borrowing from the future").

Keynes's point is not simply that "unnatural" crediting by way of "un-covered" money, inflation, or state spending can provide the impulse which results in actual economic growth and thus enables us eventually to achieve a balance whereby we settle accounts at a much higher level of economic prosperity. Keynes concedes that the moment of some final "settling of accounts" would be a catastrophe, that the entire system would collapse. Yet the art of economic politics is precisely to prolong the virtual game and thus to postpone ad infinitum the moment of final settlement. In this precise sense capitalism is a "virtual" system: it is sustained by a purely virtual keeping of accounts; debts are incurred which will never be cleared. However, although purely fictitious, this "balancing" must be preserved as a kind of Kantian "regulative Idea" if the system is to survive. What Marx as well as strict monetarists commonly hold against Keynes is the conviction that sometimes, sooner or later, the moment will arrive when we actually shall have to "settle accounts," reimburse debts and thus place the system on its proper, "natural" foundations.[45] Lacan's notion of the debt that pertains to the very notion of the symbolic order is strictly homologous to this capitalist debt: sense as such is never "proper"; it is always advanced, "borrowed from the future"; it lives on the account of the virtual future sense. The Stalinist Communist who gets caught in a vicious circle by justifying his present acts, including the sacrifice of millions of lives, with reference to a future Communist paradise brought about by these acts, i.e., who cites beneficent future consequences as what will retroactively re-deem present atrocities, simply renders visible the underlying temporal structure of sense as such.

PART II

ERGO *The Dialectical Nonsequitur*

3 On Radical Evil and Related Matters

■

"Kant with Bentham"

Today, when Kant's antinomies of pure reason enjoy the status of a philosophical commonplace which long ago ceased to be perceived as a threat to the entire philosophical edifice, it requires a considerable effort to imagine them "in their becoming," as Kierkegaard would put it, and to resuscitate their original scandalous impact. One way to achieve this goal is to concentrate on how the antinomies differ from the logic of big cosmic oppositions: yin / yang, masculine / feminine, light / darkness, repulsion / attraction, etc. There is nothing subversive about such a notion of the universe as an organism whose life force hinges on the tension of two polar principles; what Kant had in mind, however, was something quite different and incomparably more unsettling: there is no way for us to imagine in a consistent way the universe as a Whole; that is, as soon as we do it, we obtain two antinomical, mutually exclusive versions of the universe as a Whole. And— as I shall try to demonstrate—it is here, in this antinomy, that sexual difference is at work: the antagonistic tension which defines sexuality is not the polar opposition of two cosmic forces (yin / yang, etc.), but a certain crack which prevents us from even consistently imagining the universe as a Whole. Sexuality points toward the supreme ontological scandal of the nonexistence of the universe.

To get a clear idea of the scandalous impact of Kantian antinomies, let us recall Philip Dick's *Time Out of Joint*, a science fiction novel whose action seems to take place in a proverbial American small town toward the end of the fifties (when the novel was actually written). A series of strange experiences (for example, when he unexpectedly returns to the backyard of his house, he finds there, instead of the object which was there a minute ago—a garden bench—a sheet with the inscription on it "bench," as in the well-known painting by Magritte) enable the hero to arrive, step by step, at what is actually going on: he lives in the seventies; some mysterious government agency brainwashed him and resettled him in an artificially re-created town of the fifties in order to test a scientific hypothesis. (One of the myths about the KGB is that they actually built such an exact replica of a typical American small town somewhere in the Ukrainian plain, so that future agents could get used to everyday American life.) Psychoanalytical theory has an exact term for such a sheet which fills in the gap in reality, standing in for the missing object: *Vorstellungs-Repraesentanz,* the signifying representative of the missing representation.[1]

And Kant's theory of transcendental constitution amounts to something quite similar. That is to say, what is the fundamental feature of our "sense of reality," of what we usually refer to as our "common-sense realism"? We automatically assume a continuity between our field of vision and its invisible beyond: when I see the front of an actual house, I automatically assume that—even if I do not perceive it at this moment—the same house has its reverse, that behind it there is another house or some kind of landscape, etc. In short, it is an inherent part of our "common-sense realism" that we humans are part of the world which exists in itself as a (finite or infinite) Whole. On the contrary, Kant's basic premise is that the "universe" as the totality of beings, which includes us as its part, does not exist; therein lies the ultimate sense of his thesis that any use of categories (a priori forms of thought constitutive of what we experience as "reality") beyond the limits of our possible phenomenal experience is illegitimate: as soon as we try to imagine the "universe" as the totality of things-in-themselves, our reason gets entangled in irreconcilable antinomies. What we must especially bear in mind here is the difference between Kant and traditional skepticism. Kant's point is not a simple doubt concerning things-in-themselves, i.e., the fact that, since our experience is limited to phenomena, we can never be sure if things-in-themselves are of the same order as phenomena. The whole point of Kant's antinomies is that we can positively demonstrate that things-in-themselves *cannot* be of the same nature as phenomena: phenomena are constituted, their texture is structured, by transcendental categories; as soon as we apply these categories to things-in-themselves, to something that can never become an object of possible experience, antinomies emerge. The crucial point, however, is that this illusion of the universe is not something we can "realistically" renounce, but is necessary, unavoidable, if our experience is to retain its consistency: if I do not represent to myself objects in the world as entities that exist in themselves, if I do not conceive what I perceive as a partial aspect of some reality-in-itself—if, say, I do not assume that the house I see now has its back side which corresponds to its front—then my perceptual field disintegrates into an inconsistent, meaningless mess.[2] Without the sheet of paper which patches up its gaps (as in Dick's *Time Out of Joint*), reality itself falls apart; the Kantian name for this piece of paper is "transcendental Idea." So, by way of the Kantian transcendental turn, reality itself is virtualized, becomes an artifact, becomes "virtual reality" in the precise sense this term has acquired in today's computer sciences; and the Lacanian Real designates precisely the hard kernel which does not yield to this "virtualization," which is *not* a transcendental artifact. The scandalous nature of such a virtualization of reality becomes clear if we read Kant "with Bentham," i.e., against the background of Bentham's theory of fictions.

As the title of one of his "écrits"—"Kant avec Sade"—indicates, Lacan proposes to conceive of Sade as the truth of the Kantian ethics: in order to grasp the kernel of the Kantian ethical revolution, invisible to Kant himself, we must read him "with Sade." There is a homologous link between Kant's theory of the necessary transcendental *Schein* and Jeremy Bentham's theory of fictions, also one of the recurrent points of reference of Lacan.[3] In a first approach, "Kant with Bentham" seems no less absurd than "Kant with Sade": on the one hand "vulgar" utilitarianism, on the other the sublime ethic of fulfilling duty for the sake of duty. Perhaps, however, Kant = Bentham is to be understood, together with the equation Kant = Sade, as an example of the Hegelian "infinite judgment" ascertaining the coincidence of the most sublime with the lowest ("the spirit is a bone"). Within the domain of ethics, of "practical reason," Bentham prepared the ground for the Kantian revolution by way of accomplishing the same "purification" that Hume realized in the domain of theoretical reason. That is to say, what constitutes the fundamental proposition of Bentham's utilitarianism? The *instrumental* definition of the Good: to say that something is "good" means to ascertain that it is useful, that it serves some purpose; according to Bentham, the notion of "Good-in-itself" is nonsensical and self-contradictory. By emptying the field of the Good of all substantial *content*, Bentham thus cut the roots of every ethics founded upon a substantial, positive notion of the Supreme Good as an End-in-itself. The door was thus opened for the Kantian revolution whose starting point is precisely the impossibility of determining the Good-in-itself within the field of possible experience. All that remains possible is therefore to conceive of the Good at the level of *form*, as the universal form of our will.

It is theoretically even more productive to read Kant through Bentham's theory of fictions. Bentham arrived at the notion of fictions by analyzing legal discourse, which, in order to function, has to presuppose a whole series of entities whose status is obviously fictitious: the notion of a legal person (which enables us to treat an organization as a living person, attributing to it properties which actually appertain only to flesh-and-blood individuals: the state is responsible for war, the ministry promised us financial support . . .), the notion of an original "social contract" (which enables us to treat individuals subjected to law as if they were bound by contract, although they never actually made this contract), etc., up to the fundamental premise according to which ignorance of law does not absolve us from guilt (when I break the law, I cannot offer as an excuse the fact that I did not know what is prohibited: we must impute to every subject the knowledge of the corpus of laws in its entirety—without this fiction, the whole edifice of law disintegrates). Bentham's first reaction to these peculiarities of the legal discourse was, of course, that of an enlightened empiricist: fictions are fabricated by lawyers in order to obfuscate the actual state of things and thus impose upon people their own unavoidable intermediary role (homologous to the early-Enlightenment "vulgar" theory of religion as a fiction fabricated by the priests with the purpose of maintaining their power and / or the power of those whom they serve).[4] This is how Bentham arrived at the task of reducing fictions to their real ingredients, i.e., of demonstrating how fictions emerge from the wrong combinations of the elements of our real experience: "Every fictitious entity bears some relation to some real entity, and can not otherwise be understood than in so far as that relation is perceived—a conception of that relation is obtained."[5] Bentham further distinguishes fictitious entities "of the first remove," "of the second remove," etc.; in short, he was among the first to delineate the contours of the operation whose most radical version is to be found later in analytical philosophy's early heroic period (the "Viennese circle"): to accept as meaningful only those propositions which were deduced in a legitimate way from some elementary form which guarantees contact with actual experience (the "protocollary propositions" reporting on "sense-data," etc.).

However, complications soon arose and their most interesting aspect is precisely *how* things got so entangled. The key moment came when Bentham was compelled to differentiate between *two* kinds of fictions: *fictitious entities* and *imaginary (fabulous) nonentities*. It is obvious that "contract" and "golden mountain" are not entities of the same order. Although the first entity is fictitious (what "really exists" are only acts prescribed or comprised by this fiction), there is nothing imaginary about it; it is not an imaginary representation "fabricated" by my mind, and, furthermore, it serves, in its very capacity of a fiction, as a tool for bringing about a series of "real" effects ("contract" obliges me to accomplish real acts comprised by the fictitious term "obligation," or another kind of real effects comprised by the fictitious term "damages" befall me). "Golden mountain," however, is far closer to sensible reality; there is no difficulty in displaying its genesis (it unites two real representations, the representation of a mountain and the representation of gold), and yet it is in a sense "less real" than "contract," since it clearly describes something which does not exist, i.e., something which is the product of our imagination. In order not to mix up these two kinds of entities, Bentham introduced the difference between fictitious entities (contract, duty, legal person) and imaginary nonentities (unicorn, golden mountain). This way, he *produced avant la lettre the Lacanian distinction between the Symbolic and the Imaginary:* fictitious entities make up the realm of the Symbolic, whereas "unicorns," etc. are imaginary fabrications.[6] Although Bentham clung to his program of reducing fictions to their real ingredients, he had to concede that in the case of fictions *stricto sensu,* i.e., fictions as opposed to imaginary nonentities, this reduction could not be carried out; we must proceed differently and reformulate, in the form of a description of real acts, the whole situation designated by the word "contract," for example.

These and other similar impasses led Bentham to conclude that fictions are inherent to language ("discourse") as such. It is not possible to speak without making use of fictitious entities: "To language, then—to language alone—it is, that fictitious entities owe their existence—their impossible, yet indispensable, existence."[7] What Bentham has in mind here are not only legal-normative notions such as "contract," but first of all the innate propensity of language to substantiate something which, as to its original and real status, is a mere property of a thing or a process which involves it: "water is flowing" becomes "the flow of water" (although "flow" possesses no substantial reality); "this table is heavy" becomes "the table's weight," etc. In short, fictions are "those sorts of objects, which in every language must, for the purpose of discourse, be spoken of as existing."[8] Bentham was sharp enough to steer clear of the delusion that we can dispense with this fetishistic split ("I know that fictions are unreal, but I nonetheless speak of them as if they are real objects"). If we are to speak about reality in a consistent and sensible way, we have to have recourse to fictions: "Of nothing, therefore, that has place, or passes in our mind, can we speak, or so much as think, otherwise than in the way of *fiction*."[9] In other words, Lacan was fully justified in maintaining that Bentham was the first who realized that truth has the structure of a fiction: the dimension of truth is opened up by the order of discourse which loses its consistency without the support of fictions.

Bentham was thus compelled to maneuver a whole series of steps, retreats, and compromises which offer ideal stuff for a Derridean analysis: in order to save the coherency of his theoretical edifice, he had to introduce new supplementary distinctions (between fictitious entities and imaginary nonentities, etc.); the very notion of fiction got marked by an irreducible ambiguity (it oscillates incessantly between neutral and pejorative connotation: fictions are treated sometimes as the source of all evil, a confusion to be suppressed, and sometimes as an indispensable tool).[10] Underlying these troubles is the deadlock common to Bentham and Kant: it is possible to tell reality from fictions (in Bentham, the names of real entities from the names of fictions; in Kant, the legitimate use of transcendental categories in the constitution of reality from their illegitimate use which brings about "transcendental illusion"); however, as soon as we renounce fiction and illusion, we lose reality itself; *the moment we subtract fictions from reality, reality itself loses its discursive-logical consistency*. Kant's name for these fictions, of course, is "transcendental Ideas," whose status is merely regulative and not constitutive: Ideas do not simply add themselves to reality, they literally supplement it; our knowledge of objective reality can be made consistent and meaningful only by way of reference to Ideas. In short, Ideas are indispensable to the effective functioning of our reason; they are "a *natural* and inevitable *illusion*" (*CPR*, A 298): the illusion that Ideas refer to existing things beyond possible experience is "inseparable from human reason"; as such, it continues "even after its deceptiveness has been exposed" (as with Marx's famous warning that the "commodity-fetishism" persists in actual life even after its logic is theoretically revealed).[11]

Fantasy and Reality

When Lacan speaks about the "precarious" status of reality, he has in mind precisely this "transcendental illusion" qua fantasy-frame of reality. Lacan's reading of Freud is here very nuanced, so one has to be careful not to miss its accent. True, "reality" forms itself through "reality-testing," by way of which the subject differentiates between the hallucinatory object of desire and the perceived actual object; but the subject can never occupy the neutral place which would allow him or her to exclude completely the hallucinatory fantasmatic reality. In other words, although "reality" is determined by "reality-testing," *reality's frame is structured by the left-overs of hallucinatory fantasy:* the ultimate guarantee of our "sense of reality" turns on how what we experience as "reality" conforms to the fantasy-frame. (The ultimate proof of it is the experience of the "loss of reality": "our world falls apart" when we encounter something which, due to its traumatic character, cannot be integrated into our symbolic universe.)[12]

In *this* sense the status of reality *is* precarious: it depends on a delicate balance between reality-testing and the fantasy-frame. Kant's criticism took shape by refuting Swedenborg's phantasmagoria about seeing ghosts, communicating with the dead, and otherwise having immediate (that is to say: intuitive) contact with the suprasensible realm of spirits. Kant's "original insight" concerning the parallel between such fanatical "ghost-seeing" and the Leibnizean rationalist metaphysics is more than a matter of the contingent historical origins of his philosophy: as pointed out by perspicuous interpreters, the delusion of the fanatical ghost-seer remained for Kant to the very end the model for the Ideas of Reason. At first, one is thus tempted to say that Kant's criticism persists in the paradoxical intermediate position: we know and we can prove that the phenomenal universe is not reality in itself, that there is "something beyond"; but neither Reason (metaphysics) nor Intuition (ghost-seeing) can provide access to this Beyond. All we can do is delineate its empty place, constraining the domain of the phenomena without in any way extending our knowledge to the noumenal domain. However, here lurks a crucial misunderstanding: we totally miss the point if we impute to Kant the attitude of "proper measure," of avoiding both naive realism which accepts noumenal reality of the phenomena, and "ghost-seeing," which posits immediate contact with suprasensible spirits. The problem is that our most common experience of reality requires for its consistency a minimal share of regulative Ideas, of principles which reach beyond possible experience. In other words, the real choice is not the choice between naive realism and delirious ghost-seeing, since, at a certain point, *they are both on the same side:* or, as Lacan would put it, there is no reality without its fantasmatic support. In his *Opus Post-humum*, Kant quite explicitly argues that Ideas (precisely in the sense of "delirious creations," remainders of hallucinatory formations) compose the fantasmatic frame of our access to reality:

> Ideas are prime images (intuitions) created by reason which, as purely subjective things of thought, precede our knowledge of things and the elements of the latter: they are the prototypes according to which Spinoza thought that all things must be seen in God. . . . Ideas, self-created *a priori* things of thought (*entia rationis*) . . . include principles of the systematic unity of the thought of objects. We see all objects (according to Spinoza) in God: we can just as well say that, as regards their reality, they must be encountered in the world.[13]

The last sentence is crucial here: the "self-created" fantasmatic frame of the Ideas is the ultimate guarantee of the very reality of objects. This way, the ambiguous status of Ideas (at the same time noumenal Things and subjective regulative principles) appears in a new light: the point is not to dismiss this ambiguity as Kant's contradiction or inconsistency (the critique usually, albeit wrongly, attributed to Hegel), but rather to read the two determinations together, as an index of the ex-timate (intimately external) status of the Idea. "Idea" designates the point of the paradoxical immediate coincidence of the noumenal Thing with *Schein*, with the illusion which has no place in the constituted phenomenal reality. How can we fail to recall here the parallel ambiguity which from the very beginning sticks to the Freudian notion of *das Ding*: the Thing is "what hurts," the external traumatic X which derails the closed circulation of the *Lust-Ich* around hallucinatory objects, forcing the *Lust-Ich* to give up the pleasure-principle and to "confront reality"; yet the Thing is simultaneously the subject's innermost kernel of his being, what he must sacrifice in order to gain access to "external reality." And is it necessary to add that the same radical ambiguity defines the Lacanian Real?

"A Hair of the Dog That Bit You"

The fundamental paradox of symbolic fictions is therefore that, in one and the same move, they bring about the "loss of reality" *and* provide the only possible access to reality: true, fictions are a semblance which occludes reality, but if we renounce fictions, reality itself dissolves. This paradox designates the elementary dialectical structure of the symbolic order, the fact that, as Lacan put it in his *Ecrits*, "speech is able to recover the debt that it engenders"[14]—a thesis in which one must recognize all its Hegelian connotation. The debt, the "wound," opened up by the symbolic order is a philosophical commonplace, at least from Hegel onwards: with entry into the symbolic order, our immersion in the immediacy of the real is forever lost; we are forced to assume an irreducible loss; the word entails the (symbolic) murder of the thing, etc. In short, what we are dealing with here is the negative-abstractive power that pertains to what Hegel called *Verstand* (the analytical mortification-dismembering of what organically belongs together).[15] However, with regard to this wound of language, one should be careful not to miss its crucial dimension. That is to say, in his interpretation of the famous Freudian example of the child's play with the spool, accompanied by the sounds *Fort-Da*—a play which stages the process of symbolization, the subject's entry into the universe of language, at its elementary, zero level—Lacan says something quite different from what may appear at first glance. How, precisely, do things appear at first glance? The child is traumatized by his mother's unforeseeable departures which leave him helpless; as a compensation for it, he plays the game of repeatedly throwing a spool out of his field of vision and pulling it back, accompanying his movements with the signifying dyad *Fort-Da* ("away-here"). By way of symbolization, anxiety disappears, the child masters the situation, but the price for it is the "substitution of things by words," i.e., of the mother by its signifying representative (the spool), more precisely, of the mother's departures and returns by the spool's disappearances from and returns into the field of vision. The entry into the universe of symbols is therefore paid for by the loss of the incestuous object, of mother qua Thing.

Lacan, however, says something quite different and far more radical: rather than acting as a stand-in for the mother, the disappearing and reemerging spool is the sacrificed part of the subject itself; the price to be paid for entry into the symbolic universe is the subject's renunciation of his "pound of flesh." In other words, the true sacrifice does not take place "out there," in the relationship of the symbol to the object (the spool instead of the mother), but "here," in myself: *the object which compensates for the loss of the mother-Thing is part of myself;* what it truly stands for is the loss of my own substantial fullness of being, since symbolization means not only that mother ceases to be an immediate object for me, but that, *by the same token, I myself cease to be an object for her.* The moment I enter the game of *Fort-Da,* an imperceptible distance separates forever the substantial content of my person from the empty point of "self-consciousness," i.e., I am not any-more immediately identical with "what I am," with the wealth of particu-lar features in me: the axis of my self-identity shifts from S (the full, substantial, "pathological" subject) to $ (the "barred," empty subject).[16]

How, then, precisely, are we to comprehend the thesis that *logos* is able to recover its own constitutive debt, or, even more pointedly, that it is *only* speech itself, the very tool of disintegration, that can heal the wound it makes in the real—"only the spear that smote you / can heal your wound" (as Wagner puts it in *Parsifal*)? It would be easy, here, to cite exemplary answers ad infinitum, since this logic can be said to contain the quintes-sence of post-Kantian thought: from Marx, where capitalism itself brings about the force that will bury it (namely, the proletariat who will heal its wound by way of establishing a classless society); to Freud, where trans-ference, the main hindrance to the successful remembrance of the trau-matic past, becomes the lever of the psychoanalytic cure's progress; up to today's ecological crisis: if there is one thing that is clear today, it is that a return to any kind of natural balance is forever precluded; only technology and science themselves can get us out of the deadlock into which they brought us.[17] Let us, however, remain at the level of the notion. According to the postmodern *doxa,* the very idea that the symbolic order is able to square its debt in full epitomizes the illusion of the Hegelian *Aufhebung* ("sublation": negation-conservation-elevation). Language compensates us for the loss of immediate reality (for the replacement of "things" with "words") with sense which renders present the essence of things, i.e., in which reality is preserved in its notion. However—so the *doxa* goes on—the problem consists in the fact that the symbolic debt is constitutive and as such unredeemable: the emergence of the symbolic order opens up a *béance* which can never be wholly filled up by sense; for that reason, sense is never "all"; it is always truncated, marked by a stain of non-sense.

Yet contrary to the common opinion, Lacan does not follow this path; the most appropriate way to track down his orientation is to recall one of the commonplaces of antibureaucratic populism: big-government bureau-crats artificially create problems in order to offer themselves as saviors. The way out of the deadlock is therefore to ascertain how what appears as a solution is actually part of the problem. For example, within the neoliberal anti-welfare-state vision, the state bureaucracy which claims to "solve" the problems of unemployment, social security, crime, etc., actually causes these problems, due to its tax-and-spend attitude which disturbs the "nor-mal" functioning of the market mechanism. The only true solution is therefore: leave us alone with your "solutions" and the problem itself will disappear! Although there is a kind of elementary dialectics at work here (the solution retroactively creates the problem it endeavors to resolve—how not to recognize in it the obsessive attitude of providing new and newer solutions *in order to keep the problem alive?*), what Lacan (as well as Hegel) has in mind is rather the exact opposite: what, to an abstract approach, appears as a "problem" is actually a necessary constituent of the very "unproblematic," "normal" state of things we are striving for. No "unproblematic," innocent state of things exists prior to "problems"; the moment we get rid of the "problem," we lose precisely what we wanted to save, what we felt was threatened by the "problem." Let us return to neo-liberalism: what it tends to overlook is the degree to which, in today's complex economies, the very "normal" functioning of the market can be secured only by way of the state actively intervening in social security, ecol-ogy, law enforcement, etc.; left to itself, the market mechanism is bound to destroy itself. The dialectical paradox is therefore not only that the pro-posed solution can be part of the problem, reproducing its true cause, but also its reverse, i.e., that what, from our abstract, limited perspective, appears as a problem is actually its own solution. Examples abound here, up to the "absolute example" (Hegel), Christ, whose "problem," impasse, failure—death on the cross—actually is his triumph, the achievement of his true goal, the reconciliation of man and God. That is to say, how, according to Hegel, are we to conceive the death of Christ? Christ himself, in his person, already actualized the reconciliation of man and God, but in its "immediacy": as a unique spatio-temporal, historical event. There, far away, two thousand years ago, "God became man," so that his death cannot but appear as a renewed split, causing sadness and lamentation among believers. It is here that we have to accomplish the paradigmatic dialectical shift of recognizing the realized aim in what appears to be a mere striving toward it, a mere (religious) service: in the very lamentation over

Christ's death performed by the community of believers, God is here qua Spirit; reconciliation is realized in its "mediated," true form.[18]

It is against this background that one has to conceive the relationship between "empty speech (*parole vide*)" and "full speech (*parole pleine*)." Here, we immediately encounter one of the standard misapprehensions of the Lacanian theory: as a rule, empty speech is conceived as empty, non-authentic prattle in which the speaker's subjective position of enunciation is not disclosed, whereas in full speech, the subject is supposed to express his or her authentic existential position of enunciation; the relationship between empty and full speech is thus conceived as homologous to the duality of "subject of the enunciated" and "subject of the enunciation." Even if it does not devalue absolutely empty speech but regards it as "free associations" in the psychoanalytical process, i.e., as a speech emptied of imaginary identifications, such a reading misses entirely Lacan's point, which becomes manifest the moment we take into account the crucial fact that for Lacan the exemplary case of empty speech is the password (*mot-de-passage*). How does a password function? As a pure gesture of recognition, of admission into a certain symbolic space, whose enunciated content is totally indifferent: if, say, I arrange with my gangster-colleague that the password which gives me access to his hideout is "Aunt has baked the apple pie," it can easily be changed into "Long live comrade Stalin!" or whatever else. Therein consists the "emptiness" of empty speech: in this ultimate nullity of its enunciated content. And Lacan's point is that human speech in its most radical, fundamental dimension functions as a password: prior to its being a means of communication, of transmitting the signified content, speech is the medium of the mutual recognition of the speakers.[19] In other words, it is precisely the password qua empty speech which reduces the subject to the punctuality of the "subject of the enunciation": in it, he is present qua a pure symbolic point freed of all enunciated content. For that reason, full speech is never to be conceived of as a simple and immediate filling-out of the void which characterizes the empty speech (as in the usual opposition of "authentic" and "nonauthentic" speech). Quite the contrary, one must say that it is only empty speech by way of its very emptiness (of its distance toward the enunciated content which is posited in it as totally indifferent) which creates the space for "full speech," for speech in which the subject can articulate his or her position of enunciation. This is how "only the spear that smote you can heal your wound": only if you fully assume the void of the "empty speech" can you hope to articulate your truth in the "full speech." Or, in Hegelese: it is only the subject's radical estrangement from immediate substantial wealth which opens up the space for the articulation of his or her subjective content. To posit the substantial content as "my own," I must first establish myself as pure, empty form of subjectivity devoid of all positive content.

The Radical Evil

Insofar as the symbolic wound is the ultimate paradigm of Evil, the same holds also for the relationship between Evil and Good: radical Evil opens up the space for Good precisely the same way as empty speech opens up the space for full speech. What we come across here, of course, is the problem of "radical Evil" first articulated by Kant in his *Religion within the Limits of Reason Alone.*[20] According to Kant, the ultimate proof of the presence, in man, of a positive counterforce to his tendency toward Good is the fact that the subject experiences moral Law in himself as an unbearable traumatic pressure which humiliates his self-esteem and self-love—so something in the very nature of the Self must resist the moral Law, i.e., something exists which gives preference to egotistical, "pathological" leanings over the tendency to follow the moral Law. Kant emphasizes the a priori character of this propensity toward Evil (the moment which was later developed by Schelling): insofar as I am a free being, I cannot simply objectify that which in me resists the Good (by saying, for example, that it is a part of my nature for which I am not responsible). The very fact that I feel morally responsible for my evil bears witness to how, in a timeless transcendental act, I must have chosen freely my eternal character by giving preference to Evil over Good. This is how Kant conceives of "radical Evil": as an a priori, not just an empirical-contingent propensity of human nature toward Evil. However, by rejecting the hypothesis of "diabolical Evil," Kant retreats from the ultimate paradox of radical Evil, from the uncanny domain of those acts which, although "evil" as to their content, thoroughly fulfill the formal criteria of an ethical act. Such acts are not motivated by any pathological considerations, i.e., their sole motivating ground is Evil as a principle, which is why they can involve the radical abrogation of one's pathological interests, up to the sacrifice of one's life.

Let us recall Mozart's *Don Giovanni:* when, in the final confrontation with the statue of the *Commendatore,* Don Giovanni refuses to repent, to renounce his sinful past, he accomplishes something that can be properly designated only as a radical ethical stance. It is as if his tenacity mockingly reverses Kant's own example from the *Critique of Practical Reason* where the libertine is quickly prepared to renounce the satisfaction of his passion as soon as he learns that the price to be paid for it is the gallows:[21] Don Giovanni persists in his libertine attitude at the very moment when he knows very well that what awaits him is *only* the gallows and none of the satisfactions. That is to say, from the standpoint of pathological interests, the thing to do would be to accomplish the formal gesture of penitence: Don Giovanni knows that death is close, so that by atoning for his deeds he stands to lose nothing, only to gain (i.e., to save himself from posthumous torments), and yet "on principle" he chooses to persist in his defiant stance of the libertine. How can one avoid experiencing Don Giovanni's unyielding "No!" to the statue, to this living dead, as the model of an intransigent *ethical* attitude, notwithstanding its "evil" content?[22]

If we accept the possibility of such an "evil" ethical act, then it is not sufficient to conceive of radical Evil as something that pertains to the very notion of subjectivity on a par with a disposition toward Good; one is compelled to take one step further and to conceive of radical Evil as something that ontologically precedes Good by way of opening up the space for it. That is to say, what, precisely, *is* Evil? Evil is another name for the "death-drive," for the fixation on some Thing which derails our customary life-circuit. By way of Evil, man wrests himself from animal instinctual rhythm, i.e., Evil introduces the radical reversal of the "natural" relationship.[23] Here, therefore, Kant's and Schelling's standard formula reveals its insufficiency. That formula holds that the possibility of Evil is founded in man's freedom of choice on account of which he can invert the "normal" relationship between universal principles of Reason and his pathological nature by way of subordinating his suprasensible nature to his egotistical inclinations. When Hegel, in his *Lectures on the Philosophy of Religion,* conceives of the very act of becoming-human, of passage of animal into man, as the Fall into sin, he is more penetrating: the possible space for Good is opened up by the original choice of radical Evil which disrupts the pattern of the organic substantial Whole.[24] The choice between Good and Evil is thus in a sense not the true, original choice: the truly first choice is the choice between (what will later be perceived as) yielding to one's pathological leanings and choosing radical Evil, i.e., an act of suicidal egoism which "makes place" for the Good, i.e., which overcomes the domination of pathological natural impulses, by way of a purely negative gesture of suspending the life-circuit. Or, to refer to Kierkegaard's terms, Evil is Good itself "in the mode of becoming": it "becomes" as a radical disruption of the life-circuit; the difference between Good and Evil concerns a purely formal conversion from the mode of "becoming" into the mode of "being."[25] This is how "only the spear that smote you can heal the wound": the wound is healed when the place of Evil is filled out by a "good" content. Good qua "the mask of the Thing (i.e., of radical Evil)" (Lacan) is thus an ontologically secondary, supplementary attempt to reestablish the lost balance; its ultimate paradigm in the social sphere is the corporatist endeavor to (re)construct society as a harmonious, organic, nonantagonistic edifice.

Suffice it to recall Thomas More, the Catholic saint who resisted the pressure of Henry VIII to approve of his divorce. It is easy for us today to eulogize him as a "man for all seasons," to admire his inexorable sense of rectitude, his perseverance in his convictions although the price to be paid for it was his life. What is far more difficult to imagine is the way his stubborn perseverance must have struck the majority of his contemporaries: from a "communitarian" point of view, his rectitude was an "irrational" self-destructive gesture which was "evil" in the sense that it cut into the texture of the social body, threatening the stability of the crown and thereby of the entire social order. So, although the motivations of Thomas More were undoubtedly "good," *the very formal structure of his act was "radically evil"*: his was an act of radical defiance which disregarded the Good of community. And was it not the same with Christ himself, whose activity was experienced by the traditional Hebrew community as destructive of the very foundations of their life? Did he not come "to divide, not to unite," to set son against father, brother against brother?

We can see, now, how "substance becomes subject" by way of passing into its predicates. Let us take the case of capitalism: from the standpoint of the precapitalist corporate society, capitalism is Evil, disruptive, it unsettles the delicate balance of the closed precapitalist economy—why, precisely? Because it presents a case of a "predicate"—a secondary, subordinated moment of the social totality (money)—which, in a kind of *hubris*, "runs amok" and elevates itself into an End-in-itself. However, once capitalism achieves a new balance of its self-reproductive circuit and becomes its own mediating totality, i.e., once it establishes itself as a system which "posits its own presuppositions," the site of "Evil" is radically displaced: what *now* counts as "evil" are precisely the left-overs of the previous "Good"—islands of resistance of precapitalism which disturb the untroubled circulation of Capital, the new form of Good. The standard image of the "dialectical process" where the substance, the inner essence, alienates-externalizes itself and then internalizes its "otherness" by way of self-mediation is thus deeply misleading: the substance which at the end again "totalizes" the derailed process is not "the same" as the substance disintegrated by the initial derailment. The new balance is achieved when what was originally a subordinated moment of the organic totality establishes itself as the new medium of universality, the new mediating totality. What was at the outset the nonalienated substantial unity does not "return to *itself*" in "desalination"; instead, it changes into a subordinated moment of a new totality that grew out of a partial aspect of the initial unity.

The thesis that the possibility of choosing Evil pertains to the very notion of subjectivity must therefore be radicalized by a kind of self-reflective inversion: *the status of the subject as such is evil*, i.e., insofar as we are "human," in a sense we *always-already have chosen Evil*. Far more than direct references to Hegel, the Hegelian stance of the early Lacan is confirmed by the rhetorical figures which give body to this logic of the "negation of negation." Lacan's answer to the ego-psychology's notion of the ego's "maturity" as the ability to endure frustrations, for example, is that "the ego as such is frustration in its essence":[26] insofar as the ego emerges in the process of imaginary identification with its mirror-double who is at the same time its rival and its potential paranoid persecutor, the frustration generated from the side of the mirror-double is constitutive of the ego. The logic of this reversal is strictly Hegelian: what first appears as an external hindrance frustrating the ego's striving for satisfaction is thereupon experienced as the ultimate support of its being.[27]

John Ford's *How Green Was My Valley*, usually dismissed as nostalgic kitsch, locates Evil qua ethical attitude in the very gaze of nostalgia. In a flashback narrative introduced by a voice-over, the hero, Hew Morgan, who is about to leave a Wales mining town for Argentina, recalls his idyllic childhood in the safe haven of a large patriarchal family. His gaze is obsessed by this vision of the happy past ruined by "progress," of the life in a closed community where even everyday occupations acquired the status of a ritual (coming home from the work in the shaft; Saturday family lunch). At this very point, however, the film lays a trap for the spectator: by way of narrating the story from the perspective of Hew, it renders all too visible and by the same token conceals the crucial fact that the true cause of the "green valley's" decline is not the inexorable logic of the larger economic universe but the very infatuation of the miners' community with their traditional way of life, which prevented them from adjusting to the demands of the new era. In other words, the responsibility for the decline, the true source of Evil, dwells in the very point of view from which the story is told, the nostalgic view which is able to perceive as the source of Evil only the cruel impact of the external Fate. What we have here is therefore the unique case of *a film which problematizes, "extraneates" the very perspective from which the story is narrated.*[28]

Why, then, does Kant hold back from bringing out all the consequences of his thesis on radical Evil? The answer is clear, albeit paradoxical: what prevents this move is the very logic which compelled him to articulate the thesis on radical Evil in the first place, namely the logic of "real opposition" which, as suggested by Monique David-Menard, constitutes a kind of ultimate fantasy-frame of Kant's thought.[29] By conceiving Good and Evil as contraries, as two opposed positive forces, Kant aims to undermine the traditional notion of Evil as something that lacks positive ontological consistency, i.e., as a mere absence of Good (the last great proponent of this notion was Leibniz). If Good and Evil are contraries, then what opposes Good must be some positive counterforce, not just our ignorance, our lack of insight into the true nature of Good; the proof of the existence of this counterforce lies in the fact that I experience the moral Law in myself as a traumatic agency which exerts an unbearable pressure on the very kernel of my self-identity and thus utterly humiliates my self-esteem—so there must be in the very nature of the "I" something which resists moral Law: the conceit which gives preference to "pathological" interests over the moral Law. This is how Kant conceives of the "radical Evil": as an a priori, not just empirical-contingent, propensity of human nature; it expresses itself in three forms, degrees, which all hinge on a kind of self-deceit of the subject.

The first, the mildest, form of Evil expresses itself through an appeal to the "weakness of the human nature": I know what my duty is, I fully acknowledge it, but I cannot gather enough strength to follow its call and not to succumb to "pathological" temptations. The falsity of this position, of course, resides in the underlying gesture of self-objectivization: the feebleness of my character is not part of my given nature; I have no right to assume the position of metalanguage, of an objective observer of myself, in order to ascertain what my nature allows. My "natural dispositions" determine my behavior only insofar as I qua free, autonomous being acknowledge them, so I am fully responsible for them. It is this responsibility that the first form of Evil evades.

The second form, incomparably more dangerous, inverts the first one: in the first form of Evil, the subject, while retaining the adequate notion of what his duty is, professes his inability to act accordingly; here, the subject claims to act for the sake of duty, to be motivated solely by ethical concerns, whereas he is truly led by pathological motivations. An exemplary case is a severe teacher who believes that he torments the children on behalf of their own moral upbringing, whereas he is actually satisfying his sadistic impulses. The self-deception is here deeper than in the first case, since the subject misperceives the very contours of duty.

The third form, the worst, is for the subject to totally lose the inner sense, the inner relationship toward duty qua specific moral agency, and to perceive morality as a simple external set of rules, of obstacles that society puts up in order to restrain the pursuit of egotistical "pathological" interests. This way, the very notions of "right" and "wrong" lose their meaning: if the subject does follow moral rules, it is simply in order to avoid painful consequences, but if he can "bend the law" without getting caught, all the better for him. The standard excuse of the subject with this attitude, when he is reproached for doing something cruel or immoral, is "I didn't break any laws, so get off my back!"

There is, however, a fourth possibility, excluded by Kant, the possibility of what he refers to as "diabolical Evil": the moment of the Hegelian contradiction when Evil assumes the form of its opposite, i.e., when it is not anymore externally opposed to Good but becomes the content of the latter's form. We must be careful here not to confuse this "diabolical Evil" with the second Kantian form: there, also, Evil assumes the form of Good; however, what we are concerned with here is a simple case of a pathological motivation which, by way of self-deceit, misperceives itself as fulfilling one's duty, whereas in the case of "diabolical Evil," the impetus of my activity actually *is* "nonpathological" and runs against my egotistical interests. The example that comes to mind here is the difference between right-wing corrupted authoritarian regimes and left-wing totalitarian regimes: in the case of right-wing authoritarian regimes, nobody is duped, everybody knows that behind all the patriotic rhetorics hides a simple greed for power and wealth; whereas left-wing totalitarians should not be dismissed as cases of disguising selfish interests under virtue's clothes, because they really act for the sake of what they perceive as virtue and they are prepared to stake everything, including their lives, on this virtue. The irony, of course, is that the exemplary case is the Jacobinical "dictature of virtue"; although Kant opposed the Jacobins in politics, he laid the foundations for them in his moral philosophy (it was Hegel who first detected this terrorist potential of Kantian ethics). Kant had therefore good reasons for excluding "diabolical Evil": within the parameters of his philosophy, it is indistinguishable from the Good![30]

So, to resume our argument: if moral struggle is conceived as the conflict of two opposing positive forces striving for mutual annihilation, it becomes unthinkable that one of the forces—Evil—not only opposes the other, endeavoring to annihilate it, but also *undermines it from within, by way of assuming the very form of its opposite.* Whenever Kant approaches this possibility (apropos of "diabolical Evil" in practical philosophy; apropos of the trial against the monarch in the doctrine of law), he quickly dismisses it as unthinkable, as an object of ultimate abhorrence. It is only with Hegel's logic of negative self-relating that this step can be accomplished.[31]

The proof that what Kant calls "diabolical Evil" (evil as an ethical principle) *is* a necessary consequence of Kant's notion of "radical Evil," i.e., the proof that Kant, when he rejects the hypothesis of "diabolical Evil," shirks the consequences of his own discovery, is provided by Kant himself. In his *Religion within the Limits of Reason Alone,* Kant points out how, apropos of some really evil person, we can see that Evil pertains to his very eternal character: this person did not yield to evil under the influence of bad circumstances; Evil lies in his very "nature." At the same time, of course, he is—like every human being—radically *responsible* for his character. The necessary implication of it is that, in an "eternal," timeless, transcendental act, he must have chosen Evil as the basic feature of his being. The transcendental, a priori character of this act means that it could not have been motivated by pathological circumstances; the original choice of Evil had to be a purely ethical act, the act of elevating Evil into an ethical principle.

There Are Pipes and Pipes

This diabolical Evil, the "unthought" of Kant, is *stricto sensu* unrepresentable: it entails the breakdown of the logic of representation, i.e., the radical incommensurability between the field of representation and the unrepresentable Thing. Flaubert's description of the first encounter of Madame

Bovary and her lover[32] condenses the entire problematic which, according to Foucault, determines the post-Kantian episteme of the nineteenth century: the new configuration of the axis power-knowledge caused by the incommensurability between the field of representation and the Thing, as well as the elevation of sexuality to the dignity of the unrepresentable Thing. After the two lovers enter the coach and tell the driver just to circulate around the city, we hear nothing about what goes on behind the coach's safely closed curtains: with an attention to detail reminiscent of the later *nouveau roman*, Flaubert limits himself to lengthy descriptions of the city environment through which the coach aimlessly wanders, the stone-paved streets, the church arches, etc.—only in one short sentence mentioning that, for a brief moment, a naked hand pierced through the curtain. This scene is made as if to illustrate Foucault's thesis, from the first volume of his *History of Sexuality,* that the very speech whose "official" function is to conceal sexuality actually engenders the appearance of its secret, i.e., that, to make use of the very terms of psychoanalysis against which Foucault's thesis is aimed, the "repressed" content is an effect of repression: the more the writer's gaze is restricted to irrelevant and boring architectural details, the more we, the readers, are tormented, greedy to learn what goes on in the space behind the closed curtains of the coach. The public prosecutor walked into this trap in the trial against *Madame Bovary* when he quoted precisely this passage as one instance of the obscene character of the book: it was easy for Flaubert's defense lawyer to point out that there is nothing obscene in the neutral descriptions of paved streets and old houses. Any obscenity is entirely constrained to the reader's (in this case: prosecutor's) imagination obsessed by the "real thing" behind the curtain. It is perhaps no mere accident that today this procedure of Flaubert's strikes us as eminently *cinematic:* it is as if it plays upon what cinema theory designates as *hors-champ,* the externality of the field of vision which, in its very absence, organizes the economy of what can be seen: if (as was long ago proven by the classical analyses of Eisenstein) Dickens introduced into the literary discourse the correlatives of what later became the elementary cinematic procedures—the triad of establishing shots, "American" pans and close-ups, the parallel montage, etc.—Flaubert took a step further toward an externality which eludes the standard exchange of field and counter-field, i.e., an externality which has to remain excluded if the field of what can be represented is to retain its consistency.[33]

The crucial point, however, is not to mistake *this* incommensurability between the field of representation and sexuality for the censorship of the description of sexuality already at work in the preceding epochs. If *Madame Bovary* were to have been written a century earlier, the details of sexual activity would also have remained unmentioned, for sure, yet what we would have read after the two lovers' entry into the secluded space of the coach would have been a simple short statement like: "Finally alone and hidden behind the curtains of the coach, the lovers yielded to passion." There, the lengthy descriptions of streets and buildings would have been totally out of place; they would have been perceived as lacking any function, since, in this pre-Kantian universe of representations, no radical tension could arise between the represented content and the traumatic Thing behind the curtain. Against this background, one is tempted to propose one of the possible definitions of "realism": a naive belief that, behind the curtain of representations, some full, substantial reality actually exists (in the case of *Madame Bovary*, the reality of sexual superfluity). "Postrealism" begins with a doubt as to the existence of this reality "behind the curtain," i.e., with the foreboding that the very gesture of concealment creates what it pretends to conceal.

An exemplary case of such "postrealist" playfulness, of course, are the paintings of René Magritte. Today, when one says "Magritte," the first association, of course, is the notorious drawing of a pipe with an inscription below it: "Ceci n'est pas une pipe" ("This is not a pipe"). Taking as a starting point the paradoxes implied by this painting, Michel Foucault wrote a perspicacious little book of the same title.[34] Yet, perhaps another of Magritte's paintings can serve even more appropriately to establish the elementary matrix that generates the uncanny effects pertaining to his work: *La lunette d'approche* from 1963, the painting of a half-open window where, through the windowpane, we see the external reality (blue sky with some dispersed white clouds), yet what we see in the narrow opening which gives direct access to the reality beyond the pane is nothing, just a nondescript black mass. In Lacanese, the painting would translate thus: the frame of the windowpane is the fantasy-frame which constitutes reality, whereas through the crack we get an insight into the "impossible" Real, the Thing-in-itself.[35]

This painting renders the elementary matrix of the Magrittean paradoxes by way of staging the "Kantian" split between (symbolized, categorized, transcendentally constituted) reality and the void of the Thing-in-itself, of the Real, which gapes open in the midst of reality and confers upon it a fantasmatic character. The first variation that can be generated from this matrix is the presence of some strange, inconsistent element which is "extraneous" to the depicted reality, i.e., which, uncannily, has its place in it, although it does not "fit" in it: the gigantic rock which floats in the air close to a cloud as its heavy counterpart, its double, in *La Bataille de l'Argonne* (1959); the unnaturally large bloom which fills out the entire room in *Tombeau des lutteurs* (1960). This strange element "out of joint" is precisely the fantasy-object filling out the blackness of the real that we perceived in the crack of the half-open window in *La lunette d'approche*. The effect of uncanniness is even stronger when the "same" object is redoubled, as in *Les deux mystères*, a later variation (from 1966) on the famous *Ceci n'est pas une pipe:* the pipe and the inscription underneath it "Ceci n'est pas une pipe" are both depicted as drawings on a blackboard; yet on the left of the blackboard, the apparition of *another* gigantic and massive pipe floats freely in a nonspecified space. The title of this painting could also have been "A pipe is a pipe," for what is it if not a perfect illustration of the Hegelian thesis on tautology as the ultimate contradiction: the coincidence between the pipe located in a clearly defined symbolic reality, and its phantomatic, uncanny double, strangely afloat nearby. The inscription under the pipe on the blackboard bears witness to the split between the two pipes: the pipe which forms part of reality and the pipe as real, i.e., as a fantasy-apparition, are distinguished by the intervention of the symbolic order: it is the emergence of the symbolic order which splits reality into itself and the enigmatic surplus of the real, each one "derealizing" its counterpart.

The Lacanian point to be made here, of course, is that such a split can occur only in an economy of desire: it designates the gap between the inaccessible object-cause of desire, the "metonymy of nothingness"—the pipe floating freely in the air—and the "empirical" pipe which, although we can smoke it, is never "that." (The Marx Brothers version of this painting would be something like "This looks like a pipe and works like a pipe, but this should not deceive you—this *is* a pipe!")[36] The massive presence of the free-floating pipe, of course, turns the depicted pipe into a "mere painting," yet, simultaneously, the free-floating pipe is opposed to the "domesticated" symbolic reality of the pipe on the blackboard and as such acquires a phantomlike, "surreal" presence—like the emergence of the "real" Laura in Otto Preminger's *Laura*. The police detective (Dana Andrews) falls asleep staring at the portrait of the allegedly dead Laura; upon awakening, he finds at the side of the portrait the "real" Laura, well and alive. This presence of the "real" Laura accentuates the fact that the portrait is a mere "imitation"; on the other hand, the very "real" Laura emerges as a nonsymbolized fantasmatic surplus, a ghostlike apparition; beneath the portrait, one can easily imagine the inscription "This is not Laura." A somewhat homologous effect of the real occurs at the beginning of Sergio Leone's *Once Upon a Time in America:* a phone goes on ringing endlessly; when, finally, a hand picks up the receiver, *the phone continues to ring.* The first sound belongs to "reality," whereas the ringing which goes on even after the receiver is picked up comes out of the nonspecified void of the Real.[37]

But this splitting between symbolized reality and the surplus of the Real renders only the most elementary matrix of the way the Symbolic and the Real are intertwined; a further dialectical "turn of the screw" is introduced by what Freud called *Vorstellungs-Repraesentanz*, the symbolic representative of an originally missing, excluded ("primordially repressed") representation.[38] This paradox of the *Vorstellungs-Repraesentanz* is perfectly staged by Magritte's *Personnage marchant vers l'horizon* (1928–29): the portrait of an unremarkable elderly gentleman in a bowler-hat, seen from behind, situated near five thick, formless blobs which bear the italicized words "nuage," "cheval," "fusil," etc. Here words are the signifier's representatives which stand in for the absent representation of the things. Foucault is quite right in remarking that this painting functions as a kind of inverted rebus: in a rebus, pictorial representations of things stand for the words which designate these things, whereas here words themselves fill out the void of the absent things. It would be possible for us to continue with the variations generated by this elementary matrix (*The Fall of the Evening*, for example, where the evening literally falls through the window and breaks the pane—a case of realized metaphor, i.e., of the intrusion of the Symbolic into the Real); yet it suffices to ascertain how behind all these paradoxes the same matrix emerges, the same basic fissure whose nature is ultimately Kantian: "reality" is never given in its totality; there is always a void gaping in its midst, filled out by monstrous apparitions.

The Non-intersubjective Other

The impenetrable blackness that can be glimpsed through the crack of the half-opened window thus opens up the space for the uncanny apparitions of an Other who precedes the Other of "normal" intersubjectivity. Let us recall here a detail from Hitchcock's *Frenzy* which bears witness to his genius: in a scene that leads to the second murder, Babs, the soon-to-be victim, a young girl who works in a Covent Garden pub, after a quarrel with the owner leaves her working place and steps out onto the busy market street; the street noise which for a brief moment hits us is quickly suspended (in a totally "nonrealistic" way) when the camera approaches Babs for a close-up, and the mysterious silence is then broken by an uncanny voice coming from an indefinite point of absolute proximity, as if from behind her and at the same time from within her, a man's voice softly saying "Need a place to stay?" Babs moves off and looks back; standing behind her is an old acquaintance who, unbeknownst to her, is the "necktie-murderer." After a couple of seconds, the magic evaporates and we hear again the sound tapestry of "reality," of the market street bustling with life. This voice which emerges in the suspension of reality is none other than the *objet petit a,* and the figure which appears behind Babs is experienced by the spectator as supplementary with regard to this voice: it gives body to it, and, simultaneously, it is strangely intertwined with Babs's body, as her body's shadowy protuberance (not unlike the strange double body of Leonardo's Madonna, analyzed by Freud; or, in *Total Recall,* the body of the leader of the underground resistance movement on Mars, a kind of parasitic protuberance on another person's belly). It is easy to offer a long list of similar effects; thus, in one of the key scenes of *Silence of the Lambs,* Clarice and Lecter occupy the same positions when engaged in a conversation in Lecter's prison: in the foreground, the close-up of Clarice staring into the camera, and on the glass partition-wall behind her, the reflection of Lecter's head germinating behind—out of her—as her shadowy double, simultaneously less and more real than her. The supreme case of this effect, however, is found in one of the most mysterious shots of Hitchcock's *Vertigo,* when Scottie peers at Madeleine through the crack in the half-opened backdoor of the florist's shop. For a brief moment, Madeleine watches herself in a mirror close to this door, so that the screen is vertically split: the left half is occupied by the mirror in which we see Madeleine's reflection, while the right half is sliced by a series of vertical lines (the doors); in the vertical dark band (the crack of the half-opened door) we see a fragment of Scottie, his gaze transfixed on the "original" whose mirror reflection we see in the left half. A truly "Magrittean" quality clings to this unique shot: although, as to the disposition of the diegetic space, Scottie is here "in reality," whereas what we see of Madeleine is only her mirror image, the effect of the shot is exactly the reverse: Madeleine is perceived as part of reality and Scottie as a phantomlike protuberance who (like the legendary dwarf in Grimm's *Snow-white*) lurks behind the mirror. This shot is Magrittean in a very precise sense: the dwarflike mirage of Scottie peeps out of the very impenetrable darkness which gapes in the crack of the half-open window in *La lunette d'approche* (the mirror in *Vertigo*, of course, corresponds to the windowpane in Magritte's painting). In both cases, the framed space of the mirrored reality is traversed by a vertical black rift.[39] As Kant puts it, there is no positive knowledge of the Thing-in-itself; one can only designate its place, "make room" for it. This is what Magritte accomplishes on a quite literal level: the crack of the half-open door, its impenetrable blackness, makes room for the Thing. And by locating in this crack a gaze, Hitchcock supplements Magritte in a Hegelian-Lacanian way: "if beyond appearance there is no thing in itself, there is the gaze."[40]

In his Bayreuth production of *Tristan und Isolde*, Jean-Pierre Ponelle changed Wagner's original plot, interpreting all that follows Tristan's death—the arrival of Isolde and King Marke, Isolde's death—as Tristan's mortal delirium: the final appearance of Isolde is staged so that the dazzlingly illuminated Isolde grows luxuriantly *behind* him, while Tristan stares at us, the spectators, who are able to perceive his sublime double, the protuberance of his lethal enjoyment. This is also how Bergman, in his version of *The Magic Flute*, often shot Pamina and Monostatos: a close-up of Pamina, who stares intensely into the camera, with Monostatos appearing behind her as her shadowy double, as if belonging to a different level of reality (illuminated with pointedly "unnatural" dark-violet colors), with his gaze also directed into the camera. This disposition, in which the subject and his or her shadowy, ex-timate double stare into a common third point (materialized in us, the spectators), epitomizes the relationship of the subject to an Otherness which is prior to intersubjectivity. The field of intersubjectivity where subjects, within their shared *reality*, "look into each other's eyes," is sustained by the paternal metaphor, whereas the reference to the absent *third point* which attracts the two gazes changes the status of one of the two partners—the one in the background—into the sublime embodiment of the *real* of enjoyment.[41]

What all these scenes have in common on the level of purely cinematic procedure is a kind of formal correlative of the reversal of face-to-face intersubjectivity into the relationship of the subject to his shadowy double which emerges behind him or her as a kind of sublime protuberance: *the condensation of the field and counter-field within the same shot*. What we have here is a paradoxical kind of communication: not a "direct" communication of the subject with his fellow creature *in front of* him, but a communication with the excrescence *behind* him, mediated by a third gaze, as if the counter-field were to be mirrored back into the field itself. It is this third gaze which confers upon the scene its hypnotic dimension: the subject is enthralled by the gaze which sees "what is in himself more than himself." And the analytical situation itself—the relationship between analyst and analysand—does it not ultimately also designate a kind of return to this pre-intersubjective relationship of the subject (analysand) to his shadowy other, to the externalized object in himself? Is not this the whole point of the spatial disposition of analysis: after the so-called preliminary interviews, the analysis proper begins when the analyst and the analysand no longer confront each other face to face, but the analyst sits *behind* the analysand, who, stretched on the divan, stares into the void in front of him? Does not this very disposition locate the analyst as the analysand's *object small a*, not his dialogical partner, not another subject?[42]

The Object of the Indefinite Judgment

At this point, we should return to Kant: in his philosophy, this crack, this space where such monstrous apparitions can emerge, is opened up by the distinction between negative and indefinite judgment. The very example used by Kant to illustrate this distinction is telltale: the positive judgment by means of which a predicate is ascribed to the (logical) subject—"The soul is mortal"; the negative judgment by means of which a predicate is denied to the subject—"The soul is not mortal"; the indefinite judgment by means of which, instead of negating a predicate (i.e., the copula which ascribes it to the subject), we affirm a certain non-predicate—"The soul is not-mortal." (In German also, the difference is solely a matter of punctuation: "Die Seele ist nicht sterbliche"—"Die Seele ist nichtsterbliche"; Kant enigmatically does not use the standard "unsterbliche." See *CPR*, A 72–73.) This distinction, as hair-splitting as it may appear, nevertheless plays a crucial role in Kant's endeavor to distinguish different modalities of opposition and / or negation:

    —First, the *real opposition:* the conflict between two positive forces, a force and its complementary counterforce, which cancel each other out. This opposition is real in the precise sense of designating the feature constitutive of the very notion of "reality": what we experience as "reality" is structured by the all-present antagonism of a force and its counterforce (attraction and repulsion, positive and negative poles in magnetism, etc.). The opposite of a positive force is not nothing, the absence, the lack of this positive force, but *another* force which possesses its own positive ontological actuality: the result of the conflict is o when opposite forces of equal strength cancel each other, like a rope which remains at a standstill when two groups of boys of equal strength pull it in opposite directions. Kant baptized this "zero" of real opposition *nihil privativum*: it is the outcome of the mutual "privation" of the two opposite forces. The crucial feature which distinguishes real opposition is the presupposed common ground: the opposition of positive and negative poles occurs only within a magnetic field. For that reason, the fact that an object is not magnetically positive does not automatically entail that it is magnetically negative—it can simply lie outside the sphere of magnetism.

–Real opposition is not to be confused with *logical contradiction*, whose outcome is a different type of "zero," *nihil negativum*: it occurs when the very notion of the object under consideration contradicts itself and thereby cancels itself. What Kant has in mind here are notions like "square circle," "wooden iron," etc. We cannot arrive at an intuition of such objects (we cannot imagine what a "square circle" looks like), since they are cases of what Kant refers to as *Unding*: a "non-thing," an *empty object devoid of its notion* and as such, due to its self-contradictory character, logically impossible.

–There is, however, a third type of negation, irreducible to either real opposition or logical contradiction: *antinomy*. Kant praised himself for being the first to articulate its specific character. There are namely objects which, although not logically self-contradictory, nevertheless a priori cannot be intuited, i.e., imagined as objects of our experience, as parts of what we experience as reality. These objects are clearly not logically impossible, yet for all that, we cannot consider them as "possible" insofar as the domain of what counts as "possible" is delineated by the horizon of our experience. They are not empty objects devoid of their notions, but quite on the contrary *empty notions devoid of their (intuited) objects*. As such, they cannot be subsumed under the notion of *Unding*, since it is easy to imagine them without any contradiction. The problem is precisely that while it is easy to imagine them, we can never fill out their notion with positive, intuited content. For that reason, Kant baptized such an object *Gedankending*, an object-of-thought (*ens rationis*). Exemplary cases involve notions which abound in traditional metaphysics and which involve us in transcendental antinomies: the universe in its totality, the soul, God. All these notions can be rationally imagined or constructed, but we can never experience them as part of reality (in our spatio-temporal reality, we never actually stumble upon "God" or "soul").[43]

This difference between contradiction and antinomy, i.e., the specific status of antinomy as irreducible to contradiction, brings into play the *transcendental* dimension: the "zero" of contradiction is logical (the very notion of the object cancels itself), whereas the "zero" of antinomy is transcendental, that is to say, we have to focus here on the notion of an object which remains forever "empty" since it can never become an object of our sensible intuition, of our possible experience. And, according to Kant, the way to resolve the "scandal" of transcendental antinomies is precisely to conceive of them as antinomies, not as contradictions. In the case of logical contradiction, one of its poles is necessarily true: yesterday I did read Hegel's *Logic* or I did not do it; *tertium non datur*, the falsity of one pole automatically entails the truth of its opposite. This, however, is the very trap we must avoid apropos of antinomies: the moment we conceive of a transcendental antinomy as contradiction, we are compelled to conclude that one of its poles must be true—the universe is either finite or infinite; the linear causal chain determines and englobes everything or there is freedom, i.e., the possibility of an autonomous activity which cannot be reduced to its conditions. What escapes us thereby is a third possibility: what if the very problem, the apparently exhaustive alternative, is false, since the common ground of the dispute (universe as a totality of phenomena, soul) does not exist as an object of our possible experience? In this case, either both poles of the antinomy are false (universe as a totality is a pure *Gedankending* which, due to our finitude, can never be filled out with intuited content—Kant's solution of mathematical antinomies), or both poles are true since each of them concerns a different ontological level (universal causality is limited to the field of phenomena, whereas freedom defines our noumenal soul). Kant's solution of mathematical antinomies is therefore very audacious: he breaks with the entire tradition of *Weltanschauung*, of the "worldview" (or, more accurately, world intuition): the world (universe, cosmos) is something which is never given in an intuition, i.e., *stricto sensu* it does not exist.

The notion of *Gedankending* concerns objects about which we can possess no knowledge since they transcend the limits of our experience. Nonetheless, we are compelled to refer to such objects on account of the irreducible finitude of our experience. We cannot *know* them, but we must *think* them: "As sensible intuition does not extend to all things without distinction, a place remains open for other and different objects" (*CPR*, A 288). In other words, all our (finite) thought can do is to draw a certain limit, restrict the field of our knowledge, without making any positive statements about its Beyond; the "Thing-in-itself" is given only as pure absence, in the guise of a certain place which, on account of the finitude of our experience, must forever remain empty. And it is here that we encounter the difference between negative and indefinite / limiting judgment: noumena are objects of indefinite-limiting judgment. By saying "the Thing *is* non-phenomenal," we do *not* say the same as "the Thing *is not* phenomenal"; we do not make any positive claim about it, we only draw a certain limit and locate the Thing in the wholly nonspecified void beyond it.[44]

Along this line of thought, Kant introduces in the second edition of the *Critique of Pure Reason* the distinction between positive and negative meanings of "noumenon": in the positive meaning of the term, noumenon is "an object of a nonsensible intuition," whereas in the negative meaning, it is "a thing insofar as it is not an object of our sensible intuition" (*CPR*, B 307). The grammatical form should not mislead us here: the positive meaning is expressed by the negative judgment and the negative meaning by the indefinite judgment. In other words, when one determines the Thing as "an object of a nonsensible intuition," one immediately negates the positive judgment which determines the Thing as "an object of a sensible intuition": one accepts intuition as the unquestioned base or genus; against this background, one opposes its two species, sensible and nonsensible intuition. Negative judgment is thus not only limiting, it also delineates a domain beyond phenomena where it locates the Thing—the domain of the nonsensible intuition—whereas in the case of the negative determination, the Thing is excluded from the domain of our sensible intuition, without being posited in an implicit way as the object of a nonsensible intuition; by leaving in suspense the positive status of the Thing, negative determination saps the very genus common to affirmation and negation of the predicate.

Herein lies also the difference between "is not mortal" and "is not-mortal": what we have in the first case is a simple negation, whereas in the second case, a *non-predicate is affirmed*. The only "legitimate" definition of the noumenon is that it is "not an object of our sensible intuition," i.e., a wholly negative definition which excludes it from the phenomenal domain;

this judgment is "infinite" since it does not imply any conclusions as to where, in the infinite space of what remains outside the phenomenal domain, the noumenon is located. What Kant calls "transcendental illusion" ultimately consists in the very (mis)reading of infinite judgment as negative judgment: when we conceive the noumenon as an "object of a nonsensible intuition," the subject of the judgment remains the same (the "object of an intuition"); what changes is only the character (nonsensible instead of sensible) of this intuition, so that a minimal "commensurability" between the subject and the predicate (i.e., in this case, between the noumenon and its phenomenal determinations) is still maintained.

A Hegelian corollary to Kant is that limitation is to be conceived of as prior to what lies "beyond" it, so that ultimately Kant's own notion of the Thing-in-itself remains too "reified." Hegel's position on this point is subtle: what he claims by stating that the Suprasensible is "appearance qua appearance" is precisely that the Thing-in-itself is *the limitation of the phenomena as such.* "Suprasensible objects (objects of suprasensible intuition)" belong to the chimerical "topsy-turvy world"; they are nothing but an inverted presentation, projection, of the very content of sensible intuition in the form of another, nonsensible intuition—or, to recall Marx's ironic critique of Proudhon in *The Poverty of Philosophy:* "Instead of the ordinary individual with his ordinary manner of speaking and thinking, we have nothing but this ordinary manner purely and simply—without the individual."[45] (The double irony of it, of course, is that Marx intended these lines as a mocking rejection of Proudhon's Hegelianism, i.e., of his effort to supply economic theory with the form of speculative dialectics!) This is what the chimera of "nonsensible intuition" is about: instead of ordinary objects of sensible intuition, we get the same ordinary objects of intuition, without their sensible character.

This subtle difference between negative and indefinite judgment figures in a certain type of witticism where the second part does not immediately invert the first part by negating its predicate but repeats it with the negation displaced onto the subject. The judgment "He is an individual full of idiotic features," for example, can be negated in a standard mirror way, i.e., replaced by its contrary "He is an individual with no idiotic features"; yet its negation can also be given the form of "He is full of idiotic features without being an individual." This displacement of the negation from the predicate onto the subject provides the logical matrix of what is often the unforeseen result of our educational efforts to liberate the pupil from the constraint of prejudices and clichés: the result is not a person capable of expressing himself or herself in a relaxed, unconstrained way, but an automatized bundle of (new) clichés behind which we no longer sense the presence of a "real person." Let us just recall the usual outcome of psychological training intended to deliver the individual from the constraints of his or her everyday frame of mind and to set free his or her "true self," with all its authentic creative potentials (transcendental meditation, etc.): once the individual gets rid of the old clichés which were still able to sustain the dialectical tension between themselves and the "personality" behind them, what take their place are new clichés which abrogate the very "depth" of personality behind them. In short, the individual becomes a true monster, a kind of "living dead." Samuel Goldwyn, the old Hollywood mogul, was right: what we need are indeed some new, original clichés.

Invoking the "living dead" is no accident here: in our ordinary language, we resort to indefinite judgments precisely when we endeavor to comprehend those borderline phenomena which undermine established differences, such as those between living and being dead. In the texts of popular culture, the uncanny creatures which are neither alive nor dead, the "living dead" (vampires, etc.), are referred to as "the undead"; although they are not dead, they are clearly not alive like us, ordinary mortals. The judgment "he is undead" is therefore an indefinite-limiting judgment in the precise sense of a purely negative gesture of excluding vampires from the domain of the dead, without for that reason locating them in the domain of the living (as in the case of the simple negation "he is not dead"). The fact that vampires and other "living dead" are usually referred to as "things" has to be rendered with its full Kantian meaning: a vampire is a Thing which looks and acts like us, yet it is not one of us. In short, the difference between the vampire and the living person is the difference between indefinite and negative judgment: a dead person loses the predicates of a living being, yet he or she remains the same person; an undead, on the contrary, retains all the predicates of a living being without being one. As in the above-quoted Marxian joke, what we get with the vampire is "the ordinary manner of speaking and thinking purely and simply—without the individual."

One is tempted to affirm that this logic of infinite judgment contains *in nuce* Kant's entire philosophical revolution: it delineates transcendentally constituted *reality* from the uncanny, prohibited / impossible, *real* domain of the Thing which had to remain unthought since in it Good overlaps with radical Evil. In short, Kant replaced the traditional philosophical opposition of appearance and essence with the opposition of phenomenal reality and the noumenal Thing which follows a radically different logic: what appears as "essential" (moral law in ourselves) is possible and thinkable only within the horizon of our finitude, of our limitation to the domain of phenomenal reality; if it were possible for us to trespass this limitation and to gain a direct insight into noumenal Thing, we would lose the very capacity which enables us to transcend the limits of sensible experience (moral dignity and freedom).

Ate *and Its Beyond*

For a closer determination of this uncanny domain opened up by the indefinite judgment, let us turn again to Hollywood. Fritz Lang's *noir* western *Rancho Notorious* (1950) begins where a Hollywood story usually ends: with the passionate kiss of a couple awaiting their marriage. Immediately thereupon, brutal bandits rape and kill the bride, and the desperate bridegroom (played by Arthur Kennedy) commits himself to inexorable revenge. His only clue as to the identity of the bandits is "chuck-a-luck," a meaningless signifying fragment. After a long search, he unearths its secret: "Chuck-a-luck" designates a mysterious place whose very name it is dangerous to pronounce in public, a ranch in a hidden valley beyond a narrow mountain pass, where Marlene Dietrich, an aged saloon singer, ex-fatal beauty, reigns, offering refuge to robbers for a percentage of their loot. What accounts for the irresistible charm of this film? Undoubtedly the fact that, beneath the usual western plot, *Rancho Notorious* stages another mythical narrative, the one articulated in its pure form in a series of adventure novels and films whose action is usually set in Africa (*King Solomon's Mines, She, Tarzan*): the story of an expedition into the very heart of the black continent where white man had never set foot (the voyagers are lured into this risky trip by some incomprehensible or ambiguous signifying fragment: a message in a bottle, a fragment of burned paper, or the confused babbling of some madman hinting that beyond a certain frontier wonderful and / or horrible things are taking place). On the way, the expedition confronts diverse dangers; it is menaced by aborigines who at the same time strive desperately to make the foreigners understand that they should not trespass a certain frontier (river, mountain pass, abyss), since beyond it lies a damned place from which nobody has yet returned. After a series of adventures, the expedition goes beyond this frontier and finds itself in the

Other Place, in the space of pure fantasy: a mighty black kingdom (*King Solomon's Mines*), the realm of a beautiful and mysterious queen (*She*), the domain where man lives in full harmony with nature and speaks with animals (*Tarzan*). Another mythical landscape of this kind was of course Tibet: the Tibetan theocracy served as a model for the most famous image of the idyllic world of wisdom and balance, Shangri-La (in *Lost Horizon*), which can be reached only through a narrow mountain passage; nobody is allowed to return from it, and the one person who does escape pays for his success by madness, so that nobody believes him when he prattles about the peaceful country ruled by wise monks.[46] The mysterious "Chuck-a-luck" from *Rancho Notorious* is the same forbidden place: it is by no means accidental that all the crucial confrontations in the film take place at the narrow mountain pass which marks the frontier separating the everyday reality from the valley where "She" reigns—in other words, at the very place of *passage* between reality and the fantasy's "other place."[47]

What is crucial here is the strict formal homology between all these stories: in all cases, the structure is that of a Möbius band—if we progress far enough on the side of reality, we suddenly find ourselves on its reverse, in the domain of pure fantasy.[48] Let us, however, pursue our line of associations: do we not encounter the same inversion in the development of a great number of artists, from Shakespeare to Mozart, where the gradual descent into despair, when it reaches its nadir, suddenly changes into a kind of heavenly bliss? After a series of tragedies which mark the lowest point of despair (*Hamlet*, *King Lear*, etc.), the tone of Shakespeare's plays unexpectedly changes and we enter the realm of a fairy-tale harmony where life is governed by a benevolent Fate which brings to a happy conclusion all conflicts (*The Tempest*, *Cymbeline*, etc.). After *Don Giovanni*, this ultimate monument to the *impossibility* of the sexual relationship, to the antagonism of the relation between sexes, Mozart composed *The Magic Flute*, a hymn to the harmonious couple of Man and Woman (note the paradox of how the criticism *precedes* the panegyric!).[49]

The horrifying, lethal, and at the same time fascinating borderline that we approach when the reversal into bliss is imminent is what Lacan, apropos of Sophocles's *Antigone*, endeavors to indicate by means of the Greek word *ate*.[50] There is a fundamental ambiguity to this term: *ate* simultaneously denotes a horrifying limit which cannot ever be reached, i.e., whose touch means death, and *the space beyond it*. The crucial point here is the primacy of the limit over the space: we do not have two spheres (that of reality and that of pure fantasy) which are divided by a certain limit; what we have is just reality and its limit, the abyss, the void around which it is structured. The fantasy-space is therefore strictly secondary; it "gives body," it materializes a certain limit, or, more precisely, it changes the *impossible* into the *prohibited*. The limit marks a certain fundamental impossibility (it cannot be trespassed, if we come too close to it, we die), while its Beyond is prohibited (whoever enters it cannot return, etc.).[51] Thereby we have already produced the formula of the mysterious reversal of horror into bliss: by means of it, the *impossible limit* changes into the *forbidden place*. In other words, the logic of this reversal is that of the transmutation of Real into Symbolic: the impossible-real changes into an object of symbolic prohibition. The paradox (and perhaps the very function of the prohibition as such) consists of course in the fact that, as soon as it is conceived as prohibited, the real-impossible changes into something *possible,* i.e., into something that cannot be reached, not because of its inherent impossibility but simply because access to it is hindered by the external barrier of a prohibition. Therein lies, after all, the logic of the most fundamental of all prohibitions, that of incest: incest is inherently impossible (even if a man "really" sleeps with his mother, "this is not *that*"; the incestuous object is by definition lacking), and the symbolic prohibition is nothing but an attempt to resolve this deadlock by a transmutation of impossibility into prohibition. *There is One* which is the prohibited object of incest (mother), and its prohibition renders accessible all other objects.[52]

The trespassing of the Frontier in the above-mentioned series of adventure films follows the same logic: the forbidden space beyond *ate* is again constituted by the transmutation of impossibility into prohibition. On another level, the same paradoxical reversal characterizes the "national revival" under conditions of colonial repression: it is only the colonial repression ("prohibition") that stirs up resistance and thus renders possible the "national revival." The "spontaneous" idea that we are salvaging the remains of a previous tradition from under the yoke of colonial repression corresponds precisely to what Hegel calls "the illusion of (external) reflection": what we overlook insofar as we are victims of this illusion is that nation, national identity, *comes to be* through the experience of the threat to its existence—previous to this experience, it did not exist at all. This goes not only for the classical anticolonial struggle but also for the current ethnic tensions in the ex-Soviet Union: although the people experience themselves as a return to the pre-Communist tradition, it was the very Communist "repression" which, by means of prohibition, *opened up their space*, i.e., posited them as *possible*.

By means of the reversal of (impossible) limit into (prohibited) space, of *Don Giovanni* into *Magic Flute,* we thus elude the real qua impossible: once we enter the domain of fantasy, the trauma of the inherent impossibility is replaced by a fairy beatitude. Mozart's *Magic Flute,* its image of the amorous couple forming a harmonious Whole, exemplifies perfectly the Lacanian thesis that fantasy is ultimately always the fantasy of a successful sexual relationship: after the couple of Tamino and Pamina successfully undergoes the ordeal of fire and water, i.e., trespasses the limit, the two of them enter symbolic bliss. And it is reference to the anticolonial national revival which enables us to locate more precisely the dreamlike character of this beatitude: the agents of the anticolonialist national-liberation struggle necessarily fall prey to the illusion that, by means of their struggle, they "realize the ancient dreams of their oppressed ancestors." Therein consists one of the fundamental mechanisms of ideological legitimization: to legitimize the existing order by presenting it as a realization of a dream—*not of our dream, but of the Other's, the dead ancestor's dream,* the dream of previous generations. That was, for example, the reference that determined the "progressive" Western attitude toward the Soviet Union in the twenties and thirties: in spite of the poverty and wrongs, numerous Western visitors were fascinated by this very drab Soviet reality—why? Because it appeared to them as a kind of palpable materialization of the dream of millions of past and present workers from all around the world. Any doubt about the Soviet reality thus entailed instant guilt: "True, they in the Soviet Union make numerous mistakes, but when you criticize with ironic disdain their efforts, you are making fun of and betraying the dream of millions who suffered and risked their lives for what they are realizing now!"[53] The situation here is not unlike that of Zhuang Zi, who dreamt of being a butterfly, and after his awakening posed this question to himself: How does he know that he is not *now* a butterfly dreaming of being Zhuang Zi?[54] In the same way, postrevolutionary ideology endeavors to make us understand that what we live now is a dream of our ancestors come true; the worker in the Soviet Union, for example, was a prerevolutionary fighter dreaming to be a worker in the Socialist paradise—if we complain too much, we might disturb his dream. This detour through the dead Other is necessary for the ideological legitimization of the present to take effect. On another level, the fantasy of the harmonious love couple from Mozart's

Magic Flute follows the same logic: the dreary bourgeois everyday reality undergoes a kind of transubstantiation and acquires a sublime dimension as soon as it is conceived as the actualization of a prerevolutionary dream of a free love couple.

Wherein consists the logic of this reversal? Yet another formal homology might move us further down the right track: do we not encounter the same matrix in Freud's most famous dream, that of Irma's injection?[55] Do not the three stages of this dream correspond to the imaginary dual-relationship, its "aggravation" into an unbearable antagonism which announces the encounter of the Real, and the final "appeasement" via the advent of the symbolic order? In the first phase of the dream, Freud is "playing with his patient";[56] his dialogue with Irma is "totally stuck within the imaginary conditions which limit it."[57] This dual, specular relationship culminates in a look into her open mouth:

> There's a horrendous discovery here, that of the flesh one never sees, the foundation of things, the other side of the head, of the face, the secretory glands *par excellence,* the flesh from which everything exudes, at the very heart of the mystery, the flesh in as much as it is suffering, is formless, in as much as its form in itself is something which provokes anxiety. Spectre of anxiety, identification of anxiety, the final revelation of *you are this—You are this, which is so far from you, this which is the ultimate formlessness.*[58]

Suddenly, this horror changes miraculously into "a sort of ataraxia" defined by Lacan precisely as "the coming into operation of the symbolic function,"[59] exemplified by the production of the formula of trimethylamin; the subject floats freely in symbolic bliss—as soon as the dreamer (Freud) renounces its narcissistic perspective. Jacques-Alain Miller was quite right to subtitle this chapter of Lacan's *Seminar II* simply "The Imaginary, the Real and the Symbolic."[60] The trap to be avoided here is of course to oppose this symbolic bliss to some "hard reality": the fundamental thesis of the Lacanian psychoanalysis is that what we call "reality" constitutes itself against the background of such a "bliss," i.e., of such an exclusion of some traumatic Real. This is precisely what Lacan has in mind when he says that fantasy is the ultimate support of reality: "reality" stabilizes itself when some fantasy-frame of a "symbolic bliss" closes off the view into the abyss of the Real. Far from being a kind of dreamlike cobweb that prevents us from "seeing reality as it effectively is," fantasy constitutes what we call reality: the most common bodily "reality" is constituted via a detour through the cobweb of fantasy. In other words, we pay a price to gain access to "reality": something—the real of the trauma—must be "repressed."

What strikes the eye here is the parallel between the dream of Irma's injection and another famous Freudian dream, that of the dead son who appears to his father and addresses him with the reproach, "Father, can't you see that I'm burning?" In his interpretation of the dream of Irma's injection, Lacan draws our attention to the appropriate remark by Eric Ericson that after the look into Irma's throat, after this encounter of the Real, Freud *should have awakened*—as did the dreaming father, upon encountering the horrifying apparition of his burning son. Confronted with the Real in all its unbearable horror, the dreamer awakens, i.e., escapes into "reality." A radical conclusion emerges from this parallel between the two dreams: *what we call "reality" is constituted exactly upon the model of the asinine "symbolic bliss" that enables Freud to continue to sleep after the horrifying sight of Irma's throat.* The dreaming father who awakens into reality in order to avoid the traumatic Real of his burning son's reproach proceeds the same way as Freud, who, after the look into Irma's throat, "changes the register," i.e., escapes into the fantasy which veils the Real.

The Symbolic Beatitude

At this point, one is tempted to extend the formal homology a step further: does not this reversal of the horror into symbolic bliss procure also the matrix of the Hegelian "triad"? A homologous shift, changing impasse into "pass," occurs at the very beginning of the Hegelian system, namely in the passage of Being into Nothing. What does it mean, precisely, that Nothing is to be conceived as the "truth" of Being? Being is first posited as the subject (in the grammatical sense), and one endeavors to accord it some predicate, to determine it in any way possible. Yet every attempt fails: one cannot say anything determinate about Being; one cannot attribute to it any predicate, and thus Nothing qua the truth of Being functions as *a positivization, a "substantialization," of this impasse.* Such a positivization of an impossibility is at work in every Hegelian passage from one category to another which functions as the first category's "truth": the Hegelian development is never simply a descent toward a more profound and concrete essence; the logic of the notional passage is by definition that of a reflective positivization of a failure, i.e., of the impossibility of the passage itself. Let us take a moment X: all attempts to grasp its concealed essence, to determine it more concretely, end in failure, and the subsequent moment only positivizes this failure; in it, failure as such assumes positive existence. In short, one fails to determine the truth of X, and this failure *is* the truth of X. Therein lies the accent of Hegel's interpretation of the inexistence of movement in Zeno's philosophy: Zeno strives to prove the existence of self-identical, immovable Being beyond the false appearance of Movement; yet this Being is in itself empty, so the passage beyond the appearance of Movement fails; one can only describe the self-sublation of Movement, i.e., notional movement of self-suppression of Movement, which is why the Heraclitic movement is the truth of the Eleatic Being.

As a rule, one overlooks how closely the elementary Lacanian triad *need-demand-desire* follows the inner logic of the Hegelian "negation of negation." First, we have a mythical, quasi-natural starting point of an immediate *need*—the point which is always-already *presupposed*, never given, "posited," experienced "as such." The subject needs "natural," "real" objects to satisfy his needs: if we are thirsty, we need water, etc. However, as soon as the need is articulated in the symbolic medium (and it always-already *is* articulated in it), it starts to function as a *demand:* a call to the Other, originally to the Mother qua primordial figure of the Other. That is to say, the Other is originally experienced as he or she who can satisfy our need, who can give us the object of satisfaction, deprive us of it, or hinder our access to it. This intermediary role of the Other subverts the entire economy of our relationship toward the object: on the literal level, the demand aims at the object supposed to satisfy our need; the demand's true aim, however, is the love of the Other, who has the power to procure the object. If the Other complies with our demand and provides the object, this object does not simply satisfy our need, but at the same time testifies to the Other's love for us. (When, for example, a baby cries for milk, the true aim of his demand is that his mother should display her love for him by providing milk. If the mother does comply with the demand, but in a cold, indifferent way, the baby will remain unsatisfied; if, however, she bypasses the literal level of the demand and simply hugs the baby, the most likely result is the child's complacency.) It is in no way accidental that, to denote this inversion, Lacan resorts to the Hegelian notion of *Aufhebung* (sublation): "The demand sublates (*aufhebt*) the particularity of everything that can be granted by transmuting it into a proof of love."[61] By means of the transformation of a need into a demand, i.e., into a signifier addressed to the Other, the particular, material object of the need is "sublated": it is annulled in its immediacy and posited as something "mediated," as a medium through which a dimension transcendent to its immediate reality (that of love) finds its expression. This reversal is strictly homologous to that described by Marx apropos of the commodity-form: as soon as a product of human labor assumes the form of a commodity, its immediate particularity (its "use-value," the effective, actual properties by means of which it satisfies certain human needs) starts to function as the form of appearance of its "exchange-value," i.e., of a nonmaterial intersubjective relationship—the same as with the passage from need to demand, whereby the particular object of need starts to function as the form of appearance of the Other's love.

This reversal is then the first moment, the moment of "negation," which necessarily culminates in a deadlock, in the unsolvable antagonistic relationship between need and demand: every time the subject gets the object he demanded, he undergoes the experience of "This is not *that!*" Although the subject "got what he asked for," the demand is not fully satisfied, since its true aim was the Other's love, not the object as such, in its immediate particularity. This vicious circle of need and demand finds its ultimate expression in the nursling's anorexia ("pathological" refusal of food): its "message" is precisely that the true aim of his demand for food was not food itself but Mother's love. The only way open to him to point out this difference is by *refusing* food, i.e., the object of demand in its particular materiality. This impasse where a demand for the Other's love can only be articulated through the demand for an object of need which, however, is never "that" is resolved by means of the introduction of a *third* element which adds itself to need and demand: *desire*. According to Lacan's precise definition, "desire is neither the appetite for satisfaction, nor the demand for love, but the difference that results from the subtraction of the first from the second."[62] Desire is what in demand is irreducible to need: if we subtract need from demand, we get desire. In a formulation typical of the anti-Hegelian attitude of his late teaching, Lacan speaks here of "a reversal that is not simply a negation of the negation"[63]—in other words, one that *is* still a kind of "negation of the negation," although not a "simple" one (as if, with Hegel himself, the "negation of the negation" is ever "simple"!). This "reversal" is a "negation of the negation" insofar as it entails a *return to the object* annulled by the passage from need to demand: it produces a new object which replaces the lost-sublated object of need—*objet petit a*, the object-cause of desire. This paradoxical object "gives body" to the dimension because of which demand cannot be reduced to need: it is as if the surplus of the demand over its (literal) object—over what the demand immediately-literally demands—again embodies itself in an object. *Objet a* is a kind of "positivization," filling out, of the void we encounter every time we are struck by the experience of "This is not *that!*" In it, the very inadequacy, deficiency, of every positive object assumes positive existence, i.e., becomes an object.

Crucial here is the effect of "appeasement" that results from the conversion of demand into desire: the emergence of the object-cause of desire resolves the antagonistic deadlock between need and demand. This *resolving of the antagonistic deadlock by means of symbolic "appeasement"* also gives us the elementary matrix according to which the ill-famed triad of "thesis-antithesis-synthesis"[64] functions: its *imaginary* starting point is the complementary relationship of the opposed poles; thereupon follows the outbreak of the *real* of their antagonism.[65] The illusion of their mutual completion evaporates, each pole passes immediately into its opposite; this extreme tension is finally resolved by means of *symbolization* when the relationship of the opposites is posited as differential, i.e., when the two poles are again united, but this time against the background of their common lack.

The notion that "thesis" contains "antithesis" somewhere deep in its interior and that, consequently, one has somehow to "extract" the latter from its "implicit" state within "thesis" is wholly erroneous: the "antithesis" is on the contrary what the "thesis" *lacks* in order to "concretize" itself, i.e., to actualize its notional content. In other words, the "thesis" is in itself *abstract*: it presupposes its "mediation" by the "antithesis"; it can attain its ontological consistency only by means of its opposition to the "antithesis." This, however, in no way implies that "synthesis" denotes a mutual completion, a complementary relationship between the two opposed poles, that is to say, the conjunction of the type "no X without Y" (there is no man without woman, no love without hate, no harmony without chaos . . .). What Hegel calls "the unity of the opposites" subverts precisely the false appearance of such a complementary relationship: the position of an extreme is not simply the negation of its other. Hegel's point is rather that *the first extreme, in its very abstraction from the other, is this other itself.* An extreme "passes over" into its other at the very moment when it radically opposes itself to this other; the "unity" of Being and Nothing, for example, does not consist in the fact that they presuppose each other, that there is no Being without Nothing and vice versa: Being reveals itself as Nothing at the very moment when we endeavor to grasp it in its pureness, as radically opposed to Nothing. Or, to refer to a more "concrete" example from the domain of politics: the "unity" of universal and particular Will does not consist in their codependence, but in the dialectical reversal of the universal Will into its opposite: insofar as the universal Will is opposed to the multitude of particular Wills, it turns into the utmost particular Will of those who pretend to embody it (since it *excludes* the wealth of particular Wills). In this way, we are caught in an "immediate exchange" between the extremes, between the opposite poles (pure love turns into the supreme form of hate, pure Good into supreme Evil, radical anarchy coincides with the utmost terror, etc.); by means of this immediate passage of an extreme into its opposite, we surpass the level of *external* negativity: each of the extremes is not only the negation of the other but *a negation which refers to itself*, its own negation. The impasse of this "immediate exchange" between thesis and antithesis is resolved by the advent of *synthesis*.

What defines the imaginary order is the appearance of a complementary relationship between thesis and antithesis, the illusion that they form a harmonious Whole, filling out each other's lack: what the thesis lacks is provided by the antithesis and vice versa (the idea that Man and Woman form a harmonious Whole, for example). This false appearance of a mutual completion is shattered by the immediate passage of an extreme into its opposite: how can an extreme fill out the lack of its other, when it is itself, in its very opposition to its other, this other? It is only the synthesis which conveys "appeasement": in it, the imaginary opposition is *symbolized,* i.e., transformed into a symbolic dyad. The flow of immediate exchange between the two extremes is suspended; they are again "posited" as distinct, but this time as "sublated," "internalized"—in other words, as elements of a signifying network: if an extreme does not render to its other what this other lacks, what can it return to it if not *the lack itself?* What "holds together" the two extremes is therefore not the mutual filling out of their respective lacks but *the very lack they have in common:* the opposites of a signifying dyad "are one" against the background of some common lack that they return to each other. Therein consists also the definition of a symbolic exchange: in it, the place of the "object of exchange" is occupied by the lack itself, i.e., any "positive" object which circulates among the terms is nothing but the embodiment of a lack.

What is thus "internalized" by the advent of symbolization is ultimately lack itself. This is why "synthesis" does not affirm the identity of the extremes, their common ground, the space of their opposition, but on the contrary *their difference as such:* what "links up" the elements of a signifying network is their very difference. Within a differential order, the identity of each of the elements consists in the bundle of differential features which discern it from all other elements. The "synthesis" thus delivers the difference from the "compulsion to identify": the contradiction is resolved when we acknowledge the "primacy of the difference," i.e., when we conceive identity as an effect of the tissue of differences. In other words, the immediate passage of an extreme into its opposite, this pure, utmost form of contradiction, is precisely an index of our submission to the "compulsion to identify": "Contradiction is nonidentity under the aspect of identity; the dialectical primacy of the principle of contradiction makes the thought of unity the measure of heterogeneity."[66] In this precise sense the synthesis "sublates" contradiction: not by establishing a new unity encompassing both poles of a contradiction, but by retracting the very frame of identity and affirming the difference as constitutive of identity. The idea that the concluding moment of a dialectical process ("synthesis") consists of the advent of an Identity which encompasses the difference, reducing it to its passing moment, is thus totally misleading: *it is only with "synthesis" that the difference is acknowledged as such.*

The "rational kernel" of the Hegelian triad consists therefore in the symbolization of the imaginary oppositions: the "aggravation" of the imaginary opposition into the antagonistic relation where the two poles pass immediately one into another; the resolution of this tension via internalization of the lack. The passage of "antithesis" into "synthesis" is the passage of the external negativity (of the power which strives to negate the object from outside, in an immediate way, i.e., to destroy it in its physical reality) into the "absolute" (self-referring) negativity which "posits" the object anew, but qua symbolized—that is to say, against the background of a certain loss, of an incorporated, internalized negativity. This inversion of external into "absolute" negativity means that the object need not anymore be negated, destroyed, annulled, since it is already its very "positive" presence which functions as the form in which negativity assumes existence: the "symbolized" object is an object the very presence of which "gives body" to an absence; it is the "absence embodied."

4 Hegel's "Logic of Essence" as a Theory of Ideology

■

The Principle of the Insufficient Ground

"Love lets us view imperfections as tolerable, if not adorable. *But it's a choice.* We can bristle at quirks, or we can cherish them. A friend who married a hot-shot lawyer remembers, 'On the first date, I learned that he could ride out rough hours and stiff client demands. On the second, I learned that what he couldn't ride was a bicycle. *That's* when I decided to give him a chance.'"

The lesson of the so-called "endearing foibles" referred to in this quote from *Reader's Digest* is that a choice is an act which *retroactively grounds its own reasons.* Between the causal chain of reasons provided by knowledge (S_2, in Lacanian mathems) and the act of choice, the decision which, by way of its unconditional character, concludes the chain (S_1), there is always a gap, a leap which cannot be accounted for by the preceding chain.[1] Let us recall what is perhaps the most sublime moment in melodramas: a plotter or a well-meaning friend tries to convince the hero to leave his sexual partner by way of enumerating the latter's weak points; yet, unknowingly, he thereby provides reasons for continued loyalty, i.e., his very counterarguments function as arguments for (*"for that very reason* she needs me even more").[2] This gap between reasons and their effect is the very foundation of what we call transference, the transferential relationship, epitomized by love. Even our sense of common decency finds it repulsive to enumerate the reasons we love somebody. The moment I can say "I love this person for the following reasons . . . ," it is clear beyond any doubt that this is not love proper.[3] In the case of true love, apropos of some feature which is in itself negative, i.e., which offers itself as reason against love, we say "For this very reason I love this person even more!" *Le trait unaire*, the unary feature which triggers love, is always an *index of an imperfection*.

This circle within which we are determined by reasons, but only by those which, retroactively, we recognize as such, is what Hegel has in mind when he talks about the "positing of presuppositions." The same retroactive logic is at work in Kant's philosophy, in the guise of what, in the Anglo-Saxon literature on Kant, is usually referred to as the "Incorporation Thesis":[4] there is always an element of autonomous "spontaneity" which pertains to the subject, making him irreducible to a link in the causal chain. True, one can conceive of the subject as submitted to the chain of causes which determine his conduct in accordance with his "pathological" interests; therein consists the wager of utilitarianism (since the subject's conduct is wholly determined by seeking the maximum of pleasure and the minimum of pain, it would be possible to govern the subject, to predict his steps, by controlling the external conditions which influence his decisions). What eludes utilitarianism is precisely the element of "spontaneity" in the sense of German Idealism, the very opposite of the everyday meaning of "spontaneity" (surrendering oneself to the immediacy of emotional impulses, etc.). According to German Idealism, when we act "spontaneously" in the everyday meaning of the word, we are not free from but prisoners of our immediate nature, determined by the causal link which chains us to the external world. True spontaneity, on the contrary, is characterized by the moment of reflexivity: reasons ultimately count only insofar as I "incorporate" them, "accept them as mine"; in other words, the determination of the subject by the other is always the subject's self-determination. A decision is thus simultaneously dependent on and independent of its conditions: it "independently" posits its own dependence. In this precise sense, the subject in German Idealism is always the subject of self-consciousness: any immediate reference to my nature ("What can I do, I was made like this!") is false; my relationship to the impulses in me is always a mediated one, i.e., my impulses determine me only insofar as I recognize them, which is why I am fully responsible for them.[5]

Another way to exemplify this logic of "positing the presuppositions" is the spontaneous ideological narrativization of our experience and activity: whatever we do, we always situate it in a larger symbolic context which is charged with conferring meaning upon our acts. A Serbian fighting the

Muslim Albanians and Bosnians in today's ex-Yugoslavia conceives of his fight as the last act in the centuries-old defense of Christian Europe against Turkish penetration; the Bolsheviks conceived of the October Revolution as the continuation and successful conclusion of all previous radical popular uprisings, from Spartacus in ancient Rome to Jacobins in the French Revolution (this narrativization is tacitly assumed even by some critics of Bolshevism who, for example, speak of the "Stalinist Thermidor"); the Khmer Rouge in Kampuchea or the Sendero Luminoso in Peru conceive of their movement as a return to the old glory of an ancient empire (Inca's empire in Peru, the old Khmer kingdom in Cambodia); etc. The Hegelian point to be made is that such narratives are always retroactive reconstructions for which we are in a way responsible; they are never simple given facts: we can never refer to them as a found condition, context, or presupposition of our activity. Precisely as presuppositions, such narratives are always-already "posited" by us. Tradition is tradition insofar as we constitute it as such.

What we must bear in mind here is the ultimate *contingency* of this act of "positing the presuppositions." In ex-Yugoslavia, the Communist censorship was neither too harsh nor too permissive. For example, films with direct religious content were allowed, but not if their subject was Christian: we saw de Mille's *Ten Commandments,* but there were problems with Wyler's *Ben Hur.* The censor resolved his dilemma (how to obliterate Christian references in this "tale of Christ" and yet preserve the story's narrative consistency?) in a very imaginative way: he cut out of the first two-thirds the few scattered oblique references to Christ, while simply cutting off the entire last third where Christ plays the central role. The film thus ends immediately after the famous horse-race scene in which Ben Hur wins over Massala, his evil Roman archenemy: Massala, all in blood, wounded to death, spoils Ben Hur's triumph by letting him know that his sister and mother, allegedly dead, are still alive, yet confined to a colony of lepers, crippled beyond recognition. Ben Hur returns to the race ground, now silent and empty, and confronts the worthlessness of his triumph—the end of the film. The censor's achievement is here truly breathtaking: although undoubtedly he had not the slightest notion of the tragic existentialist vision, he made out of a rather insipid Christian propaganda piece an existential drama about the ultimate nullity of our accomplishments, about how in the hour of our greatest triumph we are utterly alone. And how did he pull it off? He added nothing: he brought about the effect of "depth," of a profound existential vision, by simply *mutilating* the work, by depriving it of its crucial parts. This is the way meaning emerges from nonsense.

These paradoxes enable us to specify the nature of "self-consciousness" in German Idealism. In his critical remarks on Hegel, Lacan as a rule equates self-consciousness with self-transparency, dismissing it as the most blatant case of a philosophical illusion bent on denying the subject's constitutive decenteredness. However, "self-consciousness" in German Idealism has nothing whatsoever to do with any kind of transparent self-identity of the subject; it is rather another name for what Lacan himself has in mind when he points out how every desire is by definition the "desire of a desire": the subject never simply finds in himself a multitude of desires, he always entertains toward them a reflected relationship; i.e., by way of actual desiring, the subject implicitly answers the question, "which of your desires do you desire (have you chosen)."[6] As we have already seen apropos of Kant, self-consciousness is positively founded upon the nontransparency of the subject to itself: the Kantian transcendental apperception (i.e., the self-consciousness of pure I) is possible only insofar as I am unattainable to myself in my noumenal dimension, qua "Thing which thinks."[7]

There is, of course, a point at which this circular "positing of the presuppositions" reaches a deadlock; the key to this deadlock is provided by the Lacanian logic of non-all (*pas-tout*).[8] Although "nothing is presupposed which was not previously posited" (i.e., although, for every *particular* presupposition, it can be demonstrated that it is "posited," not "natural" but *naturalized*), it would be wrong to draw the seemingly obvious *universal* conclusion that "*everything* presupposed is posited." The presupposed X which is "nothing in particular," totally substanceless yet nevertheless resistant to retroactive "positing," is what Lacan calls the *Real*, the unattainable, elusive *je ne sais quoi*. In *Gender Trouble*, Judith Butler demonstrates how the difference between sex and gender—the difference between a biological fact and a cultural-symbolic construction which, a decade ago, was widely used by feminists in order to show that "anatomy is not destiny," i.e., that "woman" as a cultural product is not determined by her biological status—can never be unambiguously fixed, presupposed as a positive fact, but is always-already "posited": how we draw the line separating "culture" from "nature" is always determined by a specific cultural context. This cultural overdetermination of the dividing line between gender and sex should not however push us into accepting the Foucauldian notion of sex as the effect of "sexuality" (the heterogeneous texture of discursive practices); what gets lost thereby is precisely the deadlock of the Real.[9] Here we see the thin, but crucial, line that separates Lacan from "deconstruction": simply because the opposition between nature and culture is always-already culturally overdetermined, i.e., that no particular element can be isolated as "pure nature," does not mean that "everything is culture." "Nature" qua Real remains the unfathomable X which resists cultural "gentrification." Or, to put it another way: the Lacanian Real is the gap which separates the Particular from the Universal, the gap which prevents us from completing the gesture of universalization, blocking our jump from the premise that every particular element is P to the conclusion that all elements are P.

Consequently, there is no logic of Prohibition involved in the notion of the Real qua the impossible-nonsymbolizable: in Lacan, the Real is not surreptitiously consecrated, envisioned as the domain of the inviolable. When Lacan defines the "rock of castration" as real, this in no way implies that castration is excepted from the discursive field as a kind of untouchable sacrifice. Every demarcation between the Symbolic and the Real, every exclusion of the Real qua the prohibited-inviolable, is a symbolic act par excellence; such an inversion of impossibility into prohibition-exclusion *occults the inherent deadlock of the Real.* In other words, Lacan's strategy is to prevent any tabooing of the Real: one can "touch the real" only by applying oneself to its symbolization, up to the very failure of this endeavor. In Kant's *Critique of Pure Reason*, the only proofs that there are Things beyond phenomena are paralogisms, inconsistencies in which reason gets entangled the moment it extends the application of categories beyond the limits of experience; in exactly the same way, in Lacan "le réel"—the real of *jouissance*—"ne saurait s'inscrire que d'une impasse de la formalisation"— can be discerned only by way of the deadlocks of its formalization.[10] In short, *the status of the Real is thoroughly non-substantial:* it is a product of failed attempts to integrate it into the Symbolic.

The impasse of "presupposing" (i.e., of enumerating the presuppositions—the chain of external causes / conditions—of some posited entity) is the reverse of these "troubles with the non-all." An entity can easily be reduced to the totality of its presuppositions. What is missing from the series of presuppositions, however, is simply the performative act of formal conversion which retroactively posits these presuppositions, making them into what they are, into the presuppositions of . . . (such as the above-mentioned act which retroactively "posits" its reasons). This "dotting of the i" is the tautological gesture of the Master-Signifier which constitutes the entity in question as One. Here we see the asymmetry between positing and presupposing: *the positing of presuppositions chances upon its limit in the "feminine" non-all, and what eludes it is the Real; whereas the enumeration of the presuppositions of the posited content is made into a closed series by means of the "masculine" performative.*

Hegel endeavors to resolve this impasse of positing the presuppositions ("positing reflection") and of the presuppositions of every positing activity ("external reflection") by way of determining reflection; this logic of the three modalities of reflection (positing, external, and determining reflection)[11] renders the matrix of the entire logic of essence, i.e., of the triads which follow it: identity, difference, contradiction; essence / form, form / matter, content / form; formal, real, complete ground; etc.[12] The aim of the ensuing brief examination of Hegel's logic of essence is thus double: to articulate the successive more and more concrete forms of "determining reflection"—the Hegelian counterpart of what Kant calls "transcendental synthesis"—and, simultaneously, to discern in them the same pattern of an elementary ideological operation.

Identity, Difference, Contradiction

In dealing with the theme "Hegel and identity," one should never forget that identity emerges only in the logic of essence, as a "determination-of-reflection": what Hegel calls "identity" is not a simple self-equality of any notional determination (red is red, winter is ·winter . . .), but the identity of an essence which "stays the same" beyond the ever-changing flow of appearances. How are we to determine this identity? If we try to seize the thing as it is "in itself," irrespective of its relationship to other things, its specific identity eludes us, we cannot say anything about it, the thing coincides with all other things. In short, *identity hinges upon what makes a difference.* We pass from identity to difference the moment we grasp that the "identity" of an entity consists of the cluster of its differential features. The social identity of a person X, for example, is composed of the cluster of its social mandates which are all by definition differential: a person is "father" only in relation to "mother" and "son"; in another relation, he is himself "son," etc. Here is the crucial passage from Hegel's *Logic* in which he brings about the passage from difference to contradiction apropos of the symbolic determination "father":

Father is the other of son, and son the other of father, and each only *is* as this other of the other; and at the same time, the one determination only is, in relation to the other. . . . The father also has an existence of his own apart from the son-relationship; but then he is not father but simply man. . . . Opposites, therefore, contain contradiction in so far as they are, in the same respect, negatively related to one another or *sublate each other* and are *indifferent* to one another.[13]

The inattentive reader may easily miss the key accent of this passage, the feature which belies the standard notion of the "Hegelian contradiction": "contradiction" does *not* take place between "father" and "son" (here, we have a case of simple opposition between two codependent terms); it also does *not* turn on the fact that in one relation (to my son) I am "father" and in another (to my own father) I am myself "son," i.e., I am "simultaneously father and son." If this were the Hegelian "contradiction," Hegel would be effectively guilty of logical confusion, since it is clear that I am not both in the same respect. The last phrase in the quoted passage from Hegel's *Logic* locates the contradiction clearly *inside "father" himself*: "contradiction" designates the antagonistic relationship between what I am "for the others"—my symbolic determination—and what I am "in myself," abstractedly from my relations to others. It is the contradiction between the void of the subject's pure "being-for-himself" and the signifying feature which represents him for the others, in Lacanian terms: between $\$$ and S_1. More precisely, "contradiction" means that it is my very "alienation" in the symbolic mandate, in S_1, which retroactively makes $\$$—the void which eludes the hold of the mandate—out of my brute reality: I am not only "father," not only this particular determination, yet beyond these symbolic mandates I am nothing but the void which eludes them (and, as such, their own retroactive product).[14] It is the very symbolic representation in the differential network which evacuates my "pathological" content, i.e., which makes out of S, the substantial fullness of the "pathological" subject, the barred $\$$, the void of pure self-relating.

What I am "for the others" is condensed in the signifier which represents me for other signifiers (for the "son" I am "father," etc.). Outside of my relations to the others I am nothing, I am only the cluster of these relations ("the human essence is the entirety of social relations," as Marx would have said), but this very "nothing" is the nothing of pure self-relating: I am only what I am for the others, yet simultaneously I am the one who self-determines myself, i.e., who determines which network of relations to others will determine me. In other words, I am determined by the network of (symbolic) relations precisely and only insofar as I, qua void of self-relating, self-determine myself this way. We encounter here again spontaneity qua self-determination: in my very relating to the other I relate myself to myself, since I determine the concrete form of my relating to the other. Or, to put it in the terms of Lacan's scheme of discourse:[15]

$$\frac{S_1}{\$} \longrightarrow S_2$$

We must be careful, therefore, not to miss the logic of this passing of opposition into contradiction: it has nothing to do with coincidence or codependence of the opposites, with one pole passing into its opposite, etc. Let us take the case of man and woman: one can endlessly vary the motif of their codependence (each is only as the other of the other; its being is mediated by the being of its opposite, etc.), but as long as we continue to set this opposition against the background of some neutral universality (the human genus with its two species, male and female), we are far from "contradiction." In "male chauvinist" terms, we arrive at contradiction only when "man" appears as the immediate embodiment of the universal-human dimension, and woman as "truncated man"; this way, the relationship of the two poles ceases to be symmetrical, since man stands for the genus itself, whereas woman stands for specific difference as such. (Or, to put it in the language of structural linguistics: we enter "contradiction" proper when one of the terms of the opposition starts to function as "marked," and the other as "non-marked.")

Consequently, we pass from opposition to contradiction through the logic of what Hegel called "oppositional determination": when the universal, common ground of the two opposites "encounters itself" in its oppositional determination, i.e., in. one of the terms of the opposition. Let us recall Marx's *Capital,* in which the supreme case of "oppositional determination" is capital itself: the multitude of capitals (invested in particular companies, i.e., productive units) necessarily contains "finance capital," the immediate embodiment of capital in general as opposed to particular capitals. "Contradiction" designates therefore the relationship between capital in general and the species of capital which embodies capital in general (finance capital). An even more outright example appears in the Introduction to *Grundrisse:* production as the structuring principle of the whole of production, distribution, exchange, and consumption "encounters itself" in its oppositional determination; the "contradiction" is here between production as the encompassing totality of the four moments and production as one of these four moments.[16]

In this precise sense, contradiction is also the contradiction between the position of enunciation and the enunciated content: it occurs when the enunciator himself, by way of the illocutory force of his speech, accomplishes what, at the level of locution, is the object of his denunciation. A textbook case from political life: when a political agent criticizes rival parties for considering only their narrow party interests, he thereby offers his own party as a neutral force working for the benefit of the whole nation. Consequently, he does what he charges the other with, i.e., he promotes in the strongest way possible the interest of his own party: the dividing line that structures his speech runs between his own party and all the rest. What is at work here is again the logic of "oppositional determination": the alleged universality beyond petty party interests encounters itself in a particular party—*that* is "contradiction."

At the end of the credits of *The Great Dictator*, Chaplin revises the standard disclaimer concerning the relationship between diegetic reality and "true" reality ("any resemblance is purely coincidental") to read: "Any resemblance between the dictator Hynkel and the Jewish barber is purely coincidental." *The Great Dictator* is ultimately a film about this coincidental *identity*: Hynkel-Hitler, this all-pervasive Voice, is the "oppositional determination," the shadowy double, of the poor Jewish barber. Suffice it to recall the scene in the ghetto in which loudspeakers transmit the ferocious anti-Semitic speech by Hynkel—the barber runs down the street, as if persecuted by the multiplied echoes of his own voice, as if running away from his own shadow. Therein lies a deeper insight than might at first be apparent: the Jewish barber in *The Great Dictator* is not depicted primarily as a Jew, but rather as the epitome of "a little man who wants to live his modest, peaceful everyday life outside of political turmoils," and (as has been demonstrated by numerous analyses) nazism is precisely the enraged reverse of this "little man," which erupts when his customary world is thrown off the rails. In the ideological universe of the film, the same paradoxical equation is articulated in another implicit identity of the opposites: Austria = Germany. That is to say, which country in the film plays the role of the victim and at the same time the idyllic counterpart of "Tomania"-Germany? "Austerlic"-Austria, the small wine-growing country of happy innocent people living together like a large family, in short: the land of "fascism with a human face."[17] The fact that the same music (the Prelude to Wagner's *Lohengrin*) accompanies both the barber's final speech and Hynkel's famous playing with the globe-balloon acquires thereby an unexpected ominous dimension: at the end, the barber's words about the need for love and peace correspond perfectly to what Hitler-Hynkel himself would say in his sentimental petit bourgeois mood.

Form / Essence, Form / Matter, Form / Content

As we start losing ground in an argument, our last recourse is usually to insist that "despite what has been said, things are essentially what we think them to be." This, precisely, is what Hegel has in mind when he speaks of the essence in its immediacy: "essence" designates here the immediate inwardness, the "essence of things," which persists irrespective of the external form. Cases of such an attitude, best exemplified by the stupidity of the proverb "a leopard cannot change his spots," abound in politics. Suffice it to recall the usual right-wing treatment of ex-Communists in the East: irrespective of what they actually do, their democratic "form" should in no way deceive us, it is mere form; "essentially" they remain the same old totalitarians, etc.[18] A recent example of such a logic of "inner essence," which sticks to its point notwithstanding the changes of the external form, was the judgment of the distrustful on Gorbachev in 1985: nothing will change, Gorbachev is even more dangerous than ordinary hard-line Communists, since he provides the totalitarian system with a seductive "open," "democratic" front; his ultimate aim is to strengthen the system, not to change it radically. A Hegelian point to be made here is that this statement is probably true: in all likelihood, Gorbachev "really" did want only to improve the existing system. However, notwithstanding his intentions, his acts set in motion a process which transformed the system from top to bottom: the "truth" resided in what not only Gorbachev's distrustful critics but also Gorbachev himself took to be a mere external form.

"Essence," thus conceived, remains an empty determination whose adequacy can be tested only by verifying the extent to which it is expressed, rendered manifest, in the external form. We thus obtain the subsequent couple form / matter in which the relationship is inverted: form ceases to be a passive expression-effect behind which one has to look for some hidden "true essence," and becomes instead the agency which individuates the otherwise passive-formless matter, conferring on it some particular determination. In other words, the moment we become aware of how the entire determinatedness of the essence resides in its form, then essence, conceived abstractedly from its form, changes into a formless substratum of the form, in short: into *matter*. As Hegel put it concisely, the moment of determination and the moment of subsistence thereby fall apart, are posited as distinct: where a thing is concerned, "matter" is the passive moment of subsistence (its substantial substratum-ground), whereas "form" is what provides for its specific determination, what makes this thing what it is.

The dialectic which hampers this seemingly straight opposition is not limited to the fact that we never encounter "pure" matter devoid of any form (the clay out of which a pot is made must already possess properties which make it appropriate for some form and not for another—for a pot, not for a needle, for example), so that "pure" formless matter passes into its opposite, into empty form-receptacle bereft of any concrete, positive, substantial determination; and vice versa, of course. But what Hegel has in mind here is something more radical: the inherent contradiction of the notion of form which designates both the principle of universalization and the principle of individuation. Form is what makes out of some formless matter a particular, determinate thing (say, a cup out of clay); but it is at the same time the abstract Universal common to different things (paper cups, glass cups, china cups, and metal cups are all "cups" on account of their common *form*). The only way out of this deadlock is to conceive matter not as something passive-formless, but as something which already in itself possesses an inherent structure, i.e., something which stands opposite form furnished with its *own content*. However, in order to avoid regression into the initial abstract counter-position of inner essence and externally imposed form, one has to keep in mind that *the couple content / form (or, more pointedly, content as such) is just another name for the tautological relationship by which form is related to itself.* What is "content" if not, precisely, *formed matter*? One can thus define "form" as the way some content is actualized, realized, in matter (by means of the latter's adequate *formation*): "the same content"—the story of Caesar's murder, for example—can be told in different forms, from Plutarch's historiographical report through Shakespeare's play to Hollywood movie. In the alternative, one can define form as the universality which unites the multitude of diverse contents (the form of the classical detective novel, for example, functions as the skeleton of codified genre rules which set a common seal on the works of authors as different as

Agatha Christie, E. S. Gardner, etc.). In other words, insofar as matter stands for the abstract Other of the form, "content" is the way matter is mediated by form, and inversely, "form" is the way content finds its expression in matter. In both cases, the relationship content / form, in contrast to the relationship matter / form, is *tautological:* "content" is form itself in its oppositional determination.

With a view to the totality of this movement from essence / form to content / form, it is easy to perceive how its logic announces in a condensed way the triad of notion, judgment, and syllogism from the "subjective logic," the third part of Hegel's *Logic:* the couple essence / form remains on the level of notion; that is, essence is the simple in-itself of the notion, of the substantial determination of an entity. The next step literally brings about the *Ur-Teilung,* judgment qua "original division," falling apart, of the essence into its two constitutive moments which are thereby "posited" as such, explicated, but in the mode of externality, i.e., as external, indifferent to each other: the moment of subsistence (matter qua substratum) and the moment of determination (form). A substratum acquires determination when a form is predicated to it. The third step, finally, renders manifest the ternary structure of mediation, the distinguishing mark of syllogism, with form as its middle term.

Formal, Real, Complete Ground

There is something almost uncanny about the "prophetic" dimensions of this apparently modest subdivision of Hegel's *Logic.* It is as if we can truly comprehend it only if we know the history of philosophy, and especially the crucial Hegel-critiques, of the next 150 years, inclusive of Althusser. Among other things, this subdivision anticipates both the young Marx's critique of Hegel and the concept of overdetermination which was developed by Althusser precisely as an alternative to the allegedly Hegelian notion of "expressive causality."

Formal ground repeats the tautological gesture of the immediate reference to "true essence": it does not add any new content to the phenomenon to be explained, it just translates, transposes, the found empirical content into the form of ground. To comprehend this process, one need only recall how doctors sometimes respond when we describe our symptoms: "Aha, clearly a case of . . ." What then follows is a long, incomprehensible Latin term which simply translates the content of our complaints into medicalese, adding no new knowledge. Psychoanalytical theory itself offers one of the clearest examples of what Hegel has in mind with "formal ground," namely the way it sometimes uses the notion of death-drive: explaining the so-called "negative therapeutic reaction" (more generally, of the phenomena of aggressivity, destructive rage, war, etc.) by invoking *Todestrieb* is a tautological gesture which only confers upon the same empirical content the universal form of law—e.g., people kill each other because they are driven to it by the death-drive. The principal target of Hegel himself is here a certain simplified version of Newtonian physics: this stone is heavy—why? On account of the force of gravity, etc. However, the bountiful sneers in Hegel's comments on formal ground should not blind us to its positive side, for the necessary, constitutive function of this formal gesture of converting the contingent content which was simply found into the form of ground. It is easy to deride the tautological emptiness of this gesture, but Hegel's point lies elsewhere: by means of its very formal character, this gesture renders possible the search for the real ground. Formal causality qua empty gesture opens up the field of the analysis of content—as in Marx's *Capital,* in which the formal subsumption of the process of production under capital precedes, opens up the way for, the material organization of production in accordance with the requirements of capital (i.e., first, the precapitalist material organization of production which was simply found—individual artisans, etc.—is formally subsumed under capital—the capitalist provides the artisan with raw materials, etc.; then, gradually, production is materially restructured into a collective man-ufacturing process directly run by the capitalist).

Hegel further demonstrates how such tautological explanations, in or-der to conceal their true nature and to create an appearance of positive content, fill out again the empty form of ground with some fantasized, imaginary content, conceived as a new, special kind of actual empirical content: we thus obtain "aether," "magnetism," "flogiston," and other similar mysterious "natural forces" in which empty determinations-of-thought assume the form of positive, determinate content—in short, we obtain the inverted "topsy-turvy world" in which the determinations-of-thought appear under the guise of their opposite, of positive empirical objects. (An exemplary case within philosophy itself, of course, is Des-cartes' placing of the link connecting body and soul within the pineal gland: this gland is nothing but a quasi-empirical positivization of the fact that Descartes was unable to *grasp conceptually* the mediation of thinking and extended substance in man.) For Hegel, the inverted "topsy-turvy world" does not consist in presupposing, beyond the actual, empirical world, the kingdom of suprasensible ideas, but in a kind of double inversion by means of which these suprasensible ideas themselves assume again sensible form, so that the very sensible world is redoubled: as if, by the side of our ordinary sensible world, there exists another world of "spiritual materiality" (of aether qua fine stuff, etc.). Why are Hegel's considerations of such interest? They articulate in advance the motif Feuerbach, young Marx, and Althusser proclaim as the "critique of speculative idealism": the hidden obverse and "truth" of speculative idealism is positivism, enslavement to contingent empirical content; i.e., idealism only confers speculative form on the empirical content simply found there.[19]

The supreme case of such a quasi-empirical object which positivizes the subject's inability to think a purely conceptual relationship is provided by Kant himself, who, in his *Opus Posthumum,* proposes the hypothesis of "aether."[20] If space is full, Kant reasoned, movement from one place in space to another is not possible since "all places are already taken"; if, however, space is empty, no contact, no interaction can occur between two bodies separated by space since no force can be transmitted via pure void. From this paradox, Kant drew the conclusion that space is possible only if sustained by "aether" qua all-pervasive, all-penetrating world-stuff which is practically the same as space itself hypostatically conceived: an all-present element which is space itself, which continuously fills it out and is as such the medium of the interaction of all other "ordinary" positive forces and / or objects in space. This is what Hegel has in mind apropos of the "topsy-turvy world": Kant solves the opposition of empty space and the objects filling it out by way of presupposing a "matter" which is its opposite, i.e., thoroughly transparent, homogeneous, and continuous—as in primitive religions with their notion of the suprasensible as an aetherical-material Beyond. (The need for this hypothesis evaporates, of course, as soon as one accepts the post-Newtonian notion of nonhomogeneous space.)[21]

Consequently, formal ground is followed by real ground: the difference between ground and grounded ceases to be purely formal, it is displaced into content itself and conceived as the distinction between two of its constituents. In the very content of the phenomenon to be explained, one has to isolate some moment and to conceive of it as the "ground" of all other moments which thereby appear as what is "grounded." In traditional Marxism, for example, the so-called "economical basis," the structure of the process of production, is the moment which, notwithstanding the inconveniences of the notorious "last instance," determines all other moments (political and ideological superstructure). Here, of course, the question emerges immediately: why *this* moment and not some other? That is to say, as soon as we isolate some moment from the whole and conceive of it as its "ground" we must also take into account the way ground itself is determined by the totality of relations within which it functions as ground: "ground" can only exert its grounding function within a precisely defined network of conditions. In short, we can only answer the question "Why *this* moment and not some other?" through the detailed analysis of the entire network of relations between the ground and the grounded, which explains why it is precisely this element of the network which plays the role of ground. What is thus accomplished is the step to the next, final modality of ground, to complete ground. It is crucial to grasp the precise nature of Hegel's accomplishment: he does *not* put forward another, even "deeper" supra-Ground which would ground the ground itself; he simply grounds the ground in the totality of its relations to the grounded content. In this precise sense, complete ground is the unity of formal and real ground: it is the real ground whose grounding relationship to the remaining content is again grounded in what?—*in itself,* i.e., *in the totality of its relations to the grounded.* The ground grounds the grounded, but this grounding role must be itself grounded in the relationship of the ground to the grounded. Thus, we again arrive at the tautology (the moment of formal ground), but not at the empty tautology, as in the case of formal ground: now, the tautology contains the moment of contradiction in the precise above-mentioned Hegelian sense, it designates the identity of the Whole with its "oppositional determination": the identity of a moment of the Whole—the real ground—with the Whole itself.

In *Reading Capital,*[22] Louis Althusser endeavored to articulate the epistemological break of Marxism by means of a new concept of causality, "overdetermination": the very determining instance is overdetermined by the total network of relations within which it plays the determining role. Althusser opposed this notion of causality to both mechanical, transitive causality (the linear chain of causes and effects whose paradigmatic case is classical, pre-Einsteinian physics) and expressive causality (the inner essence which expresses itself in the multitude of its forms-of-appearance). "Expressive causality," of course, targets Hegel, in whose philosophy the same spiritual essence—"zeitgeist"—allegedly expresses itself at the different levels of society: in religion as Protestantism, in politics as the liberation of civil society from the chains of medieval corporatism, in law as the rule of private property and the emergence of free individuals as its bearers. This triad of expressive-transitive-overdeterminate causality parallels the Lacanian triad Imaginary-Real-Symbolic: expressive causality belongs to the level of the Imaginary, it designates the logic of an identical imago which leaves its imprint at different levels of material content; overdetermination implies a symbolic totality, since such retroactive determination of the ground by the totality of the grounded is possible only within a symbolic universe; transitive causality designates the senseless collisions of the real. Today, in the midst of ecological catastrophe, it is especially important that we conceive this catastrophe as a meaningless real *tuche,* i.e., that we do not "read meanings into things," as is done by those who interpret the ecological crisis as a "deeper sign" of punishment for our merciless exploitation of nature, etc. (Suffice it to recall the theories on the homology between the soul's innerworld and the outerworld of the universe which are again fashionable within the so-called "New Age consciousness"—the exemplary case of a new rise of "expressive causality.")

It should be clear, now, that the Althusserian critical attribution to Hegel of "expressive causality" misses the target: Hegel himself articulated in advance the conceptual framework of Althusser's critique; i.e., his triad of formal, real, and complete ground corresponds perfectly to the triad of expressive, transitive, and overdetermined causality. What is "complete ground" if not the name for a "complex structure" in which the determining instance itself is (over)determined by the network of relations within which it exerts its determining role?[23] In *Hegel ou Spinoza?*[24] Pierre Macherey paradoxically maintained that Spinoza's philosophy must be read as a critique of Hegel—as if Spinoza read Hegel and was able in advance to answer the latter's critique of "Spinozism." The same could be said of Hegel in relation to Althusser: Hegel outlined in advance the contours of the Althusserian critique of (what Althusser presents as) "Hegelianism"; moreover he developed the element that is missing in Althusser and prevents him from thinking out the notion of overdetermination—the element of subjectivity which cannot be reduced to imaginary (mis)recognition qua effect of interpellation, that is to say, the subject as $, the "empty," barred subject.

From "In-itself" to "For-itself"

Let us stop here and abstain from discerning the same matrix up to the end of the second part of *Logic;* suffice it to ascertain that the fundamental antagonism of the entire logic of essence is the antagonism between *ground* and *conditions*, between the inner essence ("true nature") of a thing and the external circumstances which render possible the realization of this essence, i.e., the impossibility of reaching a common measure between these two dimensions, of coordinating them in a "higher-order synthesis." (It is only in the third part of *Logic*, the "subjective logic" of Notion, that this incommensurability is surpassed.) Therein consists the alternative between positing and external reflection: do people create the world they live in from within themselves, autonomously, or does their activity result from external circumstances? Philosophical common sense would here impose the compromise of a "proper measure": true, we have the possibility of choice, we can realize our freely conceived projects, but only within the framework of tradition, of the inherited circumstances which delineate our field of choices; or, as Marx put it in his *Eighteenth Brumaire of Louis Bonaparte:* "Men make their own history; but they do not make it just as they please; they do not make it under circumstances chosen by themselves, but under circumstances directly encountered, given and transmitted from the past."[25]

However, it is precisely such a "dialectical synthesis" that Hegel declines. The whole point of his argument is that we have no way of drawing a line between the two aspects: every inner potential can be translated (its form can be converted) into an external condition, and vice versa. In short, what Hegel does here is something very precise: he undermines the usual notion of the relationship between the inner potentials of a thing and the external conditions which render (im)possible the realization of these potentials *by positing between these two sides the sign of equality.* The consequences are far more radical than they appear; they concern above all the radically anti-evolutionary character of Hegel's philosophy, as exemplified in the notional couple *in-itself/for-self.* This couple is usually taken as the supreme proof of Hegel's trust in evolutionary progress (the development from "in-itself" into "for-self"); yet a closer look dispels this phantom of Evolution. The "in-itself" in its opposition to "for-self" means at one and the same time (1) what exists only potentially, as an inner possibility, contrary to the actuality wherein a possibility has externalized and realized itself, *and* (2) actuality itself in the sense of external, immediate, "raw" objectivity which is still opposed to subjective mediation, which is not yet internalized, rendered-conscious; in this sense, the "in-itself" is actuality insofar as it has not yet reached its Notion.

The simultaneous reading of these two aspects undermines the usual idea of dialectical progress as a gradual realization of the object's inner potentials, as its spontaneous self-development. Hegel is here quite outspoken and explicit: the inner potentials of the self-development of an object and the pressure exerted on it by an external force are *strictly correlative;* they form the two parts of the same conjunction. In other words, the potentiality of the object must also be present in its external actuality, under the form of heteronomous coercion. For example (the example here is of Hegel himself), to say that a pupil at the beginning of the process of education is somebody who potentially knows, somebody who, in the course of his development, will realize his creative potentials, *equals saying* that these inner potentials must be present from the very beginning in external actuality as the authority of the Master who exerts pressure upon his pupil. Today, one can add to this the sadly famous case of the working class qua revolutionary subject: to affirm that the working class is "in-itself," potentially, a revolutionary subject, equals the assertion that this potentiality must already be actualized in the Party, which knows in advance about the revolutionary mission and therefore exerts pressure upon the working class, guiding it toward the realization of its potentials. Thus, the "leading role" of the Party is legitimized; it is thus its right to "educate" the working class in accordance with its potentials, to "implant" in this class its historical mission.

We can see, now, why Hegel is as far as possible from the evolutionist notion of the progressive development of in-itself into for-itself: the category of "in itself" is strictly correlative to "for us," i.e., for some consciousness external to the thing-in-itself. To say that a clod of clay is "in itself" a pot equals saying that this pot is already present in the mind of the craftsman who will impose the form of pot on the clay. The current way of saying "under the right conditions the pupil will realize his potentials" is thus deceptive: when, in excuse of his *failure* to realize his potentials, we insist that "he would have realized them, if only the conditions had been right," we commit thereby an error of cynicism worthy of Brecht's famous lines from *The Threepenny Opera:* "We would be good instead of being so rude, if only the circumstances were not of this kind!" For Hegel, external circumstances are not an impediment to realizing inner potentials, but on the contrary *the very arena in which the true nature of these inner potentials is to be tested:* are such potentials true potentials or just vain illusions about what might have happened? Or, to put it in Spinozean terms: "positing reflection" observes things as they are in their eternal essence, *sub specie aeter-*

nitatis, whereas "external reflection" observes them *sub specie durationis*, in their dependence on a series of contingent external circumstances. Here, everything hinges on *how* Hegel overcomes "external reflection." If his aim were simply to reduce the externality of contingent conditions to the self-mediation of the inner essence-ground (the usual notion of "Hegel's idealism"), then Hegel's philosophy would truly be a mere "dynamized Spinozism." But what does Hegel actually do?

Let us approach this problem via Lacan: in what precise sense can we maintain that Lacan of the late forties and early fifties was a Hegelian? In order to get a clear idea of his Hegelianism, it suffices to take a closer look at how he conceives the analyst's "passivity" in the psychoanalytical cure. Since "the actual is rational," the analyst does not have to force his interpretations upon the analysand, all he has to do is clear the way for the analysand to arrive at his own truth by means of a mere punctuation of his speech. This is what Hegel has in mind when he speaks of the "cunning of reason": the analyst does not seek to undermine the analysand's self-deceit, his attitude of the "Beautiful Soul," by way of directly confronting him with the "true state of things," but by way of giving him a free rein, of removing all obstacles that may serve as an excuse, thus compelling him to reveal "the stuff he is actually made of." In this precise sense "the actual is rational": our—the Hegelian philosopher's—trust into the inherent rationality of the actual means that actuality provides the only testing ground for the reasonableness of the subject's claims; i.e., the moment the subject is bereft of external obstacles which can be blamed for his failure, his subjective position will collapse on account of its inherent inauthenticity. What we have here is a kind of cynicized Heideggerianism: since the object is in itself inconsistent, since what allows it to retain the appearance of consistency is the very external hindrance which allegedly restrains its inner potentials, the most effective way to destroy it, to bring about its collapse, is precisely to renounce any claims of domination, to remove all hindrances and to "let it be," i.e., to leave the field open for the free deployment of its potentials.[26]

However, does the Hegelian notion of the "cunning of reason" not entail a "regression" to the pre-Kantian rationalist metaphysics? It is a philosophical commonplace to oppose here Kant's critique of the ontological proof of God's existence to Hegel's reaffirmation of it, and to quote Hegel's reaffirmation as the supreme proof of Hegel's return to the domain of classical metaphysics. The story goes somewhat like this: Kant demonstrated that existence is not a predicate, since, at the level of predicates which define the notional content of a thing, there is absolutely no difference between 100 actual tollars and a mere notion of 100 tollars—and, mutatis mutandis, the same holds for the notion of God. Furthermore, one is even tempted to see in Kant's position a kind of prefiguration of the Lacanian eccentricity of the real with reference to the symbolic: existence is real insofar as it is irreducible to the network of notional-symbolic determinations. Nevertheless, this commonplace has to be rejected thoroughly.

Kant's actual line of argumentation is far more refined; he proceeds in two basic steps (see *CPR*, A 584–603). First, he demonstrates that there is still a hidden if-clause at work in the ontological proof of God's existence: true, "God" does designate a being whose existence is implied in its very notion; but we still must presuppose that such a being exists (i.e., all that the ontological proof actually demonstrates is that, *if* God exists, he exists necessarily), so that it remains possible that there is simply no such being whose notion would entail existence. An atheist would even quote such a nature of God as an argument *against* His existence: there is no God precisely because one cannot imagine in a consistent way a being whose notion would entail existence. Kant's next step aims at the same point: the only legitimate use of the term "existence" is to designate the phenomenal reality of the objects of possible experience; however, *the difference between Reason and Intuition is constitutive of reality*: the subject accepts that something "exists in reality" only insofar as its representation is filled out by the contingent, empirical content provided by intuition, i.e., only insofar as the subject is passively affected by senses. Existence is not a predicate, i.e., part of the notion of an object, precisely because, in order to pass from the notion to actual existence, one has to add the passive element of intuition. For that reason, the notion of "necessary existence" is self-contradictory— *every existence is by definition contingent.*[27]

What is Hegel's answer to all this? Hegel in no way returns to traditional metaphysics: he refutes Kant within the horizon opened up by Kant himself. He so to speak approaches the problem from the opposite end: how does the "coming-to-notion" (*zum-Begriff-kommen*) affect the existence of the object in question? When a thing "reaches its notion," what impact does this have on its existence? To clarify this question, let us recall an example which confirms Lacan's thesis that Marxism is not a "worldview,"[28] namely the idea that the proletariat becomes an *actual* revolutionary subject by way of integrating the *knowledge* of its historical role:[29]

historical materialism is not a neutral "objective knowledge" of historical development, since it is an act of self-knowledge of a historical subject; as such, it implies the proletarian subjective position. In other words, the "knowledge" proper to historical materialism is self-referential, it changes its "object." It is only via the act of knowledge that the object becomes what it truly "is." So, the rise of "class consciousness" produces the effect in the existence of its "object" (proletariat) by way of changing it into an actual revolutionary subject. And is it not the same with psychoanalysis? Does the interpretation of a symptom not constitute a direct intervention of the Symbolic in the Real, does it not offer an example of how the word can affect the Real of the symptom? And, on the other hand, does not such an efficacy of the Symbolic presuppose entities whose existence literally hinges on a certain non-knowledge: the moment knowledge is assumed (through interpretation), existence disintegrates? Existence is here not one of the predicates of a Thing, but designates the way the Thing relates to its predicates, more precisely: the way the Thing *is related to itself* by means of (through the detour of) its predicates-properties.[30] When a proletarian becomes aware of his "historical role," *none of his actual predicates changes;* what changes is just the way he relates to them, and this change in the relationship to predicates radically affects his existence.

To designate this awareness of "historical role," traditional Marxism makes use of the Hegelian couple "in-itself/for-itself": by way of arriving at its "class consciousness," the proletariat changes from a "class-in-itself" to a "class-for-itself." The dialectic at work here is that of a *failed encounter:* the passage to "for itself," to the Notion, involves the loss of existence. Nowhere is this failed encounter more obvious than in a passionate love affair: its "in itself" occurs when I simply yield to the passion, unaware of what is happening to me; afterwards, when the affair is over, *aufgehoben* in my recollection, it becomes "for itself"—I retroactively become aware of what I had, of what I lost. This awareness of what I lost gives birth to the fantasy of the impossible conjunction of being and knowledge ("if only I could have known how happy I was . . ."). But is the Hegelian "In-and-for-itself" (*An-und-Fuer-sich*) really such an impossible conjunction, the fantasy of a moment when I am happy and I know it? Is it not rather the unmasking of the illusion of the "external reflection" that still pertains to "for-itself," the illusion that, in the past, I actually *was* happy without knowing it, i.e., the insight into how "happiness" by definition comes to be retroactively, by means of the experience of its loss?

This illusion of the external reflection can be further exemplified by *Billy Bathgate*, the movie based upon E. L. Doctorow's novel. The film is fundamentally failed and the impression it arouses is that what we see is a pale, distorted reflection of a far superior literary source. There is, however, an unpleasant surprise in store for those who, after seeing the movie, set to read the novel: the novel is far closer to the insipid happy end (in it, Billy pockets the hidden wealth of Dutch Schultz); numerous delicate details which the spectator unacquainted with the novel experiences as fragments happily not lost in the impoverishing process of transposition to cinema, fragments that miraculously survived the shipwreck, actually turn out to be added by the scriptwriter. In short, the "superior" novel evoked by the film's failure is not the preexistent actual novel upon which the film is based, but a retroactive chimera aroused by the film itself.[31]

Ground versus Conditions

This conceptual background allows us to reformulate the vicious circle of ground and conditions. Let us recall the usual mode of explaining outbreaks of racism, which invokes the categorical couple of ground and conditions-circumstances: one conceives of racism (or, more generally, so-called "outbreaks of irrational mass-sadism") as a latent psychic disposition, a kind of Jungian archetype which comes forth under certain conditions (social instability and crisis, etc.). From this point of view the racist disposition is the "ground" and current political struggles the "circumstances," the conditions of its effectuation. However, what counts as ground and what counts as conditions is ultimately contingent and exchangeable, so that one can easily accomplish the Marxist reversal of the above-mentioned psychologist perspective and conceive the present political struggle as the only true determining ground. In the present civil war in ex-Yugoslavia, for example, the "ground" of Serbian aggression is not to be sought in any primitive Balkan warrior archetypes, but in the struggle for power in post-Communist Serbia (the survival of the old Communist state apparatus). The status of eventual Serbian bellicose dispositions and other similar archetypes (the "Croatian genocidal character," the "perennial tradition of ethnic hatreds in the Balkans," etc.) is precisely that of the conditions / circumstances in which the power struggle realizes itself. The "bellicose dispositions" are precisely that, i.e., latent dispositions which are actualized, drawn forth from their shadowy half-existence by the recent political struggle qua their determining ground. One is thus fully justified in saying that "what is at stake in the Yugoslav civil war are not archaic ethnic conflicts: these perennial hatreds are inflamed only on account of their function in the recent political struggle."[32]

How, then, are we to eschew this mess, this exchangeability of ground and circumstances? Let us take another example: *Renaissance,* i.e., the rediscovery ("rebirth") of antiquity which exerted a crucial influence on the break with the medieval way of life in the fifteenth century. The first, obvious explanation is that the influence of the newly discovered antique tradition brought about the dissolution of the medieval "paradigm." Here, however, a question immediately pops up: why did antiquity begin to exert its influence at precisely that moment and not earlier or later? The answer that offers itself, of course, is that due to the dissolution of medieval social links, a new zeitgeist emerged which made us responsive to antiquity; something must have changed in "us" so that we became able to perceive antiquity not as a pagan kingdom of sin but as the model to be adopted. That's all very well, but we still remain locked in a vicious circle, since this new zeitgeist itself took shape precisely through the discovery of antique texts as well as fragments of classical architecture and sculpture. In a way, everything was already there, in the external circumstances; the new zeitgeist formed itself through the influence of antiquity which enabled renaissance thought to shatter the medieval chains; yet for this influence of antiquity to be felt, the new zeitgeist must already have been active. The only way out of this impasse is therefore the intervention, at a certain point, of a tautological gesture: the new zeitgeist had to constitute itself by literally *presupposing itself in its exteriority,* in its external conditions (in antiquity). In other words, it was not sufficient for the new zeitgeist retroactively to posit these external conditions (the antique tradition) as "its own," it had to (presup)pose itself as already present in these conditions. *The return to external conditions (to antiquity) had to coincide with the return to the foundation, to the "thing itself," to the ground.* (This is precisely how the Renaissance conceived itself: as the return to the Greek and Roman foundations of our Western civilization.) We do not thus have an inner ground the actualization of which depends on external circumstances; the external relation of presupposing (ground presupposes conditions and vice versa) is surpassed in a pure tautological gesture by means of which the thing *presupposes itself.* This tautological gesture is "empty" in the precise sense that it does not contribute anything new, it only retroactively ascertains that the thing in question *is already present in its conditions*, i.e., that the totality of these conditions *is* the actuality of the thing. Such an empty gesture provides us with the most elementary definition of the *symbolic* act.

Here we see the fundamental paradox of "rediscovering tradition" at work in the constitution of national identity: a nation finds its sense of self-identity by means of such a tautological gesture, i.e., by way of discovering itself as already present in its tradition. Consequently, the mechanism of the "rediscovery of national tradition" cannot be reduced to the "positing of presuppositions" in the sense of the retroactive positing of conditions as "ours." The point is rather that, in the very act of returning to its (external) conditions, *the (national) thing returns to itself.* The return to conditions is experienced as the "return to our true roots."

The Tautological "Return of the Thing to Itself"

Although "really existing socialism" has already receded into a distance which confers upon it the nostalgic magic of a postmodern lost object, some of us still recall a well-known joke about what socialism is: a social system that is the dialectical synthesis of all previous history. From the prehistoric classless society, it took primitivism, from antiquity slave labor, from medieval feudalism ruthless domination, from capitalism exploitation, *and from socialism the name.* This is what the Hegelian tautological gesture of the "return of the thing to itself" is all about: one must include along with the definition of the object its name. That is to say, after we decompose an object into its ingredients, we look in vain in them for some specific feature which holds together this multitude and makes of it a unique, self-identical thing. As to its properties and ingredients, a thing is wholly "outside itself," in its external conditions; every positive feature is already present in the circumstances which are not yet this thing. The supplementary operation which produces from this bundle a unique, self-identical thing is the purely symbolic, tautological gesture of positing these external conditions as the conditions-components of the thing and, simultaneously, of presupposing the existence of ground which holds together this multitude of conditions.

And, to throw our Lacanian cards on the table, this tautological "return of the thing to itself" which renders forth the concrete structure of self-identity is what Lacan designates as the "point de capiton," the "quilting point" at which the signifier "falls into" the signified (as in the above-mentioned joke on socialism, where the name itself functions as part of the designated thing). Let us recall an example from popular culture: the killer shark in Spielberg's *Jaws*. A direct search for the shark's ideological meaning evokes nothing but misguided questions: does it symbolize the threat of the Third World to America epitomized by the archetypal small town? is it the symbol of the exploitative nature of capitalism itself (Fidel Castro's interpretation)? does it stand for the untamed nature which threatens to disrupt the routine of our daily lives? In order to avoid this lure, we have to shift our perspective radically: the daily life of the common man is dominated by an inconsistent multitude of fears (he can become the victim of big business manipulations; Third World immigrants seem to intrude into his small orderly universe; unruly nature can destroy his home; etc.), and the accomplishment of *Jaws* consists in an act of purely formal conversion which provides a common "container" for all these free-floating, inconsistent fears by way of anchoring them, "reifying" them, in the figure of the shark.[33] Consequently, the function of the fascinating presence of the shark is precisely to *block* any further inquiry into the social meaning (social mediation) of those phenomena that arouse fear in the common man. To say that the murderous shark "symbolizes" the above-mentioned series of fears is to say too much and not enough at the same time. It does not symbolize them, since it literally annuls them by occupying itself the place of the object of fear. It is therefore "more" than a symbol: it becomes the feared "thing itself." Yet, the shark is decidedly less than a symbol, since it does not point toward the symbolized content but rather blocks access to it, renders it invisible. In this way, it is homologous with the anti-Semitic figure of the Jew: "Jew" is the explanation, offered by anti-Semitism for the multiple fears experienced by the "common man" in an epoch of dissolving social links (inflation, unemployment, corruption, moral degradation)— behind all these phenomena lies the invisible hand of the "Jewish plot." The crucial point here, again, is that the designation *"Jew" does not add any new content:* the entire content is already present in the external conditions (crisis, moral degeneration . . .); the name "Jew" is only the supplementary feature which accomplishes a kind of transubstantiation, changing all these elements into so many manifestations of the same *ground,* the "Jewish plot." Paraphrasing the joke on socialism, one could say that anti-Semitism takes from the economy unemployment and inflation, from politics parliamentary corruption and intrigue, from morality its own degeneration, from art "incomprehensible" avant-gardism, *and from the Jew the name.* This name enables us to recognize behind the multitude of external conditions the activity of the same *ground*.

Here we also find at work the dialectic of contingency and necessity: as to their content, they fully coincide (in both cases, the only positive content is the series of conditions that form part of our actual life experience: economic crisis, political chaos, the dissolution of ethical links . . .); the passage of contingency into necessity is an act of purely formal conversion, the gesture of adding a *name* which confers upon the contingent series the mark of necessity, thereby transforming it into the expression of some hidden ground (the "Jewish plot"). This is also how later—at the very end of the "logic of essence"—we pass from absolute necessity to freedom. To comprehend properly this passage, one has to renounce thoroughly the standard notion of "freedom as comprehended necessity" (after getting rid of the illusions of free will, one can recognize and freely accept one's place in the network of causes and their effects). Hegel's point is, on the contrary, that *it is only the subject's (free) act of "dotting the i" which retroactively installs necessity*, so that the very act by means of which the subject recognizes (and thus constitutes) necessity is the supreme act of freedom and as such the self-suppression of necessity. *Voilà pourquoi Hegel n'est pas spinoziste:* on account of this tautological gesture of retroactive performativity. So "performativity" in no way designates the power of freely "creating" the designated content ("words mean what we want them to mean," etc.): the "quilting" only structures the material which is found, externally imposed. The act of naming is "performative" only and precisely insofar as *it is always-already part of the definition of the signified content.*[34]

This is how Hegel resolves the deadlock of positing and external reflection, the vicious circle of positing the presuppositions and of enumerating the presuppositions of the posited content: by means of the tautological return-upon-itself of the thing in its very external presuppositions. And the same tautological gesture is already at work in Kant's analytic of pure reason: the synthesis of the multitude of sensations in the representation of the object which belongs to "reality" implies an empty surplus, i.e., the positing of an X as the unknown substratum of the perceived phenomenal sensations. Suffice it to quote Findlay's precise formulation:

> We always refer appearances to a Transcendental Object, an X, of which we, however, know nothing, but which is none the less the objective correlate of the synthetic acts inseparable from thinking self-

consciousness. The Transcendental Object, thus conceived, can be called a Noumenon or thing of thought [*Gedankending*]. But the reference to such a thing of thought does not, strictly speaking, use the categories, but is something like *an empty synthetic gesture* in which nothing objective is really put before us.[35]

The transcendental object is thus the very opposite of the *Ding-an-sich:* it is "empty" insofar as it is devoid of any "objective" content. That is to say, to obtain its notion, one has to abstract from the sensible object its entire sensible content, i.e., all sensations by means of which the subject is affected by *Ding*. The empty X which remains *is the pure objective correlate / effect of the subject's autonomous-spontaneous synthetic activity.* To put it paradoxically: the transcendental object is the "in-itself" insofar as it is for the subject, posited by it; it is pure "positedness" of an indeterminate X. This "empty synthetic gesture"—which adds to the thing nothing positive, no new sensible feature, and yet, in its very capacity of an empty gesture, constitutes it, makes it into an object—is the act of *symbolization* in its most elementary form, at its zero-level. On the first page of his book, Findlay points out that the transcendental object *"is not for Kant different* from the object or objects which appear to the senses and which we can judge about and know . . . but it is the *same* object or objects conceived in respect of certain intrinsically unapparent features, and which is in such respects incapable of being judged about or known."[36]

This X, this irrepresentable surplus which adds itself to the series of sensible features, is precisely the "thing-of-thought" (*Gedankending*): it bears witness to the fact that the object's unity does not reside within it, but is the result of the subject's synthetic activity. (As with Hegel, where the act of formal conversion inverts the chain of conditions into the unconditional Thing, founded in itself.) Let us briefly return to anti-Semitism, to the "synthetic act of apperception" which, out of the multitude of (imagined) features of Jews, constructs the anti-Semitic figure of "Jew." To pass for a true anti-Semite, it is not enough to claim that we oppose Jews because they are exploitative, greedy intriguers. That is, it is not sufficient for the signifier "Jew" to designate this series of specific, positive features; one has to accomplish the crucial step further by saying "they are like that (exploitative, greedy . . .) *because* they are Jews." The "transcendental object" of Jewishness is precisely that elusive X which "makes a Jew into a Jew" and for which we look in vain among his positive properties. This act of pure formal conversion, i.e., the "synthetic act" of uniting the series of positive features in the signifier "Jew" and thereby transforming them into so many manifestations of the "Jewishness" qua their hidden ground, *brings about the appearance of an objectal surplus,* of a mysterious X which is "in Jew more than Jew," in other words: of the transcendental object.[37] In the very text of Kant's *Critique of Pure Reason,* this void of the synthetic gesture is indicated by an exception in the use of the pair constitutive / regulative:[38] in general, "constitutive" principles serve to construct objective reality, whereas "regulative" principles are merely subjective maxims which guide reason without giving access to positive knowledge. However, when he speaks of existence (*Dasein*), Kant makes use of the pair constitutive / regulative in the midst of the very domain of the constitutive, by way of linking it to the couple mathematical / dynamical: "In the application of pure conceptions of understanding to possible experience, the employment of their synthesis is either *mathematical* or *dynamical*; for it is concerned partly with the mere *intuition* of an appearance in general, partly with its *existence*" (*CPR*, B 199).

In what precise sense, then, are dynamical principles "merely regulative principles, and [are] distinguished from the mathematical, which are constitutive" (*CPR*, B 223)? The principles of the mathematical use of categories refer to the intuited phenomenal content (to phenomenal properties of the thing); it is only the dynamical principles of synthesis which guarantee that the content of our representations refers to some objective existence, independent of the flux of perceiving consciousness. How, then, are we to explain the paradox of making objective existence dependent not on "constitutive" but on "regulative" principles? Let us return, for the last time, to the anti-Semitic figure of the Jew. Mathematical synthesis can only gather together phenomenal properties attributed to the Jew (greediness, intriguing spirit, etc.); then dynamical synthesis accomplishes the reversal by means of which this series of properties is posited as the manifestation of an inaccessible X, "Jewishness," that is to say, of something *real,* really existing. At work here are regulative principles, since dynamical synthesis is not limited to phenomenal features, but refers them to their underlying-unknowable substratum, to the transcendental object; in this precise sense, the existence of "Jew" as irreducible to the series of predicates, i.e., his existence as pure positing (*Setzung*) of the transcendental object qua substratum of phenomenal predicates, hinges on dynamical synthesis. In Lacanian terms, dynamical synthesis posits the existence of an X as the transphenomenal "hard kernel of being" beyond predicates (which is why the hatred of Jews does not concern their phenomenal properties but aims at their hidden "kernel of being")—a new proof of how "reason" is at work in the very heart of "understanding," in the most elementary positing of an object as "really existing." It is therefore deeply significant that, throughout the subdivision on the second analogy of experience, Kant consistently uses the word *Objekt* (designating an intelligible entity) and not *Gegenstand* (designating a simple phenomenal entity): the external, objective existence achieved by the synthetic use of dynamic regulative principles is "intelligible," not empirical-intuitive; i.e., it adds to the intuitive-sensible features of the object an intelligible, nonsensible X and thus makes an object out of it.

In this precise sense Hegel remains within Kant's fundamental framework. That is to say, in what resides the fundamental paradox of Kant's transcendentalism? Kant's initial problem is the following one: given that my senses bombard me with a confused multitude of representations, how am I to distinguish, in this flux, between mere "subjective" representations and objects that exist independently of the flux of representations? The answer: my representations acquire "objective status" via transcendental synthesis which changes them into the objects of experience. What I experience as "objective" existence, the very "hard kernel" of the object beneath the ever-changing phenomenal fluctuations, independent of the flux of my consciousness, thus results from my (the subject's) own "spontaneous" synthetic activity. And, mutatis mutandis, Hegel says the same thing: the establishment of absolute necessity equals its self-cancellation, i.e., it designates the act of freedom which retroactively "posits" something as necessary.

The "Absolute Unrest of Becoming"

The trouble with contingency resides in its uncertain status: is it ontological, i.e., are things *in themselves* contingent, or is it epistemological, i.e., is contingency merely an expression of the fact that *we do not know* the complete chain of causes which brought about the allegedly "contingent" phenomenon? Hegel undermines the common supposition of this alternative, namely the external relationship of being and knowledge: the notion of "reality" as something that is simply given, that exists "out there," prior and external to the process of knowledge; the difference between the ontological and the epistemological version is only that, in the first case, contingency is part of this reality itself, whereas in the second case, reality is wholly determined by necessity. In contrast to both these versions, Hegel affirms the basic thesis of speculative idealism: the process of knowledge, i.e., our comprehending the object, is not something external to the object but inherently determines its status (as Kant puts it, the conditions of possibility of our experience are also the conditions of possibility of the objects of experience). In other words, contingency does express the incompleteness of our knowledge, but *this incompleteness also ontologically defines the object of knowledge itself*—it bears witness to the fact that the object itself is not yet ontologically "realized," fully actual. The merely epistemological status of contingency is thus invalidated, without us falling back into ontological naiveté: behind the appearance of contingency there is no hidden, not-yet-known necessity, but *only the necessity of the very appearance that, behind superficial contingency, there is an underlying substantial necessity*—as in the case of anti-Semitism, where the ultimate appearance is the very appearance of the underlying necessity, i.e., the appearance that, behind the series of actual features (unemployment, moral disintegration . . .), there is the hidden necessity of the "Jewish plot." Therein consists the Hegelian inversion of "external" into "absolute" reflection: in external reflection, appearance is the elusive surface concealing its hidden necessity, whereas in absolute reflection, appearance is the appearance of this very (unknown) Necessity behind contingency. Or, to make use of an even more "Hegelian" speculative formulation, if contingency is an appearance concealing some hidden necessity, then this necessity is *stricto sensu an appearance of itself.*

This inherent antagonism of the relationship between contingency and necessity offers an exemplary case of the Hegelian triad: first the "naive" ontological conception which locates the difference in things themselves (some events are in themselves contingent, others necessary), then the attitude of "external reflection" which conceives of this difference as purely epistemological, i.e., dependent upon the incompleteness of our knowledge (we experience as "contingent" an event when the complete causal chain that produced it remains beyond our grasp), and, finally,—what? What is the third term besides the seemingly exhaustive choice between ontology and epistemology? *The very relationship between possibility (qua subjective seizing of actuality) and actuality (qua the object of conceptual seizing).* Both contingency and necessity are categories which express the dialectical unity of actual and possible; they are to be distinguished only insofar as contingency designates this unity conceived in the mode of subjectivity, of the "absolute unrest" of becoming, of the split between subject and object, and "necessity" this same content conceived in the mode of objectivity, of determinate being, of the identity of subject and object, of the rest of the Result.[39] In short, we are again at the category of pure *formal conversion*; the change concerns only the modality of form: "This *absolute unrest* of the *becoming* of these two determinations is *contingency*. But just because each immediately turns into its opposite, equally in this other it simply *unites with itself*, and this identity of both, of one in the other, is *necessity*."[40]

Hegel's counterposition here was adopted by Kierkegaard, in his notion of the two different modalities of observing a process: from the standpoint of "becoming" and from the standpoint of "being."[41] "After the fact," history can always be read as a process governed by laws, i.e., as a meaningful succession of stages; however, insofar as we are history's agents, embedded, caught in the process, the situation appears—at least at the turning points when "something is happening"—open, undecidable, far from the exposition of an underlying necessity. We must bear in mind here the lesson on the mediation of the subjective attitude with objectivity: we cannot reduce one perspective to another by claiming, for example, that the "true" picture is that of necessity discovered by the "backward view," that freedom is just an illusion of the immediate agents who overlook how their activity is a small wheel within the large causal mechanism; or, conversely, by embracing a kind of Sartrean existentialist perspective and affirming the subject's ultimate autonomy and freedom, conceiving the appearance of determinism as the later "practico-inert" objectivization of the subject's spontaneous *praxis*. In both cases, the ontological unity of the universe is saved, whether in the form of substantial necessity pulling the strings behind the subject's back or in the form of the subject's autonomous activity "objectivizing" itself in substantial unity. What gets lost is the ontological scandal of the ultimate *undecidability* between the two choices. Here Hegel is far more subversive than Kierkegaard, who escapes the deadlock by giving preference to possibility over actuality and thus announces the Bergsonian notion of actuality qua mechanical congelation of the life-process.[42]

In this undecidability lies the ultimate ambiguity of Hegel's philosophy, the index of an impossibility by way of which it "touches the real": how are we to conceive of the dialectical re-collection?[43] Is it a retroactive glance enabling us to discern the contours of inner necessity where the view immersed in the events can only perceive an interplay of accidents, i.e., as the "sublation" (*Aufhebung*) of this interplay of accidents in underlying logical necessity? Or is it, on the contrary, a glance enabling us to resuscitate the openness of the situation, its "possibility," its irreducible contingency, in what afterwards, from objective distance, appears as a necessary objective process? And does not this undecidability bring us back to our starting point: is not this ambiguity again the way sexual difference is inscribed into the very core of Hegel's logic?

Insofar as the relationship between contingency and necessity is that of becoming and being, it is legitimate to conceive of *objet a*, this pure semblance, as a kind of "anticipation" of being from the perspective of becoming. That is to say, Hegel conceives of matter as correlative to incomplete form, i.e., to form which still is a "mere form," a mere anticipation of itself qua complete form. In this precise sense, it can be said that *objet a* designates that remainder of matter which bears witness to the fact that form did not yet fully realize itself, that it did not become actual as the concrete determination of the object, that it remains a mere anticipation of itself. The spatial anamorphosis has to be supplemented here by the temporal anamorphosis (what is anticipation if not a temporal anamorphosis in which we produce an image of the object distorted by the hasty, overtaking glance?). Spatially, *a* is an object whose proper contours are discernible only if we glimpse it askance; it is forever indiscernible to the straightforward look.[44] Temporally, it is an object which exists only qua anticipated or lost, only in the modality of not-yet or not-anymore, never in the "now" of a pure, undivided present. Kant's transcendental object (his term for *a*) is therefore a kind of *mirage* which gives body to the inequality of the form to itself, not an index of the surplus of the material in-itself over form.

What we encounter here is again the ultimate ambiguity of Hegel. According to the standard *doxa*, the telos of the dialectical process is the absolute form that abolishes any material surplus. If, however, this is truly the case with Hegel, how are we to account for the fact that the Result effectively throws us back into the whirlpool, that it is nothing but the totality of the route we had to travel in order to arrive at the Result? In other words, is not a kind of leap from "not-yet" to "always-already" constitutive of the Hegelian dialectics: we endeavor to approach the Goal (the absolute form devoid of any matter), when, all of a sudden, we establish that all the time we were already there? Is not the crucial shift in a dialectical process the reversal of anticipation—not into its fulfillment, but—into retroaction? If, therefore, the fulfillment never occurs in the Present, does this not testify to the irreducible status of *objet a*?

Actuality of the Possible

The ontological background of this leap from "not-yet" to "always-already" is a kind of "trading of places" between possibility and actuality: possibility itself, in its very opposition to actuality, possesses an actuality of its own—in what precise sense? Hegel always insists on the absolute primacy of actuality: true, the search for the "conditions of possibility" abstracts from the actual, calls it into question, in order to (re)constitute it on a rational basis; yet in all these ruminations actuality is presupposed as something given. In other words, nothing is stranger to Hegel than Leibnizean speculation about the multitude of possible worlds out of which the Creator picks out the best: speculation on possible universes always takes place against the background of the hard fact of actual existence. On the other hand, there is always something traumatic about the raw factuality of what we encounter as "actual"; actuality is always marked by an indelible brand of the (real as) "impossible." The shift from actuality to possibility, the suspension of actuality through inquiry into its possibility, is therefore ultimately an endeavor to avoid the trauma of the real, i.e., to integrate the real by means of conceiving it as something that is meaningful within our symbolic universe.[45]

Of course, this squaring of the circle of possible and actual (i.e., first the suspension of actuality and then its derivation from the conceptual possibility) never works out, as proven by the very category of contingency: "contingency" designates an actual content insofar as it cannot be wholly grounded in its conceptual conditions of possibility. According to philosophical common sense, contingency and necessity are the two modalities of actuality: something actual is necessary insofar as its contrary is not possible; it is contingent insofar as its contrary is also possible (insofar as things could also have turned out otherwise). The problem, however, resides in the inherent antagonism that pertains to the notion of possibility: possibility designates something "possible" in the sense of being able to actualize itself, as well as something "merely possible" as opposed to being actual. This inner split finds its clearest expression perhaps in the diametrically opposed roles played by the notion of possibility in moral argumentation. On the one hand, we have the "empty possibility," the external excuse of the weak: "If I really wanted to, I could have . . . (stopped smoking, etc.)." In challenging this claim, Hegel again and again points out how the true nature of a possibility (is it a true possibility or a mere empty presumption?) is confirmed only by way of its actualization: the only effective proof that you really can do something is simply to do it. On the other hand, the possibility of acting differently exerts pressure on us in the guise of the "voice of conscience": when I offer the usual excuses ("I did all that was possible, there was no choice"), the superego voice keeps gnawing at me, "No, you could have done more!" This is what Kant has in mind when he insists that freedom is actual already as possibility: when I gave way to pathological impulses and did not carry out my duty, the *actuality* of my freedom is attested to by my awareness of how I *could have* acted otherwise.[46] And this is also what Hegel aims at when maintaining that the actual (*das Wirkliche*) is not the same as that which simply exists (*das Bestehende*): my conscience pricks me when my act (of giving way to pathological impulses) was not "actual," did not express my true moral nature; this difference exerts pressure on me in the guise of "conscience."

One can discern the same logic behind the recent revival of the conspiracy theory (Oliver Stone's *JFK*): who was behind Kennedy's murder? The ideological cathexis of this revival is clear: Kennedy's murder acquired such traumatic dimensions retroactively, from the later experience of the Vietnam War, of the Nixon administration's cynical corruption, of the revolt of the sixties that opened up the gap between the young generation and the establishment. This later experience transformed Kennedy into a person who, had he remained alive, would have spared us Vietnam, the gap separating the sixties generation from the establishment, etc. (What the conspiracy theory "represses," of course, is the painful fact of Kennedy's *impotence:* Kennedy himself would not have been able to prevent the emergence of this gap.) The conspiracy theory thus keeps alive the dream of another America, different from the one we came to know in the seventies and eighties.[47]

Hegel's position with regard to the relationship of possibility and actuality is thus very refined and precise: possibility is simultaneously less and more than what its notion implies; conceived in its abstract opposition to actuality, it is a "mere possibility" and, as such, it coincides with its opposite, with impossibility. On another level, however, possibility already possesses a certain actuality *in its very capacity of possibility,* which is why any further demand for its actualization is superfluous. In this sense, Hegel points out that the idea of freedom realizes itself through a series of failures: every particular attempt to realize freedom may fail; from its point of view, freedom remains an empty possibility; but the very continuous striving of freedom to realize itself bears witness to its "actuality," i.e., to the fact that freedom is not a "mere notion" but manifests a tendency that pertains to the very essence of reality. On the other hand, the supreme case of "mere possibility" is the Hegelian "abstract universal"; what I have in mind here is the well-known paradox of the relationship between universal judgment and judgment of existence in the classical Aristotelian syllogism: judgment of existence implies the existence of its subject, whereas universal judgment can also be true even if its subject does not exist, since it concerns only the notion of the subject. If, for example, one says "At least one man is (or: some men are) mortal," this judgment is true only if at least one man exists; if, on the contrary, one says "A unicorn has only one horn," this judgment remains true even if there are no unicorns, since it concerns solely the immanent determination of the notion of "unicorn." Far from its relevance being limited to pure theoretical ruminations, this gap between the universal and the particular has palpable material effects—in politics, for example. According to the results of a public opinion poll in the fall of 1991, in the choice between Bush and a nonspecified Democratic candidate, the nonspecified Democrat would win easily; however, in the choice between Bush and any concrete, individual Democrat, provided with face and name (Kerrey, Cuomo . . .), Bush would have an easy win. In short, the Democrat in general wins over Bush, whereas Bush wins over any concrete Democrat. To the misfortune of the Democrats, there was no "Democrat in general."[48]

The status of possibility, while different from that of actuality, is thus not simply deficient with regard to it. *Possibility as such exerts actual effects which disappear as soon as it "actualizes" itself.* Such a "short-circuit" between possibility and actuality is at work in the Lacanian notion of "symbolic castration": the so-called "castration-anxiety" cannot be reduced to the psychological fact that, upon perceiving the absence of the penis in woman, man becomes afraid that "he also might lose it."[49] "Castration anxiety" rather designates the precise moment at which the possibility of castration takes precedence over its actuality, i.e., the moment at which the very possibility of castration, its mere threat, produces actual effects in our psychic economy. This threat as it were "castrates" us, branding us with an irreducible loss. And it is this same "short-circuit" between possibility and actuality which defines the very notion of power: power is *actually* exerted only in the guise of a *potential* threat, i.e., only insofar as it does not strike fully but "keeps itself in reserve."[50] Suffice it to recall the logic of paternal authority: the moment a father loses control and displays his full power (starts to shout, to beat a child), we necessarily perceive this display as impotent rage, i.e., as an index of its very opposite. In this precise sense symbolic authority always, by definition, hinges on an irreducible potentiality-possibility, on the actuality-effectivity that pertains to possibility qua possibility: we leave behind the "raw," pre-symbolic real and enter the symbolic universe the moment possibility acquires actuality of its own. (This paradox is at work in the Hegelian struggle for recognition between the (future) Lord and Bondsman: to say that the impasse of their struggle is resolved by way of the Lord's *symbolic* victory and the Bondsman's *symbolic* death equals saying that the mere *possibility* of victory is sufficient. The symbolic pact at work in their struggle enables them to stop before the actual physical destruction and to accept the possibility of victory as its actuality.) The Master's potential threat is far worse than his actual display of power. This is what Bentham counts on in his fantasy-matrix of Panopticon: the fact that the Other—the gaze in the central observing tower—*can* watch me; my radical uncertainty as to whether I am being observed or not at any precise moment gives rise to an anxiety far greater than that aroused by the awareness that I am actually observed. This surplus of what is "in the possibility more than a mere possibility" and which gets lost in its actualization is *the real qua impossible.*[51]

It is precisely on account of this potential character of his power that a Master is always, by definition, an impostor, i.e., somebody who illegitimately occupies the place of the lack in the Other (the symbolic Order). In other words, the emergence of the figure of the Master is of a strictly *metonymical* nature: a Master never fully "measures up to its notion," to Death qua "absolute Master" (Hegel). He remains forever the "metonymy of Death"; his whole consistency hinges upon the deferral, the keeping-in-reserve, of a force that he falsely claims to possess.[52] It would be wrong, however, to conclude—from the fact that anyone who occupies the place of the Master is an impostor and a clown—that the perceived imperfections of the Master subvert his authority. The whole artifice of "playing a Master" consists in knowing how to use this very gap (between the "notion" of the Master and its empirical bearer) to our advantage: the way for a Master to strengthen his authority is precisely to present himself as "human like the rest of us," full of little weaknesses, a person with whom it is quite possible to "talk normally" when he is not compelled to give voice to Authority. At a different level, this dialectic was widely exploited by the Catholic church, which was always ready to condone small infringements if they stabilized the reign of Law: prostitution, pornography, etc., are sins, yet not only can they be pardoned, they can be commended if they help preserve marriage: better a periodic visit to a brothel than divorce.[53]

This primacy of possibility over actuality enables us also to articulate the difference between the phallic signifier and the fetish. This difference may seem elusive since, in both cases, we have to do with a "reflective" element which supplements a primordial lack (the fetish fills out the void of the missing maternal phallus; the phallus is the signifier of the very lack of the signifier). However, as the signifier of pure possibility, the phallus is never fully actualized (i.e., it is the empty signifier which, although devoid of any determinate, positive meaning, stands for the potentiality of any possible future meaning), whereas a fetish always claims an actual status (i.e., it pretends actually to substitute for the maternal phallus). In other words, insofar as a fetish is an element that fills in the lack of (the maternal) phallus, the most concise definition of the phallic signifier is that it is a *fetish of itself*: phallus qua *"signifier of castration"* as it were gives body to *its own lack*.

PART III

SUM *The Loop of Enjoyment*

5 "The Wound Is Healed Only by the Spear That Smote You"

■

Opera took shape as a musical form around 1600 (Monteverdi's *Orfeo*, the earliest opera "still alive" today, was composed in 1603) and ended somewhere after 1900 (among the numerous candidates for the title of the "last true opera," there are Puccini's *Turandot*, some of Richard Strauss's operas, Berg's *Wozzeck* . . .). At its beginning stands the recitative (the great invention of Monteverdi), the not-yet-aria, and at its end *Sprachgesang*, the "spoken song," the no-longer-aria. In between—in the epoch which broadly coincides with that of modern-age subjectivity—it was possible to sing on stage, as part of the staging of some dramatic event. One is tempted, therefore, to look in the history of opera for traces of the trends and shifts that make up the history of subjectivity.

This end of classical subjectivity, of course, is the very point of the emergence of the modern hysterical subject. In this precise sense, the history of the opera can be said to belong to the prehistory of psychoanalysis: it is by no accident that the end of the opera coincides with the emergence of psychoanalysis. The predominant motif of Schoenberg which drove him into the atonal revolution, the content which it was not anymore possible to articulate in the classical tonal operatic aria, was precisely the feminine hysteria (Schoenberg's *Erwartung*, his first atonal masterpiece, depicts the hysterical longing of a lone woman). And, as is well known, the first analysands were female hysterics; that is to say, psychoanalysis was originally an interpretation of female hysteria.

The Answer of the Real

At the origins of opera there is a precisely defined intersubjective constellation: the relationship of the subject (in both senses of the term: autonomous agent as well as the subject of legal power) to his Master (King or Divinity) is revealed through the hero's recitative (the counterpoint to the collectivity embodied in the chorus), which is basically a supplication addressed to the Master, a call to him to show mercy, to make an exception, or otherwise forgive the hero his trespass.[1] The first, rudimentary form of subjectivity is this voice of the subject beseeching the Master to suspend, for a brief moment, his own Law. A dramatic tension in subjectivity arises from the ambiguity between power and impotence that pertains to the gesture of grace by means of which the Master answers the subject's entreaty. As to the official ideology, grace expresses the Master's supreme power, the power to rise above one's own law: only a really powerful Master can afford to distribute mercy. What we have here is a kind of symbolic exchange between the human subject and his divine Master: when the subject, the human mortal, by way of his offer of self-sacrifice, surmounts his finitude and attains the divine heights, the Master responds with the sublime gesture of Grace, the ultimate proof of *his* humanity.[2] Yet this act of grace is at the same time branded by the irreducible mark of a forced empty gesture: the Master ultimately makes a virtue out of necessity, in that he promotes as a free act what he is in any case compelled to do; if he refuses clemency, he takes the risk that the subject's entreaty will turn into open rebellion. It is here that we already encounter the intricacies of the dialectic of Master and Servant elaborated later by Hegel: is not the Master, insofar as he depends on the other's recognition, effectively his own servant's servant?

For that reason, the temporal proximity of the emergence of opera to Descartes' formulation of *cogito* is more than a fortuitous coincidence: one is even tempted to say that the move from Monteverdi's *Orfeo* to Gluck's *Orpheus and Euridice* corresponds to the move from Descartes to Kant. At the formal level, this move entails a shift from recitative to aria; at the level of dramatic content, what Gluck contributed was a new form of subjectivization. In Monteverdi we have sublimation in its purest: after Orpheus turns to cast a glance at Euridice and thus loses her, the Divinity consoles him: true, he has lost her as a flesh-and-blood person, but from now on, he will be able to discern her beautiful features everywhere, in the stars in the sky, in the glistening of the morning dew. Orpheus is quick to accept the narcissistic profit of this reversal: he becomes enraptured with the poetic glorification of Euridice that lies ahead of him. (This, of course, throws another light on the eternal question of why he looked back and thus screwed things up. What we encounter here is simply the link between the death-drive and creative sublimation: Orpheus's backward gaze is a perverse act *stricto sensu;* he loses her intentionally in order to regain her as the object of sublime poetic inspiration.)[3] With Gluck, the denouement is completely different: after looking back and thus losing Euridice, Orpheus sings his famous aria "Che faro senza Euridice," announcing his intention to kill himself. At this precise point of total self-abandonment, Love intervenes and gives him back his Euridice.[4] This specific form of subjectivization—the intervention of Grace not as a simple answer to the subject's entreaty, but as an answer in the very moment when the subject decides to put his life at stake—is the twist added by Gluck.[5]

Opera's development thus reaches its first full circle: all the elements for Mozart are present in Gluck. That is to say, Mozart's "fundamental matrix" consists of precisely such a gesture of subjectivization whereby the assertion of the subject's autonomy (our readiness to sacrifice ourselves, to go to the end, to die, to lose all) gives rise to a gesture of mercy in the Other. This matrix is at work in its purest in his first two masterpieces, the opera seria *Idomeneo* and the *Singspiel Abduction* from *The Seraglio:* when, in *Seraglio,* the two lovers, prisoners of Pasha Selim, express their fearless readiness to die, Pasha Selim shows mercy and lets them go. All Mozart's subsequent operas can be read as so many variations or permutations on this matrix. In *Le Nozze di Figaro,* for example, the relationship is reversed: the Master—Count Almaviva—is not prepared to grant mercy to his wife and Figaro when he thinks that he has caught them in adultery. Yet when he walks into the trap set to expose his own deceit, he is himself forced to beg for mercy; and the community of subjects does forgive him. Thus occurs a unique utopian moment of reconciliation, of integration of the Master into the community of equals. *Don Giovanni* brings this logic of mercy to its inherent negation: in it, we find neither entreaty nor mercy. Don Giovanni proudly refuses the Stone Guest's call to repent, and what then befalls him instead of clemency is the most cruel punishment, he is swallowed by the flames of Hell.[6] The ideal balance of autonomy and mercy is here perturbed by the emergence of an autonomy so radical that it leaves no space open for mercy, an autonomy in which it is not difficult to discern the contours of what Kant called "radical Evil." After this moment of utter despair, when the whole economy of mercy is suspended, the register miraculously changes and, with *The Magic Flute*, we enter the domain of fairy bliss. Here we also twice encounter the gesture of subjectivization through a readiness to die (both Pamina and Papageno are about to commit suicide), yet the agency that intervenes and prevents the accomplishment of the act is not an imposing Master or Divinity but the three *Wunderknaben*.

The temptation to be avoided here is to conceive this Mozartian codependence of autonomy and mercy as a compromise formation, as an illusory point of equilibrium between the not-yet-subject who still relies on the Master's grace (the subject of enlightened absolutism in his relationship to the Monarch), and the fully autonomous subject, master of his own fate. If we succumb to this temptation, we lose the fundamental paradox of how *autonomy itself, in its very self-affirmation, relies on "mercy," on a sign of the Other, on an "answer of the real"*: "The empirical mind sees the response of mercy as an alien caprice, or just coincidence. Bondage to fate can, absurdly enough, be broken only by the favor of fate; the individual can round his existence into a whole only, as Goethe put it, 'if quite unexpected things from outside come to his aid.' Piously believing it and bitterly accepting it, Goethe entrusted self-realization in his life to the 'daemon,' in his major work to the devil."[7] In Mozart, of course, the bourgeois subject, with his utilitarian, instrumental cunning dexterity, is hard at work from the very beginning (the element of *opera buffa*). The motto "Help yourself and God will help you" receives here its full value: the subject is never a mere applicant; by way of his subterfuge, he prepares the ground in advance, arranging the plot, so that all that is left for the God-Master is to nod his assent after the fact, like the Hegelian monarch. But the more it becomes clear that, at the level of content, the subject's subterfuge has already taken care of the final outcome, the more the true enigma of form becomes palpable: why does the subject still need mercy, why does he not also assume the formal act of decision, why does he still rely on the Other?

The further feature which apparently contradicts the cunning dexterity is that the Other intervenes at the very moment when, in a suicidal act of abandonment, the subject expresses his readiness to put all at stake in a gesture of defiant renunciation and thus disavows all the cheap tricks of instrumental reason. As long as I endeavor to bargain, as long as I propose my self-sacrifice so to speak with my fingers crossed, counting on the last-minute intervention of grace, the Other will not respond. Grace is a case of what Jon Elster called "states which are essentially a by-product":[8] it occurs at the very moment when we abandon all hope and cease to count on it. The situation is here ultimately the same as that of Abraham's acceptance of God's command to sacrifice his son: because he accepted it, he did not have to carry it out; *but he could not know that in advance.* And does not the same paradox define so-called "mature love": our partner will really appreciate our love only if we somehow let him know that we are not childishly dependent on him, that we are able to survive without him? Therein consists the ordeal of true love: I pretend that I'll leave you, and only if and when you demonstrate your ability to endure my loss do you become worthy of my love. As was pointed out by Claude Lefort,[9] a similar confidence in the answer of the real is at work in democracy, which entails the symbolic dissolution of social links (in the act of elections, the future fate of society is made dependent on a play of numeric contingency); the underlying hypothesis that—in the long term, at least—the result will be in the best interests of society can never be directly proven, it always relies on a minimum of miraculous coincidence; i.e., to refer to the Kantian terms, the status of this hypothesis is strictly regulative, not constitutive, like that of teleology in Kant. (It is precisely this gap which opens up the space for the totalitarian temptation directly to impose on society the solution which is "in its best interest.")

One of the most common "postmodern" myths concerns the phantom of the so-called "Cartesian paradigm of subjectivity": the era of modernity now reaching its end was allegedly marked by the all-devouring monster of the absolute, self-transparent Subject, reducing every Otherness to an object to be "mediated," "internalized," dominated by technological manipulation, etc., the ultimate result of which is the present ecological crisis. Here, reference to the history of the opera allows us to denounce this myth by way of demonstrating how, far from postulating an "absolute subject," philosophy from Kant to Hegel, this apogee of "modern-age subjectivity," struggled desperately to articulate the paradoxical conjunction of autonomy and Grace, i.e., the dependence of the very assertion of the subject's autonomy on the sympathetic response of an Otherness.[10]

Subjectivity and Grace

This "answer of the Real" on which we rely, this support in the big Other whose gesture of response "subjectivizes" the abyss of the pure subject, is what Hegel has in mind when he speaks of the "cunning of reason." The subject's readiness to "sacrifice everything" is conceived by Hegel as "the return of consciousness into the depths of the night of the I = I, which distinguishes and knows nothing besides itself. This feeling is therefore in fact the loss of substance and its standing over and against consciousness."[11] The commonplace reproach to Hegel is that, in the "closed economy" of his idealism, this loss reverts automatically into the new positivity of the self-identical Subject-Substance. But we must be particularly careful not to miss the paradox of this inversion. On the one hand, the sacrifice is in no way feigned, i.e., it is not part of the game in which one can rely on the Absolute's guaranteeing a happy outcome. Hegel is here quite clear and unambiguous: what dies in this experience of the return into the night of the I = I is ultimately Substance itself, i.e., God qua transcendent agency which pulls the strings behind the stage. What dies is thus precisely God qua Reason, which, by way of its "cunning," guarantees the happy outcome of the historical process—in short, absolute Subject-Reason, the notion of which is usually imputed to Hegel. Hegel's interpretation of Christianity is here far more subversive than it may appear. How does Hegel conceive the Christian notion of the becoming-man of God; at what level does he place the sign of equality between God and man? At the radical opposite of the usual view which conceives the "divine" in man as that which in him is eternal, noble, etc. When God becomes man, he identifies with man qua suffering, sinful mortal. In this sense, the "death of God" means that the subject verily finds himself alone, without any guarantee in substantial Reason, in the big Other.

On the other hand, however—and therein consists the paradox—we are here as far as possible from any kind of existential despair, from the "openness" of the radical risk ("when everything is put at stake, Grace can either intervene or not"): the reversal into mercy follows automatically; it takes place as soon as we *truly* put everything at stake. Why? More precisely: why is the standard Derridean question ("What if the reversal does *not* arrive, what if no 'answer of the Real' follows the radical loss?") here totally out of place? There is only one explanation possible: the reversal of loss into salvation by way of Grace is an act of purely formal conversion; i.e., *the intervention of Grace is not something distinct from the preceding loss, but is this very loss, the same act of self-renunciation, conceived from a different perspective.* With regard to Christianity, this means that the death of Christ is simultaneously a day of grief and a day of joy: God-Christ had to die in order to be able to come to life again in the shape of the community of believers (the

"Holy Spirit"). Instead of the "substance" qua God-Master, the inscrutable Fate which reigns in its Beyond, we obtain the "substance" qua community of believers. In this precise sense, "the wound is healed only by the spear that smote you": the death of God *is* his resurrection, the weapon that killed Christ *is* the tool that created the Christian community of the Holy Spirit.

Subjectivity thus involves a kind of loop, a vicious circle, an economical paradox which can be rendered in a multitude of ways, Hegel's, Wagner's, Lacan's. Lacan: castration means that the Thing-*jouissance* must be lost in order to be regained on the ladder of desire, i.e., the symbolic order recovers its own constitutive debt; Wagner in *Parsifal:* the wound is healed only by the spear that smote you; Hegel: the immediate identity of the substance must be lost in order to be regained through the work of subjective mediation. What we call "subject" is ultimately a name for this economic paradox or, more accurately, short-circuit, whereby *the conditions of possibility coincide with the conditions of impossibility.* This double-bind, which constitutes the subject, was for the first time explicitly articulated by Kant: the I of transcendental apperception can be said to be "self-conscious," can experience itself as a free, spontaneous agent, to the very extent to which it is inaccessible to itself as the "Thing which thinks"; the subject of practical reason can act morally (out of duty) to the very extent to which any direct access to Supreme Good is barred to him; etc. The point of these paradoxes is that what we call "subjectivization" (recognizing oneself in interpellation, assuming an imposed symbolic mandate) is a kind of defense mechanism against an abyss, a gap, which "is" the subject. The Althusserian theory conceives the subject as the effect of ideological (mis)recognition: the subject emerges in an act which renders invisible its own causality. Reference to opera enables us to discern the contours of a certain vicious circle which defines the dimension of subjectivity, yet is not the Althusserian circle of interpellation: the Althusserian moment of the closure of the circle, of the (mis)recognition in interpellation, is not the direct effect of a "process without subject," but an attempt to heal the very wound of subjectivity.

We encounter this antagonism between subject and subjectivity in all three of Kant's critiques. In the domain of "pure reason," the subject of pure apperception—$, the *empty* "I think"—necessarily lapses into the transcendental *Schein*, mistaking itself for a "thinking *substance*," i.e., falsely assuming that, by way of self-consciousness, it has the access to itself qua

Thing-in-itself. In the domain of "practical reason," the moral subject—submitted to, constituted by, the universal *form* of categorical imperative—necessarily falls prey to the *Schein* of Supreme Good, elevating some "pathological" *content* into the aim and impetus of its moral activity. In the domain of "judgment," the reflecting subject necessarily misses the purely *regulative* nature of a teleological judgment—i.e., the fact that this judgment concerns only the subject's reflective relationship to reality, not reality itself—and misreads teleology as something that pertains to reality itself, as its *constitutive* determination. The crucial feature in all three cases is an irreducible *splitting* of the subject: between $\mathcal{S}$ and the substantial "person" in pure reason, between fulfilling duty for the sake of duty and serving some Supreme Good in practical reason, between the sublime experience of the gap that separates phenomena from the suprasensible Idea and the "gentrification" of this gap via beauty and teleology in the capacity of judgment. In all three cases, the "lapse" designates the shift from subject into subjectivization: in my capacity as knowing subject, I "subjectivize" myself by way of recognizing myself as "person" in the fullness of its content; in my capacity as moral subject, I "subjectivize" myself by way of submitting myself to some substantial Supreme Good; in my capacity as reflecting, judging subject, I "subjectivize" myself by way of identifying my place in a teleological, harmonious structure of the universe. In all three cases, the logic of this "lapse" is that of an illusion which, even when its mechanism is exposed, continues to operate: I (may) know that teleological judgments have the status of a mere subjective reflection, not of a genuine knowledge of reality, yet nonetheless I cannot *abstain from making teleological observations;* etc. In all three cases, the Kantian subject is therefore caught in a kind of double-bind: in practical reason, it is evident that the true superego-reverse of the Kantian "Du kannst, denn du sollst!" ("You can, because you must!") is "You must, although you know that you cannot, that it is not possible!"—i.e., an impossible demand which can never be satisfied and as such condemns the subject to an eternal split. In teleology, on the contrary, "you know you should not do it, yet you cannot not do it."

To put it yet another way, the "lapse" (into teleology, into the substantial notion of Supreme Good) is an endeavor to heal the wound of the subject qua $\mathcal{S}$, to fill in the gap which renders the Thing inaccessible: it reinstates the subject into the "great chain of being." And far from acting as a stumbling block, this very double-bind served as a lever for the further development of philosophical problematic. In other words, Kant's merit consists thus of the very feature that is the usual target of his critics: *by means of one and the same gesture, his philosophy opens up the space (the possibility, the need) for a thing and makes this thing inaccessible and / or impossible to accomplish*—as if the opening is possible only at the price of the instantaneous crossing-out.[12] Maimon, Kant's contemporary, was the first to point out that Kant's dualism between reason and sense both creates the need for the transcendental turn (to escape Hume's skepticism) and makes it impossible; along the same lines, Kant is usually reproached for conceiving Things-in-themselves as a necessary presupposition of our knowledge (providing the "material" to be formed by the transcendental grid), but at the same time making them inaccessible to our knowledge; on another level, the pure ethical act is unconditionally imposed by the moral imperative *and* something that, for all practical purposes, remains impossible to accomplish, since one can never be quite certain of the total absence of "pathological" considerations in any of our acts. This entity, necessary and impossible in one and the same movement, is the Lacanian Real.[13] And the line separating Kant from Hegel is here far thinner than it may appear: all Hegel did was to bring to its conclusion this coincidence of conditions of possibility with conditions of impossibility: if positing and prohibiting coincide absolutely, then there is no need for Thing-in-itself; i.e., then the mirage of In-itself is created by the very act of prohibiting.

And does not this same absolute simultaneity of positioning and prohibiting define the Lacanian *objet petit a,* the object-cause of desire? In this precise sense, Lacan can be said to accomplish the Kantian critical project by supplementing it with a fourth critique, the "critique of pure desire," the foundation of the first three critiques.[14] Desire becomes "pure" the moment it ceases to be conceived as the desire for a "pathological" (positively given) object, the moment it is posited as the desire for an object whose emergence coincides with its withdrawal, i.e., which is nothing but the trace of its own retreat. What must be borne in mind here is the difference between this Kantian position and the traditional "spiritualist" position of striving after infinity, freed from every attachment to sensible particularity (the Platonic model of love which elevates itself from love for an individual person toward love for the Idea of Beauty as such): far from amounting to another version of such spiritualized-ethereal desire, the Kantian "pure desire" is confined to the paradox of the subject's finitude. If the subject were able to trespass the limitations of his finitude and to accomplish the step into the noumenal domain, the very sublime object which constitutes his desire as "pure" would be lost (we encounter the same paradox in Kant's practical philosophy: it is the very inaccessibility of the Thing which makes us capable of moral acts).

From Mozart to Wagner

Yet the story is far from over at this point. The line of Mozart's operas, from its fundamental matrix through its variations to the final reversal into the bliss of *The Magic Flute*, is repeated, on a different level, in the operas of Richard Wagner. The missing link between Mozart and Wagner is provided by Beethoven's *Fidelio*. On the one hand, we find the intervention of Mercy which follows the gesture of self-sacrificing subjectivization in its purest: when Pizarro, the evil governor of the prison, wants to dispose of the noble Florestan, Leonora, Florestan's faithful wife, masked as a man and employed as the jailer assistant under the false name of "Fidelio," interposes herself between the two, shielding Florestan with her own body, and reveals her true identity. At the very moment when Pizzaro threatens to kill her, a trumpet sounds, announcing the arrival of the Minister, the messenger of the good King who comes to free Florestan. On the other hand, we already encounter here the key moment of Wagner's fundamental matrix: man's redemption through woman's willing self-sacrifice.[15] One is even tempted to say that all of *Fidelio*, this apogee of the exaltation of the bourgeois couple, is directed toward the sublime moment of the woman's redemptive sacrifice, the consequences of which are double. Because of this exalted ethical enthusiasm, *Fidelio* has always been surrounded by a kind of magical aura (as late as 1955, when its performance marked the opening of the renovated Vienna opera, wild rumors began to circulate in Vienna about cripples regaining their ability to walk and blind men their sight). Yet this very obsession with the ethical gesture entails a kind of "ethical suspension of the esthetic" which seems to sap the opera's stage potential: at the crucial moment, the curtain falls and the opera proper is supplanted by a symphonic interlude, alone capable of rendering the intensity of the sublime exaltation (the overture *Leonora III*, usually performed between the denouement—the Minister's arrival—and the jubilant finale)—as if this exaltation fails to meet the "considerations of representability," as if something in it resists the mise-en-scène.[16]

For the shift to Wagner's universe to take place, we only have to stain both man and woman with a certain "pathology": the man to be delivered is no longer an innocent hero, but a suffering sinner, a kind of Wandering Jew who is not allowed to die, since he is condemned, for some unspeakable past transgression, to rove unendingly in the domain between the two deaths. (In contrast to Florestan, who in his famous aria which opens the second act of *Fidelio,* prior to the phantasmagorical appearance of Leonora, repeats almost obsessively how he "has accomplished his duty" [*ich habe meine Pflicht getan*], the Wagnerian hero *failed* to act in accordance with his "duty," his ethical mandate.) The counterpoint to this failed interpellation is that the woman, the hero's redeemer, acquires the unmistakable features of hysteria, so that we obtain a kind of redoubled, mirrored fantasy. On the one hand, *The Flying Dutchman* "could be reduced to the moment when the Dutchman steps beneath—one could almost say, steps out from—his picture, as Senta, who has conjured him up as Elsa had conjured up the knight [in *Lohengrin*], stands gazing into his eyes. The entire opera is nothing more than the attempt to unfold this moment in time."[17] (And is not the great last act of *Tristan und Isolde* an inversion of this phantasmagoria? Is not Isolde's appearance conjured up by the dying Tristan? For that reason, the two recent stagings of Wagner which displaced part of the action into the phantasmagoria of one of the persons on stage are deeply justified: Harry Kupfer's interpretation of the Dutchman as Senta's hysterical vision; Jean-Pierre Ponelle's interpretation of Isolde's arrival and ecstatic death as the vision of the dying Tristan.)[18] On the other hand, this figure of the woman ready to sacrifice herself is clearly an ostentatious male phantasmagoria, in this case a phantasmagoria of Wagner himself. Suffice it to quote the following passage from his letter to Liszt apropos of his love affair with Mathilde Wesendonk: "The love of a tender woman has made me happy; she dared to throw herself into a sea of suffering and agony so that she should be able to say to me "I love you!" No one who does not know all her tenderness can judge how much she had to suffer. We were spared nothing—but as a consequence I am redeemed and she is blessedly happy because she is aware of it."[19] For that reason, one is quite justified in conceiving of *The Flying Dutchman* as the first "true" Wagner opera: the suffering man, condemned to wander in the domain "between the two deaths," is delivered by the woman's self-sacrifice. It is here that we encounter the fundamental matrix in its purest, and all Wagner's subsequent operas can be generated from it via a set of variations.[20] Here, also, the elementary form of the song is the entreaty—man's complaint, whose first paradigmatic case is the Flying Dutchman's monologue in which we learn about his sad fate, eternally sailing on a ghost-ship. The most powerful moments in *Parsifal*, Wagner's last opera, are also the two supplications of the Fisher King Amfortas; here, as in the case of the Dutchman, the content of the entreaty is almost the exact opposite of the entreaty which opens the history of opera: in Wagner, the hero bemoans his very inability to find peace in death, i.e., his fate of eternal suffering.[21] The gesture of Grace, the "answer of the Real," which closes *Parsifal* is an act of Parsifal himself, who intervenes at the last minute, preventing the knights from slaughtering Amfortas and delivering him by lance from his torments. Here is the outline of the story:

The Holy Grail, the vessel with Christ's blood, is kept in the castle Montsalvat; yet its ruler Amfortas, the Fisher King, is maimed: he betrayed the sanctity of the Grail by letting himself be seduced by Kundry, a slave to the evil magician Klingsor, who castrated himself in order to be able to resist the sexual urge. While Amfortas was in Kundry's embrace, Klingsor snatched away from him the sacred spear (the one with which Longinus smote Christ on the cross) and wounded him in his thigh; this wound condemns Amfortas to a life of eternal suffering. The young Parsifal enters the domain of Montsalvat and kills a swan, unknowingly committing a crime; the wise old Gurnemanz recognizes in him the pure fool who—so the prophecy goes—will deliver Amfortas; he takes him into the temple of the Grail, where Parsifal witnesses the ritual of the Grail's disclosure painfully performed by Amfortas. Disappointed that Parsifal is unable to make anything out of this ritual, Gurnemanz chases him away. In act 2, Parsifal enters Klingsor's magic castle where Kundry endeavors to seduce him; in the very moment of her kiss, Parsifal suddenly feels compassion for the suffering Amfortas and pushes her away; when Klingsor throws the sacred lance at him, Parsifal is able to stop it by raising his hand—since he resisted Kundry's seduction, Klingsor has no power over him. By making the sign of the cross with the lance, Parsifal dispels Klingsor's magic and the castle falls into a desert. In act 3 Parsifal, after many years of wandering, returns on Good Friday to Montsalvat and reveals to Gurnemanz that he has recovered the stolen lance; Gurnemanz anoints him as the new king; Parsifal baptizes the repentant Kundry, experiences the inner peace and elevation of Good Friday, then again enters the temple of the Grail, where he finds Amfortas surrounded by enraged knights like a trapped, wounded animal. The knights want to force him to perform the Grail ritual; unable to do so, he implores them to kill him and thus relieve him of his suffering; but at the last moment, Parsifal enters, heals his wound by a touch of the lance ("The wound is healed only by the spear that smote you"), proclaims himself the new king and orders the Grail to remain revealed forever, while Kundry silently drops dead. How can one avoid here, as a first spontaneous reaction, the amazement over such a strange set of central characters expressed by Thomas Mann (among others): "One advanced and offensive degenerate after another: a self-castrated magician; a desperate double personality, composed of a Circe and a repentant Magdalene, with cataleptic transition stages; a lovesick high-priest, awaiting the redemption that is to come to him in the person of a chaste youth; the youth himself, 'pure' fool and redeemer."[22]

The way to introduce some order into this apparent mess is by simple reference to the four elements of the Lacanian discourse-matrix: the maimed king Amfortas as S_1, the Master; the magician Klingsor as the semblance of knowledge, S_2 (the semblance pertaining to Klingsor's status is attested to by the phantasmagorical character of his magic castle: as soon as Parsifal makes the sign of the cross, it collapses);[23] Kundry as $\$$, the split hysterical woman (what she demands from the other is precisely to refuse her demand, i.e., to resist her conquest); Parsifal, the "pure fool," as *objet petit a*, the object-cause of Kundry's desire, yet totally insensitive to feminine charms.[24] The further uncanny feature is the lack of any proper action in the opera. What actually takes place is a succession of negative or empty, purely symbolic gestures: Parsifal *fails to understand* the ritual; he *refuses* Kundry's advances; he *makes the sign* of the cross with the spear; he *proclaims* himself king. Therein consists the most sublime dimension of *Parsifal*: it dispenses wholly with the usual "action" (with positively "doing something") and limits itself to the most elementary opposition between the act of renunciation / refusal and the empty symbolic gesture.[25] Parsifal makes two decisive gestures: in act 2 he rejects Kundry's advances, and in act 3, in what is perhaps the crucial turning point of the opera, he proclaims himself king, accompanied by the fourfold beat of the drum (". . . that he may greet me today as king"). In the first case, we have the act qua repetition by means of which Parsifal identifies with Amfortas's suffering, taking it upon himself; in the second case, we have the act qua performative by means of which Parsifal assumes the symbolic mandate of the king, the keeper of the Grail.[26] So, what can this set of eccentrics and their (non-) deeds tell us?

"I Am Going to Talk to You about the Lamella . . ."

Let us begin by taking a closer look at the mysterious wound which prevents Amfortas from finding peace in death. This wound, of course, is another name for its opposite, for a certain surplus of *jouissance*. To delineate more precisely its contours, let us take as our starting point a new book on Lacan, Richard Boothby's *Death and Desire*.[27] Its central thesis, although ultimately false, is deeply satisfying in the sense of a demand for symmetry: it is as if it provides the missing element of a puzzle. The triad Imaginary-Real-Symbolic renders the fundamental coordinates of the Lacanian theoretical space; but these three dimensions can never be conceived simultaneously, in pure synchronicity, i.e., one is always forced to choose one pair at a time (as with Kierkegaard's triad of the aesthetical-ethical-religious): the Symbolic versus the Imaginary, the Real versus the Symbolic. The hitherto predominating interpretations of Lacan tended to accent either the axis Imaginary-Symbolic (symbolization, symbolic realization, against imaginary self-deception in the Lacan of the fifties) or the axis Symbolic-Real (the traumatic encounter of the Real as the point at which symbolization fails in the late Lacan). What Boothby offers as a key to the entire Lacanian theoretical edifice is simply the third, not yet exploited axis: the Imaginary versus the Real. That is to say, according to Boothby, the theory of the mirror-stage is not only chronologically Lacan's first contribution to psychoanalysis but designates also the original fact which defines the status of man: the alienation in the mirror image, due to man's premature birth and his/her helplessness in the first years of life, this fixation on *imago* interrupts the supple life-flow, it introduces an irreducible *béance*, gap, separating forever the imaginary ego—the wholesome yet immobile mirror image, a kind of halted cinematic picture—from the polymorphous, chaotic sprout of bodily drives—the real Id. From this perspective, the Symbolic is of a strictly secondary nature with regard to the original tension between the Imaginary and the Real: its place is the void opened up by the exclusion of the polymorphous wealth of bodily drives. Symbolization designates the subject's endeavor, always fragmentary and ultimately doomed to fail, to bring to the light of the day, by way of symbolic representatives, the Real of bodily drives excluded by imaginary identification; it is therefore a kind of compromise-formation by way of which the subject integrates fragments of the ostracized Real.

In this sense, Boothby interprets the death-drive as the reemergence of what was ostracized when the ego constituted itself by way of imaginary identification: the return of the polymorphous impulses is experienced by the ego as a mortal threat, since it actually entails the dissolution of its imaginary identity. The foreclosed Real thus returns in two modes: as a wild, destructive, nonsymbolized raging, or in the form of symbolic media-tion, i.e., "sublated" (*aufgehoben*) in the symbolic medium. The elegance of Boothby's theory turns on interpreting the death-drive as its very opposite: as the return of the life-force, of the part of Id excluded by the imposition of the petrified mask of the ego. Thus, what reemerges in the "death-drive" is *ultimately life itself,* and the fact that the ego perceives this return as a death threat precisely confirms the ego's perverted "repressive" character. The "death-drive" means that life itself rebels against the ego: the true represen-tative of death is ego itself, as the petrified *imago* which interrupts the flow of life.

Against this background, Boothby also reinterprets Lacan's distinction between the two deaths: the first death is the death of the ego, the dissolu-tion of its imaginary identifications, whereas the second death designates the interruption of the pre-symbolic life-flow itself. Here, however, prob-lems begin with this otherwise simple and elegant construction: the price to be paid is that Lacan's theoretical edifice is ultimately reduced to the opposition which characterizes the field of *Lebensphilosophie,* i.e., to the opposition between an original polymorphous life-force and its later coag-ulation, confinement to the Procrustian bed of *imagos.* For this reason, Boothby's scheme has no place for the fundamental Lacanian insight ac-cording to which the symbolic order "stands for death" in the precise sense of "mortifying" the real of the body, of subordinating it to a foreign autom-atism, of perturbing its "natural," instinctual rhythm, *thereby producing the surplus of desire, i.e., desire AS a surplus:* the very symbolic machine which "mortifies" the living body produces by the same token the opposite of mortification, the immortal desire, the Real of "pure life" which eludes symbolization.

To clarify this point, let us turn to an example which, in a first approach, may seem to confirm Boothby's thesis: Wagner's *Tristan und Isolde.* What precise effect does the philtre provided by Isolde's faithful maid Brangäne have on the future lovers? "Wagner never intends to imply that the love of Tristan and Isolde is the *physical consequence* of the philtre, but only that the pair, having drunk what they imagine to be the draught of Death and believing that they have looked upon earth and sea and sky for the last time, feel themselves free to confess, when the potion begins its work within them, the love they have so long felt but have concealed from each other and almost from themselves."[28] The point is, therefore, that after drinking the philtre, Tristan and Isolde find themselves in the domain "between the two deaths," alive, yet delivered of all symbolic ties. *Only in such a subjective position are they able to confess their love.* In other words, the "magical effect" of the philtre is simply to suspend the "big Other," the symbolic reality of social obligations (honors, vows . . .). Does this thesis not fully accord with Boothby's view of the domain "between the two deaths" as the space where imaginary identification, as well as the symbolic identities attached to it, are all invalidated, so that the excluded Real (pure life-drive) can emerge in all its force, although in the form of its opposite, the death-drive? According to Wagner himself, the passion of Tristan and Isolde expresses the longing for the "eternal peace" of death. The trap to be avoided here, however, is conceiving of this pure life-drive as a substantial entity subsisting prior to its being captured in the symbolic network: this "optical illusion" renders invisible how it is the very mediation of the symbolic order that transforms the organic "instinct" into an unquenchable longing which can find solace only in death. In other words, this "pure life" beyond death, this longing that reaches beyond the circuit of generation and corruption, is it not the *product* of symbolization, so that symbolization itself engenders the surplus which escapes it? By conceiving of the symbolic order as an agency which fills out the gap between the Imaginary and the Real opened up by the mirror-identification, Boothby avoids its constitutive paradox: the Symbolic itself opens up the wound it professes to heal.

What one should do here, in the space of a more detailed theoretical elaboration, is to approach in a new way the Lacan-Heidegger relationship. In the fifties, Lacan endeavored to read the "death-drive" against the background of Heidegger's "being-toward-death" (*Sein-zum-Tode*), conceiving of death as the inherent and ultimate limit of symbolization, which accounts for its irreducible temporal character. With Lacan's shift toward the Real from the sixties onward, it is the indestructible life sprouting in the domain "between the two deaths" that emerges as the ultimate object of horror. Lacan delineates its contours toward the end of chapter 15, of his *Four Fundamental Concepts of Psycho-Analysis* where he proposes his own myth, constructed upon the model of Aristophanes' fable from Plato's *Symposium*, the myth of *l'hommelette* (little female-man—omelette[29]):

Whenever the membranes of the egg in which the foetus emerges on its way to becoming a new-born are broken, imagine for a moment that something flies off, and that one can do it with an egg as easily as with a man, namely the *hommelette,* or the lamella.

The lamella is something extra-flat, which moves like the amoeba. It is just a little more complicated. But it goes everywhere. And as it is something . . . that is related to what the sexed being loses in sexuality, it is, like the amoeba in relation to sexed beings, immortal—because it survives any division, any scissiparous intervention. And it can run around.

Well! This is not very reassuring. But suppose it comes and envelopes your face while you are quietly asleep . . .

I can't see how we would not join battle with a being capable of these properties. But it would not be a very convenient battle. This lamella, this organ, whose characteristic is not to exist, but which is nevertheless an organ . . . is the libido.

It is the libido, qua pure life instinct, that is to say, immortal life, or irrepressible life, life that has need of no organ, simplified, indestructible life. It is precisely what is subtracted from the living being by virtue of the fact that it is subject to the cycle of sexed reproduction. And it is of this that all the forms of the *objet a* that can be enumerated are the representatives, the equivalents. The *objets a* are merely its representatives, its figures. The breast—as equivocal, as an element characteristic of the mammiferous organization, the placenta for example—certainly represents that part of himself that the individual loses at birth, and which may serve to symbolize the most profound lost object.[30]

What we have here is an Otherness prior to intersubjectivity: the subject's "impossible" relationship to this amoebalike creature is what Lacan is ultimately aiming at by way of his formula $S \lozenge a$.[31] The best way to clarify this point is perhaps to allow ourselves the string of popular-culture associations that Lacan's description must evoke. Is not the *alien* from Ridley Scott's film of the same title "lamella" in its purest? Are not all the key elements of Lacan's myth contained in the first truly horrifying scene of the film when, in the womblike cave of the unknown planet, the "alien" leaps from the egglike globe when its lid splits off and sticks to John Hurt's face? This amoebalike, flattened creature, which envelops the subject's face, stands for the irrepressible life beyond all the finite forms that are merely its representatives, its figures (later in the film, the "alien" is able to assume a multitude of different shapes), immortal and indestructible (it suffices to recall the unpleasant thrill of the moment when a scientist cuts with a scalpel into a leg of the creature which envelops Hurt's face: the liquid that drips from it falls onto the metal floor and corrodes it immediately; nothing can resist it).[32]

The second association which brings us back to Wagner is a detail from Syberberg's film version of *Parsifal:* Syberberg depicts Amfortas's wound as externalized, carried by the servants on a pillow in front of him, in the form of a vaginalike partial object out of which blood drips in a continuous flow (as, *vulgari eloquentia*, a vagina in an unending period). This palpitating opening—an organ which is at the same time the entire organism (let us just recall a homologous motif in a series of science fiction stories, like the gigantic eye living a life of its own)—this opening epitomizes life in its indestructibility: Amfortas's pain consists in the very fact that he is unable to die, that he is condemned to an eternal life of suffering; when, at the end, Parsifal heals his wound with "the spear that smote it," Amfortas is finally able to rest and die. This wound of Amfortas's, which persists outside himself as an *undead* thing, is the "object of psychoanalysis."[33]

The Wagnerian Performative

If, then, *The Flying Dutchman* renders the fundamental matrix of Wagner's universe—man's redemption through woman's self-sacrifice—*Parsifal*, his last opera, is to be conceived as the concluding point of a series of variations, the same blissful point of exception as Mozart's *Magic Flute*.[34] The parallel between *The Magic Flute* and *Parsifal* is a commonplace. Suffice it to recall a nice detail from Bergman's film version of *The Flute:* during the break between acts 1 and 2, the actor who sings Sarastro studies the score of *Parsifal.* In both cases, a youthful, initially ignorant hero, after successfully enduring the test, takes the place of the old ruler of the temple (Sarastro is replaced by Tamino and Amfortas by Parsifal); Jacques Chailley even composed a unique narrative in which all we have to do in order to obtain the story of either *The Magic Flute* or *Parsifal* is to insert the proper variables: "(Parsifal / Tamino), a prince from the East, has left his (mother / father) in search of the unknown (knights / kingdom)," etc.[35] What is even more crucial than these parallels in the narrative content is the *initiatory* character of both operas: events which, at first glance, are nothing but meaning-less peripeteias (Parsifal's bringing down of the swan, Tamino's fight with the dragon, the momentary loss of consciousness which follows this con-frontation; etc.) become intelligible the moment we conceive of them as elements of an initiatory ritual. In both *The Magic Flute* and *Parsifal,* the price to be paid for the reversal into bliss is thus the "transubstantiation" of the action: external events change into mysterious signs to be deciphered. Most interpreters fall into this trap of allegorization and try to provide a secret code for the reading of *Parsifal* (Chailley sees in it the staging of the Free Masonic initiatory ritual, while Robert Donnington offers a Jungian reading: *Parsifal* is an allegory of the transmutations of the hero's psyche, of his inner journey from the initial breaking out of the incestuous closure to the final reconciliation with the "eternally feminine"; etc.). Our aim, how-ever, is to *resist* the temptation of decoding. How, then, are we to proceed?

One way is offered by the Lévi-Straussian differential approach: our attention should focus on those features which differentiate *Parsifal* from Wagner's previous operas, as well as from the traditional version of the Grail myth. The difference from the *Dutchman* is that here the suffering hero—the Fisher King Amfortas—is delivered by a "pure fool," Parsifal, not by the woman. Whence the difference, the misogynist reversal? The main enigma of—and at the same time the key to—Wagner's *Parsifal* is that Wagner leaves unexploited the crucial component of the original legend of Parsifal, the so-called Question Test. According to the original legend, when Parsifal first witnesses the Grail ceremony, he is perplexed by what he sees—the maimed king, the display of a strange, magic vessel—but out of respect and consideration he abstains from inquiring about the meaning of it all. Later, he learns that he thereby committed a fateful mistake: were he to ask Amfortas what is wrong with him and for whom the Grail is intended, Amfortas would be delivered from his torment. After a series of ordeals, Parsifal again visits the Fisher King, asks the proper question, and thus delivers him. Furthermore, Wagner simplifies the Grail ceremony by reducing it to the display of the Grail vessel. He leaves out the original legend's uncanny dreamlike scene in which a young squire frantically and repeatedly runs across the hall of the Fisher King's castle during the dinner, displaying the lance with drops of blood dripping from its point and thus provoking ritualistic cries of horror and grief from the attending knights.

What we have here is the compulsive-neurotic ritual in its purest form, similar to that of a thirty-year-old married woman, noted by Freud: "She ran from her room into another neighbouring one, took up a particular position there beside a table that stood in the middle, rang the bell for her housemaid, sent her on some indifferent errand or let her go without one, and then ran back into her own room."[36] The interpretation: during her wedding night, her husband had been impotent; he had come running repeatedly from his room into hers to try once more. Next morning, out of shame that the housemaid would not find traces of blood (the sign of his success in deflowering the bride), he poured some red ink over the sheet. The key to the present ritualistic symptom is that on a table beside which the woman stationed herself was a big stain. By taking up this strange position, the woman wanted to prove to the Other's gaze (epitomized by the housemaid) that "the stain is there," i.e., her aim was literally to attract the Other's gaze to a certain stain, a little fragment of the real which proves the husband's sexual potency. (At the time that the symptom occurred, the woman was in the process of obtaining a divorce from her husband: the aim of the symptom was to protect him from malicious gossip about the true cause of the divorce, i.e., to prevent the Other from registering his impotence.) And, perhaps, the compulsive displaying of the bleeding lance in the traditional version of the Parsifal myth is to be read along the same lines, as proof of the King's potency (if we accept the interpretation of the bleeding lance as the condensation of two opposing features: not only the weapon which deals the wound and thus causes the King's paralysis, but at the same time the phallus which, as is proven by the blood on its tip, successfully performed the deflowering).

By virtue of the Question Test, *Parsifal* functions as a complementary opposite to Wagner's *Lohengrin*, the opera centered on the theme of the forbidden question, i.e., on the paradox of self-destructive female curiosity. In *Lohengrin*, a nameless hero saves Elsa von Brabant and marries her, but enjoins her not to ask him who he is or what his name is; as soon as she does so, he will be obliged to leave her (the famous air "Nie solst du mich befragen" from act 1). Unable to resist temptation, Elsa asks him the fateful question; so, in an even more famous air ("In fernem Land," act 3), Lohengrin tells her that he is a knight of the Grail, the son of Parsifal from the castle of Montsalvat, and then departs on a swan, while the unfortunate Elsa falls dead.[37] How not to recall here Superman or Batman, where we find the same logic: in both cases, the woman has a presentiment that her partner (the confused journalist in *Superman*, the eccentric millionaire in *Batman*) is really the mysterious public hero, but the partner puts off as long as possible the moment of revelation. What we have here is a kind of forced choice attesting to the dimension of castration: man is split, divided into the weak everyday fellow with whom a sexual relation is possible and the bearer of the symbolic mandate, the public hero (knight of the Grail, Superman, Batman). We are thus obliged to choose: if we are to maintain the possibility of sexual relation, we have to abstain from probing into our partner's "true identity"; as soon as we force the sexual partner to reveal his symbolic identity, we are bound to lose him.[38] Here, it would be possible to articulate a general theory of the "Wagnerian performative" reaching from *The Flying Dutchman* (when, at its end, the offended unknown captain publicly announces that he is the "flying Dutchman" wandering the oceans for centuries in search of a faithful wife, Senta throws herself from a cliff to her death) to *Parsifal* (when Parsifal takes over the function of the king and reveals the Grail, Kundry drops dead). In all these cases, the performative gesture by means of which the hero openly assumes his symbolic mandate, revealing his symbolic identity, proves incompatible with the very being of woman. The paradox of *Parsifal*, however, concerns its reversal of the Question Test in *Lohengrin*: the fateful consequences of a *failure* to ask the required question.[39] How are we to interpret it?

Beyond the Phallus

What we encounter in the Question Test is a pure case of the logic of the symptom in its relationship to the big Other qua symbolic order: the bodily wound—symptom—can be healed by being put into words; i.e., the symbolic order can produce an effect upon the real. Parsifal thus stands for the big Other in its ignorant neutrality: the enunciation of a simple "What's wrong with you?", somewhat like Bugs Bunny's famous "What's up, Doc?", would trigger the avalanche of symbolization and the king's wound would be healed by being integrated into the symbolic universe, i.e., by way of its symbolic realization.[40] Perhaps a symptom, in its most elementary definition, is not a question without an answer but rather an answer without its question, i.e., bereft of its proper symbolic context. This question cannot be asked by the knights themselves, it must come from outside, from somebody who epitomizes the big Other in its blessed ignorance. One is tempted to evoke an everyday experience: a stuffy atmosphere in a closed community where the tension is suddenly broken once a stranger asks the naive question about what is actually going on.[41]

Yet Wagner left this line unexploited: why? The first, superficial yet quite accurate answer is: the second act. That is to say, it would be easy to transpose the traditional myth into an opera in two acts; what takes place between Mozart and Wagner is simply *the second act:* between Mozart's traditional two acts (the formula followed also by Beethoven in *Fidelio*) creeps in another act, and it is here, in the second act (of *Lohengrin, Walkyre, The Twilight of the Gods, Parsifal . . .*), that the crucial shift occurs, namely the step into "hystericization" which confers on the action the "modern" touch.[42] One is thus even tempted to arrange the inherent logic of the three acts of *Parsifal* by reference to Lacanian logical time.[43] The first act involves the "instant of looking": Parsifal looks, witnesses the ritual, but understands nothing; the second act marks the "time for understanding": through meeting Kundry, Parsifal perceives the meaning of Amfortas's suffering; the third act brings about the "moment for concluding," the performative decision: Parsifal delivers Amfortas from his suffering and takes his place.

The cause of this interpolation of a supplementary act is a certain change in the status of the big Other.[44] In Wagner, the "pure fool" Parsifal is no longer a stand-in for the big Other, but—what? Here, a comparison between *Parsifal* and *The Magic Flute* can be of some help. In *The Magic Flute* the old king Sarastro retires in full splendor and dignity, whereas in *Parsifal*, Amfortas is maimed and therefore unable to officiate, to perform his—let us say—bureaucratic duty; *The Magic Flute* is a hymn to the bourgeois couple in which, notwithstanding the numerous male-chauvinist "wisdoms," it is ultimately the woman—Pamina—who leads her man through the fire-and-water ordeal, whereas in *Parsifal* woman is rejected—the hero's capacity to resist her is precisely what is at stake in the ordeal. (Also in *The Magic Flute*, Tamino's crucial test concerns his ability to keep his silence when faced with Pamina's desperate pleas and thus to endure her symbolic loss; yet this loss functions as a step toward the constitution of the couple.)[45] In *Parsifal*, the woman is literally reduced to a symptom of man—she is caught in a cataleptic torpor, aroused only by her master's voice or injunction.

"Woman is a symptom of man" seems to be one of the most notoriously "antifeminist" theses of Lacan. But a fundamental ambiguity arises from this thesis, reflecting the shift in the notion of the symptom within Lacanian theory. If we conceive of the symptom as a *ciphered message*, then, of course, woman-symptom appears as the sign, the embodiment of Man's

Fall, attesting to the fact that Man "gave way as to his desire." For Freud, the symptom is a compromise-formation: in the symptom, the subject gets back, in the form of a ciphered, unrecognized message, the truth about his desire, the truth that he betrayed or was not able to confront. So, if we read the thesis "Woman is a symptom of man" against this background, we inevitably approach the position that was most forcefully articulated by Otto Weininger, Freud's contemporary, a notorious Viennese antifeminist and anti-Semite from the turn of the century, who wrote the extremely influential bestseller *Sex and Character*[46] and then committed suicide at the age of twenty-four. Weininger's position is that, according to her very ontological status, woman is nothing but a materialization of man's Sin: in herself, she doesn't exist, which is why the proper way to be rid of her is not to fight her actively or to destroy her; it is enough for Man to purify his desire, to rise to pure spirituality, and, automatically, woman loses the ground under her feet, she disintegrates. No wonder, then, that Wagner's *Parsifal* was the basic reference for Weininger and that Wagner was for him the greatest man after Christ: when Parsifal purifies his desire and rejects Kundry, she loses her speech, changes into a mute shadow and finally drops dead—proof that she existed only insofar as she attracted the male gaze.

This tradition, which may appear extravagant and outdated, reemerged more recently in *film noir*, where the *femme fatale* also changes into a formless, mucuous slime without proper ontological consistency the moment the hard-boiled hero rejects her, i.e., breaks her spell upon him. Witness the final confrontation of Sam Spade with Brigid O'Shaughnessy in Hammett's *Maltese Falcon*. We have thus the male world of pure spirituality and undistorted communication, communication without constraint (if we may be permitted to use this Habermasian syntagm), the universe of ideal intersubjectivity, and Woman is *not* an external, active cause which lures Man into Fall; she is just a *consequence*, a result, a materialization of Man's fall. So, when Man purifies his desire of the pathological remainders, Woman disintegrates in precisely the same way as a symptom dissolves after successful interpretation, after we have symbolized its repressed meaning. Does not Lacan's other notorious thesis—the claim that "Woman doesn't exist"—point in the same direction? Woman doesn't exist in herself, as a positive entity with full ontological consistency, but only as a symptom of Man. Weininger was also quite outspoken about the desire compromised or betrayed when Man falls prey to a woman: the death-drive. After all the talk about man's superior spirituality, which is inaccessible to women, etc., he proposes, in the last pages of *Sex and Character*, collective suicide as the only path of salvation open for humanity.

If, however, we conceive the symptom as it was articulated in Lacan's last writings and seminars—as, for example, when he speaks about "Joyce-the-symptom"—namely, as a particular signifying formation which confers on the subject its very ontological consistency, enabling it to structure its basic, constitutive relationship toward *jouissance*, then the entire relationship between the symptom and the subject is reversed: if the symptom is dissolved, the subject loses the ground under his feet, he disintegrates. In this sense, "Woman is a symptom of man" means that *Man himself exists only through woman qua his symptom:* all his ontological consistency hangs on, is suspended from, is "externalized" in his symptom. In other words, man literally *ex-sists:* his entire being lies "out there," in woman. Woman, on the other hand, does *not* exist, she *insists,* which is why she does not come to be only through man. Something in her escapes the relation to Man, the reference to the phallic enjoyment; and, as is well known, Lacan endeavored to capture this excess by the notion of a *"non-all" feminine jouissance.*[47] This, however, opens up the possibility of a different reading of *Parsifal:* Syberberg was again right when, after the crucial moment of conversion (i.e., after Parsifal refuses Kundry's kiss), he replaced the male actor playing Parsifal with a woman. Woman is the symptom of man, caught in the hysterical game of demanding that he refuse her demand, precisely to the extent to which she is submitted to the phallic enjoyment. Wagner's fundamental matrix appears thereby in a different perspective: *woman redeems man by renouncing phallic enjoyment.*[48] (What we have here is the exact opposite to Weininger where man redeems-destroys woman by overcoming his phallicity.) This is what Wagner was not able to confront, and the price to be paid for this avoidance fully to assume the "feminization" of Parsifal after he enters the domain "beyond the phallus" was the fall into perversion.[49]

More precisely, what Wagner was not able to confront is the "feminine" nature of Parsifal's identification with Amfortas at the moment of Kundry's kiss: far from being reducible to a case of successful (symbolic) communication, this "compassion" is founded on the identification with the *real* of Amfortas's suffering; it involves the *repetition* of Amfortas's pain in the Kierkegaardian sense.[50] On that account, Syberberg's decision to alternate two actors, a male and a female, in the role of Parsifal should in no way trap us into the Jungian ideology of hermaphroditism according to which the figure of mature Parsifal stands for the reconciliation between male and female "principles." This alternation functions instead as a critical sting aimed at Wagner, a reminder that *Parsifal is not feasible as a unique, psychologically "coherent" personality:*[51] he is split into himself and "what is in him more than himself," his sublime shadowy double (Parsifal-woman first appears in the background as the ethereal double of Parsifal-man and then gradually takes over his place).[52] In the course of this transmutation *the voice remains the same* (Parsifal continues to be sung by a tenor); we thus obtain a kind of negative of Norman-Mrs. Bates from Hitchcock's *Psycho:* the monstrous apparition of an apathetically cold woman using a man's voice (the true opposite to the caricature image of a transvestite, of a man dressing up as a woman and imitating the heightened feminine voice). Syberberg's Parsifal-woman is a man who has cast off the phallic semblance, like a snake getting rid of its skin. What is subverted thereby is the ideology of "femininity as masquerade" according to which man is "man as such," the embodiment of the human genus, whereas woman is a man from whom something is missing (who is "castrated") and who resorts to masquerade in order to conceal this lack. But, on the contrary, it is the phallus, the phallic predicate, whose status is that of a semblance, so that when we throw off its mask, a woman appears.

Here, again, the key is provided by comparison with the history of the opera: in Gluck, Orpheus is sung by a woman, and this sexual ambiguity continues up through Mozart in whose *Le Nozze di Figaro* the role of Cherubino, the principal rival and "obstructionist" of the Count, this agent of pure sexuality, is sung by a soprano.[53] Perhaps we could conceive the couple Amfortas-Parsifal as the last permutation of the couple Count-Cherubino: in *Le Nozze,* the counterpoint to the Count (to this helpless, yet in no way crippled, but quite on the contrary prepotent Master) is *a man with a feminine voice,* whereas in *Parsifal,* the counterpoint to the maimed king Amfortas is *a woman with a masculine voice.* This change allows us to measure the historical shift that separates the end of the eighteenth century from the end of the nineteenth century: the objectal surplus which sticks out from the intersubjective network is no longer the elusive semblance of pure phallic sexuality[54] but rather the embodiment of the saintly-ascetic *jouissance* beyond phallus.

Safe-keeping God's Jouissance

The parallel between the gestures of Grace preventing the hero's suicide in *The Magic Flute* and in *Parsifal* should therefore not blind us to the crucial difference: in *Parsifal,* the subjectivization is strictly perverse, it equals its opposite, namely self-objectivization, conceiving oneself as an instrument of the *jouissance* of the big Other. It is here, in this notion of the Other's *jouissance,* that we should seek the roots of Wagner's anti-Semitism: what he resisted was the idea of a formal, empty Law, i.e., the Jewish prohibition to fill out God's Name with a positive content. As Lacan put it, pre-Jewish, pagan Gods belong to the Real: we gain access to them only through sacred *jouissance* (ritualistic orgies); their domain is that of the Unnameable. What the Jewish religion accomplishes is the radical evacuation of *jouissance* from the divine domain, the crucial consequence of which is a kind of reflective reversal of the prohibition: the prohibition to name the divine-sacred Real is inverted into the prohibition to fill out God's Name with a positive bearer, with His image. In short, what is now prohibited is not naming the unnameable Real but attaching to the Name any positive reality: *the Name must remain empty.* This reversal concerns, among other things, the very notion of democracy: as was shown by Claude Lefort, democracy implies the distinction between the empty symbolic locus of power and the reality of those who, temporarily, exercise power; for democracy to function, the locus of power must remain empty; nobody is allowed to present himself as possessing the immediate, natural right to exercise power.[55] And the idea of the Grail as the vessel containing the blood of Christ has to be read against this background: this blood which continues to shine and give life, what is it ultimately if not *the "little piece of the real" which immediately legitimizes power,* i.e., which "naturally" belongs to and defines the locus of power? This part of Christ which remained alive, which did *not* expire on the cross, designates the surplus of the divine *jouissance,* the part of it which was *not* evacuated from the domain of the big Other. In short, to spell out the theological consequences of such a view: Wagner's radically perverse idea was to "get Christ down from the Cross, or rather stop him from getting on it": "I have no doubt that Robert Raphael is right when he says that Parsifal, 'having now redeemed himself by insight and empathy, symbolizes a Christ who *does not have to die,* but lives.' The point about not having to die is that Wagner . . . is repelled by the idea of the Second Person of the Holy Trinity dying in order that the First Person should allow man into Heaven."[56] This is what Wagner ultimately has in mind by the "redemption of the redeemer": Christ does not have to die in order to redeem us. In Christianity proper, Christ redeems us by way of his death on the Cross, whereas for Wagner, the source of redemption is precisely that part of Christ which remained alive, which did *not* expire on the Cross.

Parsifal thus bears witness to a deep perturbance in the "normal" relationship of life and death: the denial of the will to life, yet simultaneously the phantasmagoria of a life beyond death, beyond the circuit of generation and corruption. The death toward which the Wagnerian hero tends is the "second death," the denial not of the "natural" life-circuit but of the "lamella," of the indestructible libido. The gulf separating Wagner from Christianity is here effectively insurmountable: in Christianity, eternal life is the life beyond death, the life in the Holy Spirit, and as such an object of adoration; whereas in Wagner, this indestructible life entails a vision of endless suffering. Now we can see why, enraptured by the magic of Good Friday, Parsifal is able to perceive the innocence of nature: this nature, caught in the simple circuit of generation and corruption, is delivered from the pressure of the indestructible drive which persists beyond death.[57] The political consequences of these seemingly abstract ruminations affect us all: the replacement of Amfortas by Parsifal is the replacement of the traditional patriarchal authority by the totalitarian object-instrument of the Other's *jouissance,* the safekeeper of God's Enjoyment (epitomized by the Grail).

This political background emerges in precisely those features of *Parsifal* which pose such a problem to traditional interpreters, since they stick out as a kind of uncanny surplus, disturbing the apparent symmetry between the two kingdoms, the bright kingdom of the Grail and Klingsor's kingdom of the dark, attesting to an obscene, dark obverse of the kingdom of the Grail itself. According to Lucy Beckett, for example, *Parsifal* twice reverts to an incomprehensible, out-of-place morbidity: the cruel, inexorable pressure exerted by the Grail knights on Amfortas in the finale of act 3 (they encircle him as if he were a wounded animal), which runs counter to the peaceful, blessed nature of the Grail community; the morbid dialogue between Amfortas and his father Titurel in the finale of act 1 (Titurel demands of Amfortas that he perform the required ritual and uncover the Grail in order that he be able to survive—Titurel qua living dead no longer lives off earthly food but solely off the enjoyment procured by the sight of the Grail; Amfortas desperately proposes that Titurel himself perform the ritual and that he be allowed to die). This dialogue attests to the inherently anti-Oedipal character of the Grail kingdom:[58] instead of the son killing the father, who then returns as the Name, in the guise of the symbolic authority of the dead father (the standard Oedipal scenario) we have the son who wants to die so that his father can stay alive and continue to bathe in his enjoyment. In Titurel, we thus have the purest personification of the superego: he is literally a living dead, lying in a coffin, kept alive by the sight of the Redeemer's blood, i.e., by the substance of pure enjoyment; never seen on stage, he is present as *la voix acousmatique,* a free-floating voice without a bearer[59] which persecutes his son with the unconditional injunction, "Accomplish your duty! Perform the ritual!"—the injunction Titurel pronounces *in order to procure his own enjoyment.* The obscenity of Klingsor's "black magic" has therefore its strict correlative in the superego-obscenity of Titurel's "white magic": Titurel is undoubtedly the most obscene figure in *Parsifal,* a kind of undead father, parasitic on his own son.[60] This morbid, cruel side of the Grail's temple is what Christian interpreters quite justly are leery of, since it manifests the true nature of *Parsifal:* a work whose ultimate accomplishment is to confer upon a Christian content the form of pagan ritual.[61]

With the new notion of the hero—an innocent, ignorant, pure fool, who eludes the splitting constitutive of subjectivity—the circle is in a way closed; we find ourselves again in the domain of unconditional authority: Parsifal's becoming king is not a result of his heroic deeds, he is not qualified for it by any positive feature; quite the contrary, he was able to withstand Kundry's advances because, from the very beginning, he was the Chosen One. However, this new authority differs from the traditional one in its relationship to the big Other of the Law: the traditional authority addressed by the hero's entreaty, from Monteverdi to Mozart, was capable of effectively stepping on its own shoulders and suspending its own Law in the act of Mercy. Thus the agency of the Law coincides with the agency of its momentary suspension, i.e., the Other is at the same time the Other of the Other, whereas already in Wagner's *Ring,* the God (Wotan), interpellated by the two giants in *Rhinegold* as the guarantor of the social contract, gets so entangled in his own inconsistencies that the only solution he can envisage is an act of redemption accomplished by a totally ignorant hero who will have nothing to do with the domain of the Gods. Therein consists Wagner's crucial shift: "the wound can be healed" only by a free act which, in a radical sense, *comes from the outside,* i.e., is not engendered by the symbolic system itself.

Nagel refers to Kierkegaard's famous reading of Mozart's *Don Giovanni* in order to be able to jump immediately to modern totalitarianism, via Kierkegaard's reaffirmation of blind, unconditional authority:

After Kierkegaard, the disabled self survives the annihilation of the autonomous subject, which it announces, by excepting itself (as a political theologian or mythologist) from the common fate: to be the self-appointed spokesman of mute domination. It prophesies, propagates a new world of sacrifice, whose murderous law is impenetrability—and whose murderous impenetrability will be called law. Soon, Franz Kafka's tales and Carl Schmitt's jurisprudence will mock the enlightened demand for clear and accessible laws as liberal hairsplitting; indeed such querulous claims of the individual will constitute, for the court of mythical willfulness, proof of his guilt, the very reason for his condemnation.[62]

Wagner's *Parsifal* thus provides the answer to the question: what happens when the subject takes upon himself the symbolic gesture, the "prerogative of mercy," which, in Mozart and Beethoven, still belonged to the big Other? The assumption of this gesture is paid for by the loss of "actual" power: all that is left to the subject is the empty, formal act of assent, the tautological performative by means of which he appoints himself the "spokesman of mute domination." What is thus missing in Nagel's account is the place of Wagner as what fills in the gap between the apotheosis of the bourgeois couple in *The Magic Flute* and *Fidelio* and the totalitarian symbolic economy discernible in the works of Kafka and Schmitt.

The Perverse Loop

At the level of libidinal economy, totalitarianism is defined by a perverse self-objectivization (self-instrumentalization) of the subject. But what, then, is the difference between perversion and the most elementary ideological act of self-legitimization in which we also encounter a kind of "redemption of the redeemer"? Lincoln's Gettysburg Address is deservedly so famous because it accomplishes in an exemplary way this act of self-legitimization. It first defines its task: we are here to commemorate the dead at the sacred place of their death ("We have come to dedicate a portion of that field as a final resting place for those who here gave their lives that that nation might live"). Then it proceeds to invoke the inherent impossibility of performing this task: "in a larger sense" we cannot do it, since those who died here have already done it with their glorious deeds in a way far superior to what we can do with mere words; their sacrifice has already dedicated this battlefield and it would be arrogant for us even to pretend that we are in a position to dedicate it ("But in a larger sense we can not dedicate—we can not consecrate—we can not hallow—this ground. The brave men living and dead who struggled here have consecrated it far above our poor power to add or detract"). What then follows is the crucial reflective inversion of subject and object: "it is for us the living rather to be dedicated here to the unfinished work which they who fought here have thus far so nobly advanced," that is to say, to dedicate ourselves to the task of continuing their work, so that they "shall not have died in vain." (For that reason, it is not sufficient here to distinguish the two levels by saying that "in a narrower sense" we dedicate the battlefield, whereas "in a larger sense" we dedicate ourselves: this "larger sense" is simply *the sense tout court*, i.e., it is this very reflexive reversal which brings about the sense-effect.) The result of this inversion is a circle of dedication whereby the two poles support each other: by dedicating ourselves to the task of successfully bringing to an end the work of those who sacrificed their lives, we will make sure that their sacrifice was not in vain, that they will continue to live in our memory; in this way, we will effectively commemorate them; if we do not accomplish this task of ours, they will be forgotten, they will have died in vain. So, by dedicating the place to their memory, what we actually do is dedicate, legitimize ourselves as the continuators of their work—we legitimize our own role. This gesture of self-legitimization through the other is ideology in its purest: the dead are our redeemers, and by dedicating ourselves to continuing their work we redeem the redeemers. In a sense, Lincoln makes himself seen to the dead; his message to them is "here we are, ready to go on . . ."—therein consists the ultimate sense of the Gettysburg Address.

Yet is Lincoln for all that a pervert? Does he conceive of himself as an object-instrument of the *jouissance* of the Other, i.e., of the dead heroes? No: the crucial point here is to maintain the difference between this traditional ideological vicious circle and the loop of the perverse sacrifice. Let us recall our first example of it: Orpheus who looked back and thus intentionally sacrificed Euridice in order to regain her as the sublime object of poetic inspiration. This, then, is the logic of perversion: it is quite normal to say to the beloved woman, "I would love you even if you were wrinkled and mutilated!"; a perverse person is the one who intentionally mutilates the woman, distorts her beautiful face, so that he can then continue to love her, thereby proving the sublime nature of his love. An exemplary case of this short-circuit is Patricia Highsmith's early masterpiece, the short story

"Heroine," about a young governess extremely eager to prove her devotion to the family whose child she is taking care of; since her everyday acts pass unnoticed, she ends by setting the house on fire, so that she has the opportunity to save the child from the flames. This closed loop is what defines perversion.[63] And is not the same closed loop at work in the Stalinist sacrificial production of enemies: since the Party fortifies itself by fighting rightist and leftist deviations, one is forced to produce them in order to fortify Party unity.

Kant himself gets caught in this circle of perversion in his *Critique of Practical Reason:* at the end of Part One, he asks himself why God created the world in such a way that things in themselves are unknowable to man, that the Supreme Good is unattainable to him because of the propensity to radical Evil that pertains to human nature. Kant's answer is that this impenetrability is the positive condition of our moral activity: if man were to know things in themselves, moral activity would become impossible and superfluous at the same time, since we would follow moral commands not out of duty but out of simple insight into the nature of things. So, since the ultimate goal of the creation of the universe is morality, God had to act precisely like the heroine from the Highsmith story and create man as a truncated, split being, deprived of insight into the true nature of things, exposed to the temptation of Evil.[64] Perversion is simply the fulfillment of this sacrificial act which establishes the conditions of Goodness. Therein also lies the secret shared by initiatory circles like the Grail community at Montsalvat: the perverse reverse of Christianity, the intentional killing of Christ, enabling him to play the role of the Redeemer.[65]

Consequently, Parsifal's "the wound is healed only by the spear that smote you" amounts to something quite different from what this same phrase may have meant within the horizon of Kant and Hegel. Insofar as, in Kant, the "wound" can only be the inaccessibility of the Thing and its "healing" the teleological *Schein*, the point here is that what appears as "wound" is actually a positive condition of "healing": the inaccessibility of the Thing is a positive condition of our freedom and moral dignity. Yet for that very reason, Kant is as far as possible from allowing any finite subject to assume the role of the instrument which "smote you" in order to enable realization of the Good. *This, however, is precisely what takes place in Wagner,* where we witness the emergence of the perverse subject who willingly assumes the "dealing of the wound," accomplishing the crime which paves the way for the Good.

And—to conclude—it is precisely the reference to this logic of perversion which enables us to throw some light on one of the most obscure points of Lacanian theory: what, precisely, is the role of *objet petit a* in the drive, say, in the scopic drive, as opposed to desire? The key is provided by Lacan's clarification, in his *Four Fundamental Concepts,* that the essential feature of the scopic drive is *"se faire voir"* (making oneself seen).[66] However, as Lacan immediately points out, this "making oneself seen" which characterizes the circularity, the constitutive loop, of the drive, must not be confused with the narcissistic "looking at oneself through the other," i.e., through the eyes of the big Other, from the point of the Ego-Ideal in the Other, in the form in which I appear to myself worthy of love: what is lost when I "look at myself through the other" is the radical heterogeneity of the object qua gaze to which I expose myself in "making oneself seen." In the ideological space proper, an exemplary case of this narcissistic satisfaction provided by "looking at oneself through the other" (Ego-Ideal) is the reporting on one's own country as seen through the foreign gaze (e.g., the obsession of the American media today with how America is perceived— admired or despised—by the Other: the Japanese, Russians . . .). The first exemplary case, of course, is Aeschylus' *Persians,* where the Persian defeat is rendered as seen through the eyes of the Persian royal court: the amazement of King Darius at what a magnificent people the Greeks are, etc., provides deep narcissistic satisfaction for the Greek spectators. Yet—again— this is *not* what "making oneself seen" is about; what, then, *does* constitute it?

Let us recall Hitchcock's *Rear Window,* which is often cited as an exemplary staging of the scopic drive. Throughout most of the film, the logic of desire predominates: this desire is fascinated, propelled by its object-cause, the dark window in the opposite courtyard which gazes back at the subject. When, in the course of the film, does "the arrow come back toward the subject"? At the moment, of course, when the murderer in the house opposite James Stewart's rear window returns Stewart's gaze and catches him red-handed in his act of voyeurism: at this precise moment when James Stewart does not "see himself seeing himself," but *makes himself seen to the object of his seeing* (i.e., to that stain which drew his gaze to the dark room across the courtyard), we pass from the register of desire into that of drive. That is to say, we remain within the register of desire as long as, by way of assuming the merely inquisitive attitude of a voyeur, we are looking for the fascinating X, for some trace of what is hidden "behind the curtain"; *we* "change gear" into the drive the moment we make ourselves seen to this stain in the picture, to this impervious foreign body in the frame, to this point which attracted our gaze. This reversal is what defines the drive: insofar as I cannot see the point in the other from which I'm gazed at, the only thing that remains for me to do is to make myself visible to that point. The difference between this gaze and the narcissistic looking at oneself from the point of the Ego-Ideal is clear: in the case of the gaze, the point to which the subject makes himself seen retains its traumatic heterogeneity and nontransparency, it remains an object in a strict Lacanian sense, not a symbolic feature. This point to which I make myself visible in my very capacity of looking is the object of drive, and in this way, one can perhaps clarify a little bit the difference between the status of *objet a* in desire and in drive (as we all know, when Jacques-Alain Miller asks Lacan about this point in the *Four Fundamental Concepts,* the answer he gets is chiaroscuro, at best).

What can further clarify this crucial distinction is another feature of the final scene of *Rear Window* which stages in its purest this transmutation of desire into drive: the desperate defense of James Stewart who attempts to stop the murderer's advance by setting off multiple flash-bulbs. This apparently nonsensical gesture must be read precisely as a *defense against the drive,* against "making oneself seen"—Stewart endeavors frantically to blind the other's gaze.[67] (The key to this scene of confrontation is that the murderer gives body to the question emanating from the Other—"Che vuoi?", What do you want from me? By repeatedly asking what does Stewart want, what is his stake, his interest in this affair, the murderer confronts Stewart with his own unacknowledged desire. Stewart's defense is therefore a desperate attempt to elude the truth of his desire.)[68] What befalls Stewart when the murderer throws him through the window is precisely the inversion which defines drive: by falling through the window, he in a radical sense *falls into his own picture,* into the field of his own visibility. In Lacanian terms, he changes into a *stain in his own picture,* he makes himself seen in it, i.e., within the space defined as his own field of vision.[69]

Those magnificent scenes toward the end of *Who Framed Roger Rabbit* are another variation on the same motif, where the hard-boiled detective falls into the universe of cartoons: he is thereby confined to the domain "between the two deaths" where there is no death proper, just unending devouring and / or destruction. Yet another left-paranoiac variation on this theme is to be found in *Dreamscape,* a sci-fi movie about an American president troubled by bad dreams about the nuclear catastrophe he may trigger; the dark militarist plotters try to circumvent his pacifist plans by making use of a criminal who can transpose himself into another person's dream and act in it. The idea is to scare the President so much in his dream that he dies of a heart attack.

In the final scene of Chaplin's *Limelight* we also have the reversal of desire into drive; the apparent melodramatic simplicity of this scene should not deceive us. It is centered upon a magnificent backwards tracking-shot, from the close-up of the dead clown Calvero behind the stage to the establishing shot of the entire stage where the young girl, now a successful ballerina and his great love, is performing. Just before this scene, the dying Calvero expresses to the attending doctor his desire to see his love dancing; the doctor taps him gently on the shoulders and comforts him: "You shall see her!" Thereupon Calvero dies, his body is covered by a white sheet, and the camera withdraws so that the screen comprises the dancing girl on the stage, while Calvero is reduced to a tiny, barely visible white stain in the background. What is here of special significance is the way the ballerina enters the frame: from behind the camera, like the birds in the famous "God's-view" shot of Bodega Bay in Hitchcock's *The Birds*—yet another white stain which materializes out of the mysterious intermediate space separating the spectator from the diegetic reality on the screen. We encounter here the function of the gaze qua object-stain in its purest: the doctor's forecast is fulfilled. Precisely insofar as Calvero is dead, i.e., insofar as he cannot *see* the young girl anymore, he *looks at her.* For that reason, the logic of this backwards tracking-shot is thoroughly Hitchcockian: by way of it, a piece of reality is transformed into an amorphous stain (a white blot in the background), yet a stain around which the entire field of vision turns, a stain which "smears over" the entire field (as in the backwards tracking-shot in *Frenzy*). In other words, what confers upon this scene its melodramatic beauty is the spectator's awareness that *without knowing that Calvero is already dead, the ballerina is dancing for him, for that stain which he has become* (the melodramatic effect always hinges on such an ignorance of the agent); it is this stain, this white smudge in the background, which guarantees the sense of the scene. Where, precisely, is the transmutation of desire into drive? We remain within the register of desire as long as the field of vision is organized, supported, by Calvero's desire to see for the last time his love dancing; we enter the register of drive the moment Calvero is reduced to a stain-object in his own picture. For that precise reason, it is not sufficient to say that it is simply she, the ballerina, his love, who makes herself seen to him; the point is rather that, simultaneously, he acquires the presence of a stain, so that both of them appear within the same field of vision.[70]

Scopic drive always designates such a closing of the loop whereby I get caught in the picture I'm looking at, lose distance toward it; as such, it is never a simple reversal of desire to see into a passive mode. "Making oneself seen" is inherent to the very act of seeing: drive is the loop which connects them. The ultimate exemplifications of drive are therefore the visual and temporal paradoxes which materialize the nonsensical, "impossible" vicious circle: Escher's two hands drawing each other or the waterfall which runs in a closed perpetuum-mobile; the time-travel loop whereby I visit the past in order to create myself (to organize the coupling of my parents).

Perhaps even better than by the arrow invoked by Lacan, this "loop formed by the outward and return movement of the drive" can be exemplified by the first free association which this formulation resuscitates, namely the boomerang where "hitting the target" changes over into "making oneself hit." That is to say, when I throw the boomerang, its "goal," of course, is to hit the target (the animal); yet the true art of throwing depends upon being able to catch the boomerang when, upon our *missing* the goal, the boomerang flies back; the true aim is to miss the goal, so that the boomerang returns to us (the most difficult part of learning how to handle the boomerang is therefore mastering the art of catching it properly, i.e., of avoiding being hit by it, of blocking the potentially suicidal dimension of throwing it). The handling of the boomerang stages the elementary hysterical splitting: the subject's catching of the boomerang hinders the realization of the true aim of its throwing, the "making oneself hit" as a display of the death-drive. The boomerang thus designates the very moment of the emergence of "culture," the moment when instinct is transformed into drive: the moment of splitting between goal and aim, the moment when the true aim is no longer to hit the goal but to maintain the very circular movement of repeatedly missing it.

6 Enjoy Your Nation as Yourself!

■

Why was the West so fascinated by the disintegration of Communism in Eastern Europe? The answer seems obvious: what fascinated the Western gaze was the *reinvention of Democracy*. It is as if democracy, which in the West shows more and more signs of decay and crisis and is lost in bureaucratic routine and publicity-style election campaigns, is being rediscovered in Eastern Europe in all its freshness and novelty. The function of this fascination is thus purely ideological: in Eastern Europe, the West seeks for its own lost origins, its own lost original experience of "democratic invention." In other words, Eastern Europe functions for the West as its Ego-Ideal (*Ich-Ideal*): the point from which West sees itself in a likable, idealized form, as worthy of love. The real object of fascination for the West is thus the *gaze*, namely the supposedly naive gaze by means of which Eastern Europe stares back at the West, fascinated by its democracy. It is as if the Eastern gaze is still able to perceive in Western societies its own *agalma*, the treasure that causes democratic enthusiasm and that the West has long ago lost the taste of.

The reality emerging now in Eastern Europe is, however, a disturbing distortion of this idyllic picture of the two mutually fascinated gazes: the gradual retreat of the liberal-democratic tendency in the face of the growth of corporate national populism which includes all its usual elements, from xenophobia to anti-Semitism. To explain this unexpected turn, we have to rethink the most elementary notions about national identification—and here, psychoanalysis can be of help.

The "Theft of Enjoyment"

The element which holds together a given community cannot be reduced to the point of symbolic identification: the bond linking together its members always implies a shared relationship toward a Thing, toward Enjoyment incarnated.[1] This relationship toward the Thing, structured by means of fantasies, is what is at stake when we speak of the menace to our "way of life" presented by the Other: it is what is threatened when, for example, a white Englishman is panicked because of the growing presence of "aliens." What he wants to defend at any price is *not* reducible to the so-called set of values that offer support to national identity. National identification is by definition sustained by a relationship toward the Nation qua Thing. This Nation-Thing is determined by a series of contradictory properties. It appears to us as "our Thing" (perhaps we could say *cosa nostra*), as something accessible only to us, as something "they," the others, cannot grasp; nonetheless it is something constantly menaced by "them." It appears as what gives plenitude and vivacity to our life, and yet the only way we can determine it is by resorting to different versions of the same empty tautology. All we can ultimately say about it is that the Thing is "itself," "the real Thing," "what it really is about," etc. If we are asked how we can recognize the presence of this Thing, the only consistent answer is that the Thing is present in that elusive entity called "our way of life." All we can do is enumerate disconnected fragments of the way our community organizes its feasts, its rituals of mating, its initiation ceremonies, in short, all the details by which is made visible the unique way a community *organizes its enjoyment.* Although the first, so to speak, automatic association that arises here is of course that of the reactionary sentimental *Blut und Boden,* we should not forget that such a reference to the "way of life" can also have a distinctive "leftist" connotation. Note George Orwell's essays from the war years, in which he attempted to define the contours of an English patriotism opposed to the official, stuffy imperialist version of it. His points of reference were precisely those details that characterize the "way of life" of the working class (the evening gathering in the local pub, etc.).[2]

It would, however, be erroneous simply to reduce the national Thing to the features composing a specific "way of life." The Thing is not directly a collection of these features; there is "something more" in it, something that *is present* in these features, that *appears* through them. Members of a community who partake in a given "way of life" *believe in their Thing,* where this belief has a reflexive structure proper to the intersubjective space: "I believe in the (national) Thing" equals "I believe that others (members of my community) believe in the Thing." The tautological character of the Thing—its semantic void which limits what we can say about the Thing to "It is the real Thing," etc.—is founded precisely in this paradoxical reflexive structure. The national Thing exists as long as members of the community believe in it; it is literally an effect of this belief in itself. The structure is here the same as that of the Holy Spirit in Christianity. The Holy Spirit *is* the community of believers in which Christ lives after his death: *to believe in Him equals believing in belief itself,* i.e., believing that I'm not alone, that I'm a member of the community of believers. I do not need any external proof or confirmation of the truth of my belief: by the mere act of my belief in others' belief, the Holy Spirit is here. In other words, the whole meaning of the Thing turns on the fact that "it means something" to people.

This paradoxical existence of an entity which "is" only insofar as subjects believe (in the other's belief) in its existence is the mode of being proper to ideological causes: the "normal" order of causality is here inverted, since it is the Cause itself which is produced by its effects (the ideological practices it animates). Significantly, it is precisely at this point that the difference between Lacan and "discursive idealism" emerges most forcefully: Lacan does not reduce the (national, etc.) Cause to a performative effect of the discursive practices that refer to it. The pure discursive effect does not have enough "substance" to compel the attraction proper to a Cause—and the Lacanian term for the strange "substance" which must be added so that a Cause obtains its positive ontological consistency, the only substance acknowledged by psychoanalysis, is of course *enjoyment* (as Lacan states it explicitly in *Encore*[3]). A nation *exists* only as long as its specific *enjoyment* continues to be materialized in a set of social practices and transmitted through national myths that structure these practices. To emphasize in a "deconstructionist" mode that Nation is not a biological or transhistorical fact but a contingent discursive construction, an overdetermined result of textual practices, is thus misleading: such an emphasis overlooks the remainder of some *real,* nondiscursive kernel of enjoyment which must be present for the Nation qua discursive entity-effect to achieve its ontological consistency.[4]

Nationalism thus presents a privileged domain of the eruption of enjoyment into the social field. The national Cause is ultimately nothing but the way subjects of a given ethnic community organize their enjoyment through national myths. What is therefore at stake in ethnic tensions is always the possession of the national Thing. We always impute to the "other" an excessive enjoyment: he wants to steal our enjoyment (by ruining our way of life) and / or he has access to some secret, perverse enjoyment. In short, what really bothers us about the "other" is the peculiar way he organizes his enjoyment, precisely the surplus, the "excess" that pertains to this way: the smell of "their" food, "their" noisy songs and dances, "their" strange manners, "their" attitude to work. To the racist, the "other" is either a workaholic stealing our jobs or an idler living on our labor, and it is quite amusing to notice the haste with which one passes from reproaching the other with a refusal to work to reproaching him for the theft of work. The basic paradox is that our Thing is conceived as something inaccessible to the other and at the same time threatened by him. According to Freud, the same paradox defines the experience of castration, which, within the subject's psychic economy, appears as something that "really cannot happen," but we are nonetheless horrified by its prospect. The ground of incompatibility between different ethnic subject positions is thus not exclusively the different structure of their symbolic identifications. What categorically resists universalization is rather the particular structure of their relationship toward enjoyment:

> Why does the Other remain Other? What is the cause for our hatred of him, for our hatred of him in his very being? It is hatred of the enjoyment in the Other. This would be the most general formula of the modern racism we are witnessing today: a hatred of the particular way the Other enjoys. . . . The question of tolerance or intolerance is not at all concerned with the subject of science and its human rights. It is located on the level of tolerance or intolerance toward the enjoyment of the Other, the Other as he who essentially steals my own enjoyment. We know, of course, that the fundamental status of the object is to be always already snatched away by the Other. It is precisely this theft of enjoyment that we write down in shorthand as minus Phi, the mathem of castration. The problem is apparently unsolvable as the Other is the Other in my interior. The root of racism is thus hatred of my own enjoyment. There is no other enjoyment but my own. If the Other is in me, occupying the place of extimacy, then the hatred is also my own.[5]

What we conceal by imputing to the Other the theft of enjoyment is the traumatic fact that *we never possessed what was allegedly stolen from us:* the lack ("castration") is originary, enjoyment constitutes itself as "stolen," or, to quote Hegel's precise formulation from his *Science of Logic*, it "only *comes to be* through being *left behind*."[6] The late Yugoslavia offers a case study of such a paradox, in which we witness a detailed network of "decantations" and "thefts" of enjoyment. Every nationality has built its own mythology narrating how other nations deprive it of the vital part of enjoyment the possession of which would allow it to live fully. If we read all these mythologies together, we obtain Escher's well-known visual paradox of a network of basins where, following the principle of *perpetuum mobile,* water pours from one basin into another until the circle is closed, so that by moving the whole way downstream, we find ourselves back at our starting point. Slovenes are being deprived of their enjoyment by "Southerners" (Serbians, Bosnians . . .) because of their proverbial laziness, Balkan corruption, dirty and noisy enjoyment, and because they demand bottomless economic support, stealing from Slovenes their precious accumulation of wealth by means of which Slovenia should otherwise have already caught up with Western Europe. The Slovenes themselves, on the other hand, allegedly rob the Serbs because of Slovenian unnatural diligence, stiffness, and selfish calculation. Instead of yielding to life's simple pleasures, the Slovenes perversely enjoy constantly devising means of depriving Serbs of the results of their hard labor by commercial profiteering, by reselling what they bought cheaply in Serbia. The Slovenes are afraid that Serbs will "inundate" them, and that they will thus lose their national identity. Meanwhile, the Serbs reproach Slovenes for their "separatism," which means simply that Slovenes refuse to recognize themselves as a subspecies of Serb. To mark Slovenian difference from the "Southerners," recent Slovenian popular historiography is bent on proving that Slovenes are not really of Slavic but of Etruscan origin; Serbs, on the other hand, excel in showing how Serbia was a victim of a "Vatican-Komintern conspiracy": their *idée fixe* is that a secret joint plan between Catholics and Communists aims to destroy Serbian statehood. The basic premise of both Serb and Slovene is of course "We don't want anything foreign, we just want what rightfully belongs to us!"—a reliable sign of racism, since it claims to draw a clear line of distinction where none exists. In both cases, these fantasies are clearly rooted in hatred of one's own enjoyment. Slovenes, for example, repress their own enjoyment by means of obsessional activity, and it is this very enjoyment which returns in the real, in the figure of the dirty and easygoing "Southerner."[7]

This logic is, however, far from being limited to the "backward" Balkan conditions. How the "theft of enjoyment" (or, to use a Lacanian technical term, imaginary castration) functions as an extremely useful tool for analyzing today's ideological processes can be further exemplified by a feature of American ideology of the eighties: the obsessive idea that there might still be some American POWs alive in Vietnam, leading a miserable existence, forgotten by their own country. This obsession articulated itself in a series of macho-adventures in which a hero undertakes a solitary rescue mission (*Rambo II, Missing in Action*). The underlying fantasy-scenario is far more interesting. It is as if down there, far away in the Vietnam jungle, America had lost a precious part of itself, had been deprived of an essential part of its very life substance, the essence of its potency; and because this loss became the ultimate cause of America's decline and impotence in the post-Vietnam Carter years, recapturing this stolen, forgotten part became an element of the Reaganesque reaffirmation of a strong America.[8]

Capitalism without Capitalism

What sets in motion this logic of the "theft of enjoyment" is of course not immediate social reality—the reality of different ethnic communities living closely together—but the *inner antagonism inherent in these communities.* It is possible to have a multitude of ethnic communities living side by side without racial tensions (like the Amish and neighboring communities in Pennsylvania); on the other hand, one does not need a lot of "real" Jews to impute to them some mysterious enjoyment that threatens us (it is a well-known fact that in Nazi Germany, anti-Semitism was most ferocious in those parts where there were almost no Jews; in today's ex-East Germany, the anti-Semitic Skinheads outnumber Jews by ten to one). Our perception of "real" Jews is always mediated by a symbolic-ideological structure which tries to cope with social antagonism: the real "secret" of the Jew is our own antagonism. In today's America, for example, a role resembling that of the Jew is played more and more by the Japanese. Witness the obsession of the American media with the idea that Japanese don't know how to enjoy themselves. The reason for the growing Japanese economic superiority over the U.S.A. is located in the somewhat mysterious fact that the Japanese don't consume enough, that they accumulate too much wealth. If we look closely at the logic of this accusation, it soon becomes clear that what American "spontaneous" ideology really reproaches the Japanese for is not simply their inability to take pleasure but rather the fact that their very relationship between work and enjoyment is strangely distorted. *It is as if they find an enjoyment in their very renunciation of pleasure,* in their zeal, in their inability to "take it easy," relax, and enjoy—and it is this attitude which is perceived as a threat to American supremacy. Thus the American media report with such evident relief how Japanese are finally learning to consume, and why American TV depicts with such self-satisfaction Japanese tourists staring at the wonders of the American pleasure-industry: finally, they are "becoming like us," learning our way of enjoying.

It is too easy to dispose of this problematic by pointing out that what we have here is simply the transposition, the ideological displacement, of the effective socioeconomic antagonisms of today's capitalism. The problem is that, while this is undoubtedly true, *it is precisely through such a displacement that desire is constituted.* What we gain by transposing the perception of inherent social antagonisms into the fascination with the Other (Jew, Japanese . . .) is the fantasy-organization of desire. The Lacanian thesis that enjoyment is ultimately always enjoyment of the Other, i.e., enjoyment supposed, imputed to the Other, and that, conversely, the hatred of the Other's enjoyment is always the hatred of one's own enjoyment, is perfectly exemplified by this logic of the "theft of enjoyment."[9] What are fantasies about the Other's special, excessive enjoyment—about the black's superior sexual potency and appetite, about the Jew's or Japanese's special relationship toward money and work—if not precisely *so many ways, for us, to organize our own enjoyment?* Do we not find enjoyment precisely in fantasizing about the Other's enjoyment, in this ambivalent attitude toward it? Do we not obtain satisfaction by means of the very supposition that the Other enjoys in a way inaccessible to us? Does not the Other's enjoyment exert such a powerful fascination because in it we represent to ourselves our own innermost relationship toward enjoyment? And, conversely, is the anti-Semitic capitalist's hatred of the Jew not the hatred of the excess that pertains to capitalism itself, i.e., of the excess produced by its inherent antagonistic nature? Is capitalism's hatred of the Jew not the hatred of its own innermost, essential feature? For this reason, it is not sufficient to point out how the racist's Other presents a threat to our identity. We should rather inverse this proposition: the fascinating image of the Other gives a body to our own innermost split, to what is "in us more than ourselves" and thus prevents us from achieving full identity with ourselves. *The hatred of the Other is the hatred of our own excess of enjoyment.*

The national Thing functions thus as a kind of *"particular Absolute" resisting universalization,* bestowing its special "tonality" upon every neutral, universal notion. It is for that reason that the eruption of the national Thing in all its violence has always taken by surprise the devotees of international solidarity. Perhaps the most traumatic case was the debacle of the international solidarity of the worker's movement in the face of "patriotic" euphoria at the outbreak of the First World War. Today, it is difficult to imagine what a traumatic shock it was for the leaders of all currents of social democracy, from Edouard Bernstein to Lenin, when the social-democratic parties of all countries (with the exception of the Bolsheviks in Russia and Serbia) gave way to chauvinist outbursts and "patriotically" stood behind "their" respective governments, oblivious of the proclaimed solidarity of the working class "without country." This shock, the *powerless fascination* felt by its participants, bears witness to an encounter with the Real of enjoyment. That is to say, the basic paradox is that these chauvinist outbursts of "patriotic feeling" were far from unexpected. Years before the actual outbreak of the war, social democracy alerted workers to how imperialist forces were preparing for a new world war, and warned them against yielding to "patriotic" chauvinism. Even at the very outbreak of the war, i.e., in the days following the Sarajevo assassination, the German social democrats cautioned workers that the ruling class would use the assassination as an excuse to declare war. Furthermore, the Socialist International adopted a formal resolution obliging all its members to vote against war credits in the case of war. With the outbreak of the war, international solidarity vanished into thin air. An anecdote about how this overnight reversal took Lenin by surprise is significant: when he saw the daily newspaper of German social democracy, announcing on its front page that the social-democratic deputies had voted for the war credits, he was at first convinced that this issue was fabricated by German police to lead workers astray!

And it is the same in today's Eastern Europe. The "spontaneous" presupposition was that what is "repressed" there, what will burst forth once the lid of "totalitarianism" is removed, will be *democratic desire* in all its forms, from political pluralism to a flourishing market economy. What we are getting instead, now that the lid *is* removed, are more and more ethnic conflicts, based upon constructions of different "thieves of enjoyment"—as if, beneath the Communist surface, glimmered a wealth of "pathological" fantasies, waiting for their moment to arrive—a perfect exemplification of the Lacanian notion of communication where the speaker gets back from the addressee his own message in its true, inverted form. The emergence of ethnic causes breaks the narcissistic spell of the West's complacent recognition of its own values in the East: Eastern Europe is returning to the West the "repressed" truth of its democratic desire. And what we should point out is again the *powerless fascination* of (what remains of) the critical leftist intellectuals when faced with this outburst of national enjoyment. They are, of course, reluctant to fully embrace the national Cause; they are desperately trying to maintain a kind of distance from it. This distance is, however, false, a disavowal of the fact that their desire is already *implied*, caught in the Cause.

Far from being produced by the radical break occurring now in Eastern Europe, the obsessive adherence to the national Cause is precisely what *remains the same* throughout this process—what, for example, is shared in common by Ceauşescu and the radical rightist-nationalist tendencies gaining momentum in Romania. Here we encounter the Real, that which "always returns to its place" (Lacan), the kernel that persists unchanged in the midst of the radical upheavals in the society's symbolic identity. It is therefore wrong to conceive of this rise of nationalism as a kind of "reaction" to the alleged Communist betrayal of national roots—the idea being that because Communist power ripped apart the entire traditional fabric of society, the only remaining point on which to rally is national identity. It was already the Communist power that *produced* the compulsive attachment to the national Cause. This attachment was all the more exclusive the more the power structure was "totalitarian"; we find its extreme cases in Ceauşescu's Romania, in the Khmer Rouge of Kampuchea, in North Korea, and in Albania.[10] The ethnic Cause is thus the left-over that persists once the Communist ideological fabric disintegrates. We can detect this Cause in how the figure of the Enemy is constructed in today's Romania, for example: Communism is treated as a foreign organism, as the intruder which poisoned and corrupted the sound body of the nation, as something that really could not have its origins in the nation's own ethnic tradition and which therefore must be cut out for the health of the nation's body to be restored. The anti-Semitic connotation is here unmistakable: in the Soviet Union, the Russian nationalist organization Pamyat likes to count the number of Jews in Lenin's Politbureau to prove its "non-Russian" character. A popular pastime in Eastern Europe is not anymore simply to put all the blame on Communists but to play the game "who was *behind* the Communists?" (Jews for Russians and Romanians, Croatians and Slovenes for Serbs, etc.). This construction of the Enemy reproduces in its pure, so to speak, distilled form the way the Enemy was constructed in the late Communist nationalist-totalitarian regimes: once we overthrow the Communist symbolic form, what we get is the underlying relation to the ethnic Cause, stripped of this form.

So, why this unexpected disappointment? Why does the authoritarian nationalism overshadow the democratic pluralism? Why the chauvinist obsession with the "theft of enjoyment" instead of openness toward ethnic diversity? Because, at this point, the standard analysis of the causes of ethnic tensions in the "real socialist" countries proposed by the Left has proved wrong. The leftist thesis was that ethnic tensions were instigated and manipulated by the ruling Party bureaucracy as a means of legitimizing the Party's hold on power. In Romania, for example, the nationalist obsession, the dream of Great Romania, the forceful assimilation of Hungarian and other minorities, created a constant tension which legitimized Ceaușescu's hold on power; in Yugoslavia, the tensions between Serbs and Albanians, Croats and Serbs, Slovenes and Serbs, etc., seemed a showcase of how corrupted local bureaucracies can prolong their power by presenting themselves as the sole defenders of national interests. However, this hypothesis was refuted in a most spectacular way by recent events: once the rule of the Communist bureaucracies was broken, ethnic tensions emerged even more forcefully. So, why does this attachment to the ethnic Cause *persist* even after the power structure that produced it has collapsed? Here, a combined reference to classical Marxist theory of capitalism and to Lacanian psychoanalysis might be of some help.

The elementary feature of capitalism consists of its *inherent structural imbalance,* its innermost antagonistic character: the constant crisis, the constant revolutionizing of its conditions of existence. Capitalism has no "normal," balanced state: its "normal" state is the permanent production of an excess; the only way for capitalism to survive is to expand. Capitalism is thus caught in a kind of loop, a vicious circle, that was clearly designated already by Marx: producing more than any other socioeconomic formation to satisfy human needs, capitalism nonetheless also produces even more needs to be satisfied; the greater the wealth, the greater the need to produce more wealth. It should be clear, therefore, why Lacan designated capitalism as the reign of the *discourse of the hysteric:*[11] this vicious circle of a desire, whose apparent satisfaction only widens the gap of its dissatisfaction, is what defines hysteria. A kind of structural homology exists between capitalism and the Freudian notion of the superego. The basic paradox of the superego also concerns a certain structural imbalance: the more we obey its command, the more we feel guilty, so that renunciation entails only a demand for more renunciation, repentance more guilt—as in capitalism, where an increase in production to fill out the lack only widens the lack.

It is against this background that we should grasp the logic of what Lacan calls the (discourse of the) *Master:* its role is precisely to introduce *balance,* to *regulate the excess.* Precapitalist societies were still able to dominate the structural imbalance proper to the superego insofar as their dominant discourse was that of the Master. In his last works, Michel Foucault showed how the ancient Master embodied the ethics of self-mastery and "just measure": the entire precapitalist ethics aimed to prevent the excess proper to the human libidinal economy from exploding. With capitalism, however, this function of the Master becomes suspended, and the vicious circle of the superego spins freely.

Now, it should also be clear where the corporatist temptation comes from, i.e., why this temptation is the necessary reverse of capitalism. Let us take the ideological edifice of fascist corporatism: the fascist dream is simply to have *capitalism without its "excess," without the antagonism that causes its structural imbalance.* Which is why we have, in fascism, on one hand, the return to the figure of the Master—Leader—who guarantees the stability and balance of the social fabric, i.e., who again saves us from society's structural imbalance; while, on the other hand, the reason for this imbalance is attributed to the figure of the Jew whose "excessive" accumulation and greed are the cause of social antagonism. Thus the dream is that, since the excess was introduced from outside, i.e., is the work of an alien intruder, its elimination would enable us to obtain again a stable social organism whose parts form a harmonious corporate body, where, in contrast to capitalism's constant social *displacement,* everybody would again occupy his *own place.* The function of the Master is to dominate the excess by locating its cause in a clearly delimited social agency: "It is *they* who steal our enjoyment, who, by means of their excessive attitude, introduce imbalance and antagonism." With the figure of the Master, the antagonism *inherent* in the social structure is transformed into a relationship of *power,* a struggle for *domination* between *us* and *them,* those who cause antagonistic imbalance.

Perhaps this matrix also helps us to grasp the reemergence of nationalist chauvinism in Eastern Europe as a kind of "shock-absorber" against the sudden exposure to the capitalist openness and imbalance. It is as if, in the very moment when the bond, the chain preventing free development of capitalism, i.e., a deregulated production of the *excess,* was broken, it was countered by a *demand for a new Master* who will rein it in. What one demands is the establishment of a stable and clearly defined social body which will restrain capitalism's destructive potential by cutting off the "excessive" element; and since this social body is experienced as that of a nation, the cause of any imbalance "spontaneously" assumes the form of a "national enemy."

When the democratic opposition was still fighting against the Communist power, it united under the sign of "civil society" all "antitotalitarian" elements, from the Church to the leftist intellectuals. Within the "spontaneous" experience of the unity of this fight, the crucial fact passed unnoticed: the same words used by all participants referred to two fundamentally different languages, to two different worlds. Now that the opposition has won, this victory necessarily assumes the shape of a split: the enthusiastic solidarity of the fight against Communist power has lost its mobilizing potential and the fissure separating the two political universes cannot be concealed anymore. This fissure is of course that of the well-known couple *Gemeinschaft / Gesellschaft:* the traditional, organically linked community versus the "alienated" society which dissolves all organic links. The problem of Eastern Europe's nationalist populism is that it perceives Communism's "threat" from the perspective of *Gemeinschaft,* as a foreign body corroding the organic texture of the national community; this way, nationalist populism actually imputes to Communism the crucial feature of capitalism itself. In its moralistic opposition to the Communist "depravity," the nationalist-populist Moral Majority unknowingly *prolongs* the thrust of the previous Communist regime toward State qua organic community. The desire at work in this symptomatic substitution of Communism for capitalism is a desire for capitalism cum *Gemeinschaft,* a desire for capitalism without the "alienated" civil society, without the formal-external relations between individuals. Fantasies about the "theft of enjoyment," the re-emergence of anti-Semitism, etc., are the price to be paid for this impossible desire.

The Blind Spot of Liberalism

Paradoxically, we could say that what Eastern Europe needs most now is *more alienation:* the establishment of an "alienated" State which would maintain its distance from the civil society, which would be "formal," "empty," i.e., which would not embody any particular ethnic community's dream (and thus keep the space open for them all). Is, then, the solution for Eastern Europe's present woes simply a larger dose of liberal democracy? The picture we have presented seems to point in this direction: Eastern Europe cannot start to live in peace and true pluralist democracy because of the specter of nationalism, i.e., because the disintegration of Communism opened up the space for the emergence of nationalist obsessions, provincialism, anti-Semitism, hatred of all that comes from abroad, ideology of a threat to the nation, antifeminism, and a postsocialist moral majority inclusive of a pro-life movement—in short, *enjoyment* in its entire "irrationality." Yet what is deeply suspicious about this attitude, about the attitude of an antinationalist, liberal Eastern European intellectual, is the already-mentioned obvious fascination exerted on him by nationalism: liberal intellectuals refuse it, mock it, laugh at it, yet at the same time stare at it with powerless fascination. The intellectual pleasure procured by denouncing nationalism is uncannily close to the satisfaction of successfully explaining one's own impotence and failure (which always was a trademark of a certain kind of Marxism). On another level, Western liberal intellectuals are often caught in a similar trap: the affirmation of their own autochthonous tradition is for them a red-neck horror, a site of populist protofascism (for example, in the U.S.A., the "backwardness" of the Polish, Italian, etc. communities, the alleged brood of "authoritarian personalities" and similar liberal scarecrows), whereas such intellectuals are at once ready to hail the autochthonous ethnical communities *of the other* (African Americans, Puerto Ricans . . .). Enjoyment is good, on condition that it not be too close to us, on condition that it remain the *other's* enjoyment.

As to the ultimate inefficiency of this "enlightened," "socially conscious" critical analysis, suffice it to recall Clint Eastwood's *Dirty Harry* series: the first film of the series unabashedly stages and thereby endorses the right-wing, populist fantasy (a lone avenger breaking the corrupted, inefficient law in order to "get things done," a masochist, sexually ambiguous criminal, etc.), whereas in the following installments, it seems as if Eastwood somehow incorporated a liberal critic's reflections on the first film. Already the first one to follow, *Magnum Force*, rebukes the logic of a "lone avenger" and insists on unconditional respect for the letter of the Law; *Sudden Impact* gives the logic of the lone avenger almost a feminist touch, with Harry setting free the female killer, a rape victim, since she was not able to obtain justice from the male-chauvinist legal system; *Tightrope* alludes to the dark parallelisms between the murderer and the law-enforcing inspector. And yet in spite of this self-reflective incorporation of the liberal, "socially conscious" ingredients, *the fantasy remains thoroughly the same*, its efficiency in structuring our space of desire intact. The truly radical critique of ideology should therefore go beyond the self-congratulatory "social analyses" which continue to participate in the fantasy that sustains the object of their critique and to search for ways to sap the force of this underlying fantasy-frame itself—in short, to perform something akin to the Lacanian "going-through the fantasy."[12] The general lesson to be drawn from it with reference to how ideology works concerns the gap that separates ideology qua discursive formation from its fantasy-support: an ideological edifice is of course submitted to incessant retroactive restructurations, the symbolic-differential value of its elements shifting all the time, but fantasy designates the hard kernel which resists symbolic "perlaboration," i.e., which as it were anchors an ideology in some "substantial" point and thus provides a constant frame for the symbolic interplay. In other words, it is on account of fantasy that an ideology cannot be reduced to a network of elements whose value wholly depends on their respective differential position within the symbolic structure.

The positive expression of this ambivalence toward the other's fantasmatic enjoyment is the obsessive attitude that one can easily detect in what is usually referred to as "PC," political correctness: the compulsive effort to uncover ever new, ever more refined forms of racial and / or sexual violence and domination (it is not PC to say that the president "smokes a peace-pipe" since this involves a patronizing irony toward Native Americans, etc., etc.). The problem, here, is simply "how can one be a white, heterosexual male and still retain a clear conscience"? All other positions can affirm their specificity, their specific mode of enjoyment, only the white-male-heterosexual position must remain empty, must sacrifice its enjoyment. The weak point of the PC attitude is thus the weak point of the neurotic compulsion: the problem is not that it is too severe, too fanatic, but quite on the contrary that *it is not severe enough*. That is to say, at first glance, the PC attitude involves the extreme self-sacrifice, the renunciation of everything that sounds sexist and racist, the unending effort to unearth traces of sexism and racism in oneself, an effort not unworthy of the early Christian saint who dedicated his life to discovering in himself ever new layers of sin.[13] Yet all this effort should not dupe us; it is ultimately a stratagem whose function is to conceal the fact that the PC type is not ready to renounce what really matters: "I'm prepared to sacrifice everything *but that*"—but what? The very gesture of self-sacrifice. In other words, the PC attitude implies the same antagonism between the enunciated content and the position of enunciation that Hegel denounced apropos of the ascetic self-humiliation: it conceals a patronizing elevation over those whose injuries from discrimination are allegedly compensated. In the very act of emptying the white-male-heterosexual position of all positive content, the PC attitude retains it as a universal form of subjectivity. As such, the PC attitude is an exemplary case of the Sartrean *mauvaise foi* of the intellectuals: it provides new and newer answers *in order to keep the problem alive*. What this attitude really fears is that the problem will disappear, i.e., that the white-male-heterosexual form of subjectivity will actually cease to exert its hegemony. The guilt displayed by the PC attitude, the apparent desire to get rid of "incorrect" elements, is therefore the form of appearance of its exact opposite: it bears witness to the inflexible will to stick to the white-male-heterosexual form of subjectivity. Or, to put it in clear, old-fashioned political terms: far from being a disguised expression of the extreme Left, the PC attitude is the main ideological protective shield of the bourgeois liberalism against a genuine leftist alternative.[14]

What truly disturbs liberals is therefore *enjoyment* organized in the form of self-sufficient ethnic communities. It is against this background that we should consider the ambiguous consequences of the politics of school busing in the U.S.A., for example. Its principal aim, of course, was to surmount racist barriers: children from black communities would widen their cultural horizons by partaking in the white way of life, children from white communities would experience the nullity of racial prejudices by way of contacts with blacks, etc. Yet, inextricably, another logic was entwined in this project, especially where school busing was externally imposed by the "enlightened" state bureaucracy: to destroy the enjoyment of the closed ethnic communities by abrogating their boundaries. For this reason, school busing—insofar as it was experienced by the concerned communities as imposed from outside—reinforced or to some extent even generated racism where previously there was a desire of an ethnic community to maintain the closure of its way of life, a desire which is *not* in itself "racist" (as liberals themselves admit through their fascination with exotic "modes of life" of others).[15] What one should do here is to call into question the entire theoretical apparatus that sustains this liberal attitude, up to its Frankfurt-school-psychoanalytical *pièce de résistance,* the theory of the so-called "authoritarian personality": the "authoritarian personality" ultimately designates that form of subjectivity which "irrationally" insists on its specific way of life and, in the name of its self-enjoyment, resists liberal proofs of its supposed "true interests." The theory of the "authoritarian personality" is nothing but an expression of the ressentiment of the left-liberal intelligentsia apropos of the fact that the "non-enlightened" working classes were not prepared to accept its guidance: an expression of the intelligentsia's inability to offer a positive theory of this resistance.[16]

The impasses of school busing also enable us to delineate the inherent limitation of the liberal political ethic as it was articulated in John Rawls's theory of distributive justice.[17] That is to say, school busing fully meets the conditions of distributive justice (it stands the trial of what Rawls calls the "veil of ignorance"): it procures a more just distribution of social goods, it equalizes the chances for success of the individuals from different social strata, etc. Yet the paradox is that everyone, including those deemed to profit most by busing, somehow felt cheated and wronged—why? The dimension infringed upon was precisely that of *fantasy.* The Rawlsian liberal-democratic idea of distributive justice ultimately relies on "rational" individuals who are able to abstract their particular position of enunciation, to look upon themselves from a neutral place of pure "metalanguage" and thus perceive their "true interests." Such individuals are the supposed subjects of the social contract which establishes the coordinates of justice. What is thereby a priori left out of consideration is the fantasy-space within which a community organizes its "way of life" (its mode of enjoyment): within this space, what "we" desire is inextricably linked to (what we perceive as) the other's desire, so that what "we" desire may turn out to be the very destruction of our object of desire (if, in this way, we deal a blow to the other's desire). In other words, human desire, insofar as it is always-already mediated by fantasy, can never be grounded in (or translated back into) our "true interests": the ultimate assertion of our desire, sometimes the only way to assert its autonomy in the face of a "benevolent" other providing for our Good, is to act *against* our Good.[18]

Every "enlightened" political action legitimized by the reference to "true interests" encounters sooner or later the resistance of a particular fantasy-space: in the guise of the logic of "envy," of the "theft of enjoyment." Even such a clear-cut issue like the Moral Majority pro-life movement is in this respect more ambiguous than it may seem: one aspect of it is *also* the reaction to the endeavor of the "enlightened" upper-middle-class ideology to penetrate the lower-class community life. And, on another level, was not the same attitude at work in the uneasiness of the wide circle of English leftist-liberal intellectuals apropos of the great miner's strike in 1988? One was quick to renounce the strike as "irrational," an "expression of an outdated working-class fundamentalism," etc.; while all this was undoubtedly true, the fact remains that this strike was also a desperate form of resistance from a certain traditional working-class way of life. As such, it was perhaps more "postmodern," on account of the very features perceived by its critics as "regressive," than the usual "enlightened" liberal-leftist criticism of it.[19]

The fear of "excessive" identification is therefore the fundamental feature of the late-capitalist ideology: the Enemy is the "fanatic" who "over-identifies" instead of maintaining a proper distance toward the dispersed plurality of subject-positions. In short: the elated "deconstructionist" logomachy focused on "essentialism" and "fixed identities" ultimately fights a straw-man. Far from containing any kind of subversive potentials, the dispersed, plural, constructed subject hailed by postmodern theory (the subject prone to particular, inconsistent modes of enjoyment, etc.) simply designates *the form of subjectivity that corresponds to late capitalism*. Perhaps the time has come to resuscitate the Marxian insight that Capital is the ultimate power of "deterritorialization" which undermines every fixed social identity, and to conceive of "late capitalism" as the epoch in which the traditional fixity of ideological positions (patriarchal authority, fixed sexual roles, etc.) becomes an obstacle to the unbridled commodification of everyday life.

Spinozism, or, the Ideology of Late Capitalism

As to this ideological matrix of late capitalism, it is rewarding to reread the last pages of Lacan's *Seminar XI*, in which he provides a concise account of the Spinozist position: "What, quite wrongly, has been thought of in Spinoza as pantheism is simply the reduction of the field of God to the universality of the signifier, which produces a serene, exceptional detachment from human desire. . . . [Spinoza] institutes this desire in the radical dependence of the universality of the divine attributes, which is possible only through the function of the signifier."[20] That is to say, what does this Spinozist "universality of the signifier" consist of? In Lacanian terms, Spinoza accomplishes a kind of leveling of the signifying chain, he gets rid of the gap that separates S_2, the chain of knowledge, from S_1, the signifier of injunction, of prohibition, of *NO!*: the Spinozist substance designates universal Knowledge as having no need for support in a Master-Signifier, i.e., as being the metonymical universe of "pure positivity" prior to the intervention of the negativizing cut of the paternal metaphor. The attitude of the Spinozist "wisdom" is therefore defined by the reduction of deontology to ontology, of injunction to rational knowledge, and, in terms of speech-acts-theory, of performative to constative. An exemplary case is Spinoza's treatment of God's warning to Adam and Eve, "Don't eat the apple from the tree of knowledge!": this pronouncement appears as a prohibition only to the finite mind unable to grasp the chain of causes which lie behind its message; injunctions and prohibitions are justified only where we have to deal with primitive minds which lack rational insight. A mind which has access to rational truth understands God's announcement not as a prohibition but as an insight into the state of things: this apple has properties injurious to health, which is why it is not advisable to eat it. The contemporary version of Spinoza's reading of God's message would therefore run as follows: "Warning! This apple can be harmful to your health, since the tree was sprinkled with pesticides."[21]

This is then what observing phenomena *sub specie aeternitatis* ultimately amounts to: by way of surmounting the *béance* of our finitude, we conceive phenomena as the elements of a universal symbolic network. This network is universal in the precise sense that it has no use for the exceptional element that Lacan baptized the "Master-Signifier": that element which brings about the closure of an ideological field by way of designating the Supreme Good (God, Truth, Nation, etc.). According to Spinoza, this exceptional element conveys no positive knowledge of causal connections: the imaginary glitter, the power of fascination that pertains to this figure, simply gives body to the void of our ignorance. "God," understood as a transcendent sovereign imposing his aims on the world, bears witness to our inability to grasp the world in its immanent necessity. Kant, on the contrary, affirms the primacy of practical over theoretical reason, which means that *the fact of injunction is irreducible:* we, as finite subjects, cannot ever assume the contemplative position which would enable us to reduce imperative to constative.

This opposition between Spinoza and Kant, of course, has radical consequences for the status of the subject. The Spinozean contemplation of the universe *sub specie aeternitatis* implies an attitude which Lacan, in his first two seminars, wrongly attributes to the Hegelian "absolute knowledge": an attitude achieved through the subject's self-annihilation, by means of which the universe appears to be a self-sufficient mechanism that can be contemplated in supreme beatitude, since we are relieved of all responsibility for it. In contrast to this universe of pure positivity in which nothing is to be punished and only causal links are to be grasped, Kant introduces the radical responsibility of the subject: I am ultimately responsible for everything; even those features which may seem to be part of my inherited nature were chosen by me in a timeless, transcendental act.[22]

And it seems as if today we live in an age of new Spinozism: the ideology of late capitalism is, at least in some of its fundamental features, "Spinozist." Suffice it to recall the predominant attitude which replaces punishment and responsibility with illumination of the causes of our socially unacceptable behavior ("guilt" is nothing but an obsolete term for my ignorance of the causes which drove me into destructive behavior); or consider the labels on food cans full of pseudoscientific data—this soup contains so much cholesterol, so many calories, so much fat . . . (Lacan, of course, would discern behind this replacement of direct injunction by the allegedly neutral information the superego-imperative "*Enjoy!*").

We should not be led astray here by the inspired argumentation of contemporary Spinozists (Deleuze, for example) who endeavor to unearth in Spinoza a theory of communication that breaks completely with the Cartesian problematic of contact between self-conscious monadic individuals: individuals do not form a community through the mutual recognition of the ego and its Other, but through the mechanism of affective identification, through the intermixture of partial affects where one "passion" echoes another and thus reinforces its intensity—a process labeled by Spinoza *affectum imitatio*. Far from being an autonomous bearer of this process, the subject is rather a place, a passive ground for the network of partial lateral links: *communication does not take place between subjects, but directly between affects.* "I" recognize myself as an autonomous, self-sufficient Subject precisely insofar as I overlook—misrecognize—this network of partial objectal identifications-imitations which determine me and traverse the boundaries of my self-identity.[23] All this may appear very "subversive," if measured by the standard of the classical ideological notion of "autonomous subject"—but isn't this very Spinozist mechanism at work in what we call the "postindustrial society of consumption"; i.e., isn't the so-called "postmodern subject" the passive ground traversed by partial affective links, reacting to images which regulate his or her "passions," unable to exert control over this mechanism?

In her article "Nuclear Sublime," Frances Ferguson[24] registered the growing claustrophobia displayed by a series of features in our everyday life: from the awareness of how smoking endangers not just smokers themselves but nonsmokers in their company, through the obsession with child abuse, up to the revival of the theory of seduction in (the critique of) psychoanalysis (Masson's *The Assault on Truth*).²⁵ What lurks in the background of these features is the Spinozist idea that, imperceptibly, at a presubjective level, we are entangled in a network by way of which others encroach upon us: ultimately, the very presence of others as such is perceived as violence. However, in order for this enhanced awareness of how others threaten us, of how we are totally "exposed" to them, to emerge, a certain solipsist shift had to occur which defines the "postmodern" subject: this subject has as it were withdrawn from the big Other, maintaining a protopsychotic distance toward the Other; i.e., this subject perceives himself as an out-Law, lacking the common ground shared with others. And for this reason, every contact with others is perceived and experienced as a violent encroachment.

The so-called "fundamentalism" on which today's mass media more and more confer the role of the Enemy par excellence (in the guise of self-destructive "radical Evil": Saddam Hussein, the narco-cartels . . .) is to be grasped as a reaction to the ruling Spinozism, as its inherent Other. The result is sad enough, although theoretically very instructive: it is as if today the usual opposition of Good qua unyielding ethical attitude, the readiness to risk all rather than compromise one's sense of justice, and of Evil qua opportunist giving way under the pressure of circumstances, is inverted and thus attains its hidden truth. Today, "fanaticism," any readiness to put everything at stake, is as such suspicious, which is why *a proper ethical attitude survives only in the guise of "radical Evil."* The only true dilemma today is whether or not the late-capitalist Spinozism is our ultimate horizon: is all that seems to resist this Spinozism mere "remainders of the past," simply limited, "passive" knowledge, unable to contemplate the Capital-Substance *sub specie aeternitatis*, as a self-sufficient machinery, or can we effectively call this Spinozism into question?

Dreams of Nationalism, Explained by the Dream of Radical Evil

Where, then, are we to look for the way out of this vicious circle of late-capitalist Spinozism? Needless to stress, we are far from advocating that fundamentalist overidentification is "anticapitalist": the point is precisely that the contemporary forms of "paranoiac" overidentification are the inherent reverse of Capital's universalism, an inherent reaction to it. *The more the logic of Capital becomes universal, the more its opposite will assume features of "irrational fundamentalism."* In other words, there is no way out as long as the universal dimension of our social formation remains defined in terms of Capital. The way to break out of this vicious circle is not to fight the "irrational" nationalist particularism but to invent forms of political practice that contain a dimension of universality beyond Capital; their exemplary case today, of course, is the ecological movement.

And where does this leave us with regard to Eastern Europe? The liberal point of view which opposes liberal-democratic "openness" to nationalist-organic "closure"—the view sustained by the hope that a "true" liberal-democratic society will arise once we get rid of the protofascist nationalistic constraints—falls short, since it fails to take into account the way the supposedly "neutral" liberal-democratic framework produces nationalist "closure" as its inherent opposite.[26] The only way to prevent the emergence of protofascist nationalist hegemony is to call into question the very standard of "normality," the universal framework of liberal-democratic capitalism—as was done, for a brief moment, by the "vanishing mediators" in the passage from socialism into capitalism.

In the ethnic tensions emerging in Eastern Europe, the Western gaze upon the East encounters its own uncanny reverse usually qualified (and by the same token disqualified) as "fundamentalism": the end of cosmopolitanism, liberal democracy's impotence in the face of this return of tribalism. It is precisely here that, for the sake of democracy itself, one has to gather strength and repeat the exemplary heroical gesture of Freud, who answered the threat of Fascist anti-Semitism by depriving Jews of their founding father: *Moses and Monotheism* is Freud's answer to Nazism. What Freud did was therefore the exact opposite of Arnold Schoenberg, for example, who scornfully dismissed Nazi racism as a pale imitation of the self-comprehension of the Jews as the elected people: by way of an almost masochistic inversion, Freud targeted Jews themselves and endeavored to prove that their founding father, Moses, was Egyptian. Notwithstanding the historic (in)accuracy of this thesis, what really matters is its discursive strategy: to demonstrate that Jews are already in themselves "decentered," that their "originality" is a bricolage. The difficulty does not reside in Jews but in the transference of the anti-Semite who thinks that Jews "really possess it," *agalma,* the secret of their power: the anti-Semite is the one who "believes in the Jew," so the only way effectively to undermine anti-Semitism is to contend that *Jews do not possess "it."*[27]

In a similar move, one has to detect the flaw of liberal democracy which opens up a space for "fundamentalism." That is to say, there is ultimately only one question which confronts political philosophy today: is liberal democracy the ultimate horizon of our political practice, or is it possible effectively to comprise its inherent limitation? The standard neoconservative answer here is to bemoan the "lack of roots" that allegedly pertains to liberal democracy, to this kingdom of the Nietzschean "last man" where no place is left for ethical heroism, where we are more and more submerged in the idiotic routine of everyday life regulated by the pleasure-principle, etc.: within this perspective, "fundamentalism" is a simple reaction to this "loss of roots," a perverted, yet desperate search for new roots in an organic community. Yet this neoconservative answer falls short by failing to demonstrate how the very project of formal democracy, conceived in its philosophical founding gesture, opens up the space for "fundamentalism."

The structural homology between Kantian formalism and formal democracy is a classical topos: in both cases, the starting point, the founding gesture, consists of an act of radical emptying, evacuation. With Kant, what is evacuated and left empty is the locus of the Supreme Good: every positive object destined to occupy this place is by definition "pathological," marked by empirical contingency, which is why the moral Law must be reduced to the pure Form bestowing on our acts the character of universality. Likewise, the elementary operation of democracy is the evacuation of the locus of Power: every pretender to this place is by definition a "pathological" usurper; "nobody can rule innocently," to quote Saint-Just. And the crucial point is that "nationalism" as a specifically modern, post-Kantian phenomenon designates the moment when the Nation, the national Thing, usurps, fills out, the empty place of the Thing opened up by Kant's "formalism," by his reduction of every "pathological" content. The Kantian term for this filling-out of the void, of course, is the fanaticism of *Schwärmerei:* does not "nationalism" epitomize fanaticism in politics?

In this precise sense, it is the very "formalism" of Kant which, by way of its distinction between negative and indefinite judgment, opens up the space for the "undead" and similar incarnations of some monstrous radical Evil. It was already the "pre-critical" Kant who used the dreams of a ghost-seer to explain the metaphysical dream;[28] today, one should refer to the dream of the "undead" monsters to explain nationalism. The filling-out of the empty place of the Thing by the Nation is perhaps the paradigmatic case of the inversion which defines radical Evil. As to this link between philosophical formalism (the emptying of the "pathological" content) and nationalism, Kant presents a unique point: by discerning the empty place of the Thing, he effectively circumscribes the space of nationalism, yet at the same time prohibits us from taking the crucial step into it (this was done later by way of the "aesthetization" of the Kantian ethic, in Schiller, for example). In other words, the status of nationalism is ultimately that of the transcendental illusion, the illusion of a direct access to the Thing; as such, it epitomizes the principle of fanaticism in politics. Kant remains a "cosmopolite" precisely insofar as he was not yet ready to accept the possibility of "diabolical" Evil, of Evil as an ethical attitude. This paradox of filling-out the empty place of the Supreme Good defines the modern notion of Nation. The ambiguous and contradictory nature of the modern *nation* is the same as that of vampires and other living dead: they are wrongly perceived as "leftovers from the past"; their place is constituted by the very break of modernity.

This pathological "stain" also determines the deadlocks of today's liberal democracy. The problem with the liberal democracy is that a priori, for structural reasons, it cannot be universalized. Hegel said that the moment of victory of a political force is the very moment of its splitting: the triumphant liberal-democratic "new world order" is more and more marked by a frontier separating its "inside" from its "outside"—a frontier between those who manage to remain "within" (the "developed," those to whom the rules of human rights, social security, etc., apply) and the others, the excluded (the main concern of the "developed" apropos of them is to contain their explosive potential, even if the price to be paid for such containment is the neglect of elementary democratic principles).[29] This opposition, not the one between the capitalist and the socialist "bloc," is what defines the contemporary constellation: the "socialist" bloc was the true "third way," a desperate attempt at modernization outside the constraints of capitalism. What is effectively at stake in the present crisis of postsocialist states is precisely the struggle for one's place, now that the illusion of the "third way" has evaporated: who will be admitted "inside," integrated into the developed capitalist order, and who will remain excluded from it? Ex-Yugoslavia is perhaps the exemplary case: every actor in the bloody play of its disintegration endeavors to legitimize its place "inside" by presenting itself as the last bastion of European civilization (the current ideological designation for the capitalist "inside") in the face of oriental barbarism. For the right-wing nationalist Austrians, this imaginary frontier is Karavanke, the mountain chain between Austria and Slovenia: beyond it, the rule of Slavic hordes begins. For the nationalist Slovenes, this frontier is the river Kolpa, separating Slovenia from Croatia: we are *Mitteleuropa*, while Croatians are already Balkan, involved in the irrational ethnic feuds which really do not concern us; we are on their side, we sympathize with them, yet in the same way one sympathizes with a third world victim of aggression. For Croatians, the crucial frontier, of course, is the one between them and Serbians, i.e., between the Western Catholic civilization and the Eastern Orthodox collective spirit which cannot comprehend the values of Western individualism. Serbians, finally, conceive of themselves as the last line of defense of Christian Europe against the fundamentalist danger bodied forth by Muslim Albanians and Bosnians. (It should be clear, now, who, within the space of ex-Yugoslavia, effectively behaves in the civilized "European" way: those at the very bottom of this ladder, excluded from all—Albanians and Muslim Bosnians.) The traditional liberal opposition between "open" pluralist societies and "closed" nationalist-corporatist societies founded on the exclusion of the Other has thus to be brought to its point of self-reference: the liberal gaze itself functions according to the same logic, insofar as it is founded upon the exclusion of the Other to whom one attributes the fundamentalist nationalism, etc. On that account, events in ex-Yugoslavia exemplify perfectly the properly dialectical reversal: something which first appeared within the given set of circumstances as the most backward element, a left-over of the past, all of a sudden, with the shift in the general framework, emerges as the element of the future in the present context, as the premonition of what lies ahead. The outbursts of Balkan nationalism were first dismissed as the death throes of Communist totalitarianism disguised in new nationalist clothes, as a ridiculous anachronism that truly belongs to the nineteenth-century age of nation-states, not to our present era of multinationals and world integration; however, it suddenly became clear that the ethnic conflicts of ex-Yugoslavia offer the first clear taste of the twenty-first century, the prototype of the post-cold war armed conflicts.

This antagonistic splitting opens up the field for the Khmer Rouge, Sendero Luminoso, and other similar movements which seem to personify "radical Evil" in today's politics: if "fundamentalism" functions as a kind of "negative judgment" on liberal capitalism, as an inherent negation of the universalist claim of liberal capitalism, then movements such as Sendero Luminoso enact an "infinite judgment" on it. In his *Philosophy of Right*, Hegel conceives of the "rabble" (*Pöbel*) as a necessary product of the modern society: a nonintegrated segment in the legal order, prevented from partaking of its benefits, and for this very reason delivered from any responsibilities toward it—a necessary structural surplus excluded from the closed circuit of social edifice. It seems that only today, with the advent of late capitalism, has this notion of "rabble" achieved its adequate realization in social reality, through political forces which paradoxically unite the most radical indigenist antimodernism (the refusal of everything that defines modernity: market, money, individualism . . .) with the eminently modern project of effacing the entire symbolic tradition and beginning from a zero-point (in the case of Khmer Rouge, this meant abolishing the entire system of education and killing intellectuals). What, precisely, constitutes the "shining path" of the Senderistas if not the idea to reinscribe the construction of socialism within the frame of the return to the ancient Inca empire? The result of this desperate endeavor to surmount the antagonism between tradition and modernity is a double negation: a radically anticapitalist movement (the refusal of integration into the world market) coupled with a systematic dissolution of all traditional hierarchical social links, beginning with the family (at the level of "micro-power," the Khmer-Rouge regime functioned as an "anti-Oedipal" regime in its purest, i.e., as the "dictature of adolescents," instigating them to denounce their parents). The truth articulated in the paradox of this double negation is that capitalism cannot reproduce itself without the support of precapitalist forms of social links. In other words, far from presenting a case of exotic barbarism, the "radical Evil" of the Khmer Rouge and the Senderistas is conceivable only against the background of the constitutive antagonism of today's capitalism. There is more than a contingent idiosyncrasy in the fact that, in both cases, the leader of the movement is an intellectual well skilled in the subtleties of Western culture. (Prior to becoming a revolutionary, Pol Pot was a professor at a French lycée in Phnom Penh, known for his subtle readings of Rimbaud and Mallarmé; Abimael Guzman, "presidente Gonzalo," the leader of the Senderistas, is a philosophy professor whose preferred authors are Hegel and Heidegger and whose doctoral thesis was on Kant's theory of space.) For this reason, it is too simple to conceive of these movements as the last embodiment of the millenarist radicalism which structures social space as the exclusive antagonism between "us" and "them," allowing for no possible forms of mediation; instead, these movements represent a desperate attempt to avoid the imbalance constitutive of capitalism without seeking support in some previous tradition supposed to enable us mastery of this imbalance (the Islamic fundamentalism which remains within this logic is for that reason ultimately a perverted instrument of modernization). In other words, behind Sendero Luminoso's endeavor to erase an entire tradition and to begin from the zero-point in an act of creative sublimation, there is the correct insight into the complementary relationship of modernity and tradition: any true return to tradition is today a priori impossible, its role is simply to serve as a shock-absorber for the process of modernization.

The Khmer Rouge and the Senderistas therefore function as a kind of "infinite judgment" on late capitalism in the precise Kantian sense of the term: they are to be located in a third domain beyond the inherent antagonism that defines the late-capitalist dynamic (the antagonism between the modernist drive and the fundamentalist backlash), since they radically reject both poles of the opposition. As such, they are—to put it in Hegelese—an integral part of the notion of late capitalism: if one wants to comprise capitalism as a world-system, one must take into account its inherent negation, the "fundamentalism," as well as its absolute negation, the infinite judgment on it.

It is against this background that one must judge the significance of the renewed (symbolic and real) violence against "foreigners" in the developed Western countries. Apropos of the French Revolution, Kant wrote that its world-historical significance is not to be sought in what actually happened on the streets of Paris, but in the enthusiasm this endeavor to realize freedom aroused in the educated, enlightened public: it may well be true that what actually took place in Paris was horrifying, that the most repulsive passions were let loose, yet the reverberations of these events within the enlightened public all around Europe bear witness not only to the possibility of freedom, but also to the very actuality of the tendency toward freedom qua anthropological fact.[30] The same step—the shift from the event's immediate reality to the modality of its inscription into the big Other epitomized by passive observers—is to be repeated apropos of the anti-immigrant violent outbursts in Germany in the summer of 1992 (in Rostock and other cities in the ex-East Germany): the true meaning of these events is to be sought in the fact that the neo-Nazi pogroms met with approval or at least "understanding" in the silent majority of observers—

even some top Social Democratic politicians used them as an argument for reconsidering German liberal immigrant policies. This shift in the zeitgeist is where the real danger lurks: it prepares the ground for the possible hegemony of an ideology which perceives the presence of "aliens" as a threat to national identity, as the principal cause of antagonisms that divide the political body.

What we must be particularly attentive to is the difference between this "postmodern" racism which now rages around Europe and the traditional form of racism. The old racism was direct and raw—"they" (Jews, blacks, Arabs, Eastern Europeans . . .) are lazy, violent, plotting, eroding our national substance, etc., whereas the new racism is "reflected," as it were squared racism, which is why it can well assume the form of its opposite, of the fight *against* racism. Etienne Balibar hit the mark by baptizing it "meta-racism."[31] How does a "postmodern" racist react to the outbursts in Rostock? He of course begins by expressing his horror and repulsion at the neo-Nazi violence, yet he is quick to add that these events, deplorable as they are, must be seen in their context: they are actually a perverted, distorted expression and effect of a true problem, namely that in contemporary Babilon the experience of belonging to a well-defined ethnic community which gives meaning to the individual's life is losing ground; in short, the true culprits are cosmopolitic universalists who, in the name of "multiculturalism," mix races and thereby set in motion natural self-defense mechanisms.[32] Apartheid is thus legitimized as the ultimate form of anti-racism, as an endeavor to prevent racial tensions and conflicts. What we have here is a palpable example of what Lacan has in mind when he insists that "there is no metalanguage": the distance of metaracism toward racism is void; metaracism is racism pure and simple, all the more dangerous for posing as its opposite and advocating racist measures as the very form of fighting racism.

The Eastern European "Vanishing Mediators"

This criticism of the usual Western liberal attitude opens up the way for a different, supplementary way to explain the fascinating force exerted by nationalism in Eastern Europe: the peculiarity of the "transition" from real socialism to capitalism. Let us take the case of Slovenia. If, in the recent disintegration of the "real socialism" in Slovenia, there were political agents whose role fully deserves the designation "tragic," these were the Slovenian Communists who lived up to their promise to make possible the peaceful, nonviolent transition into pluralist democracy. From the very beginning they were caught in the Freudian paradox of the superego: the more they gave way to the demands of the (then) opposition and accepted democratic rules of the game, the more violent became the opposition's accusations about their "totalitarianism," the more they were suspected of accepting democracy only "in words" while actually preparing demonic plots against it. The paradox of such accusations emerged in its purest when, finally, after many claims that the Communists' democratic commitments were not to be taken seriously, it became clear that they "meant it": far from being perplexed, the opposition simply changed the charge and accused the Communists of "unprincipled behavior"—how can you trust somebody who betrayed shamelessly his old revolutionary past and accepted democratic behavior? The demand of the opposition discernible in this paradox is an ironic repetition of the good old Stalinist demand at work in the political monster-trials where the accused were forced to admit their guilt and claim supreme punishment for themselves: for the anti-Communist opposition, the only good Communist would be the one who would first organize free multiparty elections and then voluntarily assume in them the role of the scapegoat, of a representative of totalitarian horrors who has to be beaten. In short, Communists were expected to assume the impossible position of pure metalanguage and to say, "We confess, we are totalitarian, we deserve to lose the elections!" like the victim of the Stalinist trials who confesses guilt and demands the harshest possible punishment. This shift in the public perception of Slovenian democratic Communists was truly enigmatic: up to the "point of no return" on the way to democracy, the public trembled for them, counting on them to endure the pressure of the true antidemocratic forces (Yugoslav army, Serbian populism, old hard-liners, etc.) and to organize free elections; yet once it became clear that free elections would take place, these same Communists suddenly became the Enemy.

The logic of this shift, from the "open" condition before elections into its "closure" after elections, can be conceived of by means of the term "vanishing mediator" elaborated by Fredric Jameson.[33] A system reaches its equilibrium, i.e., it establishes itself as a synchronous totality, when—in Hegelese—it "posits" its external presuppositions as its inherent moments and thus obliterates the traces of its traumatic origins. What we have here is the tension between the "open" situation when a new social pact is generated, and its subsequent "closure"—to refer to Kierkegaard's terms, the tension between possibility and necessity: the circle is closed when the new social pact establishes itself in its necessity and renders invisible its "possibility," the open, undecided process that engendered it.[34] In between, when the socialist regime was already disintegrating, yet before the new regime could stabilize itself, we witnessed a kind of opening; things were for a moment visible which immediately thereafter became invisible. To put it in a rude way, those who triggered the process of democratization and fought its heaviest battles are not those who today enjoy its rewards—not because of any usurpation or deception on the part of the present winners, but because of a deeper historical logic. Once the process of democratization had reached its peak, it buried its detonators. Who effectively triggered this process? New social movements, punk, the New Left. After the victory of democracy, all these impulses suddenly and enigmatically lost ground and more or less disappeared from the scene. Culture itself, the set of cultural preferences, changed radically: from punk and Hollywood to national poems and quasi-folkloric commercial music (in contrast to the usual idea according to which the universal American-Western culture overshadows authentic national roots). What we had was a true "primitive accumulation" of democracy, a chaotic array of punkers, students with their sit-ins, committees for human rights, etc., which literally *became invisible* the moment the new system established itself and therewith its own myth of origins. The same people who, a couple of years ago, abused the new social movements from the position of party hardliners, now, as members of the ruling anti-Communist coalition, accuse their representatives of "proto-communism."

This dialectics is especially interesting in its theoretical aspect. Roughly, we could say that in the last two decades two philosophical orientations dominated intellectual life in Slovenia: Heideggerianism among the opposition and Frankfurt-school Marxism among the "official" Party circles. So one would have expected the main theoretical fight to have taken place between these two orientations, with the third block—Lacanians and Althusserians—in the role of innocent bystanders. Yet as soon as polemics broke out, both major orientations ferociously attacked the same particular *third* author, Althusser. (And, to make the surprise even bigger, the two main proponents of this polemics, a Heideggerian and a then Frankfurt Marxist, were later both members of the ruling anti-Communist coalition.) In the seventies, Althusser actually functioned as a kind of symptomatic point, a name apropos of which all the "official" adversaries, Heideggerians and Frankfurt-Marxists in Slovenia, Praxis-philosophers and Central Committee ideologues in Zagreb and Belgrade, *suddenly started to speak the same language,* pronouncing the same accusations. From the very beginning, the starting point of the Slovene Lacanians was this observation of how the name "Althusser" triggered an enigmatic uneasiness in all camps. One is even tempted to suggest that the unfortunate event in Althusser's private life (his strangling of his wife) played the role of a welcome pretext, of a "little piece of reality" enabling his theoretical adversaries to repress the real trauma represented by his theory ("How can a theory of somebody who strangled his wife be taken seriously?"). It is perhaps more than a mere curiosity that, in Yugoslavia, Althusserians (and more generally those adopting a "structuralist" or "poststructuralist" orientation) were the only ones who remained "pure" in the fight for democracy: all other philosophical schools at some point or other sold themselves to the regime. The analytical philosophers were sending the regime the message "True, we're not Marxists, but we're also not dangerous; our thought is pure apolitical professional apparatus, so you not only have nothing to fear in us, but by leaving us alone you can even gain a reputation for allowing non-Marxism without risking your hold on political power." The message was received; they were left alone. In the republic of Bosnia, the Frankfurt school enjoyed a half-official status in the seventies, whereas in Croatia and partially in Serbia "official" Heideggerians thrived, especially in the army circles, so that cases arose where, in the university purges, someone lost his job for not understanding the subtleties of negative dialectics (as it was put in the justification after the fact), or the socialist armed forces submitted apologies written in the purest Heideggerian style ("the essence of the self-defense of our society is the self-defense of the essence of our society," etc.). The resistance to Althusser confirmed how it was precisely the Althusserian theory—often defamed as proto-Stalinist—which served as a kind of "spontaneous" theoretical tool for effectively undermining the Communist totalitarian regimes: his theory of the Ideological State-Apparatuses assigned the crucial role in the reproduction of an ideology to "external" rituals and practices with regard to which "inner" beliefs and convictions are strictly secondary. And is it necessary to call attention to the central place of such rituals in "real socialism"? What counted in it was external obedience, not "inner conviction." *Obedience coincided with the semblance of obedience,* which is why the only way to be truly "subversive" was to act "naively," to make the system "eat its own words," i.e., to undermine the *appearance* of its ideological consistency.

This disappearance of the "vanishing mediator," of course, is not a peculiarity of Slovenia. Is not the most spectacular example the role of *Neues Forum* in East Germany? An inherently *tragical* ethical dimension pertains to its fate: it presents a point at which an ideology "takes itself literally" and ceases to function as an "objectively-cynical" (Marx) legitimization of the existing power relations. *Neues Forum* consisted of groups of passionate intellectuals who "took socialism seriously" and were prepared to put everything at stake in order to destroy the compromised system and replace it with the utopian "third way" beyond capitalism and "really existing" socialism. Their sincere belief and insistence that they were not working for the restoration of Western capitalism, of course, proved to be nothing but an insubstantial illusion; however, we could say that precisely as such (as a thorough illusion without substance) it was *stricto sensu nonideological:* it didn't "reflect" in an inverted-ideological form any actual relations of power. At this point, we should correct the Marxist vulgate: contrary to the commonplace according to which an ideology becomes "cynical" (accepts the gap between "words" and "acts," doesn't "believe in itself" anymore, isn't experienced anymore as truth but treats itself as pure instrumental means of legitimizing power) in the period of the "decadence" of a social formation, it could be said that precisely the period of "decadence" opens up to the ruling ideology the possibility of "taking itself seriously" and effectively opposing its own social basis. (With Protestantism, Christian religion opposed feudalism as its social basis, the same as with *Neues Forum*, which opposed the existing socialism in the name of "true socialism.") In this way, unknowingly, the "vanishing mediators" unchained the forces of their own final destruction: once their job was done, they were "overrun by history" (*Neues Forum* scored 3 percent at the elections) and a new "scoundrel time" sets in, with people in power who were mostly silent during the Communist repression and who nonetheless now indict *Neues Forum* as "crypto-Communists."

The general theoretical lesson to be drawn from these examples is that the concept of ideology must be disengaged from the "representationalist" problematic: *ideology has nothing to do with "illusion,"* with a wrong, distorted representation of its social content. To put it succinctly: a political standpoint can be quite accurate ("true") as to its objective content and yet thoroughly ideological, and vice versa; the idea a political standpoint gives of its social content can prove totally wrong, and yet there is absolutely nothing "ideological" about it. With regard to the "factual truth," the position of *Neues Forum*—taking the disintegration of the Communist regime as the opening-up of a way to invent some new form of social space that would reach beyond the confines of capitalism—was doubtless illusory. Opposing *Neues Forum* were forces who put all their bets on the quickest possible annexation to West Germany, i.e., on the inclusion of their country into the world capitalist system; for them, the people around *Neues Forum* were nothing but a bunch of heroic daydreamers. This position proved accurate—*yet it was nonetheless thoroughly ideological.* Why? The conformist adoption of the West German model implied the ideological belief in the unproblematic, nonantagonistic functioning of the late-capitalist "social state," whereas the first stance, although illusory as to its factual content (its "enunciated"), by means of its "scandalous" and exorbitant position of enunciation attested to an awareness of the antagonism that pertains to late capitalism. This is one of the ways to conceive of the Lacanian thesis according to which truth has the structure of a fiction: in those confused months of the passage of "really existing socialism" into capitalism, *the fiction of a "third way" was the only point at which social antagonism was not obliterated.* Herein lies one of the tasks of the "postmodern" critique of ideology: to designate the elements within an existing social order which—in the guise of "fiction," i.e., of the "utopian" narratives of possible but failed alternative histories—point toward the system's antagonistic character and thus "estrange" us from the self-evidence of its established identity.

Collapse of the "Big Other"

What, then, forms the link between this "vanishing mediator" and the rise of nationalism? The democratic Communists and new social movements in general represent the moment of the "vanishing mediator," of what must disappear, become invisible, for the new order to establish its identity-with-itself. The agent who initially triggered the process must come to be perceived as its main impediment, or, to use the terms of Propp's structural analysis of fairy tales,[35] the donor must appear as the malefactor, like lady Catherine de Bourgh in Jane Austen's *Pride and Prejudice,* who, in the guise of the evil impediment to Darcy's and Elizabeth's marriage, effectively maneuvers the hand of destiny, thus enabling the happy outcome. "Nation" as the substantial support is, on the other hand, what the new ruling ideology *sees* so that it can *not see*, so that it can *overlook*, the "vanishing mediator": "nation" is a fantasy which fills out the void of the vanishing mediator. If one is to avoid the historicist trap, one must therefore learn the materialist lesson of anti-evolutionist creationism, which resolves the contradiction between the literal meaning of the Scripture (according to which the universe was created ca. 5,000 years ago) and irrefutable proofs of its greater age (million-year-old fossils, etc.) not by indulging in the usual allegorical readings of the Scripture ("Adam and Eve are not really the first couple but a metaphor for the early stages of humanity . . ."), but by sticking to the literal truth of the Scripture: the universe was created recently, i.e., only 5,000 years ago, *yet with built-in false traces of the past* (God directly created fossils, etc.).[36] The past is always strictly "synchronous," it is *the way a synchronous universe thinks its antagonism.* It suffices to recall the infamous role of the "remnants of the past" in accounting for the difficulties of the "construction of socialism." In this sense, the tale of ethnic roots is from the very beginning the "myth of the Origins": what is "national heritage" if not a kind of ideological fossil created retroactively by the ruling ideology in order to blur its *present* antagonism?

In other words, instead of marveling with traumatic disorientation at the shocking swiftness of this reversal into nationalism, it would perhaps be more appropriate to accomplish a kind of Hegelian reversal and to transpose this shock into the "thing itself," i.e., to conceive of this traumatic disorientation not as a problem but rather as a key to the solution: the recourse to nationalism emerged in order to protect us from the traumatic disorientation, from the loss of the ground under our feet, caused by the disintegration of the "really existing socialism." That is to say, the breakdown of socialism is not to be underestimated, as is usually the case when one conceives of "real socialism" as an externally imposed system which oppressed some original national life-force. True, "real socialism" was ultimately a society of "pure appearance"; the system functioned so that nobody "believed in it"—yet it is here that its true enigma emerges. This appearance was what Hegel called "an essential appearance," in which, for us, today, it is easy to recognize the contours of the Lacanian big Other: what disintegrated in Eastern Europe was *le grand Autre*, the ultimate guarantor of the social pact.[37] If one disposes of enough information, this disintegration of the big Other can be pinned down to a precise point in time and space; Ryszard Kapuscinski did it in an exemplary way apropos of the Iranian revolution of 1979: the "beginning of the end" of the Shah's regime took place at a certain Teheran crossroad where a common citizen refused to obey a policeman's order to go away. The news spread like fire and, all of a sudden, people ceased to "believe in the big Other." What we have here, of course, is a retroactive reconstruction: the event in question cannot be said simply to "be" the "beginning of the end"; it is rather something that, in view of later events, "will have been" it; yet for all that, it is nonetheless the tiny snowball which set in motion the avalanche:

> Now the most important moment, the moment that will determine the fate of the country, the Shah, and the revolution, is the moment when one policeman walks from his post toward one man on the edge of the crowd, raises his voice, and orders the man to go home. The policeman and the man on the edge of the crowd are ordinary, anonymous people, but their meeting has historic significance. They are both adults, they have both lived through certain events, they have both had their individual experiences. The policeman's experience: If I shout at someone and raise my truncheon, he will first go numb with terror and then take to his heels. The experience of the man at the edge of the crowd: At the sight of an approaching policeman I am seized by fear and start running. On the basis of these experiences we can elaborate a scenario: The policeman shouts, the man runs, others take flight, the square empties. But this time everything turns out differently. The policeman shouts, but the man doesn't run. He just stands there, looking at the policeman. It's a cautious look, still tinged with fear, but at the same time tough and insolent. So that's the way it is! The man on the edge of the crowd is looking insolently at uniformed authority. He doesn't budge. He glances around and sees the same look on other faces. Like his, their faces are watchful, still a bit fearful, but already firm and unrelenting. Nobody runs though the policeman has gone on shouting; at last he stops. There is a moment of silence. We don't know whether the policeman and the man on the edge of the crowd already realize what has happened. The man has stopped being afraid—and this is precisely the beginning of the revolution. Here it starts. Until now, whenever these two men approached each other, a third figure instantly intervened between them. That third figure was fear. Fear was the policeman's ally and the man in the crowd's foe. Fear interposed its rules and decided everything. Now

two men find themselves alone, facing each other, and fear has disappeared into thin air. Until now their relationship was charged with emotion, a mixture of aggression, scorn, rage, terror. But now that fear has retreated, this perverse, hateful union has suddenly broken up; something has been extinguished. The two men have now grown mutually indifferent, useless to each other; they can go their own ways. Accordingly, the policeman turns around and begins to walk heavily back toward his post, while the man on the edge of the crowd stands there looking at his vanishing enemy.[38]

There is, however, one point at which this formidable description has to be set right or, rather, supplemented: Kapuscinski's all too naive, immediate use of the notion of fear. The "third figure" which intervenes between us ordinary citizens and the policeman is not directly fear but the big Other: we fear the policeman insofar as he is not just himself, a person like us, since his acts are the acts of power, that is to say, insofar as he is experienced as the stand-in for the big Other, for the social order. It would be of great interest to pursue this analysis and to identify, in the recent history of each of Eastern Europe's ex-Communist countries, the precise coordinates of this moment when the big Other ceased to exist, when "the appearance was broken." Sometimes, this moment was literally a moment, lasting a couple of seconds. In Romania, for example, "the spell was broken" the moment when, at the mass rally in Bucharest convoked by Ceauşescu after the demonstrations in Timisoara in order to prove that he still enjoyed popular support, the crowd started to shout at Ceauşescu, who then raised his hands in a tragicomic and bewildered display of impotent paternal love, as if wanting to embrace them all. This moment designates the reversal by means of which a dissident—a pariah, an outlaw with whom we "ordinary" people found it somehow embarrassing to socialize, although, of course, we did not "believe in power"—miraculously changes into an object of admiration and identification. The feature common to all these moments of the big Other's collapse is their utter unpredictability: nothing really great happened, yet suddenly the spell was broken, "nothing was the same as before," reasons which a moment ago were perceived as reasons *for* (obeying the Power), now function as reasons *against*. What a moment ago evoked in us a mixture of fear and respect is now experienced as a rather different mixture of ridiculous imposture and brutal, illegitimate display of force. It is clear, therefore, how this shift is of a purely symbolic nature: it designates neither a change in social reality (there, the balance of power remains exactly the same) nor a "psychological" change, but a shift in the symbolic texture which constitutes the social bond.[39]

It is precisely this belief in the existence of the big Other which enables us to account for a paradox noted already by De La Boétie in his treatise on *servitude volontaire:*[40] the reason people are ready to renounce their freedom cannot be sought in their "pathological" motivations, fear of dying, greed, lust for material goods, etc., since—if their fanaticism is properly aroused—they are prepared to sacrifice everything, including of their life, for the despot whom they obey. Why, then, do I find it so difficult to put at stake my life in the fight against the despot, when—under certain conditions, at least—I am ready to lose everything for the despot? What, exactly, is the difference between the two sacrifices? Do we not find ourselves here in a vicious circle characteristic of obsessional neurosis: I am ready to do anything, inclusive of X (in this case self-sacrifice), only to avoid X?[41] In sacrificing myself for the despot, I retain my place in the big Other, whereas risking one's life against the despot entails the loss of my support in the big Other, i.e., my exclusion from the community, from the social order epitomized by the despot's name. The common man from Teheran found enough courage to openly oppose the despot only when the despot himself had lost his support in the big Other and was perceived as a violent impostor. What I am running away from when I voluntarily take refuge in servitude is thus the traumatic confrontation with the big Other's ultimate impotence and imposture.

The same paradox accounts for the mixture of fascination and fear aroused by the "encounters of the third kind," i.e., with extraterrestrial intelligent beings. According to the so-called "UFO conspiracy theorists," the Power is hushing up information on space invaders: NASA allegedly possesses not only irrefutable data about ET visits to Earth but also evidence of their remainders (dead bodies, parts of the alien spaceships . . .), yet NASA persistently denies any knowledge of such things—why? The ultimate ground of the fear of "aliens" is that they are usually conceived of as a force against which there is no possible defense; here, however, one has to be more precise: those who are helpless against the "aliens" are not us but those in power. An encounter with "aliens" would lay open the ultimate imposture of the Master, it would sap our (unconscious) belief in the Power's omnipotence. This experience of how "the throne is empty" (of how the big Other does not exist) is bound to trigger panic, which is why the reason usually imputed to the Power for not acknowledging any "encounters of the third kind" is that they want to "prevent panic." It is precisely insofar as "aliens" threaten to lay bare the big Other's imposture and impotence that they provide the clearest embodiment of the Lacanian *Che vuoi?*, "What do you want from me?", i.e., of the enigma, impenetrability, of the Other's desire: what makes aliens so uncanny is that we can never be quite certain about their aims, about what they see in us, about what they want from us. The ultimate root of our fear of "aliens" is not their physical menace as such but their ultimate motives and intentions, which remain completely impenetrable and unknown to us.

In today's "enlightened" world, such a belief in the Power's omnipotence seems out of date, if not outright ridiculous; however, the Power, in its functioning, relies on this very split between our conscious knowledge of the Power's impotence, our ironical distance toward it, and our unconscious belief in its omnipotence; i.e., it relies on the fact that we do not believe in our own unconscious belief in the Power's omnipotence. "Wolf-Man" himself, Freud's most famous analysand, walked into this trap: in the summer of 1951, when Austria was still occupied by Allied forces, while painting a half-abandoned building in the suburbs of Vienna, he was arrested by Russian soldiers for espionage (the building was a military station); the Russians questioned him, searched him thoroughly, and accused him of national treason (since his family name was Russian). At last they let him go, yet ordered him back in twenty-one days. During all this time, the Wolf-Man was tormented by feelings of guilt and delusions of persecution; however, when, after three weeks, he reported to the Russian military station, the officer in charge who had questioned him before was not even there. Another officer took charge who knew nothing about him; he even expressed interest in Wolf-Man's painting, they talked amicably for some time about art, and then the Russian let him go.[42] This radical oscillation — this passing from one extreme into another, where power, after displaying its "irrational" cruelty and culpabilizing us to the extreme, all of a sudden "changes the tune," shows its friendly face, wonders at our fright and endeavors to make us feel easier — provides the elementary superego-matrix of its manipulation. Anyone who has done military service knows perfectly the logic of this impossible choice: if you do not follow promptly the order of a corporal, you are bound to meet with his rage and threats; if, however, you do carry out the order as required, he sneers at you for your over-zealous attitude, for your taking things seriously where a proper distance of taking-it-easy is appropriate.

This paradox of the impossible choice points toward the insufficiency of those theories which identify the performative with the mechanism of power, of establishing a power relationship, and therefore advocate the strategy of ironical self-destructive imitation of the performative: the logic of the impossible choice is precisely the logic of a "pragmatic paradox," of a self-contradicting performative. In order to function properly, power discourse must be inherently split, it must "cheat" performatively, to disavow its own underlying performative gesture. Sometimes, therefore, the only truly subversive thing to do when confronted with a power discourse is simply to *take it at its word*.

The crucial, hitherto underestimated ideological impact of the coming ecological crisis will be precisely to make the "collapse of the big Other" part of our everyday experience, i.e., to sap this unconscious belief in the "big Other" of power: already the Chernobyl catastrophe made ridiculously obsolete such notions as "national sovereignty," exposing the power's ultimate impotence. Our "spontaneous" ideological reaction to it, of course, is to have recourse to the fake premodern forms of reliance on the "big Other" ("New Age consciousness": the balanced circuit of Nature, etc.). Perhaps, however, our very physical survival hinges on our ability to consummate the act of assuming fully the "nonexistence of the Other," of *tarrying with the negative*.

Notes

Introduction

1 There is also an opposite way to undermine the domination of a Master-Signifier. Monuments are usually "phallic": towers, spires, something that protrudes and "stands out." For that reason, the monument at the university campus in Mexico City is unique: a large jagged ring of concrete encircles the formless black undulating surface of lava. What we have here is a true monument to the Thing, to coagulated *jouissance*, substance of enjoyment—the reverse of the hole in the flag which sets in motion our sublime enthusiasm. Insofar as what we perceive through the hole in the flag is the empty sky, we might say that the relationship between the hole in the flag and the coagulated lava points toward the Heideggerian antagonism of Earth and Sky.

2 See chapter 11 of Jacques Lacan, *Le séminaire,* book 8: *Le transfert* (Paris: Editions du Seuil, 1991).

3 See Fredric Jameson, "The Existence of Italy," in *Signatures of the Visible* (New York: Routledge, 1990).

4 See Rodolphe Gasché, *The Tain of the Mirror* (Cambridge: Harvard University Press, 1986).

5 See Bernard Baas, "Le désir pur," in *Ornicar?* 38 (Paris 1985).

6 See Jacques Lacan, *Le séminaire,* book 17: *L'envers de la psychanalyse* (Paris: Editions du Seuil, 1991).

7 See Alain Badiou, *Manifeste pour la philosophie* (Paris: Editions du Seuil, 1989).

1 "I or He or It (the Thing) Which Thinks"

1 *Basic Instinct* also, in a very specific way, bears witness to a fundamental change in the logic and function of narrative frame: a decade or two ago, the effect of the sudden shift

in the last shot (the tracking from the love-making couple on the bed to a close-up of the ice-pick, the murderous tool, under the bed) would be shattering, it would cause a vertiginous turnabout compelling us to reinterpret the entire previous content; today, however, it loses its dramatic impact and basically leaves us indifferent. In short, the "Hitchcockian object," a "little piece of the real" condensing an intense intersubjective relationship, is today no longer possible. (As to this "Hitchcockian object," see Mladen Dolar, "Hitchcock's Objects," in Slavoj Žižek, *Everything You Always Wanted to Know about Lacan (But Were Afraid to Ask Hitchcock)* [London: Verso, 1992].)

2   In *Blade Runner* as well as in *Angel Heart,* this "alien" element is detectable by way of a stain in the eye (androids are identified through their unnaturally dilated irises; when the Devil discloses his true nature, his eyes take on an uncanny blue glare). This stain in the eye designates the left-over of something which had to be excluded so that what we experience as "reality" gained its consistency. Its reemergence therefore vacillates the very coordinates of "reality." Already in *Frankenstein,* the impenetrable gaze of "depth-less eyes" is the feature which distinguishes the monster. Suffice it to quote Mary Shelley's own "hideous phantasm" which was at the origin of her book: "He sleeps; but he is awakened; he opens his eyes; behold, the horrid thing stands at his bedside, opening his curtains and looking on him with yellow, watery, but speculative eyes" (Mary Shelley, *Frankenstein* [Harmondsworth: Penguin, 1992], p. 9). The nontransparent, "depthless" eye blocks our access to the "soul," to the infinite abyss of the "person," thus turning it into a soulless monster: not simply a nonsubjective machine, but rather an uncanny subject that has not yet been submitted to the process of "subjectivization" which confers upon it the depth of "personality."

3   The version released in 1992 as "director's cut" is a compromise, not yet the true director's cut: it drops the voiceover and the imbecile happy-ending, yet it abstains from disclosing Deckard's own replicant-status.

4   See Michel Foucault, *The Order of Things* (New York: Vintage, 1973).

5   All quotes from *Critique of Pure Reason (CPR)* are from Norman Kemp Smith's translation (London: Macmillan, 1992).

6   The same paradox could also be formulated by way of the ambiguous ontological status of possibility which, in its very capacity of a "mere possibility" as opposed to actuality, possesses an actuality of its own: the Kantian transcendental apperception designates a pure possibility of self-consciousness which, *qua* possibility, produces actual effects, i.e., determines the actual status of the subject. Once this possibility is actualized, we are not dealing anymore with the self-consciousness of the pure I, but with the empirical consciousness of the Self *qua* phenomenon, part of reality. Another way to formulate this difference is via the gap that separates "I" from "me": the Kantian transcendental apperception designates the I of "I think," whereas Descartes surreptitiously substantial-izes the "je pense" (I think) into "moi qui pense" (me who thinks).

7   Jacques Lacan, *Ecrits: A Selection* (New York: Norton, 1977), p. 314.

8   Which is why the expression "self-in-itself" used by some interpreters of Kant (J. N. Findlay, for example—see his *Kant and the Transcendental Object* [Oxford: Clarendon Press, 1981]) seems inherently nonsensical: insofar as we conceive Self as an intelligible Thing, it loses the very feature that defines it, namely its transcendental "spontaneity"

and autonomy which belong to it only within the horizon of finitude, i.e., of the split between intelligible and intuitive. (This is ultimately confirmed by Kant himself, who always insisted on leaving open the possibility that free human activity is actually regulated by some inaccessible intelligible Nature—God's Providence, for example—which makes use of us for the realization of its unfathomable plan.)

9   In a supreme twist of irony, the title of the subdivision in which Kant articulates this unique status of the pure I of apperception as neither a phenomenon nor a noumenon is "Of the Ground of the Division of All Objects into Phenomena and Noumena."

10 And my—Hegelian—point is here that the "I think" stands in exactly the same relationship to the Thing-in-itself: it designates a hole, a gap, in it and as such it opens up, within the domain of Things which only "truly exist" (i.e., which exist in themselves as opposed to a mere phenomenal existence), the space where phenomena can emerge, the space of our phenomenal experience. In other words, through the "I think," the Thing-in-itself is as it were split and becomes inaccessible to itself in the guise of phenomena. This is the question Kant does not ask: how does the transcendental fact of pure apperception, the "I think," concern Things-in-themselves? The truly Hegelian problem is not to penetrate from the phenomenal surface into Things-in-themselves, but to explain how, within Things, something akin to phenomena could have emerged.

11 Henry E. Allison, *Kant's Transcendental Idealism* (New Haven: Yale University Press, 1986), p. 289.

12 Ibid., pp. 289–90.

13 Toward the end of part one of *Critique of Practical Reason*, the same logic reemerges at the ethical level: if I were to have a direct insight into God's nature, this would abrogate the very notion of ethical activity. See Immanuel Kant, *Critique of Practical Reason* (New York: Macmillan, 1956), pp. 151–53: "Of the Wise Adaptation of Man's Cognitive Faculties to His Practical Vocation."

14 Beatrice Longuenesse, *Hegel et la critique de la métaphysique* (Paris: Vrin, 1981), p. 24. Therein consists the gap that separates the transcendental object from the Thing: the Thing is the unattainable substratum which affects our senses, i.e., with regard to it, we are mere passive recipients, whereas the transcendental object is an object totally devoid of any positive, intuitive, content, of any "stuff" originating in the transcendent Thing; it is an object which is in its entirety transcendentally "posited" by the subject. The axis that separates the Thing and the transcendental object is therefore that of positing and presupposing: the Thing is the pure presupposition, whereas the transcendental object is purely posited; and the ultimate identity of the Thing and the transcendental object offers another example of the Hegelian coincidence of the pure presupposition with positing.

15 How are we to render palpable the link between *objet petit a*, i.e., the *plus-de-jouir,* surplus-enjoyment, and the Marxian surplus-value? Perhaps a reference to one of the favored Hitchcock's anecdotes (retold, among others, by Truffaut in his *Hitchcock*) could be of some help. For *North-by-Northwest,* so the story goes, Hitchcock planned the following scene which was never shot: while engaged in a conversation, Cary Grant and his partner walk along the assembly line of a car factory, moving with the same pace as the assembling of a car in the background, so that behind them we can clearly observe in one

continuous shot the entire process of manufacturing a car—we see all parts that enter into its composition. At the end of the line, Grant turns toward the car, opens its door, and out of it falls a bloody corpse. The corpse is here *objet petit a*: the pure semblance, the surplus which magically emerges "out of nowhere," and simultaneously the surplus of the production process over the elements which went into it.

16   As it was demonstrated by Allison, *Kant's Transcendental Idealism*, p. 245.

17   What then is the exact relationship between transcendental object and subject? In order to provide an answer, one has to bear in mind the double nature of the Thing-in-itself in Kant: the Thing designates the totality of phenomena (inaccessible to us *qua* finite subjects) as well as their noumenal support, the unknowable X which affects us. So, the transcendental object is metonymical; it stands for the infinite series of phenomena, of the objects of possible intuition, whereas the subject obeys the logic of metaphor, i.e., its void holds the place of the inaccessible noumenal "Thing-which-thinks."

18   See Robert Pippin, *Hegel's Idealism* (Cambridge: Cambridge University Press, 1988).

19   Adorno articulates in an exemplary way this move from Kant to Hegel apropos of the failed mediation between sociology and psychology (see his "Zum Verhaeltnis von Soziologie und Psychologie," in *Gesellschaftstheorie und Kulturkritik* [Frankfurt: Suhrkamp, 1975]). In Kantian terms, their relationship is strictly antinomical: one can endeavor to deduce sociology from psychology, i.e., to conceive the struggle of "anonymous" social forces as an "objectivization" of "concrete" interpersonal relationships, individual existential "projects," etc. (the ultimate aim of various phenomenological approaches, up to Sartre's *Critique of Dialectical Reason* with its key notion of "practico-inerte"); on the other hand, one can conceive the psychological self-experience as a mere imaginary effect-reflection of objective social structures and processes (the ultimate aim of functionalist-structuralist approaches, up to the early Althusser, before the reference to "class-struggle" assumed the crucial role in his theoretical edifice). In both cases, the synthesis is false, and the attempts to bridge the gap (via notions like "social character," etc.), by means of their ultimate failure, do nothing but bear witness to its persistence. Insofar as we remain within the Kantian horizon, the looked-for unity of psychology and sociology (which we somehow feel is the necessary ingredient of any "true" theory of the social space) is thus displaced into the unattainable Beyond, i.e., it acquires the status of a Thing-in-itself. The Hegelian dialectical approach, on the contrary, allows us to grasp how, in this very failure of our endeavor to develop a consistent theoretical synthesis of psychology and sociology, we "touch the real"; this abyss that forever separates the "reified" field of social forces from the psychological self-experience is the fundamental feature of the modern society. Our very epistemological failure thus throws us into the "thing itself," since it registers an antagonism that pertains to the very kernel of the object itself.

20   As to this notion, see "Introduction" to G. W. F. Hegel, *Phenomenology of Spirit* (Oxford: Oxford University Press, 1977).

21   As to this opposition in Kant and Hegel, see Chapter 3 of the present book.

22   This chapter culminates in the motif of money, taken over later by Marx: the reign of disintegration—a society in which the stability and firmness of opposites (Good-Evil, Truth-Lie, etc.) are undermined and in which every opposite incessantly passes into its

other (Good is revealed as hypocritical mask of Evil, etc.)—emerges as the reign of money. Money is the "existing Notion," the force of negativity assuming the reified form of a particular, external object, i.e., the paradox of something which is in itself a mere dispensable object, a little piece of metal or paper in my hand, but which nonetheless possesses the power to overturn every firm determination, to provide mobility for the footless, beauty for the hideous, etc.

23   Hegel, *Phenomenology of Spirit*, p. 362.

24   And what Kant obliterates is precisely this radical "decentering" at work here: the agency which compels the subject to act morally, to follow the ethical imperative ("the voice of conscience"), is a parasitical *object*, a foreign body in his very center.

25   See Karl Marx, *Pre-Capitalist Economic Formations* (London: Lawrence and Wishart, 1964).

26   See Georg Lukács, *History and Class Consciousness* (London: New Left Books, 1969).

27   See Helmut Reichelt, *Zur logischen Struktur des Kapitalbegriffs bei Karl Marx* (Frankfurt: Suhrkamp Verlag, 1970).

28   Hegel and Kierkegaard are here far closer than may appear. The exchange of "something for nothing" by way of which the subject *qua S* emerges is namely the very act of abyssal / noneconomical sacrifice which, in Kierkegaard, defines the religious stage: the ability to accomplish this move is what distinguishes the "knight of faith": "The person who denies himself and sacrifices himself for duty gives up the finite in order to grasp on to the infinite; he is secure enough. The tragic hero gives up what is certain for what is still more certain, and the eye of the beholder rests confidently upon him. But the person who gives up the universal to grasp something still higher that is not the universal, what does he do?" (Søren Kierkegaard, *Fear and Trembling* [Harmondsworth: Penguin, 1985], p. 89).

29   See Brian Rotman, *Signifying Nothing* (London: Macmillan, 1987).

30   Ibid., p. 24.

31   Ibid., p. 25.

32   At the level of social identity, the same shift designates the so-called naturalization of immigrants: as long as they perceive themselves as Greeks, Italians, etc., who came to live in America, their identity remains particular, i.e., "American" remains an abstract-universal predicate; the crucial reversal takes place when they start to perceive themselves as Americans whose contingent ethnic roots are Greek or Italian.

33   One of the standard reproaches to Hegel is that he ventures the illegitimate leap from the thought of the finite subject into the thought of the Absolute itself: Kant's transcendental logic remains the reflective insight into the a priori forms that outline the horizon of the finite subject, whereas Hegel's logic is the reflection of the Absolute itself which appears to itself in the thought of the (finite) subject. However, "everything turns on grasping and expressing the True, not only as *Substance*, but equally as *Subject*" (*Phenomenology of Spirit*, p. 10). This does not mean that the Absolute itself is a Subject playing with us, finite humans, i.e., that, in the movement of absolute reflection, we, finite humans, make ourselves into the instrument, the medium through which the Absolute contemplates itself—this would be a simple perverse position. What Hegel has in mind is that the split between us and the Absolute (the split on account of which we are subjects) is at the same time the self-split of the Absolute itself: *we participate at the Absolute not on account of*

244 Notes to Chapter 1

our exalted contemplation of it, but by means of the very gap which forever separates us from it —
as in Kafka's novels where the fascinated gaze of the subject is already included in the
functioning of the transcendent, unapproachable agency of Law (the court, the castle).

34   See Jacques Lacan, *Ecrits: A Selection*, p. 80.

35   In this respect, Pierre Livet's "Reflexivité et extériorité dans la Logique de Hegel"
(*Archives de Philosophie*, books 47 and 48, Paris, 1984) is very instructive in its endeavor to
grasp Hegel's dialectic as an ambiguous attempt to combine two ultimately incompatible logics: the logic of self-relating (of reapplying a logical operator onto the same object
or onto itself — the "negation of negation," etc.), which points forward, in the direction of
contemporary formal logic, and the logic of subjectivity ("substance as subject," etc.),
which points backward, to the problematic inherited from Kant ("transcendental apperception" as the guarantee of the unity of thought and being, as well as the locus of
"spontaneity" of the subjective constitution of reality). According to Livet, the first logic
leads to the splitting, self-decentering process, a process by means of which the inherent
logical structure gives rise to its externality; whereas the second logic forces this externality back into the frame of the traditional philosophical problematic of the "externalization of subjectivity." What Livet does not take into account (and what the Lacanian
logic of the signifier enables us to conceptualize) is a notion of the subject at work in the
very process of reflective self-relating: Livet tacitly assumes the identity of the Hegelian
subject with the traditional notion of the "subject," thereby imputing to Hegel a duality
which simply is not there. The Hegelian subject emerges precisely by way of the
reflective, self-relating, reapplication of a logical operator, as in the worn-out joke on the
cannibal who ate the last cannibal in the tribe.

36   Hegel is here opposed by Kierkegaard, according to whom, in the eyes of the universal
public Law, the act of the religious suspension of the Ethical (Abraham's killing of his
son, for example) remains a crime; its religious significance discloses itself only from the
standpoint of the individual's pure inwardness.

37   Hegel, *The Philosophy of History* (New York: Dover, 1956), p. 33.

38   See Jacques Lacan, *Le séminaire*, book 17: *L'envers de la psychanalyse* (Paris: Editions du
Seuil, 1991).

39   Things are further complicated by the fact that, according to Lacan, the very emergence
of philosophical discourse in Plato results from a transmutation of the hysterical position
into the position of a Master: Socrates, Plato's "Master," is not yet a Master, his position
is between a hysteric and an analyst.

40   As to the notion of the "infinite / indefinite judgment," see Chapter 3 of the present
book.

41   The passage in which Hegel compares the difference between "naive" and speculative
reading of the proposition "Spirit is a bone" to that between the urinating and the
fecundating function of one and the same organ (penis) is far more ambiguous than it
may appear. That is to say, Hegel's point is in no way that we have to reject the "naive"
reading (the way phrenology conceived of itself: Spirit is this inert object, the skull; its
characteristics are to be deduced from the skull's swellings and hollows) and to take into
account only the speculative meaning (Spirit is strong enough to embrace, to mediate
entire reality, inclusive of the most inert objectivity): this speculative meaning emerges

only when we yield unreservedly to the "naive" reading and thereby experience its inherent nonsense, its absurd self-contradiction. This radical discord, incompatibility, this absolute "negative relationship" between the two terms (Spirit and bone) *is* Spirit *qua* power of negativity. In other words, *in the choice between "naive" and speculative reading, one has first to make the wrong choice if one is to arrive at the speculative truth.* This example could serve a more general purpose of warning us how *not* to read Hegel, i.e., how the very immediate counter-position of nondialectical "Understanding" and dialectical "Reason" belongs to Understanding: with regard to Hegel's phallic comparison, we remain stuck to the level of "urinating" precisely when we endeavor directly to comprehend the penis in its fecundating function. And the same goes for the relationship of Kant to Hegel: if there is a philosopher who (viewed from the Hegelian perspective) produces speculative truths in an unreflected form, that is, who "already speaks on fecundation while continuing to refer to urination," this philosopher is Kant. In all crucial passages of his system, Kant misrecognizes the speculative dimension of his own discovery, presenting it in the guise of its opposite: in Kant's philosophy, the abstractive power of absolute negativity, the Spirit's power to "tear asunder what naturally belongs together," i.e., to break apart the substantial "chain of being" and to treat nonbeing (appearance) as possessing the ontological weight of being, is misperceived as its *impotence,* as its inability to attain the transcendent Thing-in-itself; etc. Precisely at this point, however, we should not yield to the temptation of opposing the Kantian "rigid" Differences to their Hegelian speculative Mediation. The moment we do so, we regress to a point before Kant, back into pre-critical "dogmatic" attitude. What we must do, on the contrary, is to persist in being "more Kantian than Kant himself" and to assume fully the inconsistencies of the Kantian position.

42 This is also how Jacques-Alain Miller, in his unpublished seminar on "extimité" from 1985–1986, defines *objet petit a:* as the "In-itself which is for us."

43 As to this ambiguity, see chapter 5 of Slavoj Žižek, *The Sublime Object of Ideology* (London: Verso, 1990).

44 In this sense, Lacan interprets the primordial father, *Père-jouissance,* as a neurotic's myth sustained by the belief that, prior to the Prohibition, there really was a father to whom uninhibited enjoyment was accessible.

45 The reproach of Monique David-Menard—see her *La folie dans la raison pure* (Paris: Vrin, 1991).

46 Foucault's pendulum (which, by way of its irregular swinging, demonstrates that the earth itself rotates) exerts such a fascination because it effectively gives body to this logic of the Sublime. Its spectacular effect is not due solely to the fact that it literally makes us lose our footing (since ground itself, the phenomenological foundation and stable measure of our experience of movement, proves to be shifting); what is even more awesome is that *it implies a third imaginary point of absolute immobility.* The sublime point is this hypothetical point of absolute rest produced by way of the self-reference of movement, i.e., the point with reference to which both the pendulum and the earth surface are moving.

47 The opposition of Kant and Hegel with regard to the Limit and its Beyond is usually conceived in a wholly different way. According to this standard version, Kant limited the

field of phenomena, yet simultaneously prohibited the access to its Beyond (i.e., the only legitimate definition of the noumena is the purely negative one); Hegel's answer to this Kantian paradox is that the moment we conceive something as limited, implicitly, at least, we already reach beyond it, i.e., we must possess an implicit notion of what lies on the other side of the frontier. This way, Hegel throws the door wide open to the return to the traditional rationalist metaphysics. However, such a reading involves a crucial misunderstanding of Hegel's critique of Kant. According to Hegel, it is Kant who maintains the reference to some Beyond, although devoid of any positive content; for Kant, the status of this void is purely epistemological, i.e., due to our finitude, we do not know how Things-in-themselves are structured. What Hegel accomplishes here is not a "filling out" of this void, but rather the simple reversal of the epistemological void into an ontological one: the negative definition of the Thing concerns the Thing itself, since this Thing is nothing but the void of absolute negativity. In other words, Hegel does not reproach Kant with not daring to take the step into what lies beyond phenomena, but rather with sticking to the "representational" notion that the void beyond phenomena is only a negative reflection in our finite minds of some positive, inaccessible In-itself.

48   For a Lacanian reading of Magritte, see chapter 3 of the present book.

49   One of the early stories of Philip Dick, the author of *Do Androids Dream of Electric Sheep?*, upon which *Blade Runner* is based, is "The Father-thing" from 1954: Charles Walton, a ten-year-old boy, realizes that his father Ted was killed and replaced by an alien, malignant form of life. This Thing, that is "more in father than father himself," an evil embodiment of the superego, can be discerned in those rare moments when the expression of the father's face suddenly changes, losing the features of an ordinary, weary middle-class American and irradiating a kind of indifferent, impersonal Evil.

50   In this respect, the consequences of the Orlando, Florida, court ruling in September 1992 to comply with the request of the ten-year-old boy who wanted to stay with his foster parents instead of returning to his biological mother are more radical than it may appear, since they concern the very relationship of S_1 and S_2: when a child can win a divorce against his parents, as the newspapers put it, he can ultimately choose who his parents are with regard to their respective positive properties (the quality of care, etc.). This way, motherhood as well as fatherhood ultimately cease to be symbolic functions independent of positive features, i.e., the very logic of "Whatever you do, you remain my mother-father and I shall love you . . . ," of S_1 qua Master-Signifier which designates a symbolic mandate, not a simple cluster of properties, is undermined.

51   The correlate to this reduction of the father to nonphallic Knowledge, of course, is the fantasy-notion of mother qua self-reproducing monster which generates its offspring without the mediation of the phallus: it was already Marx who, in an enigmatic metaphor in *Capital III*, determined Capital as a self-reproducing Mother-Thing.

52   All these cases, of course, reproduce the structure of the liar-paradox ("What I am saying now is a lie"). According to Lacan, this paradox can articulate an authentic subjective acknowledgment which becomes visible the moment we take into account the splitting between the subject of the enunciation and the subject of the enunciated: by saying "I am lying!" I acknowledge the inauthenticity of my being, of my subjective position of enunciation, and in this sense I am telling the truth.

53 And was not the same gesture accomplished by Kierkegaard apropos of belief: we, finite mortals, are condemned to "believe that we believe"; we can never be certain that we actually believe. This position of eternal doubt, this awareness that our belief is forever condemned to remain a hazardous wager, is the only way for us to be true Christian believers: those who go beyond the threshold of uncertainty, preposterously assuming that they really do believe, are not believers at all but arrogant sinners. If, according to Lacan, the question that animates the compulsive (obsessional) neurotic is "Am I dead or alive?", and if the religious version of it is "Am I really a believer or do I just believe to believe?", here, as we can see, the question is transformed into "Am I a replicant or a human being?"

54 For such a reading, see Kaja Silverman, "Back to the Future," *Camera obscura* 27 (1991): 109–32.

55 It is Lacan himself who is ultimately responsible for this confusion, insofar as, in his early seminars, when he articulates the motif of the "mechanical" character of the unconscious, he does not yet distinguish between knowledge qua symbolic tradition and knowledge inscribed into the Real itself. However, beginning with Seminar 20 (*Encore*), which expressly posits the distinction between signifier and writing-inscription (*écrit*), every confusion is excluded. It is against this background that we can explain the failure of *The Lady in the Lake*, Robert Montgomery's film version of Raymond Chandler's novel, which, with the exception of the brief prologue and epilogue, is entirely made of subjective shots, reducing our field-of-vision to that of the detective. That is to say, why does this experiment necessarily affect us as somehow artificial, contrived, instead of creating the illusion of actually transposing us into the hero's subjective experience? The subjective shot is effective insofar as it remains a fragment framed by objective shots which provide for its context; the moment the subjective perspective "spills over" the effect is not total subjectivization but rather an uncanny mechanization: the alleged pure subjective gaze coincides with its radical opposite, with the mechanical intake of the camera. For that reason, those moments in *The Lady in the Lake* when we briefly see the hero's face (its reflection in a mirror as allegedly perceived by the hero, for example) produce the effect of a radical discord: this face, these eyes that we now see, are in no way those through which we perceive reality throughout the film. We are identified with a gaze which is obviously the gaze of an awkward machine: we, the spectators, become reduced to a "Thing which sees."

2   *Cogito* and the Sexual Difference

1 See Immanuel Kant, *The Critique of Judgement* (Oxford: Clarendon Press, 1991).

2 On radical Evil see Chapter 3 of the present book. This notion of the Sublime provides a new approach to Lacan's "Kant avec Sade," i.e., his thesis on Sade as the truth of Kant. Let us begin with an everyday question: what accounts for the (alleged) charm of sexual manuals? That is to say, it is clear that we do not really browse them to learn things; what attracts us is that the activity which epitomizes the transgression of every rule (when we are engaged in "it," we are not supposed to think, but just to yield to passions . . .) assumes the form of its opposite and becomes an object of school-like drill. (A common

piece of advice actually concerns achieving sexual excitement by imitating—during the foreplay, at least—the procedure of cold, asexual instrumental activity: I discuss with my partner in detail the steps of what we will do, we ponder the pros and cons of different possibilities—shall we begin with cunnilingus or not?—assessing every point as if we are dealing with an elaborate technical operation. Sometimes, this "turns us on.") What we encounter here is a kind of paradoxically inverted sublime: in the Kantian Sublime, the boundless chaos of sensible experience (raging storm, breathtaking abysses) renders forth the presentiment of the pure Idea of Reason whose Measure is so large that no object of experience, not even nature in the wildest and mightiest display of its forces, can come close to it (i.e., here, the Measure, the ideal Order, is on the side of the unattainable Idea, and the formless chaos on the side of sensible experience); whereas in the case of "bureaucratized sexuality," the relationship is reversed: sexual arousal, as the exemplary case of the state which eludes instrumental regimentation, is evoked by way of its opposite, by way of being treated as bureaucratic duty. Perhaps, it is (also) in this sense that Sade is the truth of Kant: the sadist who enjoys performing sex as an instrumentalized bureaucratic duty reverses and thereby brings to its truth the Kantian Sublime in which we become aware of the suprasensible Measure through the chaotic, boundless character of our experience.

3   In this precise sense, the Kantian distinction between the constitutive and the regulative dimension corresponds to the Lacanian distinction between knowledge and supposed knowledge: the teleological regulative Idea has the status of "knowledge in the real," of the inherent rational order in nature which, although theoretically unprovable, has to be presupposed if our positive knowledge (structured through constitutive categories) is to be possible.

4   The choice of Raymond Massey for the role of the superego-driven governor is deeply significant if we bear in mind his screen persona: he also played John Brown, whose name epitomizes (in the eyes of the predominant ideology) the obsession with justice which, on account of its overzealous character, turns into ravaging Evil.

5   If we are not to miss this paradox of the Christian Sublime, it is of crucial importance that we bear in mind the structure of the Möbius strip that pertains to judgment in Hegelian theory. The judgment of reflection, for example—"Socrates is mortal"—renders the identity of the two moments: the (logical) subject, a certain nonconceptual "this" pointed out, designated, by a name (standing for the immediate, indeterminate, unity-with-itself of an entity), and the predicate which is *this same unity* in its mode of alienation, i.e., separated, torn from itself, opposed to itself in the guise of a universal "reflective determination" under which the immediate "this" is subsumed ("reflective determination" of an entity is its very essence, the innermost kernel of its identity, yet conceived in the guise of its opposite, of a totally indifferent and external universal determination). Consequently, we do not have two elements united, tied up, in the common space of the judgment, but *one and the same* element which appears first in the mode of immediate-nonreflected unity-with-itself ("this," the logical subject), then in the mode of its opposite, of self-externalization, i.e., as an abstract reflective determination. Perhaps even more appropriate than this metaphor of the two surfaces of the Möbius strip is the science fiction paradox of the time-travel loop where the subject

encounters a different version of itself, i.e., runs into its own later incarnation. Therein consists Hegel's point: subject and predicate are identical, the same thing, their difference is purely topological.

6   The same paradox is repeated at the very end of the chapter on Spirit, where we pass from the objective Spirit to the sphere of the Absolute (religion, philosophy) via the resolution of the impasses of the Beautiful Soul. Significantly, Hegel here for the first time uses the term "reconciliation" (*Versöhnung*): the Beautiful Soul has to recognize its complicity with the wicked ways of the world it deplores; it has to accept the *factum brutum* of its environs as "its own."

7   In the history of modern cinema, the progressive modes of how to present "pathological" libidinal economies (hysteria, etc.) perfectly follows the matrix of this "downward-synthesis." Up to a certain point, formal procedures—extravagant as they may appear—remain "anchored" in the diegetic reality, i.e., they express the "pathology" of a diegetic personality. In the films of Alain Resnais, for example, the formal convolutions (time-loops, etc.) render the paradoxes of the memory of a diegetic personality; in John Cassavetes' work, the diegetic content—the hysteria of everyday American married life—contaminates the cinematic form itself (the camera gets "too close" to the faces, rendering in detail the repulsive facial convulsions; shots from a hand-carried camera confer upon the very cinematic frame the precipitous trembling that characterizes hysterical economy; etc.). At a certain point, however, the diegetic underpinning "explodes" and the film sets out to render directly the hysterical economy, bypassing altogether the diegetic content. It is thus impossible to distinguish three phases:

–"realism": the form is not yet contaminated by the hysterical, etc. content; no matter how pathological the diegetic content, it is rendered from a neutral distance of an "objective" narrative.

–its first negation: the hysterical content "contaminates" form itself. In many a modernist film, the form seems to narrate its own story, which undermines the film's "official" diegetic content; this antagonism between diegetic content and form, the surplus of the latter over the former, is what the standard use of the term "writing" designates. Suffice it to recall the famous Cahiers du cinema analysis of John Ford's *The Young Lincoln* in which the form registers the ominous, superego, monstrous-inhuman side of the main character, and thus runs counter to the patriotic elevation of Lincoln, the "official" theme of the film.

–the "negation of the negation": the modernist "abstract cinema" which renders its "pathological" content directly, renouncing the detour through a consistent diegetic reality.

8   See section 3 of Immanuel Kant, *Observations on the Feeling of the Beautiful and Sublime* (Berkeley: University of California, 1991). What is of special interest here are the perverse paradoxes Kant gets involved in when he endeavors to articulate the interaction of a beautiful woman and a sublime man: man's ultimate message to a woman is "even if you do not love me, I shall force you to respect me by the sheer force of my sublime grandeur," whereas woman's counter-claim is "even if you do not respect me, I shall force you to love me for my beauty." These paradoxes are perverse insofar as their underlying premise is that, in order to discover the sublime grandeur of man's moral

stance, woman must cease to love him, and vice versa, man must disdain woman for her lack of proper moral attitude if he is to experience the true character of his love for her. Along these lines, Kant even provides his own formulation of the impossibility of sexual relationship: in sexuality, man's object is either the nonspecified universality of "any woman" (if he is driven by raw bodily passion) or the fantasy-image to which no actual woman can ever correspond in reality (the romantic notion of sublime infatuation). In both cases, the real object—the actual woman in her uniqueness—is annihilated.

9   I am indebted to Joan Copjec for the crucial notion of the structural homology between Lacan's "formulae of sexuation" and the Kantian opposition of mathematical and dynamical sublime. This book in its entirety is a token of my theoretical debt to her. Cf. Joan Copjec, *Read My Desire* (Cambridge: MIT Press, 1993).

10 Lacan's F of course means the function of (symbolic) castration: "man is submitted to castration" implies the exception of "at least one," the primordial father of the Freudian myth in *Totem and Taboo,* a mythical being who has had all the women and was capable of achieving complete satisfaction. For an explication of these "formulae of sexuation," see Jacques Lacan, *Le séminaire,* book 20: *Encore* (Paris: Editions du Seuil, 1975); the two key chapters are translated in Jacques Lacan and the Ecole freudienne, *Feminine Sexuality* (London: Macmillan, 1982). For a compressed presentation of it see also chapter 3 of Slavoj Žižek, *For They Know Not What They Do* (London: Verso, 1991).

11 It is the recent revival of the "human rights" problematic which offers an opportunity to demonstrate how Lacan's opposition of masculine and feminine formulas can be of "practical use." The "masculine" approach to human rights is based on universalization: "*every human being* must enjoy the rights to . . . (freedom, property, health, etc., etc.)," with an exception always lurking in the background. It is easy, for example, simply to proclaim that every x has to enjoy these rights *insofar as she or he fully deserves the title of "human being"* (i.e., of our idealized-ideological notion of it), a move which allows us to exclude covertly those who do not fit our criteria (insane, criminals, children, women, other races . . .). The "feminine" approach, on the other hand, seems much more appropriate to our "postmodern" attitude: "there must be nobody who is *denied his or her specific rights"*—a move which guarantees that specific rights, the only ones which really matter, will not be excluded under the guise of an apparently neutral, all-embracing universality. See Renata Salecl, *The Spoils of Freedom* (London: Routledge, 1993).

12 Or, to put it in the Lacanian way, man and woman "are split differently and *this difference in splitting accounts for sexual difference"* (Bruce Fink, "There's No Such Thing as a Sexual Relationship," *Newsletter of the Freudian Field,* vol. 5, nos. 1–2 [1992]: 78).

13 There seem to be grounds for an opposite reading which would link dynamic antinomies to the feminine side of the formulae of sexuation and mathematical antinomies to the masculine side: as pointed out by Jacques-Alain Miller, feminine antinomies are antinomies of inconsistency, whereas masculine antinomies are antinomies of incompleteness—and are dynamic antinomies not about the inconsistency between universal causal links and the fact of freedom? On the other hand, do mathematical antinomies not hinge on the finitude, i.e., incompleteness, of our phenomenal experience? (See Jacques-Alain Miller, "Extimité" [unpublished seminar], Paris, 1985–86.) However, the "not-all," incomplete character of the phenomenal field in Kant does not imply that something lies

beyond or outside this field; instead, it implies the field's inherent inconsistency: phenomena are never "all," yet for all that there is no exception, nothing outside them. It is only the dynamic antinomy which deals with the opposition of phenomena and their noumenal Beyond.

14 It is on the contrary man for whom it can be said that "a part of him eludes the phallic function"—the exception constitutive of the Universal. The paradox is therefore that man is *dominated* by the phallic function insofar as there is something in him which *evades* it, whereas woman *eludes its grasp* precisely insofar as there is nothing in her which is *not* submitted to it. The solution to this paradox is that the "phallic function" is, in its fundamental dimension, the operator of exclusion.

15 For a more detailed account of it, see Chapter 3 of the present book.

16 See chapter 16 of Jacques Lacan, *The Four Fundamental Concepts of Psycho-Analysis* (New York: Norton, 1977).

17 See *The Ethics of Psychoanalysis, 1959–1960, The Seminar of Jacques Lacan,* book 7, ed. Jacques-Alain Miller (London: Routledge / Tavistock, 1992).

18 See Jacques Lacan, "Kant avec Sade," in *Ecrits* (Paris: Editions du Seuil, 1966).

19 This ethics of desire, for example, would compel us to reject Lars von Trier's *Europa* (*Zentropa*), a film which seems to realize fully Hans-Jürgen Syberberg's anti-Semitic program of aesthetics as the only medium for the reconciliation of Germany with its Nazi past. (In his recent work, Syberberg claims that those truly responsible for the German inability to "work through" their Nazi past are Jews themselves with their anti-aesthetic prohibition—Adorno's "no poetry after Auschwitz.") The aestheticist myth of Europe offered by the film is that of a continent caught in the vicious circle of self-indulging decadent *jouissance:* it is this very over-proximity of *jouissance* which suspends the efficiency of the performative, of the social link of symbolic authority. (Injunctions are inoperative: when the young American working on a German train undergoes examination for the post of the sleeping-car steward, the committee, instead of provoking anxiety, acts ridiculously with its meaningless questions and out-of-place punctuality.) The ultimate lesson of the film is that even the innocent American gaze cannot escape the decadent whirlpool of the European *jouissance* which finally draws him into itself. Although the film takes place in the autumn of 1945, immediately after the German defeat, the ruined Germany is clearly presented as a timeless metaphor for "Europe" as a continent caught in the circle of its decadent *jouissance.* The entire film is staged as a kind of hypnotic trauma masterminded by an anonymous narrator (Max von Sydow) who addresses the hero, telling him what to do and what lies ahead. The ultimate aim of psychoanalysis is precisely to deliver us from the domination of such a voice.

20 I.e., symptom. As to this notion of "sinthome," see Chapter 5 of the present book.

21 See subdivision 3 of "Introduction" in Marx's *Grundrisse,* selected and edited by David McLellan (London: Macmillan, 1980).

22 See Jacques Derrida, "Cogito and the History of Madness," in *Writing and Difference* (Chicago: University of Chicago Press, 1978).

23 Among the numerous variations on this motif of "death and the maiden," suffice it to mention the death-accident of Karen Silkwood in Mike Nichols's *Silkwood:* Meryl Streep behind the wheel of a car on a night drive, occupying the right side of the screen, her gaze

intensely fixed on the car mirror above her head through which she observes the light of a giant truck approaching her car from behind, and, on the left side of the screen, seen through the rear window of the car, the light of the truck gradually spreading into a formless dazzling spot overflowing the entire screen.

24   For a more detailed description of it, see Miran Božovič, "The Man behind His Own Retina," in Slavoj Žižek, *Everything You Always Wanted to Know about Lacan (But Were Afraid to Ask Hitchcock)* (London: Verso, 1992).

25   Sigmund Freud, *The Psychopathology of Everyday Life,* Pelican Freud Library, vol. 5 (Harmondsworth: Penguin, 1976), p. 248.

26   The Kantian split between the pure form of "I think" and the unknowable "Thing which thinks" is therefore not yet the Freudian Unconscious: the Unconscious *stricto sensu* takes place only with the choice of being; *it designates the "it thinks" which emerges the moment I "am,"* the moment the subject chooses being. In other words, Lacan's two versions of *cogito* enable us to distinguish clearly between the Unconscious and the Id (*Es*): the Unconscious is the "it thinks" in "I am, therefore it thinks," whereas the Id is the "it is" in "I think, therefore it is."

27   It is against this background that computer phobia can be properly situated: the fear of a "machine which thinks" bears witness to the foreboding that thought as such is external to the self-identity of my being.

28   Is not the exemplary case of such an object qua self-consciousness the Hitchcockian object? Is its traumatic impact not due to the fact that it *gives body to an unbearable gaze* which catches sight of the unbearable truth about the subject? Let us recall the victim's pair of glasses in the first murder in *Strangers on a Train:* while Bruno is strangling Miriam, Guy's promiscuous wife, we see the distorted reflection of the crime in her glasses, which fell to the ground when Bruno first attacked her. The glasses are the "third party," the witness to the murder, the object which gives body to a gaze. (Six years later, in *The Wrong Man,* the same role is assumed by the big table lamp, the witness of Rose's outburst against Manny. See Renata Salecl, "The Right Man and the Wrong Woman," in Žižek, *Everything You Always Wanted to Know about Lacan (But Were Afraid to Ask Hitchcock).)* For that reason, it is essential to read this scene together with the later unique scene of Bruno strangling an old society lady at a party. Bruno first engages in what is a simple, if somewhat tasteless, social game: he demonstrates to an elderly lady (who willingly offers her bare neck) how it is possible to strangle somebody so that the victim is unable to utter the slightest sound. However, things get out of control when the dual relationship is supplemented by a "third party," i.e., when Bruno perceives behind the lady he mockingly is strangling a girl with glasses (the sister of Ann, Guy's love). At this point the game suddenly takes a serious turn: as indicated by the musical score, the girl's glasses recall to Bruno's mind the scene of the first murder, and this short-circuit pushes Bruno to begin to strangle the old lady for real. This girl (played by Hitchcock's daughter Patricia) is made into "the woman who knows too much" purely on account of her glasses. What triggers the murderous drive in Bruno is the unbearable pressure exerted on him by the glasses; they are the object which "returns the gaze," i.e., because of the glasses, Bruno sees in the poor girl's surprised gaze "his ruin writ large."

29   See Mladen Dolar, "The Father Who Was Not Quite Dead," in Žižek, *Everything You Always Wanted to Know about Lacan (But Were Afraid to Ask Hitchcock).*

30 Patricia Highsmith's masterpiece *The Cry of the Owl* stages perfectly the delicate balance that defines the perverse position. A woman living alone in a country house suddenly becomes aware that she is observed by a shy voyeur hidden in the bushes behind the house; taking pity on him, she invites him into the house, offers him her friendship and finally falls in love with him—thereby inadvertently trespassing the invisible barrier that sustained his desire and thus provoking his repulsion. Therein consists the kernel of the perverse economy: a proper distance has to be maintained which prevents the subject from engaging in a "normal" sexual relationship; its transgression changes the love-object into repulsive excrement. What we have here is the zero-level of the logic of the "partial object" which, under the guise of obstructing the sexual relationship, actually conceals its inherent impossibility: the "partial object" is here reduced to the distance as such, to the invisible barrier which prevents me from consummating the sexual relation-ship; it is as if we have to do with the form of fetishism without fetish. (Patricia Highsmith is generally at her best when she renders with unmatched sensitivity the point at which compliance turns into intrusiveness: in *Dog's Ransom*, her other master-piece, the young police detective who offers his help to the couple whose dog was stolen gradually becomes an embarrassing intruder.)

31 The difference between neurotic and perverse symptom hinges upon this same point (see Colette Soler, "The Real Aims of the Analytic Act," *Lacanian Ink* 5 [1992]: 53–60). A neurotic has nothing but troubles with her symptom; it inconveniences her; she experi-ences it as an unwelcome burden, as something which perturbs her balance—in short, she *suffers* on account of her symptom (and therefore turns for help to the analyst), whereas a pervert unabashedly enjoys his symptom. Even if he is later ashamed of it or disturbed by it, the symptom as such is a source of profound satisfaction; it provides a firm anchoring point to his psychic economy and for that very reason he has no need for an analyst, i.e., there is no experience of suffering which sustains the demand for an analysis.

32 See chapter 14 of Jacques Lacan, *Le séminaire*, book 8: *Le transfert* (Paris: Editions du Seuil, 1991).

33 An example can be provided by the author of these lines who is unable to indulge alone in a rich meal in an expensive restaurant. The very idea of it gives rise to the feeling of an obscene, incestuous short-circuit; the only way to do it is in company, where having a good meal becomes part of a community ritual, i.e., where enjoying good food coincides with displaying to others that I enjoy it. An obsessional neurotic's *ethic* can be further exemplified by a patient who, apropos of every woman he tried to seduce, went to excessive pains to please her (and thus again and again succeeded in organizing his failure). When he endeavored to seduce a woman who loved deep sea diving, he immediately enrolled in a diving course (although he was personally repulsed by the very idea of it); even after this woman left him for good and he was devoting his amorous attention to a new woman who was totally indifferent toward diving, he nonetheless out of a sense of duty continued to participate in the diving course!

34 See Louis Althusser, "Ideology and Ideological State Apparatuses," in *Lenin and Philoso-phy, and Other Essays* (London: Verso, 1991).

35 An exemplary case of how somebody can "look alike" is to be found in Lubitch's *To be or not to be:* a Polish actor, as part of an intricate plot to deceive the Nazis, impersonates a

notorious Gestapo butcher; he wildly articulates and laughs, so that we, the spectators, automatically perceive his acting as a caricatural exaggeration; however, when, finally, the "original" himself—the true Gestapo butcher—enters the stage, he behaves in exactly the same way, acting as it were as *his own caricature*—in short, he "looks alike [himself]."

36   See Jacques Lacan, "Logical time and the Assertion of Anticipated Certainty," in *Newsletter of the Freudian Field*, vol. 2, no. 2 (1988).

37   And, perhaps, the (future) master is simply the one who takes a chance and is the first to make the move, i.e., to say "I am white": he becomes a new master if his bluff pays off.

38   At a different level, Rosa Luxembourg discerned a homologous anticipatory move in the matrix of a revolutionary process: if we wait for the "right moment" of a revolution, it will never occur; the "right moment" emerges only after a series of failed "premature" attempts, i.e., we attain our identity as a revolutionary subject only by way of "overtaking" ourselves and claiming this identity "before its time has arrived." For a more detailed reading of this paradox, see chapter 5 of Slavoj Žižek, *The Sublime Object of Ideology* (London: Verso, 1991).

39   See Lacan's crucial remarks in his *Séminaire*, book 20: *Encore* (Paris: Editions du Seuil, 1975), pp. 47–48. In this sense, *hysteria* designates the failure of interpellation: the hysterical question is "Why am I what you are saying that I am?", i.e., I question the symbolic identity imposed on me by the master; I resist it in the name of what is "in me more than myself," the object small *a*. Therein consists the anti-Althusserian gist of Lacan: subject qua $ is not an effect of interpellation, of the recognition in an ideological call; it rather stands for the very gesture of calling into question the identity conferred on me by way of interpellation.

40   See Paul Grice, "Meaning," in *Studies in the Way of Words* (Cambridge: Harvard University Press, 1989), pp. 377–88.

41   In our everyday experience, this gap separating different levels of intention is at work in what we call "politeness": when, upon engaging in a conversation, we say "How are you today?", we of course "do not mean it seriously"; we just offer an empty conversational form which calls for a ritualistic "OK" (the best proof of this emptiness of form is the uneasiness that emerges if our partner takes the question "seriously" and proceeds to offer an elaborate answer). It is nonetheless totally out of place to denounce this question as an insincere feigning of our concern: although its literal, first level of intention is not "meant seriously," i.e., although I am not really interested in how are you today, the question bears witness to my absolutely "sincere" intention to establish a normal, friendly communication with you.

42   In Hitchcock's films, such an element is the notorious "MacGuffin," the secret which sets in motion the narrative, although it is in itself "nothing at all": its meaning is purely self-referential; it amounts to the fact that the subjects involved in the narrative ascribe a meaning to it.

43   Phil Patton, "Marketers Battle for the Right to Profit from Malcolm's 'X,'" *New York Times,* Monday, November 8, 1992, B1 and 4.

44   Lacan's notion of Oedipus is to be opposed here to the "anti-Oedipal" notion of Oedipus qua the "repressive" force which canalizes, domestifies, the polymorphous perversion of partial drives, straining them to the Procrustian triangle of Father-Mother-Child. With

Lacan, "Oedipus" (i.e., the imposition of the Name-of-the-Father) stands for a purely negative logical operator of "deterritorialization" (see his pun in French on the homophony between *Nom-du-Père* and *Non-du-Père*): "Name-of-the-Father" is a function which brands every object of desire with the sign of a lack, i.e., which changes every attainable object into the metonymy of lack; apropos of every positive object, we experience how "That's not *it!*" (And "Mother" qua incestuous object is nothing but the reverse of this same operation: the name for that x missed by every given object.) What can be of help here is the reference to the Wittgensteinian motto "the meaning of a word equals its use": "father" qua paternal metaphor is used only and simply to introduce this gap which lurks in the background of every object of desire. We should therefore not be fascinated by the imposing *presence* of the father: the positive figure of the father merely gives body to this symbolic function, without ever fully meeting its requirements.

45 As to this virtual character of capitalist economy, see Brian Rotman, *Signifying Nothing* (London: Macmillan, 1987).

3   On Radical Evil and Related Matters

1   Here, we left out of consideration the historical tension inherent to the notion of "fifties." As it was pointed out by Fredric Jameson, this tension provides the key for the ideological background of the novel (see Fredric Jameson, "Nostalgia for the Present," in *Postmodernism* [Durham: Duke University Press, 1991]). It is by no means an accident that the ahistorical character of the "small town of the fifties" reminds us of a western set-up: the western succeeded in abolishing the discrepancy between people and their habitat, between nature and culture, which saps the "credibility" of all other "historical" genres; the cowboy outfit is not experienced as a ridiculous costume, it "naturally" blends with natural environs. The western is thus a kind of timeless past of the contemporary America: cowboy is the "natural" of the present culture, i.e., the modern citizen stripped of his urbane alienation and revealed in his "true nature." Thus, of course, the western is ideology at its purest.

2   Suffice it to recall a common experience with the word processor's screen: when we jump along the text, we automatically imagine that the text itself "rolls" in front of our eyes: we assume that the line which just entered the screen from above previously existed in an imaginary space "above" the screen, for example. The truth is, of course, that it was "created" the very moment it entered our field of vision, i.e., the frame of the screen.

3   See "A Fragment on Ontology," in *Works*, vol. 8, pp. 195–211.

4   "By the priest and the lawyer, in whatsoever shape fiction has been employed, it has had for its object or effect, or both, to deceive, and, by deception, to govern, and, by governing, to promote the interest, real or supposed, of the party addressing, at the expense of the party addressed" (ibid., p. 199).

5   Ibid., p. 197.

6   "The fictitious is not, in effect, in its essence that which deceives, but is precisely what I call the symbolic" (*The Ethics of Psychoanalysis, 1959–1960, The Seminar of Jacques Lacan*, book 7, ed. Jacques-Alain Miller [London: Routledge / Tavistock, 1992], p. 12).

7   Bentham, "A Fragment on Ontology," p. 198.

8   Ibid.

9   Ibid., p. 199.

10   For a clear presentation of Bentham's theory of fictions see chapters 2–4 of Ross Harrison, *Bentham* (London: Routledge and Kegan Paul, 1983).

11   We encounter a similar "mediation" between illusion and truth in Spinoza. In a context which, for sure, differs from Bentham's, Spinoza proposed that fiction is a determinate mode of knowledge standing between truth and simple falsehood: fiction involves untruths that are knowingly entertained as such, rather than mistaken for adequate ideas. (Later, Pierre Macherey relied on this Spinozean notion of fiction in his Althusserian elaboration of literature—literary fiction—as a specific mode of knowledge which is not yet scientific knowledge, yet nonetheless enables us to distance ourselves from our immersion in imaginary experience.) This intermediate notion of fiction determines the way Spinoza conceives of the passage from error to truth: we do not unmask error on the basis of a direct insight into truth; on the contrary, we arrive at truth through the analysis of the very reasons which caused us to err. Truth is *stricto sensu* error's truth, i.e., an insight into the process which generated error: "the mind's only recourse against these sources of error is to grasp the conditions that brought them about—the historical, causal, or linguistic factors—and thereby achieve the kind of rational grasp that converts 'passive' into 'active' understanding" (Christopher Norris, *Spinoza and the Origins of Modern Critical Theory* [Oxford: Blackwell, 1991], p. 245). This follows from Spinoza's fundamental premise that "false and fictitious ideas have nothing positive about them . . . which causes them to be called false and fictitious; they are only considered as such through the defectiveness of knowledge" ("On the Improvement of the Understanding," in *The Chief Works of Benedict de Spinoza* [New York: Dover, 1951], p. 18): the falsity of a false idea is unmasked the moment we attain true knowledge of it by way of locating it in its proper context.

12   It is against this background that we have to locate the standard paranoiac idea that, at any moment, we might pull some lever that will inadvertently set in motion the process of the disintegration of the entire reality, as in the urination-dream reported in Freud's *Interpretation of Dreams:* the tiny flow out of the child's penis grows into a stream on the street, changing the line separating the street from the sidewalk into a river's bank, then into a sea on which ocean liners sail. The author of this book experienced a similar momentary "loss of reality" during a very harsh winter in Paris a couple of years ago: after pulling the knob and flushing water in the toilet, the small stream of water in the toilet-sink was joined first by drops of water from the ceiling, then by an actual torrent literally flooding the entire toilet room. My first reaction, of course, was "What did I do wrong? Why did I have to pull that stupid knob?" (The solution of the enigma was very simple: because of the harsh winter, water in the pipes was frozen, causing some of the pipes to explode; by pulling the toilet-knob, I caused the renewed flow which broke through the holes in the pipes.) Such an object, which appears as a part of reality, yet the moment we approach it too closely, reality itself disintegrates, is the object in the strict Lacanian sense of the term.

13   Quote from J. N. Findlay, *Kant and the Transcendental Object* (Oxford: Clarendon Press, 1981), p. 274.

14 Jacques Lacan, *Ecrits: A Selection* (New York: Norton, 1977), p. 144.

15 The further step to be accomplished here, however, is to raise the question of the appropriateness of the very conceptual framework within which nature is a balanced circuit with organisms harmoniously included in their environs, whereas human culture is conceived as a "derailed" nature, nature sick unto death. Perhaps nature appears as such only to a backward glance, from the human perspective; it is the very transgression (the human excess, the derailment) which retroactively creates the appearance of a prelapsarian norm. See chapter 2 of Slavoj Žižek, *Looking Awry* (Cambridge: MIT Press, 1991).

16 Lacan, *Ecrits: A Selection*, pp. 103–4.

17 This dialectic of the spear healing its own wound enables us also to distinguish democracy from all other political systems: in order to rectify their excesses, they have to have recourse to a counteractant opposed to their fundamental principles (socialist planning economy has to allow for a minimum of market incentives, although in the form of illegal "black market economy"), whereas only democracy can emphatically claim that the only cure for the troubles brought about by democracy (corruption, alienation . . .) is *more* democracy.

18 Let us add an exemplary case from the history of music: the questionable status of act 2 in Mozart's great operas (*Le nozze di Figaro, Don Giovanni, The Magic Flute*). In all of them, act 2 (or the second part, insofar as there are good reasons to regard *Le nozze* as an opera in two parts) contains some of Mozart's highest achievements—the unjustly underrated finale of act 3 in *Le nozze*, the sextet in *Don Giovanni*, Pamina's suicide aria in *The Magic Flute*. In spite of this, however, one cannot escape the overall impression that act 1 succeeds in producing an effect of incomparable harmonious balance, whereas in act 2 supreme passages alternate with obvious "fillers" (suffice it to mention the "patched-up" character of *Don Giovanni*'s act 2). For an abstract, nondialectical approach, this fact bears witness to an inherent limitation of Mozart's art; however, as soon as we consider this limitation not as a contingent biographical feature, but as a structural necessity, this very formal "weakness" starts to function as the index of a fundamental historical truth: to put it in the good old Marxist jargon, it is this very formal limitation, the impossibility of a "successful" act 2, which registers an irreducible social antagonism, the impossibility of the utopian social synthesis Mozart was striving for.

19 Lacan, *Ecrits: A Selection*, pp. 40–56.

20 See book 1 in Immanuel Kant, *Religion within the Limits of Reason Alone* (New York: Harper and Row, 1960).

21 See Immanuel Kant, *Critique of Practical Reason* (New York: Macmillan, 1956), p. 30.

22 As to this notion of Evil qua ethical attitude, one could mention several recent thrillers which feature a kind of ethical humanization of the murderer in the last moments of his life. In *Deceived,* for example, the murderous husband, after cornering his wife, bursts into an unexpected superego-fury, repeating compulsively how he prefers not to kill, but if it has to be done, he will do it, disagreeable as it may be. We witness here a case of Evil qua ethical attitude in its purest. A somewhat similar scene occurs toward the end of *Sea of Love:* the detective holds under gun the murderer who was killing sexual partners of his ex-wife; instead of accepting his arrest, the murderer, in a pathetically suicidal

gesture, starts to cry out loudly what a humiliation it is if you are abandoned by the beloved wife and senselessly jumps toward the detective who shoots him down. What suddenly emerges in both cases is an unforeseen dimension that undermines the usual portrayal of the murderer as a cold-blooded, avaricious, or pathological being.

23   In this sense, the *femme fatale* who, in the *film noir* universe, derails man's daily routine, is one of the personifications of Evil: the sexual relationship becomes impossible the moment woman is elevated to the dignity of the Thing.

24   See G. W. F. Hegel, *Lectures on the Philosophy of Religion* (Berkeley and Los Angeles: University of California Press, 1987).

25   We must be careful here to avoid the trap of retroactive projection: Milton's Satan in his *Paradise Lost* is not yet the Kantian radical Evil—he appeared as such only to the Romantic gaze of Shelley and Blake. When Satan says "Evil, be thou my Good," this is *not* yet radical Evil, but remains simply a case of wrongly putting some Evil at the place of Good. The logic of radical Evil consists rather in its exact opposite, i.e., in saying "Good, be thou my Evil"—in filling out the place of Evil, of the Thing, of the traumatic element which derails the closed circuit of organic life, with some (secondary) Good.

26   Lacan, *Ecrits: A Selection*, p. 42. Another question opened up by this definition of ego's "maturity," of course, is that of the implicit deontological assumptions of ego-psychology: what, from the point of view of the conformist ego-psychology, appears as "immature" rebelliousness, a more "radical" psychology may conceive as a sign that the ego has outgrown primitive dependence and attained full critical autonomy; from the perspective of a "radical" psychology, it is rather the ego's capability silently to endure endless frustrations which bears witness to his "immaturity." On another level, the same goes for the ideal of "normal heterosexual relationship": in Protestant countries prior to the "sexual revolution" of the sixties, this ideal was interpreted as implying sexual activity within the confines of marriage, so that extramarital sexual activity automatically assumed symptomal status, i.e., was conceived as an index of some pathological disturbance (in more liberal environs, of course, it was the strict adherence to marital fidelity which was interpreted as an expression of "pathologically" rigid mental attitude). The Lacanian approach enables us here to change the terrain of the entire debate: "pathology" is not defined by the positive content of ethical norms but *by the way the subject relates to these norms:* do they function as traumatic injunctions? are they "repressed" or fully acknowledged? etc.

27   Lacan often makes use of the same rhetorical inversion to delineate the relationship of the ego to its symptoms: it is not sufficient to say that the ego forms its symptoms in order to maintain its precarious balance with the forces of the Id; the ego itself is, as to its essence, a symptom, a compromise-formation, a tool enabling the subject to regulate his or her desire. When we desire X, we always identify ourselves with a certain self-image ("ideal ego") of us as desiring X. For example, when we are enraptured by an old melodrama and are moved to tears by the events on the screen, we do not do it immediately; we previously identify ourselves with the image of a "naive" viewer moved to tears by this type of film. In this precise sense, our ideal-ego image is our symptom, is the tool by means of which we organize our desire: *the subject desires by means of his or her ego-symptom.* The ultimate Hegelian inversion, of course, is that between the object and

the lack: not only is the object always, by definition, lacking, but the object as such is already the place-holder, the materialization, of a lack.

28 For such a "Brechtian" reading of *How Green Was My Valley*, see Tag Gallagher, *John Ford* (Berkeley and Los Angeles: University of California Press, 1986).

29 See Monique David-Menard, *La folie dans la raison pure* (Paris: Vrin, 1991).

30 It is with regard to the "diabolical Evil" that the otherwise excellent essay by Etienne Balibar, "Ce qui fait qu'un peuple est un peuple. Rousseau et Kant" (*Revue de synthèse*, nos. 3–4 [1989]), seems to fall short. Balibar stays within the confines of Kant's self-perception when he points out how "radical Evil" cannot be reduced to the conflict between the subject's universal-rational will and its sensible-"pathological" nature: it concerns the inherent splitting of the free will between "true" freedom (submission to the moral law) and *Willkür*, the caprice and self-will of the free choice. The moral law does not exert its pressure only on our "pathological" impulses; we resist it in the name of the self-will which constitutes the innermost kernel of our Selves. This way, the opposition of morality and legality can be deduced from the inherent conflict of the free will: legality qua external pressure which, under the threat of punishment, forces me to obey laws is needed on account of the splitting of my free will. If "to act morally" were to be part of my actual nature, if I were not to experience the moral law as a humiliating pressure, I would not need the external coercion of law, of the legal system, or, to refer to Kant's own formulation, man would not be "the animal in need of a Master."

31 For a detailed account of this logic, see Chapter V of Slavoj Žižek, *For They Know Not What They Do* (London: Verso Books, 1991).

32 See Alain Abelhauser's analysis "D'un manque à saisir," in *Razpol* 3 (Ljubljana 1987).

33 One can imagine how the cinematic version of this scene would be able to rely on the contrapuntal use of sound: the camera would show the coach running along the empty streets, the fronts of old palaces and churches, whereas the soundtrack would be allowed to retain the absolute proximity to the Thing and to render the *real* of what goes on in the coach: the gasping and moaning that attests to the intensity of the sexual encounter.

34 See Michel Foucault, *This Is Not a Pipe* (Berkeley and Los Angeles: University of California Press, 1982).

35 One encounters the same paradox in Robert Heinlein's science fiction novel *The Unpleasant Profession of Jonathan Hoag*: when a window is opened, the reality previously seen through it dissolves and all we see is a dense, nontransparent slime of the Real. For a more detailed Lacanian reading of this novel, see chapter 1 of Slavoj Žižek, *Looking Awry* (Cambridge: MIT Press, 1991).

36 In Marx brothers films, we encounter three variations on this paradox of identity, i.e., of the uncanny relationship between existence and property:
   –Groucho Marx, upon being introduced to a stranger: "Say, you remind me of Emmanuel Ravelli.—But I *am* Emmanuel Ravelli.—Then, no wonder that you look like him!"
   –Groucho, defending a client before the court: "This man looks like an idiot and acts like an idiot, yet all this should not deceive you—he *is* an idiot!"
   –Groucho, courting a lady: "Everything on you reminds me of you, your nose, your eyes, your lips, your hands—everything except you!"

What lies at the heart of these paradoxes, of course, is the thesis, defended already by Russian formalists (Jakobson, for example), according to which every predicate has the status of a metaphor: describing a thing by means of a predicate ultimately equals saying what that thing resembles.

37 What we have in this scene, of course, is a kind of reflective redoubling of the external stimulus (sound, organic need, etc.) that triggers the activity of dreaming: one invents a dream integrating this element in order to prolong the sleep, yet the content encountered in the dream is so traumatic that, finally, one escapes into reality and awakens. The ringing of the phone while we are asleep is such a stimulus par excellence; its duration even after the source in reality ceased to emit it exemplifies what Lacan calls the *insistence* of the real.

38 See Sigmund Freud, "Repression," in *Standard Edition*, vol. 14, pp. 152–53, and "The Unconscious," ibid., p. 177. For a Lacanian reading of this concept, see Jacques Lacan, *The Four Fundamental Concepts of Psycho-Analysis* (New York: Norton, 1977), p. 218.

39 A similar shot is found in Fritz Lang's *Blue Gardenia*, when Anne Baxter peeps out of the crack between half-opened doors.

40 Lacan, *The Four Fundamental Concepts of Psycho-Analysis*, p. 103.

41 This third gaze also provides the key for the logic of exhibitionism: when the male exhibitionist accomplishes the legendary gesture of opening his coat in front of his victim, his aim is to produce a shock, a feeling of shame in the victim—the victim is embarrassed not because of the presence of the exhibitionist himself, but due to the imagined presence of a *third* gaze. (Accidentally, this also confirms that the aim of the exhibitionist—of the pervert sadist in general—is not to reduce the victim to the status of an object, but quite on the contrary to *subjectivize* it, to bring about in him or her the splitting (the mixture of fascination and repulsion) that characterizes the subject qua desiring.)

42 This phantomlike double, our shadow and yet "more real than ourselves," is also rendered by the famous verses from Coleridge's *Ancient Mariner* which Mary Shelley used to characterize Dr. Frankenstein's relationship to his terrifying creature: "Like one, that on a lonesome road / Doth walk in fear and dread, / And having once turned round walks on, / And turns no more his head, / Because he knows, a frightful fiend / Doth close behind him tread."

43 Within Freud's theory of dreams, this difference between *Unding* and *Gedankending* is at work in his notion of "considerations of representability" (see division D of chapter 6 of his *Interpretation of Dreams* [Harmondsworth: Penguin Books, 1977]): *Gedankending* is not in itself nonsensical, contradictory; it is simply not capable of being represented, i.e., of being experienced as an object within our field of representation.

44 In this precise sense, the Lacanian difference between reality and real repeats the Kantian difference between what is possible (what falls within the frame of possible experience, what can be imagined as an object of intuition), and between what, although not logically impossible, nevertheless can never become an object of experience: the "real" designates this uncanny intermediate domain of what "exists," sometimes even necessarily exists, in the sense of logical construction, yet can never become part of what we experience as reality. This is also what Kant has in mind when he differentiates between

Gegenstand and *Objekt: Gegenstand* is an object which belongs to the domain of possible experience, whereas *Objekt* stands for an entity which can never be intuited.

45 Karl Marx, "The Poverty of Philosophy," in Karl Marx and Friedrich Engels, *Collected Works*, volume 6 (New York: International Publishers, 1976), p. 163.

46 This utopian world is of course structured as a counterpoint to the Western aggressive, patriarchal civilization: the realm of matriarchy (*She*), of black rule (*King Solomon's Mines*), of harmonious contact with nature (*Tarzan*), of balanced wisdom (*Lost Horizon*). The message of these novels is however more ambiguous than it may seem: for the heroes who entered this idyllic world, life in the domain of saturated desire soon becomes unbearable and they strive to return to corrupted civilization; the universe of pure fantasy is a universe without surplus enjoyment, i.e., a perfectly balanced universe where the object-cause of desire cannot be brought to effect.

47 This is the reason why this pass is always shown in a way that points out its artificial character (one perceives immediately that it is a studio set, with its entire background— including the "Rancho Notorious" in the valley below—painted on a gigantic cloth); the same procedure was used by Hitchcock in his *Marnie*, among others. And do we not encounter the same matrix of a pure fantasy-space beyond the frontier in Coppola's *Apocalypse Now?* What this film stages is also a kind of "voyage beyond the end of the world": the "end of the world" is clearly represented by the burning bridge on the frontier of Vietnam and Kampuchea, this place of general confusion and dissolution where the distinction between reality and delusion is blurred. However, once we trespass this frontier and penetrate its Beyond, the ferocious violence all of a sudden gives way to an unnatural calm; we enter the pure fantasy-space, the kingdom of Kurtz, the obscene-knowing father, the reverse of the "normal" symbolic Father who constitutes reality. (As it was noted by Fredric Jameson, the role of the Mount Rushmore monument in Hitchcock's *North-by-Northwest* is also to serve as the image of the "end of the world": the view from the top of the presidents' heads into the valley below is clearly the view into the unfathomable Beyond.)

48 It is similar with the status of the "transcendental *Schein*" in Kant: although the Idea of Reason does not belong to the field of reality, of possible experience, it functions as the symbolic closure which totalizes, fills out, its field. If we progress in reality to its utmost, to its utter limit, all of a sudden we find ourselves "on the other side," in ideas to whom no reality corresponds.

49 A homological inversion in the domain of painting occurs in the work of Edvard Munch; the despair of his "expressionistic" phase is followed by a quasi-magical appeasement when Munch found support and a stable point of reference in the rhythm of Nature, the life-giving power of the sun, etc. This shift is homologous to the shift from the early to the late work of Joan Miró: one is tempted to say that the entire Miró is already contained in his early paintings, which are still figural. There the elements of the late Miró, the famous jovial, "childish" abstract colored shapes, are present in the guise of details of an overall figural canvas. Miró thus in a way "reified" his own work: he "forgot" the dialectical mediation of its elements; he abstracted them from their totality and conferred upon them the appearance of independence. Within modernism proper, the same logic is at work in the shift from expressionism into modernist formalism. Let

us recall the fate of *Sprachgesang* (stylized "speech-song") in Arnold Schoenberg's musical compositions: in *Gurre-Lieder*, *Sprachgesang* is still "contextualized"; it appears as the calming down of the unbearable pain of King Valdemar, who bemoans the death of his beloved Tove. During his nightly rides, Valdemar articulates his pain in a traditional late-romantic air, whereas the speaker celebrates the dawn of a new day which dispels nocturnal horrors in the form of *Sprachgesang*. In *Pierrot Lunaire*, Schoenberg's later work, this dialectical tension, i.e., the mediation of the *Sprachgesang* with the late-romantic chromatic air, is lost: *Sprachgesang* emancipates itself and occupies the entire field. On a more general level, the fundamental matrix of such an inversion of extreme tension into peaceful felicity is offered by the passage of modernism into postmodernism. The crucial point here is that what changes in this shift is not the perceived object or state of things but the standpoint from which the perceived state of things appears as horrifying: we pass from modernist-expressionist horror into postmodernist etheric bliss when the dimension of authentic subjectivity, the implicit standard of normality, disintegrates. The logic of the inversion is everywhere the same: the jovial childish immediacy which at first emerges as the form of expression of its opposite, i.e., as the affected manifestation of the deepest despair in which the subject is no longer able to express his or her horror directly but can only mimic an idiotic innocence, loses this "mediation" and pretends to be "true" childish innocence.

50   See chapters 20 and 21 of *The Ethics of Psychoanalysis, 1959–1960, The Seminar of Jacques Lacan*, book 7, ed. Miller.

51   Insofar as, with Kant, the frontier which separates phenomena from noumena—i.e., which simply confines, restrains the phenomenal field—is also logically prior to noumena qua positive entities; the status of the "transcendental *Schein*" is ultimately the same as that of the mysterious kingdom beyond the frontier in these films.

52   Besides the *real* impossibility and the *symbolic* prohibition there is a third, *imaginary*, version the economy of which is psychotic: incest is necessary and unavoidable since every libidinal object is incestuous. An exemplary case of it is the Catharist heresy which prohibits *every* sexual relation, claiming that intercourse with whichever libidinal object, not only with one's parents, is incestuous. As to these three modalities of incest (its impossibility, prohibition, necessity), see Peter Widmer, "Jenseits des Inzestverbots," *Riss* 2, 4, and 6 (Zurich, 1986–87).

53   Here we encounter the function of the "subject supposed to believe": the existing order is legitimized via the fact that a doubt about it would betray the naive belief of the Other (of the foreign worker who believes in the USSR, who, by means of this belief, confers meaning and consistency upon his life). As to the notion of the "subject supposed to believe," see Slavoj Žižek, *The Sublime Object of Ideology* (London: Verso Books, 1989), pp. 185–86.

54   For another reading of this paradox, see Žižek, *The Sublime Object of Ideology*, pp. 45–47.

55   See Sigmund Freud, *Interpretation of Dreams* (Harmondsworth: Penguin Books, 1977), chapter 2.

56   *The Ego in Freud's Theory and in the Technique of Psychoanalysis, The Seminar of Jacques Lacan*, book 2, ed. Miller (Cambridge: Cambridge University Press, 1988), p. 159.

57   Ibid., p. 154.

58 Ibid., pp. 154–55.

59 Ibid., p. 168.

60 Ibid., p. 161. This reversal of trauma into bliss is equivalent to a kind of symbolic lobotomy: excision of the traumatic tumor, like the operation to which Francis Farmer was submitted in order to "feel good" in the American everyday ideology.

61 Jacques Lacan, *Ecrits: A Selection* (New York: Norton, 1977), p. 286.

62 Ibid., p. 287.

63 Ibid.

64 Before accusing Hegel of applying the triad thesis-antithesis-synthesis as a formal principle of introducing order into every kind of chaotic content, one should note that the terms are not Hegel's: Hegel *never* speaks of "thesis-antithesis-synthesis"; these terms were introduced by his pupils years after his death.

65 Within a "nonantagonistic" relation, the identity-with-itself of every moment is grounded in its complementary relationship to its Other (woman is woman through her relationship to man; together, the two of them constitute a harmonious Whole, etc.), whereas in an "antagonistic" relation the Other truncates our identity, it prevents us from achieving it, from "becoming fully what we are" (the relation between the sexes thus becomes "antagonistic" when woman starts to perceive her relationship to the opposite sex as something which prevents her from fully realizing her female subjective position, from fully "being herself"). For such a notion of antagonism, see Ernesto Laclau and Chantal Mouffe, *Hegemony and Socialist Strategy* (London: Verso Books, 1985).

66 Theodor W. Adorno, *Negative Dialectics* (New York: Continuum, 1973), p. 5.

4 Hegel's "Logic of Essence" as a Theory of Ideology

1 Perspicuous theologians know very well this paradox of a decision which retroactively posits its own reasons: of course there are good reasons to believe in Jesus Christ, *but these reasons are fully comprehensible only to those who already believe in Him.*

2 It was the same with Ronald Reagan's presidency: the more the liberal journalists enumerated his slips of tongue and other faux pas, the more they strengthened his popularity; unknowingly, reasons against functioned as reasons for. As to Reagan's "teflon presidency," see Joan Copjec, "The *unervmoegender* Other: Hysteria and Democracy in America," *New Formations* 14 (London: Routledge, 1991). On another level, an exemplary case of this gap separating S_1 from S_2, the act of decision from the chain of knowledge, is provided by the institution of jury: the jury performs the formal act of decision, it delivers the verdict of "guilt" or "innocence"; then it is up to the judge to ground this decision in knowledge, to translate it into an appropriate punishment. Why can't these two instances coincide, i.e., why can't the judge himself decide the verdict? Is he not better qualified than an average citizen? Why is it repulsive to our sense of justice to leave the decision to the judge? For Hegel, the jury embodies the principle of free subjectivity: the crucial fact about the jury is that it comprises a group of citizens who allegedly are peers of the accused and who are selected by a lottery system—they stand for "anybody." The point is that I can be judged only by my equals, not by a superior agency speaking in the name of some inaccessible Knowledge beyond my reach and

comprehension. At the same time, the jury implies an aspect of contingency which suspends the principle of sufficient ground: if the concern of justice were only to be the correct application of law, it would be far more appropriate for the judge to decide on guilt or innocence. By entrusting the jury with the verdict, the moment of uncertainty is preserved; up to the end we cannot be sure what the judgment will be, so its actual pronouncement always affects us as a surprise.

3   The paradox, of course, consists in the fact that, precisely, there is *nothing* behind the series of positive, observable features: the status of that mysterious *je ne sais quoi* which makes me fall in love is ultimately that of a pure semblance. This way, we can see how a "sincere" feeling is necessarily based upon an illusion (I am "really," "sincerely" in love only insofar as I believe in your secret *agalma*, i.e., insofar as I believe that there is something behind the series of observable features).

4   As for this "Incorporation Thesis," see Henry E. Allison's *Kant's Theory of Freedom* (Cambridge: Cambridge University Press, 1990).

5   The converse procedure is also false: the attribution of personal responsibility and guilt which relieves us of the task of probing into the concrete circumstances of the act in question. Suffice it to recall the moral-majority practice of attributing a moral character to the higher crime rate among African Americans ("criminal dispositions," "moral insensitivity," etc.): this attribution precludes any analysis of the concrete social, economic, and political conditions of African Americans.

6   What we have here is thus another example of the Hegelian rhetorical inversion in Lacan: we can identify with the other's desire since our desire as such is already the desire of the other (in all meanings: our desire is a desire to be desired by the other, i.e., a desire for another's desire; what we experience as our innermost desire is structured by the decentered Other; etc.). In order to desire, the subject has to identify with the desire of the other.

7   See Chapter 1 of the present book. The ultimate proof of how this reflectivity of desire that constitutes "self-consciousness" not only has nothing whatsoever to do with the subject's self-transparency but is its very opposite, i.e., involves the subject's radical splitting, is provided by the paradoxes of love-hate. The Hollywood publicity machinery used to describe Erich von Stroheim, who in the thirties and forties regularly played sadistic German officers, as "a man you'll love to hate": to "love to hate" somebody means that this person fits perfectly the scapegoat role of attracting our hatred. At the opposite end of it, the *femme fatale* in the *noir* universe is clearly a woman one "hates to love": we know she means evil, but it is against our will that we are forced to love her, and we hate ourselves and her for it. This hate-love clearly registers a certain radical split within ourselves, the split between the side of us that cannot resist love and the side that finds this love abominable. On the other hand, the tautological cases of this reflectivity of love-hate are no less paradoxical. When, for example, I say to somebody that I "hate to hate you," this again points toward a splitting: I really love you, but for certain reasons I am forced to hate you, and I hate myself for it. Even the positive tautology "love to love" conceals its opposite: when I use it, it must usually be read as "I (would) love to love you . . . (but I cannot anymore)" — as expressing a willingness to go on, although the thing is already over. In short, when a husband or a wife tells his conjugal partner "I love to love you," one can be sure that divorce is round the corner.

8 As to this logic of the "non-all," see Chapter 2 of the present book.

9 See Judith Butler, *Gender Trouble* (New York: Routledge, 1990), the hitherto most radical attempt to demonstrate how every "presupposed" support of sexual difference (in biology, in symbolic order) is ultimately a contingent, retroactive performative effect, i.e., is already "posited"; one is tempted to summarize its result in the ironic conclusion that women are men masked as women, and men are women who escape into manhood to conceal their own femininity. As long as Butler unfolds the impasses of the standard ways to substantiate sexual difference, one can only admire her ingenuity; problems arise in the last, "programmatic" part of the book, which unfolds a positive project of an unbounded performative game of constructing multiple subject-positions which subvert every fixed identity. What is lost thereby is the dimension designated by the very title of the book—gender *trouble*: the fact that sexuality is defined by a constitutive "trouble," a traumatic deadlock, and that every performative formation is nothing but an endeavor to patch up this trauma. What one has to accomplish here is therefore a simple self-reflective reversal of the negative into the positive: there is always trouble with gender—why? *Because gender as such is a response to a fundamental "trouble":* "normal" sexual difference constitutes itself in an attempt to avoid an impasse.

10 Jacques Lacan, *Le séminaire*, book 20: *Encore* (Paris: Editions du Seuil, 1975), p. 85. Consequently, Lacan's statement that "there is no sexual relationship" does not contain a hidden normativity, an implicit norm of "mature" heterosexuality impossible to attain, in the eyes of which the subject is always, by definition, guilty. Lacan's point is quite the contrary, that in the domain of sexuality, *it is not possible to formulate any norm which should guide us with a legitimate claim to universal validity:* every attempt to formulate such a norm is a secondary endeavor to mend an "original" impasse. In other words, Lacan does not fall into the trap of invoking a cruel superego agency which knows that the subject is not able to meet its demands, thereby branding the subject's very being with a constitutive guilt: the relationship of the Lacanian subject to the symbolic Law is *not* a relationship to an agency whose demand the subject can never fully satisfy. Such a relationship to the Other of the Law, usually associated with the God of the Old Testament or with the Jansenist *Dieu obscur,* implies that the Other *knows* what it wants from us, it is only us who cannot discern the Other's inscrutable will. With Lacan, however, *the Other of the Law itself does not know what it wants.*

11 For a detailed reading of the Hegelian logic of reflection see chapter 6 of Slavoj Žižek, *The Sublime Object of Ideology* (London: Verso Books, 1989).

12 Therein consists the crucial weakness of Robert Pippin's *Hegel's Idealism* (Cambridge: Cambridge University Press, 1988), a book which otherwise announces a new epoch in Hegelian studies. Its fundamental intention is to reaffirm, against the prevalent "historicist" approach (the dismissal of Hegel's "metaphysics"—dialectical logic—as a hopelessly outdated mastodon, i.e., the notion that the only thing "still alive" in Hegel is to be found in the concrete sociohistorical analyses of *Phenomenology, Philosophy of Right, Aesthetics,* etc.), the continued relevance of Hegel's dialectical logic, and, furthermore, to demonstrate how the only way to grasp this relevance leads through Kant. Hegel's position in no way entails the regression to the "precritical" metaphysical ontology of the Absolute, but remains thoroughly confined to the Kantian criticism: Hegel's speculative idealism is Kantian criticism brought to a close. This project of Pippin deserves full

support. Yet Pippin fails at the crucial place, in his treatment of the logic of reflection. The final result of his analysis is that we are ultimately condemned to the antinomy of positing and external reflection: he repudiates "determining reflection" as an empty metaphoric formula, a failed attempt to break out of this antinomy.

13   *Hegel's Science of Logic* (Atlantic Highlands, N.J.: Humanities Press International, 1989), p. 441. Since our concern here is limited to the paradoxical structure of the notion of contradiction, we leave aside the difference between difference and opposition, i.e., the mediating role of opposition between difference and contradiction.

14   Hegel's choice of example—father, the symbolic function par excellence—is of course in no way accidental or neutral. It was already Thomas Aquinas who evokes paternity in arguing that, in order to survive, we must accept another's word for things we ourselves did not witness: "If man refused to believe anything unless he knew it himself, then it would be quite impossible to live in this world. How could a person live, if he did not believe someone? How could he even accept the fact that a certain man is his father?" (*The Pocket Thomas* [New York: Washington Square Press, 1960], p. 286). As it was pointed out by Freud (in his *Moses and Monotheism*), in contrast to maternity, paternity is from the very outset a matter of belief, i.e., a symbolic fact: the Name-of-the-Father exerts its authority only against the background of trusting the Other's word.

15   What about the fourth term of the Lacanian algebra, *a?* The *object small a* designates precisely the endeavor to procure for the subject a positive support of his being beyond the signifying representation: by way of the fantasy-relation to *a,* the subject ($) acquires an imaginary sense of his "fullness of being," of what he "truly is" independently of what he is for others, i.e., notwithstanding his place in the intersubjective symbolic network.

16   *Marx's Grundrisse,* selected and edited by David McLellan (London: Macmillan, 1980), p. 99.

17   Was Chaplin aware of the irony of the fact that Austria, Hitler's first victim, was from 1934—from Dolfuss's right-wing coup—a proto-fascist corporatist state? And does not the same hold for *The Sound of Music,* in which the force opposed to fascism assumes the form of self-sufficient Austrian provincialism, i.e., in which the politico-ideological struggle between fascism and democracy is ultimately reduced to the struggle between two fascisms, the one overtly barbarian and the one which still maintains a "human face"?

18   So whatever ex-Communists do, they are lost: if they behave aggressively, they display their true nature; if they behave properly and follow democratic rules, they are even more dangerous since they conceal their true nature.

19   The science fiction film *Hidden* provides, in its very naiveté, one of the most poignant mise-en-scènes of such a materialization of a notional relationship: everyday life goes on in today's California, until the main character puts on special green glasses and sees the true state of things—the ideological injunctions, invisible to the ordinary, conscious gaze, i.e., the inscriptions "do this, buy that . . ." which bombard the subject from all around. The fantasy of the film thus provides us with glasses which literally enable us to "see ideology" qua voluntary servitude, to perceive the hidden injunctions we follow when we experience ourselves as free individuals. The "error" of the film, of course, is to hypothesize the ordinary material existence of ideological injunctions: their status is

actually that of pure symbolic relations; it is only their effects which have material existence. (In other words, *Hidden* realizes in a slightly modified form the classical Enlightenment fantasy of ideology as the plot of the clerical caste which, in the interests of those in power, consciously deceives people.)

20 See J. N. Findlay, *Kant and the Transcendental Object* (Oxford: Clarendon Press, 1981), pp. 261–67.

21 What we must bear in mind here is that Kant is compelled to hypothesize the existence of aether by the fundamental fantasmatic frame of his philosophy, namely the logic of "real opposition": "aether" is deduced as the necessary positive opposite of the "ordinary" ponderable-compressible-cohesible-exhaustible stuff.

22 See Louis Althusser et al., *Reading Capital* (London: New Left Books, 1970), pp. 186–89.

23 This point was first made by Beatrice Longuenesse in her excellent *Hegel et la critique de la métaphysique* (Paris: Vrin, 1981).

24 See Pierre Macherey, *Hegel ou Spinoza?* (Paris: Maspero, 1975).

25 Karl Marx, "Eighteenth Brumaire of Louis Bonaparte," in Karl Marx and Friedrich Engels, *Collected Works*, volume 2, p. 103.

26 In his reference to the Hegelian Beautiful Soul, Lacan makes a deeply significant mistake by condensing two different "figures of consciousness": he speaks of the *Beautiful Soul* who, in the name of her *Law of the Heart*, rebels against the injustices of the world (see, for example, *Ecrits: A Selection*, p. 80). With Hegel, however, the "Beautiful Soul" and the "Law of the Heart" are two quite distinct figures: the first designates *the hysterical* attitude of deploring the wicked ways of the world while actively participating in their reproduction (Lacan is quite justified to apply it to Dora, Freud's exemplary case of hysteria); the "Law of the Heart and the Frenzy of Self-Conceit," on the other hand, clearly refer to a *psychotic* attitude—to a self-proclaimed Savior who imagines his inner Law to be the Law of everybody and is therefore compelled, in order to explain why the "world" (his social environs) does not follow his precepts, to resort to paranoiac constructions, to some plot of dark forces (like the Enlightened rebel who blames the reactionary clergy's propagating of superstitions for the failure of his efforts to win the support of the people). Lacan's slip is all the more mysterious for the fact that this difference between Beautiful Soul and the Law of the Heart can be perfectly formulated by means of the categories elaborated by Lacan himself: the hysterical Beautiful Soul clearly locates itself within the big Other, and it functions as a demand to the Other within an intersubjective field, whereas the psychotic clinging to the Law of one's Heart involves precisely a rejection, a suspension, of what Hegel referred to as the "spiritual substance."

27 Existence in the sense of empirical reality is thus the very opposite of the Lacanian Real: precisely insofar as God does not "exist" qua part of experiential, empirical reality He belongs to the Real.

28 Lacan, *Le séminaire*, book 20: *Encore*, p. 32.

29 This point was articulated in all its philosophical weight by Georg Lukács in his *History and Class Consciousness* (London: NLB, 1969).

30 That Kant himself already had a premonition of this link between existence and self-relating is attested to by the fact that, in the *Critique of Pure Reason*, he conferred on

dynamical synthesis (which concerns also existence, not only predicates) regulative character.

31   The role of fantasy in perversion and in neurosis offers an exemplary case of this passage of in-itself into for-itself at work in the psychoanalytic clinic. A pervert immediately "lives" his fantasy, stages it, which is why he does not entertain toward it a "reflected" relationship, he does not relate toward it qua fantasy. In Hegelian terms: fantasy is not "posited" as such, it is simply his in-itself. The fantasy of a hysteric, on the other hand, is also a perverse fantasy, but the difference consists not only in the fact that a hysteric related to it in a reflected, "mediated" way—vulgari eloquentia, that he "only fantasizes about what a pervert is actually doing." The crucial point is rather that, within the hysterical economy, fantasy acquires a different function, becomes part of a delicate intersubjective game: by means of fantasy, a hysteric conceals his or her anxiety, at the same time offering it as a lure to the other for whom the hysterical theater is staged.

32   This exchangeability could be further exemplified by the ambiguity as to the precise causal status of trauma in psychoanalytic theory: on the one hand, one is fully justified in isolating the "original trauma" as the ultimate ground which triggered the chain reaction the final result of which is the pathological formation (the symptom); on the other hand, in order for event X to function as "traumatic" in the first place, the subject's symbolic universe had already to have been structured in a certain way.

33   See Fredric Jameson, "Reification and Utopia in Mass Culture," in *Signatures of the Visible* (New York: Routledge, 1991).

34   In this precise sense Lacan conceives Master-Signifier as an "empty" signifier, a signifier without signified: an empty container which rearranges the previously given content. The signifier "Jew" does not add any new signified (all its positive signified content is derived from the previously given elements which have nothing whatsoever to do with Jews as such); it just "converts" them into an expression of Jewishness qua ground. One of the consequences to be drawn from it is that, in endeavoring to provide an answer to the question "Why were precisely Jews picked out to play the scapegoat role in anti-Semitic ideology?", we might easily succumb to the very trap of anti-Semitism, looking for some mysterious feature in them that as it were predestined them for that role: the fact that Jews who were chosen for the role of the "Jew" ultimately *is* contingent—as it is pointed out by the well-known anti-anti-Semitic joke "Jews and cyclists are responsible for all our troubles.—Why cyclists?—WHY JEWS?"

35   Findlay, *Kant and the Transcendental Object*, p. 187.

36   Ibid., p. 1.

37   Here, we must be attentive to how a simple symmetrical inversion brings about an asymmetrical, irreversible, non-specular result. That is to say, when the statement "the Jew is exploitative, intriguing, dirty, lascivious . . ." is reversed into "he is exploitative, intriguing, dirty, lascivious . . . , *because he is Jewish,*" we do not state the same content in another way. Something new is produced thereby, the *objet petit a,* that which is "in Jew more than the Jew himself" and on account of which the Jew is what he phenomenally is. This is what the Hegelian "return of the thing to itself in its conditions" amounts to: the thing returns to itself when we recognize in its conditions (properties) the effects of a transcendent Ground.

38   As to this exception, see Monique David-Menard, *La folie dans la raison pure* (Paris: Vrin, 1991), pp. 154–55.

39   This irreducible antagonism of being and becoming thus also provides the matrix for Hegel's solution of the Kantian enigma of the Thing-in-itself: *the Thing-in-itself is in the modality of "being" what the subject is in the modality of "becoming."*

40   *Hegel's Science of Logic*, p. 545. What we encounter in the tetrad *actuality–possibility–contingency–necessity* is thus the repetition, on a higher, more concrete, level, of the initial tetrad of *being–nothing–becoming–determinate being*: contingency is the "passing" of possibility into actuality, whereas necessity designates their stable unity.

41   See chapter 5 of Slavoj Žižek, *For They Know Not What They Do* (London: Verso, 1991), and chapter 3 of Slavoj Žižek, *Enjoy Your Symptom!* (New York: Routledge, 1992).

42   This Kierkegaardian opposition of "becoming" and "being" perhaps lurks in the background of Heidegger's recurrent figure apropos of the ontological difference, namely the tautological verbalization of the substantive: "worlding of the world," etc. "Worlding of the world" designates precisely "world in its becoming," in its possibility, which is not to be conceived as a deficient mode of actuality: ontological difference is the difference between (ontic) actuality and its (ontological) possibility, i.e., that surplus of possibility which gets lost the moment possibility actualizes itself. On another level, the "ordering of the [political] order" could be said to designate the "open" process of the formation of a new order, the "unrest of becoming" (epitomized, in the case of Rumania, by the hole in the center of the flag, previously occupied by the red star, the Communist symbol) which disappears, becomes invisible, the moment a new order is established via the emergence of a new Master-Signifier.

43   This undecidability also pertains to Hegel's *Phenomenology of Spirit:* one has only to bear in mind that its close, absolute knowledge coincides with the starting point of *Logic*, the point without presuppositions, the point of absolute *non-knowledge* in which all one is capable of expressing is the empty being, the form of nothingness. The path of *Phenomenology* thus appears as what it is: *a process of forgetting*, i.e., the very opposite of the gradual, progressive "remembering" of the Spirit's entire history. *Phenomenology* functions as the "introduction" to the "system" proper insofar as, by way of it, the subject has to learn to obliterate the false fullness of the non-notional (representational) content, all non-reflected presuppositions, in order to be able, finally, to begin from (being which is) nothing. It is against this background that one has to conceive the reemergence of the term "skull" on the last page of *Phenomenology*, where Hegel designates its itinerary as "the Calvary of absolute Spirit" (*Hegel's Phenomenology of Spirit* [Oxford: Oxford University Press, 1977], p. 493). The literal meaning of the German term for calvary, *Schädelstätte*, is "the site of skulls." The infinite judgment "spirit is a bone (a skull)" acquires thereby a somewhat unexpected dimension: what is revealed to the Spirit in the backwards-gaze of its *Er-Innerung*, inwardizing memory, are the scattered skulls of the past "figures of consciousness." The worn-out Hegelian formula according to which the Result, in its abstraction from the path leading to it, is a corpse, has to be inversed once again: this "path" itself is punctuated by scattered skulls.

44   See chapter 1 of Slavoj Žižek, *Looking Awry* (Cambridge: MIT Press, 1991).

45   Is not the computer-generated virtual reality an exemplary case of reality conceived

through the detour of its virtualization, i.e., of a reality wholly generated from its conditions of possibility?

46   Suffice it to recall here Kant's reflections on the meaning of the French Revolution: the very belief in the *possibility* of a free, rational social order, attested to by the enthusiastic response of the enlightened public to the French Revolution, witnesses to the *actuality* of freedom, of a tendency toward freedom as an anthropological fact. See Immanuel Kant, *The Conflict of the Faculties* (Lincoln: University of Nebraska Press, 1992), p. 153.

47   This, of course, is a leftist reading of the Kennedy murder conspiracy theory; the reverse of it is that the trauma of Kennedy's death expresses a conservative longing for an authority which is not an imposture—or, to quote one of the commentaries on the anniversary of the Vietnam War: "Somewhere within the generation now taking power, Vietnam may have installed the suspicion that leadership and authority are a fraud. That view may have subtle stunting effects upon moral growth. If sons don't learn to become fathers, a nation may breed politicians who behave less like full-grown leaders than like inadequate siblings, stepbrothers with problems of their own." Against this background, it is easy to discern in the Kennedy myth the belief that he was the last "full-grown leader," the last figure of authority which was not a fraud.

48   Another exemplary case of this paradoxical nature of the relationship between possible and actual is Senator Edward Kennedy's candidacy for presidential nomination in 1980. As long as his candidacy was still in the air, all polls showed him easily winning over any Democratic rival; yet the moment he publicly announced his decision to run for the nomination, his popularity plummeted.

49   What this notion of feminine castration ultimately amounts to is a variation on the notorious old Greek sophism "What you don't have, you have lost; you don't have horns, so you have lost them." To avoid the notion that this sophism can be dismissed as inconsequential false reasoning, i.e., to get a presentiment of the existential anxiety that may pertain to its logic, suffice it to recall the Wolf-Man, Freud's Russian analysand, who was suffering from a hypochondriacal *idée fixe:* he complained that he was the victim of a nasal injury caused by electrolysis; however, when thorough dermatological examinations established that absolutely nothing was wrong with his nose, this triggered an unbearable anxiety in him: "Having been told that nothing could be done for his nose because nothing was wrong with it, he felt unable to go on living in what he considered his irreparably mutilated state" (Muriel Gardiner, *The Wolf-Man and Sigmund Freud* [Harmondsworth: Penguin, 1973], p. 287). The logic is here exactly the same as if you do not have horns, you lost them; if nothing can be done, then the loss is irreparable. Within the Lacanian perspective, of course, this sophism points toward the fundamental feature of a structural / differential order: the unbearable absolute lack emerges at the very point when the lack itself is lacking.

50   As to this potentiality that pertains to the very actuality of power, see chapter 5 of Žižek, *For They Know Not What They Do.*

51   Another facet of this dialectical tension between possibility and actuality is the tension between a notion and its actualization: the content of a notion can be actualized only in the form of the notion's failure. Let us recall the recent Robert Harris alternative-history bestseller *Fatherland* (London: Hutchinson, 1992): its action takes place in 1964, with

Hitler having won World War II and extending his empire from the Rhine to the Ural Mountains. The trick the novel pulls is to stage what actually takes place today as the result of Hitler's victory: after his victory, Hitler organized Western Europe into the "European Community," an economic union with twelve currencies under the domination of the German mark, whose flag consists of yellow stars on blue background (German documents from the early forties actually contain such plans!). The lesson of the novel is therefore that the "notion" of Nazi Europe realized itself in the guise of the very "empirical" defeat of nazism.

52 The key question here is how this problematic of the Master qua metonymy of death is affected by Lacan's later shift toward *jouissance*, which entails the splitting of the paternal figure into the Name-of-the-Father, the pure symbolic authority beyond enjoyment (the big Other is by definition beyond enjoyment—"the big Other doesn't smell," as we may put it), and the Father-Enjoyment (*le Père-jouissance*): does the obscene Father qua Master of Enjoyment still function as "metonymy of death," or does he rather epitomize "life beyond death," the immortal, indestructible substance of enjoyment?

53 It is against this background that one is able to measure the subversive effect of a personal feature of Lacan noted by those who knew him. As is well known, he carefully cultivated the image of himself as being unbearable, demanding to the point of cruelty; yet at the same time he appeared witty and eccentric; those who knew him endeavored to penetrate to the "true person" behind this public mask, propelled by the desire for the reassuring guarantee that, beneath the mask, Lacan is "human like the rest of us." However, they were in for a bad surprise: what awaited them "behind the mask" was no "normal warm person," since even in private, Lacan stuck to his public image; he acted in precisely the same way, displaying the same mixture of courtesy and exacting cruelty. The effect of this uncanny coincidence between the public mask and private person was the exact opposite of what one would expect (obliteration of all private, "pathological," features; complete identification with the public symbolic role): the public symbolic role itself, as it were, collapsed into pathological idiosyncrasy, turned into a contingent personal tick.

5 "The Wound Is Healed Only by the Spear That Smote You"

1   I follow here Ivan Nagel's path-breaking study of Mozart's operas *Autonomy and Mercy* (Cambridge: Harvard University Press, 1991).

2   As to this symbolic exchange, see Mladen Dolar, "Filozofija v operi," *Razpol 7* (Ljubljana, 1992); the present text takes a number of instigations from Dolar's essay.

3   Such a reading of the Orpheus myth was already proposed by Klaus Theweleit in his *Buch der Koenige*, vol. 1, *Orpheus und Eurydike* (Frankfurt: Stroemfeld and Roter Stern, 1992).

4   The very words of this aria attest its aim of eliciting an answer of the Real: "O Dio, rispondi!" (O God, answer!).

5   As to this relationship between the two Orpheuses, see chapter 2 of Joseph Kerman's *Opera as Drama* (Berkeley and Los Angeles: University of California Press, 1988).

6   The standard "deconstructionist" version of Don Giovanni is that of a subject "not

bound by words," i.e., systematically violating the commitments imposed on him by the performative (illocutory) dimension of his speech (see, for example, Shoshana Felman, *Le scandale du corps parlant* [Paris: Seuil, 1978]). However, its reverse is that Don Giovanni complies with the rules of etiquette even after it becomes obvious that, by way of assuming a symbolic commitment, he got more than he asked for. Don Giovanni's dinner invitation to the statue at the graveyard, for example, was undoubtedly meant as an empty gesture, as a blasphemous act of defiance, yet when "the real answers," when the dead accepts the invitation and actually appears at Don Giovanni's home as the Stone Guest, Don Giovanni, in spite of his visible astonishment, *keeps to the form* and asks the guest to take his place at the table.

7   Nagel, *Autonomy and Mercy,* p. 26. This codependence of the subject's autonomy and the Other's grace is further exemplified by the well-known paradox of predestination: the very belief that everything is decided in advance by God's inscrutable grace, far more than the Catholic conviction that our deliverance depends on our good deeds, charges the subject with incessant frenetic activity. See chapter 6 of Slavoj Žižek, *The Sublime Object of Ideology* (London: Verso, 1989).

8   See Jon Elster, *Sour Grapes* (Cambridge: Cambridge University Press, 1982).

9   See Claude Lefort, *Democracy and Political Theory* (Minneapolis: University of Minnesota Press, 1988).

10   As we shall see later, the ultimate proof of the constitutive character of the dependence on the Other is precisely so-called "totalitarianism": in its philosophical foundation, "totalitarianism" designates an attempt on the part of the subject to surmount this dependence by taking upon himself the performative act of grace. Yet the price to be paid for it is the subject's perverse self-objectivization, i.e., his transmutation into the object-instrument of the Other's inscrutable Will.

11   G. W. F. Hegel, *Phenomenology of Spirit* (Oxford: Oxford University Press, 1977), p. 476.

12   This simultaneity of positioning and withholding finds perhaps its purest expression in Kant's theory of the Beautiful with its four consecutive crossings-out of what was first posited as the fundamental feature: finality *without* end, etc.

13   Jacob Rogozinski (in "Kant et le régicide," *Rue Descartes* 4 [Paris: Albin Michel, 1992], pp. 99–120) pointed out how, in Kant's political philosophy, this simultaneity of positioning and withholding the object assumes the form of the "antinomy of political reason." On the one hand, power belongs to the People (the totality of its subjects); nobody is allowed to appropriate it, any pretender to the place of power (king, for example) is by definition a tyrant. On the other hand, every attempt, on the part of the People, to assert itself immediately as the actual, positively given sovereign necessarily reverts into its opposite and ends in the radical Evil of Terror. This is the reason for Kant's ambiguous relation to the French Revolution, simultaneously an object of sublime enthusiasm (the affirmation of the sovereignty of the People as the sole legitimate bearer of power) and the point of unthinkable, diabolical Evil (the Jacobin Reign of Terror). The intimate link between Kant and democracy is thereby reconfirmed: what the solution of this "antinomy of political reason" amounts to is simply the democratic notion of the empty place of Power: democracy conceives of the People as the only legitimate Sovereign, yet simultaneously prevents any positive agent from occupying this place of the Sovereign.

14 See Bernard Baas, "Le désir pur," in *Ornicar?* 38 (Paris, 1985).

15 This mediating role of *Fidelio* can be established even at the biographical level: as is well known, it was the profound impression made on the young Wagner by the great soprano Wilhelmine Schroeder-Devrient in the role of Beethoven's Fidelio which made him determined to become a composer for the theater. The role of Senta in the *Dutchman* was written expressly for Schroeder-Devrient.

16 It is safe to surmise that what takes place behind the fallen curtain, in this intermediate time between the duet "Namenlose Freude . . ." (Nameless joy) and the finale, filled out by the orchestral music, is the "Big Bang," the long overdue sexual act between Florestan and Leonore. With reference to the dialectical tension between private and public, *Fidelio* marks the utopian moment when the affirmation of the conjugal couple's "private" love possesses the weight of the public act of asserting one's allegiance to political freedom.

17 Theodor W. Adorno, *In Search of Wagner* (London: Verso Books, 1991), p. 88. Let us bear in mind that phantasmagoria is at work again at the very end of *Lohengrin* when the allegedly dead Elsa's brother appears as an "answer of the real" to Lohengrin's fervent prayer.

18 Do we not encounter this logic of phantasmagoria already in *Fidelio*, in the famous aria of Florestan which opens act 2, where Leonora emerges as Florestan's vision? Is therefore her later emergence "in reality" not again a kind of "answer of the real" to his phantasmagorical desire? The place of phantasmagoria par excellence in Wagner, of course, is the locus of incestuous enjoyment: from Venusberg in *Tannhäuser* to Klingsor's flower garden in *Parsifal*: in both cases, its spell is broken, the place disintegrates, the moment the (male) hero "purifies his desire" and gains distance from it.

19 Quoted from Robert Donington, *Wagner's "Ring" and Its Symbols* (London: Faber and Faber, 1990), p. 265.

20 In *Tannhäuser*, for example, the woman is split into self-sacrificing redemptress (Elizabeth) and pernicious seductress (Venus), the cause of the hero's damnation; the truth concealed here is that they are ultimately one and the same since "the wound is healed only by the spear that smote you" (this truth is finally realized in *Parsifal*, which reunites both aspects in Kundry). *Lohengrin*, on the other hand, brings about the opposite of the subject condemned to eternal suffering: the subject who is the pure object-instrument of the Other's will, i.e., the tool of God's intervention in the world; etc. These equivalences transgress sexual difference: not only is Hans Sachs in the *Meistersingers* a new version of King Marke from *Tristan*, etc., but Kundry is the last version of the Flying Dutchman, this figure of the Wandering Jew. The crucial shift in these series of transformations, of course, occurs between the *Ring* and *Parsifal*: Siegfried, the ignorant-active hero, changes into Parsifal, the knowing-passive hero, the golden ring into the holy vessel, etc.

21 A desire for death (*"Lasciate mi morir"*) is of course at work in the operatic subject's entreaty from the very beginning, yet prior to Wagner it follows the simple logic of despair of life's calamities ("better to die than to endure this misery"), whereas the Wagnerian subject already dwells in the domain "between the two deaths."

22 Quote from Lucy Beckett, *Parsifal* (Cambridge: Cambridge University Press, 1981), p. 119.

23   Klingsor's further essential feature is his self-castration—the proof of his being unable to dominate the sexual urge. This violent abnegation of one's sexuality confirms Schelling's thesis according to which the true, demoniac Evil is far more "spiritual," hostile to sensuality, than the Good: Klingsor's spiritual domination over Kundry, his insensibility to her charms, is the very proof of his ultimate evilness.

24   The same matrix enables us to account for the uncanny shifts at the beginning of what is perhaps the crucial turning point of Mozart's *Don Giovanni*, the sextet in act 2. Four persons who successively enter the stage (Elvira, Leporello, Don Ottavio, Donna Anna) occupy the four positions of the Lacanian discourse. Donna Elvira is a split subject, confused, self-contradicting in her desire ($), although inconsistent, her speech is nonetheless deeply authentic in its very confusion—in short, *hysteric*. Leporello is also caught in contradictions, but in a nonauthentic, *compulsive* way, expressing the servant's false *knowledge* (S_2), i.e., his endeavor to slip out of every impasse by way of ingenious trickery. The remaining two positions are self-consistent. Don Ottavio's is that of a self-confident *Master* (S_1) who tries to comfort the desperate Donna Anna, but his solaces are pompous and shallow, i.e., nonauthentic: his speech is, no less than that of Leporello's, that of an *impostor*. Finally, we get the self-consistent *and* authentic subjective position, which can only be that of a *death-drive*, of "subjective destitution," of assuming freely the place of the object (*a*): in her magnificent baroque response, Donna Anna answers Ottavio that "only death" (*sol'la morte*) can console her.

25   There are two exceptions to this (Parsifal's killing of the swan; his slaying of the knights who guard Klingsor's castle), yet, significantly, both take place off-stage, and we see only the effects (the dead swan who falls on the stage; Klingsor's description of the battle).

26   It is at this precise moment that Parsifal becomes alert to the innocent beauty of nature absolved from sin (the "magic of Good Friday"): this "innocent" nature is by no means simply nature "as such," "in itself"—it appears as "innocent" only when the subject assumes the appropriate attitude toward it. Or, to put it even more pointedly: nature becomes innocent only through Parsifal's assuming the symbolic mandate of the king. Far from registering the subject's "inner purification," which enables him finally to perceive nature in its innocence, Parsifal's performative act absolves nature itself from sin. It would be interesting, here, to draw a parallel between *Parsifal* and *Meistersinger von Nuernberg*: in both cases, the crucial shift occurs in the first part of act 3, in a "private" place, and the public ritual in the second part of the act seems only to give a formal nod, to take note of what already had happened. In *Parsifal*, this shift consists in Parsifal's assuming the symbolic mandate of the new king of the Grail; in *Meistersinger*, it is—somewhat surprisingly—the resolution of the tension between Hans Sachs and Eva (after the desperate outburst of his long repressed quasi-incestuous passion, Sachs resignedly renounces her and hands her over to Walter von Stolzing). The scene of "inner peace and reconciliation" (the "magic of Good Friday" in *Parsifal*, the quintet "Morgenlich leuchtend . . .") comes in between the crucial inner shift and the public trial (Parsifal's accession to the Grail-throne; the singing contest in *Meistersinger*): although its function may be said to be to prepare the hero for the coming ordeal, it signals that everything is already decided, that the battle is already won before its official beginning.

27   Richard Boothby, *Death and Desire* (New York: Routledge, 1991).

28 Ernest Newman, *Wagner Nights* (London: The Bodley Head, 1988), p. 221.

29 Lacan, of course, alludes here to the proverbial "You cannot make an hommelette without breaking the egg."

30 Jacques Lacan, *The Four Fundamental Concepts of Psycho-Analysis* (New York: Norton, 1979), pp. 197–98.

31 Here, apropos of lamella, one should avoid the trap of identifying it precipitously with the maternal body. As Freud himself pointed out in one of his letters, the model of the double (and of lamella) is not mother but rather *placenta*—that part of the child's body that, at the moment of birth, is lost by the *newborn as well as by the mother.*

32 It is precisely this physical, tangible impact of "lamella" which gets lost in the sequel *Aliens*, which is why this sequel is infinitely inferior to the original *Alien. Alien³* is far more interesting because of two key features: first, the doubling of the "alien" motif (Ripley, herself an alien in the male penal colony, carries within her the "alien"); secondly, the suicidal gesture which concludes the film (upon learning that she already is pregnant with the "alien" which, sooner or later, is bound to jump out of her chest the way it did in the first *Alien* out of John Hurt, Ripley throws herself into the hot melted iron—the only way to destroy what is "in herself more than herself," the *a*, the surplus-object in herself).

33 The more general interest of Syberberg's *Parsifal* lies in the specific mode of subverting ideology which might be called *interpellation without identification* (the same paradox is also at work in Franz Kafka's novels; see chapter 5 of Žižek, *The Sublime Object of Ideology*): the subject finds itself interpellated without knowing what she / he is interpellated into, without any point of identification, of self-recognition, being offered. And it is precisely this "empty" interpellation, this nonspecified notion that we are addressed, summoned, lacking any clear indication of what the Other actually wants from us, that gives rise to an intense culpability. The "Che vuoi?" emanating from the Other thus remains un-fulfilled. Or, to put it a different way, Syberberg's *Parsifal* overwhelms us with a baroque profusion of symbols in which we, the spectators, look in vain for a consistent message; this overabundance paradoxically hinders the effect of meaning and brings about what Lacan baptized *jouis-sense*, enjoy-meant, enjoyment-in-meaning.

34 As a general introduction to Wagner's *Parsifal*, see Lucy Beckett, *Parsifal* (Cambridge: Cambridge University Press, 1981).

35 Jacques Chailley, *"Parsifal" de Richard Wagner: Opéra initiatique* (Paris: Editions Buchet / Chastel, 1986), pp. 44–45.

36 See Sigmund Freud, *Introductory Lectures on Psychoanalysis* (Harmondsworth: Penguin Books, 1975), pp. 300–301.

37 This myth of the curious woman asking the forbidden question (or, according to the Bluebeard myth, entering the only forbidden room in the house—see its different versions up to Hitchcock's *Notorious* and Fritz Lang's *Secret Beyond the Door*) is usually interpreted as the woman's readiness to confront the secret of her own (feminine) sexuality: "Pandora's box" ultimately stands for the female genitals. Perhaps it would be more productive to reverse the perspective by conceiving of the mystery that has to remain hidden as the impotence, the imposture, of the Master: the true "secret beyond the (forbidden) door" is that the phallus is a semblance; not only woman, man himself is

also already "castrated." It is almost superfluous to point out the key role of the figure of the humiliated master in Wagner. Suffice it to mention Alberich from his *Ring des Nibelungen* (not only Alberich's curse after he is forced to cede the ring to Wotan, but even prior to it his utter humiliation when his slaves, the Nibelungs, see him as the helpless prisoner of Gods to whom he is forced to deliver all his gold).

38   When Lacan says that the "secret of psychoanalysis" consists in the fact that "there is no sexual act, whereas there is sexuality," the act is to be conceived precisely as the performative assumption, by the subject, of his symbolic mandate, like the passage in *Hamlet* where the moment when finally—too late—Hamlet is able to act is signaled by his expression "I, Hamlet the Dane": this is what is not possible in the order of sexuality; i.e., as soon as the man proclaims his mandate, saying "I, . . . [Lohengrin, Batman, Superman]," he excludes himself from the domain of sexuality.

39   The first thing that strikes the eye here, of course, is how this opposition coincides with the sexual difference: in *Lohengrin* the woman asks the forbidden question, whereas in *Parsifal* the man abstains from asking the required question.

40   According to Lacan, the symptom always includes its addressee (every symptom that the analysand produces during his / her analysis includes the transferential relationship to the analyst as the subject supposed to "know," that is to say: to detain, the symptom's meaning). This is what Parsifal fails to grasp when he witnesses the strange Grail ritual: the fact that this ritual is staged for his gaze, that he is its addressee (as in Kafka's *Trial* where the man from the country fails to see how the door of the Law is meant only for him).

41   It is here that the insufficiency of the Jungian interpretation which centers on Parsifal's "inner development" becomes manifest: by conceiving Parsifal's ability to ask the required question as the sign of his spiritual maturity (the capacity of compassion with the other's suffering), this approach fails to take notice of the true enigma which does not concern Parsifal but the other side, the Grail community: how can the simple act of asking a question possess the tremendous healing power of restoring the health of the King and thereby of the entire community held together by the King's body? The reading of Parsifal as an allegorical staging of the hero's "inner journey" totally misses the crucial point that Parsifal functions as an "empty integer" without depth, without "psychology": a point at which innocence overlaps with unheard-of monstrosity—not really a "person" at all but rather a kind of logical operator which renders possible the healing of the community. The entire "psychology" is on the side of Amfortas and Kundry, these two suffering souls astray in the domain "between the two deaths."

42   *Lohengrin*, for example, would remain a standard romantic opera, if it were not for the "psychological" intricacies of act 2.

43   See Jacques Lacan, "Logical Time and the Assertion of Anticipated Certainty," in *Newsletter of the Freudian Field*, vol. 2, no. 2 (1988).

44   This change also accounts for Wagner's leaving out the display of the bleeding lance: this display again presupposes the big Other as its addressee.

45   This difference between the refusal of the woman in *The Magic Flute* and in *Parsifal* can be pinned down in a very precise way: in act 2 of *Parsifal*, Kundry at first manipulates Parsifal; she tries to seduce him by reminding him of his guilt toward his mother who

died of grief after he left her, and then offers her love as simultaneously maternal and sexual ("a last token of a mother's blessing, the first kiss of love"); after Parsifal's refusal, however, her manipulative seduction changes into true love's desperate attempt to reach the partner; it is only now that she starts really to appreciate him and desperately seeks in him a support that would enable her to escape her damnation. At the level of *The Magic Flute,* this second attempt would suffice: Parsifal would be now allowed to accept Kundry's "mature" love which has integrated the loss, i.e., his initial refusal; yet Parsifal again refuses even her "mature" love.

46 See Otto Weininger, *Geschlecht und Character* (Munich: Matthes und Seitz, 1980; originally published in Vienna, 1903).

47 As to this notion of the "non-all" feminine *jouissance,* see Jacques Lacan, *Le séminaire,* book 20: *Encore* (Paris: Editions du Seuil, 1975); the two key chapters are translated in Jacques Lacan and the Ecole freudienne, *Feminine Sexuality* (London: Macmillan, 1982).

48 Frank Wedekind was well aware of this dimension of the figure of Parsifal in his two Lulu dramas, *The Spirit of the Earth* and *Pandora's Box,* which later served as the basis for Alban Berg's unfinished *Lulu,* the work whose claim to the title "the last opera" is perhaps most fully justified. The parallel drawn by Wedekind is not, as one would expect, between Lulu and Kundry, but between Lulu and Parsifal. This scandalous equation, worthy of the Hegelian infinite judgment "Spirit is a bone," between Parsifal's elevated spirituality and Lulu's total apathy in which the ultimate Evil coincides with irresponsible childish innocence without any traces of hysteria, can be detected in the scene where Lulu answers the questions of the painter Schwarz concerning "higher spiritual matters" (God, soul, love) with a six-time "Ich weiss es nicht"—"I don't know it," an obvious allusion to the scene in *Parsifal* where Parsifal also answers repeatedly with "Das weiss ich nicht" when Gurnemanz questions him after his killing of the sacred swan. See Constantin Floros, "Studien zur 'Parsifal'-Rezeption," in *Musik-Konzepte 25: Richard Wagner's "Parsifal"* (Munich: Edition text + kritik, 1982), pp. 53–57.

49 This evasion of Wagner's also accounts for the ambiguous relationship between the two streams of blood in *Parsifal,* the "pure" blood of Christ in the Grail vessel and the "putrid" blood leaking from Amfortas's wound: what Wagner refuses to acknowledge is their ultimate *identity.* It is this shrinking back which accounts for the above-mentioned exceptional status of *Parsifal* among Wagner's operas: the sudden reversal into fairy-tale bliss and, accompanying it, the initiatory dimension. This shift occurs at the precise moment when the inherent logic of development would bring about the figure of the nonhystericized woman, i.e., of the woman beyond phallic enjoyment; upon approaching this borderline, Wagner "changes the register."

50 As to what, precisely, this sense is, see chapter 3 of Slavoj Žižek, *Enjoy Your Symptom!* (New York: Routledge, 1992).

51 This point was already made by Michel Chion in his *La voix au cinéma* (Paris: Cahiers du Cinéma, 1982).

52 Unfortunately, Syberberg himself falls prey to eclectic confusion and gives way to the ideology of hermaphroditism, which takes the edge off his subversive gesture: at the opera's end, following the final reconciliation, both Parsifals (male and female) are brought face to face, looking into each other's eye, and thus constitute a complementary,

harmonious couple. This, however, is precisely what never can happen: for structural reasons, the subject can never confront face to face its own objective surplus-correlative, since its very ex-sistence qua $ hinges upon the object's occultation (in topological terms, $ is the object's reverse, $ and *a* are to the opposite sides of a Möbius strip).

53   Let us not forget that in *Fidelio* we also come upon the disguise which trespasses the sexual difference: in order to be able to serve as "Fidelio," the jailer's assistant, Leonora dresses up as a man.

54   Brigid Brophy (in her *Mozart the Dramatist*, note to chapter 11 on "Who Is Cherubino, What Is He?" (London: Libris, 1988) demonstrated this phallic nature of Cherubino by way of an audacious, yet charmingly simple interpretation of his aria from the act 1, "Non so piu cosa son": "I no longer know what I am, what I do; now I'm all fire, now all ice, every woman changes my temperature, every woman makes my heart beat faster . . ." Are these words not quite literally spoken from the impossible, unthinkable, subjective position of the phallus itself? Is it not the phallus itself which makes itself heard in its uncontrollable oscillation between erected and withered state?

55   See Lefort, *Democracy and Political Theory.*

56   Michael Tanner, "The Total Work of Art," in *The Wagner Companion*, ed. P. Burbidge and R. Suton (London: Faber and Faber, 1979), p. 215.

57   In other words, nature is dying (see the "ecological" undertones of the third act with the desolate landscape around Montsalvat) because of the King's wound, because of this surplus of indestructible life which perturbs the "normal" circuit of generation and corruption.

58   Insofar as the traditional authority is Oedipal, i.e., the authority of the dead father who reigns as his Name, *Parsifal* can be conceived as anti-Oedipus. In his "De Chretien de Troyes à Richard Wagner" (l'*Avant-Scène Opéra 38–39: Parsifal* [Paris, 1982], pp. 8–15), Claude Lévi-Strauss proposed a detailed structural analysis of the opposition between *Parsifal* and the Oedipus myth: the "Oedipal" element in *Parsifal* is the antipole to the Grail temple, Klingsor's magic castle (the place of potential incest under the rule of the castrated father figure).

59   As to this *voix axousmatique*, see Chion, *La voix au cinéma.*

60   We must therefore bear in mind that the original sin which stains the kingdom of the Grail is not committed by Amfortas's yielding to the charms of Kundry and losing the holy spear, but by his father Titurel who uses the Grail as the means for his own enjoyment, for the eternal life provided by gazing at the Grail. It is this "unnatural" fixation which derails the normal life-circuit of the Grail community! And the same goes for *Hamlet:* as it was pointed out by Lacan, one of the mysteries of the play concerns the fact that Hamlet's father is not in heaven but dwells in the intermediate space "between the two deaths," like a kind of a living dead, not anymore alive, yet finding no peace in death—as the text hints, he was killed "in the blossom of his sins." So if there is something rotten in the land of Denmark, it is to be sought in the obscene reverse of Hamlet's father, of this figure otherwise presented as an ideal, model king, not in Claudius, who is a small-time crook.

61   However, if one is not to miss the point altogether, one must conceive of the notion of ritual in *Parsifal* in an appropriately broad way which exceeds by far the ritualistic

enactment of the sacred enjoyment (the Grail's disclosure): the very failure to perform the ritual properly is part of the ritual. Amfortas's lamentation, for example, is by no means a spontaneous outburst of an unbearable suffering, but a thoroughly ritualized, "formalized" performance. The proof of its "nonpsychological" character is the finale of act 1: after Titurel's superego-voice repeats the command "Disclose the Grail!" the unbearable pain miraculously passes and Amfortas is able to perform the required motions with no trouble at all. Far from being an exception, this reflective shift from the failed ritual to the ritualistic performance of a failure offers the key to the very notion of the ritual: "ritual" is originally, constitutively the formalized repetition of a failure.

62 Nagel, *Autonomy and Mercy*, pp. 147–48.

63 And since this same loop characterizes the drive, we can see why Lacan insisted that perversion deploys the structure of the drive in its purest.

64 In this respect, Kant's God therefore actually does act like Descartes' Evil Spirit: he does deceive the human subject intentionally, i.e., in order to render possible his moral activity. See the subchapter "Of the Wise Adaptation of Man's Cognitive Faculties to His Practical Vocation" in *Critique of Practical Reason* (New York: Macmillan, 1956), pp. 151–53.

65 On another level, Martin Scorcese's *Last Temptation of Christ* proposes the same thesis: Jesus himself ordered Judas to betray him, so that he was able to fulfill his destiny of the Saviour. Judas was thus a kind of a forerunner of the Stalinist traitor who commits the supreme crime against the Cause in the interest of the Cause. For a reading of it, see chapter 3 of Žižek, *The Sublime Object of Ideology*.

66 Lacan, *The Four Fundamental Concepts of Psycho-Analysis*, p. 195.

67 The same defense against the drive is at work in the famous tracking shot from Hitchcock's *Young and Innocent*: the nervous blinking of the drummer is ultimately a defense-reaction to being seen, an attempt to avoid being seen, a resistance to being drawn into the picture. The paradox, of course, is that by his very defense-reaction he inadvertently draws attention to himself and thus exposes himself, divulges, i.e., literally "renders public by beat of drum," his guilt; he is unable to endure the other's (camera's) gaze.

68 Another crucial ingredient of this scene of confrontation is a formal feature later repeated in *Marnie*. When Stewart triggers the flash, the entire field of screen is over-flown with red; the same effect occurs in *Marnie*: when Marnie catches sight of some red stain which arouses the repressed trauma, the color red so to speak boils over and covers the entire field. In both cases, the association of this stain with the subject's losing consciousness is crucial: what we encounter here is precisely the Lacanian notion of *aphanisis*, the subject's disappearance, self-erasure, when he or she is forced to confront the truth of his or her desire, the repressed kernel of his or her being.

69 We get a hint of this even in the first scene of the film, where we see for a brief moment the last snapshot taken by Stewart prior to his accident, depicting the cause of his broken leg. This shot is a true Hitchcockian counterpart to Holbein's *Ambassadors*: the oblique stain in its center is a racing-car wheel flying toward the camera, captured the split second before Stewart was hit by it. The moment rendered by this shot is the very moment when he lost his distance and was, so to speak, caught into his own picture. See Miran Božovič, "The Man behind His Own Retina," in Slavoj Žižek, *Everything You*

Always Wanted to Know about Lacan (But Were Afraid to Ask Hitchcock) (London: Verso Books, 1992).

70   What we encounter here again is the condensation of field and counter-field within the same shot. Desire delineates the field of ordinary intersubjectivity in which we look at each other face to face, whereas we enter the register of drive when, together with our shadowy double, we find ourselves on the same side, both of us staring at the same third point. Where here is the "making oneself seen" constitutive of the drive? One makes oneself seen precisely to this third point, to the gaze capable of embracing field and counter-field, i.e., capable of perceiving in me also my shadowy double, what is in me more than myself, the *object small a*. (See Chapter 3 of the present book.)

6   Enjoy Your Nation as Yourself!

1   For a detailed elaboration of this notion of the Thing see *The Ethics of Psychoanalysis, 1959–1960, The Seminar of Jacques Lacan,* book 7, ed. Jacques-Alain Miller (London: Routledge / Tavistock, 1992). What should be pointed out here is that enjoyment (*jouissance, Genuss*) is not to be equated with pleasure (Lust): enjoyment is precisely "Lust im Unlust"; it designates the paradoxical satisfaction procured by a painful encounter with a Thing that perturbs the equilibrium of the "pleasure principle." In other words, enjoyment is located "beyond the pleasure principle."

2   The way these fragments persist across ethnic barriers can be sometimes quite affecting, as, for example, with Robert Mugabe who, when asked by a journalist what was the most precious legacy of British colonialism to Zimbabwe, answered without hesitation: "Cricket"—a senselessly ritualized game, almost beyond the grasp of a Continental, in which the prescribed gestures (or, more precisely, gestures established by an unwritten tradition), the way to throw a ball, for example, appear grotesquely "dysfunctional."

3   See chapter 6 of Jacques Lacan, *Le séminaire,* book 20: *Encore* (Paris: Editions du Seuil, 1966).

4   The fact that a subject fully "exists" only through enjoyment, i.e., the ultimate coincidence of "existence" and "enjoyment," was already indicated in Lacan's early seminars by the ambiguously traumatic status of existence: "By definition, there is something so improbable about all existence that one is in effect perpetually questioning oneself about its reality" (*The Seminar of Jacques Lacan,* book 2 [Cambridge: Cambridge University Press, 1988], p. 226). This proposition becomes much clearer if we simply replace "existence" by "enjoyment": "By definition, there is something so improbable about all enjoyment that one is in effect perpetually questioning oneself about its reality." The fundamental subjective position of a *hysteric* involves posing precisely such a question about his or her existence qua enjoyment, whereas a sadist *pervert* avoids this questioning by transposing the "pain of existence" onto the other (his victim).

5   Jacques-Alain Miller, "Extimité," Paris, November 27, 1985 (unpublished lecture). The same logic of the "theft of enjoyment" determines also the relationship of the people to the State's Leader: when is the concentration and consumption of wealth in the hands of the Leader experienced as "theft"? As long as the Leader is perceived as "what is in us more than ourselves"; i.e., as long as we remain in a transferential relationship toward

him, his wealth and splendor are "our own." The transference is over when the Leader loses his charisma and changes from the embodiment of the nation's substance into a parasite on the nation's body. In postwar Yugoslavia, for example, Tito justified his splendor by the fact that "people expect it from me," that it "gives them pride"; with the loss of his charisma during the last years of his life, the same splendor was perceived as excessive dissipation of the nation's resources.

6 *Hegel's Science of Logic* (London: Allen and Unwin, 1969), p. 402.

7 The mechanism at work here is of course that of *paranoia*: at its most elementary, paranoia consists of this very externalization of the function of castration in a positive agency appearing as the "thief of enjoyment." By means of a somewhat risky generalization of the foreclosure of the Name-of-the-Father (the elementary structure of paranoia, according to Lacan), we could perhaps sustain the thesis that Eastern Europe's national paranoia results precisely from the fact that Eastern Europe's nations are not yet fully constituted as "authentic States": it is as if the failed, foreclosed State's symbolic authority "returns in the real" in the shape of the Other, the "thief of enjoyment."

8 I am indebted for this idea to William Warner's paper "Spectacular Action: Rambo, Reaganism, and the Cultural Articulation of the Hero," presented at the colloquium *Psychoanalysis, Politics, and the Image,* New York State University, Buffalo, November 8, 1989. Incidentally, *Rambo II* is in this respect far inferior to *Rambo I,* which accomplishes an extremely interesting ideological rearticulation: it condenses in the same person the "leftist" image of a lone hippy vagrant threatened by the small-town atmosphere embodied in a cruel sheriff, and the "rightist" image of a lone avenger taking the law into his hands and doing away with the corrupted bureaucratic machinery. This condensation implies of course the hegemony of the *second* figure, so that *Rambo I* succeeded in including into the "rightist" articulation one of the crucial elements of the American "leftist" political imagery.

9 Herein lies also Lacan's criticism of Hegel, of the Hegelian dialectic of lordship and bondage: contrary to Hegel's thesis that, by submitting himself to the lord, the bondsman renounces enjoyment, which thus remains reserved for the lord, Lacan claims that it is precisely enjoyment (and not the fear of death) which keeps the bondsman in servitude—enjoyment procured by the relationship toward the (hypothetical, presupposed) Master's enjoyment, by the expectation of enjoyment waiting for us at the moment of the Master's death, etc. Enjoyment is thus never immediate, it is always mediated by the presupposed enjoyment imputed to the Other; it is always enjoyment procured by the expectation of enjoyment, by the renunciation of enjoyment.

10 This attachment is not without its comical side-effects. Because of his Albanian origins, John Belushi, the very embodiment of Hollywood "decadence" who died of an overdose of drugs, enjoys today a cult status in Albania: official media praise him as a "great patriot and humanist" who was "always ready to embrace the just and progressive causes of humanity"!

11 See Jacques Lacan, *Le séminaire,* book 17: *L'envers de la psychanalyse* (Paris: Editions du Seuil, 1991).

12 The first thing to do, if we are to "go through the fantasy," is of course to get rid of the naive notion of fantasy as staging the gratification of a desire. Woody Allen's *Husbands*

and Wives ironically turns around this naive notion: as it is commonly known, in his "real life" Allen *did* sleep with his adopted daughter, thirty years his minor, whereas in the film, the sexual relationship with the young student (Juliette Lewis) is not consummated—a mocking reversal of the standard thesis of the artist who, in his fantasy-universe, fulfills sexual desires which he miserably failed to realize in his actual life. However, it is easy to demonstrate how, in this case, Freud's model of fantasy remains thoroughly valid: one has simply to take into account the *narcissistic gain* procured by the fantasy of sexual abstinence: in the film, Allen paints himself as a mature person who knows how to restrain his passion and to maintain a mature, wise distance.

13   This Christian background of the PC attitude is further confirmed by the recurrent motif of the look as a form of "sexual harassment": insofar as one can be guilty of the "provocative" look, guilt is located in the subject's *desire,* not in his actual deeds—in accordance with the Christian motto that those who sin in their minds are no less guilty than those who actually commit a sin.

14   The hysterical counterpoint to this American obsessional attitude is the position of the traditional European "critical intellectual" tormented by the question: *which legitimate power should I be allowed to obey with a clear conscience?* In other words, the traditional European Left intellectual is, even more than Jane Eyre, this ultimate example of the female hysteric, *in constant search of a Good Master:* he wants a Master, but a Master whom he could dominate, who would follow his advice. This attitude provokes a hysterical reaction, a reaction of "This is not *that!*", whenever the hysteric's side comes to power: he undertakes a desperate search for reasons that would legitimate his continuing disobedience (an exemplary case is provided by the French Left intellectuals after the electoral victory of Mitterrand's socialists in 1981: they were quick to discover in the socialist government features which made it even worse than the preceding liberal-conservative government, including signs of protofascist nationalism!).

15   Consider the success of Peter Weir's thriller *Witness,* which mostly takes place in an Amish community: are not the Amish an exemplary case of a closed community which persists in its way of life, yet without falling prey to a paranoiac logic of the "theft of enjoyment"? In other words, the paradox of the Amish is that, while they live according to the highest standards of the Moral Majority, *they have absolutely nothing to do with the Moral Majority qua politico-ideological movement,* i.e., they are as far as possible from the Moral Majority's paranoiac logic of envy, of aggressive imposition of its standards onto others. And, incidentally, the fact that the most pathetic and effective scene of the film is the collective building of a new barn testifies again to what Fredric Jameson calls the "utopian" potential of the contemporary mass-culture.

16   As it was already noted by numerous critics, the theory of "authoritarian personality" is actually a foreign body within the Frankfurt-school theoretical edifice: it is based on presuppositions undermined by the Adorno-Horkheimer theory of late-capitalist subjectivity.

17   See John Rawls, *A Theory of Justice* (Cambridge: Harvard University Press, 1971).

18   The notion of fantasy thus designates the inherent limitation of distributive justice: although the other's interests are taken into account, *his fantasy is wronged.* In other words, when the trial by "veil of ignorance" tells me that, even if I were to occupy the

lowest place in community, I would still accept my ethical choice, I move within my own fantasy-frame. *What if the "other" judges from within the frame of an absolutely incompatible fantasy?* For a more detailed Lacanian criticism of Rawls's theory of justice, see Renata Salecl, *The Spoils of Freedom* (London: Routledge, 1993).

19   The reverse of this resistance is a desire to maintain the "other" in its specific, limited form of (what our gaze perceives as) "authenticity." Let us mention the recent case of Peter Handke, who expressed doubts about Slovene independence, claiming that the notion of Slovenia as an independent state is something imposed on Slovenes from outside, not part of the inherent logic of their national development. Handke's mother was Slovene and, within his artistic universe, Slovenia functions as a mythical point of reference, a kind of maternal paradise, a country where words still directly refer to objects, somehow miraculously bypassing commodification, where people are still organically rooted in their landscape, etc. (See his *Repetition* [Wiederholung].) What ultimately bothers him is therefore simply the fact that the actual Slovenia does not want to behave according to his private myth and thus disturbs the balance of his artistic universe.

20   Jacques Lacan, *Four Fundamental Concepts of Psycho-Analysis* (New York: Norton, 1977), pp. 276–77.

21   This crucial point of Spinoza was rendered by Deleuze: "God reveals to Adam that the fruit will poison him because it will act on his body by decomposing its relations; but because Adam has a weak understanding he interprets the effect as a punishment and the cause as a moral law. Adam thinks that God has shown him a sign. In this way, morality compromises our whole conception of law, or rather moral law distorts the right conception of causes . . . And the most serious error of theology consists precisely in its having disregarded and hidden the difference between obeying and knowing, in having caused us to take principles of obedience for models of knowledge" (Gilles Deleuze, *Spinoza: Practical Philosophy* (San Francisco: City Lights Books, 1988), p. 106).

22   This shift from Spinoza to German Idealism can be best exemplified by a crucial stylistic feature. Spinoza's *Ethics* as well as Hegel's mature written works (*Encyclopaedia; Philosophy of Right*) are structured in a homologous way; they are traversed by a line that separates the main text (the deductive, purely immanent, exposition of the positive doctrine) from the multitude of remarks, footnotes, etc., which are written in a dialogical, often polemical mode, by somebody who fully participates in the ideological struggles of the day. In both cases, the main text imitates the form of another discourse; however, in the case of Spinoza, this other discourse is that of *mathematics* (axioms, etc.), whereas in Hegel the main text imitates *legal* discourse (paragraphs, etc.).

23   Notwithstanding the philosophical opposition between Spinoza and Hume, this dissolution of the subject's self-identity is homologous to that accomplished by Hume, who dissolves the Self in the heterogeneous flow of perceptions-ideas lacking any substantial self-identity. And it is against this background that we have to conceive Kant's I of pure apperception: Kant wholly takes into account the Spinozean and / or Humean disintegration of the Cartesian *res cogitans;* what he affirms is therefore the nonsubstantial empty point of self-consciousness.

24   See Frances Ferguson, "The Nuclear Sublime," *Diacritics* 7 (Summer 1984): 4–10.

25   See Jeffrey Masson, *The Assault on Truth: Freud's Suppression of the Seduction Theory* (New

York: Farrar, Straus and Giroux, 1984). One of the inherent paradoxes of the Moral Majority's anti-abortion campaign is that *it is parasitical upon the logic of its (left-liberal) adversary:* the "rights of the unborn" are simply one in the series of new rights which emerge the moment we accept the discourse of the potentially infinite extension of rights (the right not to be endangered by smoking; the child's right to avoid abuse, up to his or her right to sue parents for "divorce"; the right of the dolphins to be accorded the same dignity as humans; etc.).

26   Thereby, it repeats the mistake of the classic liberal opposition of "open" liberal and "closed" authoritarian personality: here, also, the liberal perspective fails to notice that the authoritarian personality is not an external opposite to the "open," tolerant liberal personality, a simple distortion of it, but its hidden "truth" and presupposition.

27   See Sigmund Freud, "Moses and Monotheism," in *The Standard Edition of the Complete Psychological Works of Sigmund Freud* (London: Hogarth Press, 1953–74), vol. 23. And does not Lacan make the same gesture apropos of woman? "Woman's secret" is man's fantasy, which is why the only proper feminist gesture is to assert that woman qua real does not possess the mysterious X imputed to her by man—in short, "Woman doesn't exist."

28   See Immanuel Kant, *Dreams of a Spirit-Seer, Illustrated by Dreams of Metaphysics* (London: S. Sonnenschein, 1900).

29   This split is therefore *the very form of universality of the liberal democracy:* the liberal-democratic "new world order" affirms its universal scope by way of imposing this split as the determining antagonism, the structuring principle, of inter- and intranational relations. What we have here is an elementary case of the dialectic of identity and difference: the very *identity* of the liberal-democratic "order" consists in the *scissure* which separates its "inside" from its "outside."

30   Immanuel Kant, *The Conflict of the Faculties* (Lincoln: University of Nebraska Press, 1992), p. 153.

31   See Etienne Balibar, "Is There a 'Neo-Racism'?", in Etienne Balibar and Emmanuel Wallerstein, *Race, Nation, Class* (London: Verso Books, 1991).

32   Or, to quote from a recent letter to *Newsweek* magazine: "Maybe it's fundamentally unnatural for different races or ethnic groups to live together. . . . While no one can condone the attacks against foreigners in Germany, the Germans have every right to insist that their country remain ethnically German."

33   See Fredric Jameson, "The Vanishing Mediator; or, Max Weber as Storyteller," in *The Ideologies of Theory,* vol. 2 (Minneapolis: University of Minnesota Press, 1988).

34   As to this problematic, see chapter 5 of Slavoj Žižek, *For They Know Not What They Do* (London: Verso Books, 1991). This logic of the "vanishing mediator" enables us to elucidate a crucial misunderstanding apropos of the Hegelian *Aufhebung* (sublation). The usual counterargument to Hegel is here that the movement of *Aufhebung* never "turns out," that there is always a remainder which resists it, that some traces of the nonsublated persist forever. Let us take the case of the Christian "sublation" of pagan religions: with the advent of Christianity, paganism is "re-marked," reframed, reinscribed, reinterpreted as incomplete, false religion, superstition, blasphemy, or—in the best of cases—as announcing the arrival of Christ. What, precisely, eludes this Christian *Aufhebung?* What becomes invisible once we are within the horizon of the Christian *Auf-*

hebung is not the true, original meaning of the pre-Christian religions, but rather Christianity itself "in its becoming" (as Kierkegaard would have put it), i.e., the very gesture by means of which Christianity breaks off, emerges from the pagan domain. The truly subversive move is thus not the return to pre-Christian tradition, but rather the endeavor to grasp Christianity itself "in its becoming," before its horizon of meaning was established: how did Christianity function within the pagan horizon, when it was still perceived as an unheard-of scandal? (The homology is here perfect with the "sublation" of crime in the universal Law: what eludes the grasp of Law is not some particularity of crime beyond the reach of Law but the violent founding gesture which reinstates the very reign of Law: the fact that Law "in its becoming" is nothing but universalized crime; see chapter 2 of Žižek, *For They Know Not What They Do,* and chapter 3 of Žižek, *Enjoy Your Symptom!*.) And the same goes for the disintegration of Communism: what becomes invisible once the passage into the new order is accomplished are not traces of the past but the very process of passage, the forces which actually set in motion the disintegration of Communism but are obliterated from the memory when the new order organizes its historical narrative.

35 See Vladimir Propp, *Theory and History of Folklore* (Minneapolis: University of Minnesota Press, 1984).

36 See Stephen Jay Gould, "Adam's Navel," in *The Flamingo's Smile* (Harmondsworth: Penguin Books, 1985).

37 See chapter 2 of Žižek, *Enjoy Your Symptom!*.

38 Ryszard Kapuscinski, *The Shah of Shahs* (London: Picador, 1986), pp. 109–10.

39 As to the utter unpredictability of this moment, suffice it to recall—apart from the obvious fact that anybody who five years ago were to have predicted the imminent collapse of Communism, would generally have been dismissed as a dreamer—how General Ian Hackett in his 1978 bestseller *World War III,* that is to say, just a year prior to the Iranian Revolution, conferred in his imagined scenario on Iran the role of the bastion of Western interests in the anti-Western Arabian world. Geopolitical analysts are as a rule blind to what Hegel called the "silent weaving of the spirit," for the underground disintegration of the spiritual substance of a community which precedes and prepares the way for its spectacular public collapse. In a way, we can say that the crucial thing takes place, that the mole does his work, before "anything happens," which is why the fall of a social edifice usually is not perceived as the overcoming of a mighty adversary. In a kind of implosion, the existing order somehow simply collapses into itself, magically losing its coherence. And it is not the least irony of history that those who were most blind to these "signs of the time" were precisely those Communists who pretended to speak in the name of historical progress: they supported to the end the Shah in Iran, Marcos in the Philippines, etc., misrecognizing the funereal ringing of the bells which signal that the game is over for an insignificant, minor rebellion.

40 See Etienne De La Boétie, *Slaves by Choice* (New York: Runnymede Books, 1988).

41 What we encounter here is once again the structure of the Möbius strip: while we obsessively shirk X, while we organize our entire life as an avoidance of X, this very evasion at a certain point compels us to embrace the very X we were running from.

42 See Muriel Gardiner, *The Wolf-Man and Sigmund Freud* (Harmondsworth: Penguin, 1973), pp. 350–51.

Index

Slavoj Žižek is Senior Researcher at the Institute for Social
Sciences, University of Ljubljana, Slovenia. He is the author of
numerous books, including *The Sublime Object of Ideology* and
Enjoy Your Symptom!

Library of Congress Cataloging-in-Publication Data
Žižek, Slavoj.
Tarrying with the negative : Kant, Hegel, and the critique of
ideology / Slavoj Žižek.
p.   cm. — (Post-contemporary interventions)
Includes bibliographical references and index.
ISBN 0-8223-1362-6 (hard : alk. paper). —
ISBN 0-8223-1395-2 (pbk. : alk. paper)
1. Kant, Immanuel, 1724–1804.   2. Hegel, Georg Wilhelm
Friedrich, 1770–1831.   3. Lacan, Jacques, 1901–   .
4. Ideology—History   I. Title.   II. Series.
B2798.Z59   1993
190—dc20   93-17366 CIP